Sex and Violence in 1920s Scotland

History of Crime, Deviance and Punishment

Series Editor: Anne-Marie Kilday, Vice Chancellor & Professor of Criminal History, University of Northampton, UK

Editorial Board: Neil Davie, University of Lyon II, France
Johannes Dillinger, University of Maine, Germany
Wilbur Miller, State University of New York, USA
Marianna Muravyeva, University of Helsinki, Finland
David Nash, Oxford Brookes University, UK
Judith Rowbotham, Nottingham Trent University, UK

Academic interest in the history of crime and punishment has never been greater and the *History of Crime, Deviance and Punishment* series provides a home for the wealth of new research being produced. Individual volumes within the series cover topics related to the history of crime and punishment, from the later medieval to modern period and in both Europe and North America, and seek to demonstrate the importance of this subject in furthering understanding of the way in which various societies and cultures operate. When taken together, the works in the series will show the evolution of the nature of illegality and attitudes towards its perpetration over time and will offer their readers a rounded and coherent history of crime and punishment through the centuries. The series' broad chronological and geographical coverage encourages comparative historical analysis of crime history between countries and cultures.

Published:

Policing the Factory, Barry Godfrey
Crime and Poverty in 19th-Century England, Adrian Ager
Print Culture, Crime and Justice in Eighteenth-Century London, Richard Ward
Rehabilitation and Probation in England and Wales, 1900–1950, Raymond Gard
The Policing of Belfast 1870–1914, Mark Radford
Crime, Regulation and Control during the Blitz, Peter Adey, David J. Cox and Barry Godfrey
The Italian Prison in the Age of Positivism, 1861–1914, Mary Gibson
Life Courses of Young Convicts Transported to Van Diemen's Land, Emma D. Watkins

Fair and Unfair Trials in the British Isles, 1800–1940, eds. David Nash and Anne-Marie Kilday
Photographing Crime Scenes in Twentieth-Century London, Alexa Neale
Combating London's Criminal Class, Matthew Bach
Mothers, Criminal Insanity and the Asylum in Victorian England: Cure, Redemption and Rehabilitation, Alison C. Pedley

Forthcoming:

The Forefathers of Terrorism: Violent Crime in Politics, 1300–1800, Johannes Dillinger
Feminist Campaigns against Child Sexual Abuse: Britain and India, 1860–1947, Daniel Grey
Deviance, Disorder and Music in Modern Britain and America, Cliff Williamson
Crime and Criminal Justice in Early Modern Ireland: Developing a Colonial Institution, Coleman A. Dennehy
Motor Bandits in Interwar England: Criminal Mobility in the Modern Age, Alyson Brown
Prosecuting London's Fraudsters 1760–1820: Swindlers, Tricksters and the Law, Cerian Griffiths

Sex and Violence in 1920s Scotland

Incest, Rape, Lewd and Libidinous Practices, 1918–1930

Louise Heren

BLOOMSBURY ACADEMIC
LONDON • NEW YORK • OXFORD • NEW DELHI • SYDNEY

BLOOMSBURY ACADEMIC
Bloomsbury Publishing Plc
50 Bedford Square, London, WC1B 3DP, UK
1385 Broadway, New York, NY 10018, USA
29 Earlsfort Terrace, Dublin 2, Ireland

BLOOMSBURY, BLOOMSBURY ACADEMIC and the Diana logo are trademarks of
Bloomsbury Publishing Plc

First published in Great Britain 2024
This paperback edition published in 2025

Copyright © Louise Heren, 2024

Louise Heren has asserted her right under the Copyright, Designs and Patents Act, 1988, to be identified as Author of this work.

For legal purposes the Acknowledgements on p. xi constitute an extension of this copyright page.

Cover image © Glasgow City Archives

All rights reserved. No part of this publication may be reproduced or transmitted in any form or by any means, electronic or mechanical, including photocopying, recording, or any information storage or retrieval system, without prior permission in writing from the publishers.

Bloomsbury Publishing Plc does not have any control over, or responsibility for, any third-party websites referred to or in this book. All internet addresses given in this book were correct at the time of going to press. The author and publisher regret any inconvenience caused if addresses have changed or sites have ceased to exist, but can accept no responsibility for any such changes.

A catalogue record for this book is available from the British Library.

A catalog record for this book is available from the Library of Congress.

ISBN: HB: 978-1-3502-2777-4
PB: 978-1-3502-2781-1
ePDF: 978-1-3502-2778-1
eBook: 978-1-3502-2779-8

Series: History of Crime, Deviance and Punishment

Typeset by Deanta Global Publishing Services, Chennai, India

To find out more about our authors and books visit www.bloomsbury.com and sign up for our newsletters.

For Bill, without who . . . and for Louis, as always.

Contents

List of Figures	x
Acknowledgements	xi
List of Abbreviations	xii
Glossary	xiii
1 Introduction to 1920s Scotland	1
2 Scots Criminal Law and the Prosecution Process	35

Part I Intimate violence

3 'Abhominabill vile and fylthie lust of incest': Incest	53
4 'Outrages against little girls': Sexual violence against girls under sixteen years	86
5 'Vice and virtue': Sexual violence against women over sixteen years	120

Part II Recourse to the law

6 Getting to court: Pretrial processes	155
7 Behind closed doors: Judicial processes	192
8 Sexual entitlement and arrogance: Conclusion	217
Bibliography	233
Index	249

Figures

3.1	Incest: Victims per year by age group	59
3.2	Incest: Number of cases per year by age group	59
4.1	Rape: Minors by age group	90
4.2	Attempt to Ravish: Underage victims by age group	90
4.3	Lewd and libidinous practices and behaviour: All age victims by age group	91
5.1	Rape: Adult victims over sixteen years annual counts 1885–1910	123
5.2	Rape: Adult victims over sixteen years annual counts 1918–1930	124
6.1	Non-familial indictments, total cases per year	188
7.1	Incest verdicts: All age groups	198
7.2	Rape verdicts: All age groups including adult females	201

Acknowledgements

In 1985 at the University of St Andrews, I succumbed to the god-like influence of Professor T. C. Smout, who persuaded me to take single honours Scottish History; he handed me to Dr William Knox for my honours years. Now my supervisor, I am eternally grateful to Bill for agreeing to take me on again, and for his scholarly guidance and friendship.

The thesis on which this book is based would not have reached fruition without special permission granted by the Lord President of Scotland for access to criminal proceedings papers held under the 100 years closure rules at the National Records of Scotland. Alison Lindsay, the head of the National Record's Historical and Legal Search Rooms, is due many thanks for her diligence, keen interest and warm friendship; thank you too to her team and Gillian Mapstone.

Generous financial assistance in the form of travel grants from the Society of Antiquaries of Scotland, the Economic History Society, the Royal Historical Society, the Russell Trust and lastly the Scottish History Review Trust is much appreciated. The School of History at St Andrews awarded very helpful annual and discretionary travel grants. The University of St Andrews library staff have my eternal gratitude.

Several academics – emailed out of the blue – have been most helpful: Professor Roger Davidson, Dr Kevin Crosby, Dr Carolyn Conley, Professor Randolph Roth, Professor Martin Wiener and Professor Joanna Bourke, Professor Lindsay Farmer, Dr Robert Shiels. Thanks to my supervisors, Dr James Nott and Professor Rab Houston, at St Andrews, who steered me towards completion and to my examiners, Dr Malcolm Petrie and Professor Joanna Bourke, for their constructive criticism and support. Professor Anne-Marie Kilday has been a fabulous mentor during this project, and Maddie Holder and the Bloomsbury team have held my hand throughout.

The victims, their families and the perpetrators who populate this book and who must remain anonymous are acknowledged for their unwitting contribution. Each individual's experience will never be forgotten.

Lastly, heartfelt thanks go to my husband and son for their forbearance, cheerleading and love. When this research began, Louis was in single digits – he now knows more than any teenager should about the potential for sexual violence in society.

Abbreviations

AD	Advocate Depute
CA	Crown Agent
CC	Crown Counsel
CLAA	Criminal Law Amendment Act
HCJ	High Court of Justiciary
LLPB	Lewd and libidinous practices and behaviour
LPPO	Lord President's Private Office
MPR	Multiple perpetrator rape
NRS	National Records of Scotland
NSPCC	National Society for the Prevention of Cruelty to Children
PF	Procurator Fiscal
RSSPCC	Royal Scottish Society for the Prevention of Cruelty to Children

Glossary

Advocate Depute Prosecuting law officer and assistant to the Lord Advocate.
Assoilzied Scots Law sentence effectively dismissing a panel from the bar on a verdict of either not guilty or not proven.
Complainer Scots Law term for an individual reporting a crime.
Crown Agent The principle legal adviser to the Lord Advocate and head of the Crown Office, a permanent staff of civil servants.
Crown Counsel The collective term for the Lord Advocate, Advocates Depute and Solicitor General, Scotland's prosecutorial body.
Lewd and libidinous practices and behaviour An indictment peculiar to Scots Law that is the modern equivalent of intimate touching.
Lord Advocate The chief Scottish legal officer for the Crown.
Lord President Scotland's senior judge and head of the judiciary.
Panel Scots Law term for defendant/accused.
Precognoscer Person tasked with taking down a complainer's and witnesses' testimonies.
Procurator Fiscal Public prosecutor.
Single-end A one-roomed tenement dwelling typical of late-nineteenth- and early-twentieth-century Scottish urban centres.
Youth Used throughout as alternative to young man.
Solicitor General The Lord Advocate's deputy.

Copyright notices

All graphs, © The Author, 2022

Declaration

Permission to investigate the closed High Court of Justiciary records, which form the dataset for this research, was granted by the Lord President's Private Office (LPPO), Edinburgh, 27 August 2015. The LPPO's permissions require that the dataset can only be viewed by researchers on written request to the LPPO. Under the terms of the agreement signed with the LPPO, all individuals and specific place names mentioned in the research have been anonymized.

1

Introduction to 1920s Scotland

Most historians would recognize the immediate post-Great War years and the following decade as a period of reconstruction and great societal change in the aftermath of the world's first truly global conflict.[1] From political upheaval to labour protest and unrest, to gender tensions, economic slump and depression, the 1920s were a decade of disruption to the social norm that had largely prevailed until the conflagration of the 1914–18 war. After four years of industrial-scale carnage, the evidence of which had been reported daily in the nation's newspapers, how brutalized were soldiers now returning to normal life or the public who had lived in fear and even the state which had enacted emergency legislation?[2] There is often a gulf between the people's perception of the society which they inhabit and reality. Contemporary debates concerning brutalization and social upheavals began in the last years of the war and were played out in the immediate post-war traumas between 1918 and 1921, the impact of which would continue to be felt until the next war.[3] Those traumas began with crime and labour protests across the country, notably in the port and industrial cities. On 18 January 1919, a police constable was shot and killed in Glasgow when he disturbed a burglary in progress. On 23 January, a brawl broke out among white and 'coloured' seamen in Broomielaw, Glasgow, requiring fifty policemen to restore order. Glasgow's 'Bloody Friday' riot occurred eight days later on 31 January 1919, requiring 140 police to quell a crowd variably estimated to number between 20,000 and 40,000.[4] Ostensibly a strike to achieve a forty-hour working week to accommodate returning troops in the workplace, it was partly also an attempt, as contemporary journalist Cicely Hamilton identified, to force

---

1 For wider discussion on the globalization of the Great War see H. Strachan, 'The First World War as a Global War', *First World War Studies*, 1, issue 1 (2010): 3–14; P. Clarke, *Hope and Glory: Britain in 1900-1990* (London, 1996), 77–85.
2 J. Lawrence, 'Forging a Peaceable Kingdom: War, Violence and Fear of Brutalization in Post First War Britain', *The Journal of Modern History*, 75, no. 3 (September 2003): 557.
3 Lawrence, 'Peaceable Kingdom', 560.
4 D. Grant, *The Thin Blue Line: The Story of the City of Glasgow Police* (London, 1973), 65–6.

women 'to relinquish their recent freedoms created by the war and return to domesticity to avoid male hatred'.[5]

Regional strikes and protests across Britain were followed by the crash of 1920, as the boom created by post-war short-term restocking collapsed.[6] In Scotland, the experience of unemployment was geographically concentrated, with the south-west's focus on the shipbuilding trades being particularly hard hit. Scotland experienced a consistently higher rate of unemployment than in the UK as a whole throughout the decade, with the south-west's heavy industries centred on Clydeside's urban areas experiencing 53 per cent unemployment by 1933, which was barely lower than October 1922. On the east coast, the employees in Dundee's jute industry also felt the pinch with unemployment at 50 per cent, while service-based employment in Aberdeen and Edinburgh escaped the impact of the economic depression more lightly.[7] Unemployment and labour tensions culminated in the 1926 General Strike, which war journalist Philip Gibbs feared would plunge Britain into 'bloodshed and civil disorder of the wildest kind'.[8] The Great Crash of 1929 saw the working population's prospects plummet further. The war had damaged men mentally and physically and now they were supposed to suffer the humiliation of unemployment while women were expected to return quietly to their pre-war situation: domesticity and the gendered spheres of home and social life.[9]

Against the backdrop of economic and social strife, suffragist, feminist and social observer Cicely Hamilton saw the 1920s as an 'ugly epoch'. After four years of horrific conflict, hatred had become a habit albeit with a new enemy: 'instead of hating by nation, we hated by party and by class', and, by extension, by sex. Cicely had been fearful that aggression learned in the trenches would 'be acted out in the relative security of post-war social life'.[10] Her fears were supported by Gibbs, who anticipated that returning soldiers would wreak murder and rapine on their womenfolk at home.[11] Yet other contemporaries, such as combatant and war poet Robert Graves, witnessed an 'improvement in public behaviour' due to 'the habits of discipline and cleanliness learned in the Army and Navy', with no more 'ruffianism in crowded trains and buses, at places of public entertainment,

---

5   C. Hamilton, *Life Errant* (New York, 1935), 186–7.
6   W. W. Knox, *Industrial Nation: Work, Culture and Society in Scotland, 1800-Present* (Edinburgh, 1999), 189.
7   Knox, *Industrial Nation*, 189–90.
8   P. Gibbs, *Since Then* (London, 1930), 226–33.
9   L. Bland, *Modern Women on Trial: Sexual Transgression in the Age of the Flapper* (Manchester, 2013), 2.
10 Hamilton, *Life Errant*, 186–7.
11 P. Gibbs, *Now It Can Be Told*, facsimile edition (South Carolina, 2015), 167.

and in public houses'.[12] While some feared the brutalizing effect of the war, most especially the middle and upper classes, others realized the discipline engendered by war service, and it has been argued that the violence experienced in the immediate post-war years was perpetrated not by demobilizing troops but by civilians.[13] Living 'in the moment', the chasm between perceived anxieties of violent crime and its reality was unrealizable.[14]

Gender and societal tensions were further fuelled by the enfranchisement of men and some women by the Representation of the People Act 1918, and the Sex Disqualification (Removal) Act the following year. For the first time, all men over the age of twenty-one were granted the vote, as well as women over thirty, but with certain added property qualifications. Women were also permitted to enter professions previously barred to them, such as politics and law. How these changes would affect elite male influence over politics, the law and professional life could not possibly be immediately evaluated, although it did provoke debate in Parliament as the Acts became law.[15]

Thus, there was unease among the middle and upper classes – the elites – about a society in flux. Hamilton's and Gibbs's approach conflicted with Graves's perception of their times; clearly competing narratives had emerged regarding peace-time life in Britain and the reconstruction of society at all levels which were influenced by class and elite perceptions of the lower classes as uncivilized because crime persisted among them.[16] Gibbs's anxieties concluded with a dismal description of life at home for demobilized troops, who, inspired by 'homicidal mania and secret lust', might commit 'outrages upon little girls', something that 'appalled decent-minded people' who could not 'understand the cause of this epidemic', especially when their perception romanticized earlier periods when there had supposedly been less crime.[17]

Paul Fussell, Susan Kingsley-Kent, Sandra Gilbert and Tracey Loughran have all investigated contemporary authors' interpretations of post-Great War British society and have discovered that gender antagonism and fear were dominant motifs in this period: returning soldiers unable to relate to women; separate spheres were required to segregate women from men's 'primitive instincts'; as

---

12   R. Graves and A. Hodge, *The Long Weekend: A Social History of Great Britain, 1918–1939* (London, 1995), 171.
13   R. Overy, *The Morbid Age* (London, 2010), 12; Lawrence, 'Peaceable Kingdom', 563.
14   C. Emsley, 'Violent Crime in England in 1919: Post-War Anxieties and Press Narratives', *Continuity and Change*, 23, no. 1 (2008): 189.
15   M. Takayanagi, 'Women and the Vote: The Parliamentary Path to Equal Franchise, 1918-28', *Parliamentary History*, 37, no. 1 (June 2018): 173–7.
16   Lawrence, 'Peaceable Kingdom', 559.
17   Gibbs, *Now It Can Be Told*, 167.

well as 'sexual anger' between the sexes.[18] However, it should be remembered that these post-war authors were middle-class, chaperoned women, who were unlikely to have first-hand knowledge of male violence unless they witnessed it during their charitable and philanthropic endeavours in working-class districts. Whereas the adult victims of prosecuted rape and ravishment in 1920s Scotland were working class – a group of women probably more qualified to speak of insidious male violence in their community.

Male violence is an age-old phenomenon understood by women, particularly young women, of all social strata: men are a threat to their virtue, chastity and, potentially, their physical well-being. Anxieties over male sexual abuse of females have fluctuated in intensity over centuries in response to societal influences and pressures. As such, the immense social upheaval of the post-Great War years was one period when some individuals perceived male violence as a particularly real threat.

Examining a decade of enormous social reconstruction, this book has two aims. Firstly, to describe and measure the level of indicted sexual crime and to evaluate the possible impact of socio-economic stresses on society through fluctuations in the records of prosecuted crime. And secondly, to assess the competing claims of contemporaries regarding the degree to which post-war society was 'brutalized': can a correlation between the emotional impact of the war, male unemployment and fluctuations in sexual violence against women be made? Moreover, was there a regional aspect to this, and, if so, which areas were more violent and why were the men domiciled in them more violent than elsewhere? Ultimately, was Cicely Hamilton correct to describe the post-war period as an 'ugly epoch'? The incidence of prosecuted sexual violence in Scotland is one tool by which to evaluate her claim.

Why Scotland?

Scotland has been described as 'an astonishing ensemble of contradictory narratives' ranging from the romantic Highlands to Glasgow's slums, from the poorest to the wealthiest citizens, often perceived as 'an oppressed nation' of

---

18   T. Loughran, 'A Crisis of Masculinity? Re-Writing the History of Shell-Shock and Gender in First World War Britain', *History Compass*, 11, no. 9 (2013): 728; S. Kingsley-Kent, 'The Politics of Sexual Difference: World War I and the Demise of British Feminism', *Journal of British Studies*, 27, no. 3 (July 1988): 233; S. Gilbert, 'Soldier's Heart: Literary Men, Literary Women, and the Great War', in *Behind the Lines: Gender and the Two World Wars*, eds R. Higonnet, J. Jenson, S. Michel and M. Collins Weitz (Yale, 1987), 198–9.

empire builders torn between drink and puritanism, of 'hard men but battered wives'.[19] Of those Highlanders and urban hard men, 41.5 per cent aged between fifteen and forty-five had served in the Great War, largely recruited from the industrial areas of the west before conscription was introduced.[20] Like many returning combatants, Scottish soldiers returned to a society in upheaval with burgeoning political unrest evident within weeks of the Armistice and the threat of unemployment as the requirement for munitions decreased; this was mostly centred on Glasgow.

This wealth of geographical and social diversity makes Scotland a highly attractive country for this research study for three main reasons. Firstly, because in the early twentieth century, the image of the hard drinking, smoking, opinionated man epitomized a certain type of Scot, in particular those living on the industrialized west coast; their behaviour had come to symbolize the whole country.[21] Glasgow was the 'second city of empire' building the nation's naval and commercial fleets and distributing the products of its heavy engineering industries around the world, but despite this, working-class living conditions in Glasgow and Dundee were among the worst in Europe. As Cicely Hamilton noted for 1911: 'forty-seven per cent of the Scottish people' lived in homes comprising one or two rooms, while 'south of the Tweed' only 7 per cent lived in comparable slum conditions.[22] These are the legacies of the past century.

Secondly, Scotland has been chosen because of its diversity of localities. In the 1920s, Scotland's population comprised approximately one-seventh of the UK and encompassed two major industrial cities and their satellite towns (Glasgow and the Clyde Corridor, and Dundee), a capital city (Edinburgh) and a range of smaller coastal and rural towns (Aberdeen and Inverness), as well as the remote agricultural villages of the Highlands and Islands. Other studies of historical violence in the UK have concentrated on a particular county or city or have only investigated a certain level of court, for example, magistrate or assize for a specified area; some studies have surveyed an entire country but have included sexual violence only as part of a general investigation of male violence.[23] These

---

19 L. Abrams and C. G. Brown, 'Introduction: Conceiving the Everyday in the Twentieth Century', in *A History of Everyday Life in Twentieth Century Scotland*, eds L. Abrams and C. G. Brown (Edinburgh, 2010), 2.
20 H. Strachan, 'The Scottish Soldier and Scotland, 1914–1918', in *A Global Force: War, Identities and Scotland's Diaspora*, eds D. Forsyth and W. Ugolini (Edinburgh, 2018), chapter 3.
21 H. Young, 'Being a Man: Everyday Masculinities', in *A History of Everyday Life in Twentieth Century Scotland*, eds L. Abrams and C. G. Brown (Edinburgh, 2010), 131.
22 C. Hamilton, *Modern Scotland* (London, 1937), 29.
23 L. A. Jackson, *Child Sexual Abuse in Victorian England* (London, 2000); C. Conley, 'War among Savages: Homicide and Ethnicity in the Victorian United Kingdom', *Journal of British Studies*, 44

mainly English studies have tended to assume the mantle of 'British' research and thus, by default, incorporate the Scottish experience without consulting Scottish records. However, Scotland operates under a different legal system. By conflating England with Britain, the different experiences of the constituent countries of the UK have been obscured by the English experience which is assumed to be normative for all. As Eric Hobsbawm argued, 'Scotland and Wales are socially, and by their history, traditions, and sometimes institutions, entirely distinct from England'.[24]

Therefore, thirdly, due to its relatively small size, multiple geographies and separate judicial system, Scotland provides a capsule nation, an ideal case study against which to compare other more time-delineated and geographically focused studies. It has been argued that individual micro studies can conceal wider trends by their lack of homogenous approach.[25] By investigating Scotland's experience of male sexual violence by individual indictments – incest, rape, attempt to ravish, and lewd and libidinous practices and behaviour (LLPB) – it is also possible not only to examine regional diversities within the country but to attempt to compare Scotland's national experience with trends discovered for England. This then is an ambitious and unique study, something not previously attempted for a whole country. It offers a Scottish 'one-stop-shop' from which other researchers of early twentieth-century violence can extract material to compare and contrast with their own studies.

Why deep history?

Historians require evidence, the fine and often micro details, from which to formulate ideas and arguments.[26] By examining society's legal and governmental systems, its social structures and morals, the everyday and individual historical experience can be obscured by the bigger picture.[27] However, by employing 'thick description' – the intimate reading of historical documents – the historian

---

(October 2005): 775–95; M. Wiener, *Men of Blood: Violence, Manliness and Criminal Justice in Victorian England* (Cambridge, 2006).
24 E. J. Hobsbawm, *Industry and Empire: The Birth of the Industrial Revolution* (London, 1999), 278.
25 K. Carson and H. Idzikowska, 'The Social Production of Scottish Policing 1795-1900', in *Policing and Prosecution in Britain 1750-1950*, eds D. Hays and F. Snyder (Oxford, 1989), 269.
26 Deep history is a term used by H. Rogers, 'Making their Mark: Young Offenders' Life Histories and Social Networks', in *Law, Crime and Deviance since 1700*, eds A. Kilday and D. Nash (London, 2017), 227–49; Paul Knepper has summarized Foucault's attitude towards microhistory thus: 'leading historians deal with the ideas and second-raters worry about the details'; P. Knepper, *Writing the History of Crime* (London, 2017), 167.
27 Abrams and Brown, *Twentieth Century Scotland*, 1.

delves to the furthest corners of the archive to seek out the ordinary individual's contribution which may otherwise be discarded as too particular to be significant. This is 'deep history'.[28] These are the people whose absorbing experiences of sexual violence are preserved in Scotland's High Court of Justiciary (HCJ) records. Contained in these records is 'what happened on the ground' as well as what occurred in the upper reaches of the judicial system.[29] It is probably the closest the historian can get to investigating the experiences of the participants in society's most depraved crimes.

Why sexual crime?

In legal terms, violence is defined as 'the unlawful exercise of physical force'.[30] 'Unlawful' defines violence as illegitimate in terms of the individual victim who has recourse to the law but also that institutions regulating society consider violence to be a prohibited and therefore criminal act. Sexual violence is arguably the most intimate form of interpersonal violence, and its incidence can be an index of broader sociocultural processes. In recent years, historical violence studies have enjoyed an expansion as more historians realize the value of analysis of all types of violence to an understanding of societal dynamics. Manuel Eisner's analysis of European homicide covering eight centuries provides the bedrock for comparative studies for other Westernized societies, while Martin Wiener's *Men of Blood* is the starting position for historians of English male violence.[31] In the United States, statistical work by Eric Monkkonen and Eric Johnson has produced city-specific as well as nationwide historical violence data, while in the UK, Gatrell's and Hadden's statistical analysis of nineteenth-century society provides a wealth of material.[32]

28   J. Sharpe, 'History from Below', in *New Perspectives on Historical Writing*, ed. P. Burke (Cambridge, 2001), 26.
29   Loughran, 'Crisis of Masculinity?', 733; D. Hay, P. Linebaugh, J. G. Rule, E. P. Thompson and C. Winslow, *Albion's Fatal Tree: Crime and Society in Eighteenth-Century England* (London, 2011), xvi.
30   *Oxford English Dictionary*, https://www.oed.com/view/Entry/223638?rskey=rnDtdM&result=1 &isAdvanced=false#eid, accessed April 2020.
31   M. Eisner, 'Long Term Historical Trends in Violent Crime', *Crime and Justice, A Review of Research*, 30 (2003): 83–142; 'Modernization, Self-control and Lethal Violence: The Long-Term Dynamics of European Homicide Rates in Theoretical Perspective', *British Journal of Criminology*, 41 (2001): 618–38, are a small selection of his wider work. Wiener, *Men of Blood*.
32   E. Monkkonen and E. Johnson, eds, *The Civilization of Crime: Violence in Town and Country since the Middle Ages* (Chicago, 1996), as well as Monkkonen's individual papers, for example, 'New Standards for Historical Homicide Research', *Crime History and Societies*, 5, no. 2 (2001): 5–26; 'Estimating the Accuracy of Historic Homicide Rates', *Social Science History*, 25, no. 1 (Spring 2001): 53–66. V. A. C. Gatrell and T. B. Hadden, 'Criminal Statistics and their Interpretation', in

The specialism of historical sexual violence not only allows insight into society dynamics but also provides an unsavoury yet instructive further area of scholarship through the detail captured in the legal records. For example, working hours, family size, bed sharing, leisure activities, employment type and status and neighbourhood networks. Other criminal indictments rarely contain this wealth of detail; HCJ murder records are less concerned with the environment in which the crime was committed, preferring to concentrate on the actions of the protagonists to reconstruct the crime. As a capital crime, murder mesmerized society because of the danger murderous individuals posed, supported by public displays of deterrent retribution. However, sexual violence fascinates society in an entirely different manner. How and why sexual violence is committed and how society responds to such crimes varies; the construction of sexual crime and society's tolerance for it are determined by historical time and location.[33] From the late nineteenth century, judicial, welfare and philanthropic bodies were exercised by sexual violence, because such unregulated behaviour was considered contrary to an advanced and civilized society. The HCJ records are a prime source for the study of societal responses to crime as it progressed through the prosecution process. Because this survey examines only prosecuted cases which were successful in reaching the HCJ, if not successful in their outcome, it must be acknowledged that they possess inherent limitations on what can be argued from their content. However, it is a starting point from which to examine who was committing sexual violence against whom; who reported it and how; and how the judicial authorities responded.

Why men?

Violence is a gendered crime: men commit violent crime; women do not. Throughout history and across societies men have committed the majority of violent crime and especially sexual offences.[34] If women are violent, their crimes have been largely constructed by their gender: infanticide or husband murder. Male violence constitutes the bulk of the criminal records in Western societies, and in Scotland in the 1920s, the HCJ records suggest that men are responsible

---

Nineteenth Century Society: Essays in the Use of Quantitative Methods for the Study of Social Data, ed. E. A. Wrigley (Cambridge, 1972), 336–96.
33 C. Conley, 'Sexual Violence in Historical Perspective', in *Oxford Handbook of Gender, Sex and Crime*, eds R. Gartner and B. McCarthy (Oxford, 2014), 191.
34 M. Wiener, 'The Victorian Criminalization of Men', in *Men and Violence: Gender, Honor, and Rituals in Modern Europe and America*, ed. P. Spierenburg (Ohio, 1998), 199.

for the totality of sexual crime.³⁵ Thus, the question of masculinity, what defines 'being a man', is important when examining the male monopoly of sexual crimes. Throughout history, masculinity has been hegemonic, a manifestation of undisputed patriarchy.³⁶ However, the construction of masculinity is also mediated through the lens of socio-economic status and class; it can be cultural and regional, context specific and far from static, changing over time.

Patriarchy was firmly established in public life: politically, women (and a third of men) were unenfranchised until 1919; educationally, higher academic institutions refused women until 1892 and then segregated them; in work, roles and wages were differentiated by gender; and domestically, women acted as carers and housewives while men were breadwinners. This hegemonic masculinity legitimized men's dominant role in nearly all aspects of domestic and public life. Men's physical superiority, their economic independence, political rights contrasted with women's domestic 'separate sphere' and reinforced men's sense of self-respect and status among their peers.³⁷

How men behaved in society and how they used their superior physical power has changed over time. Writing in the early 1920s, psychologist Bernard Hollander argued that 'civilization has diminished the necessity of physical aggression and defence' with a general reduction in male interpersonal violence.³⁸ Almost twenty years later, Norbert Elias's book *Über den Prozess der Zivilisation*, published in 1939, reached a similar conclusion. Elias's theory of the 'civilizing process' argued that over time male society has been self-limiting in how it utilizes violence as a means of dispute resolution. Application of normative manifestations of manliness and regulation of masculine activities, he argued, was a top-down process, which the civilized male elites gradually internalized. A reduction in violent confrontations such as brawling and duelling was countered by an increase in legal means of conflict resolution. Extensive research investigating seventeenth-century Dutch and northern European violence concluded that impulsive violence was the norm in these early societies, but that the gradual improvement in manners and behaviour percolating from the elites downwards – the 'civilizing process' – was becoming increasingly evident in the decline of

---

35 Only one rape indictment cites a female co-defendant, who had colluded in an abortion as the result of rape; AD15/21/65.
36 S. Yarrow, 'Masculinity as a World Historical Category of Analysis', in *What is Masculinity? Historical Dynamics from Antiquity to the Contemporary World*, eds J. H. Arnold and S. Brady (London, 2013), 117.
37 J. Tosh, 'The History of Masculinity: An Outdated Concept?', in *What is Masculinity? Historical Dynamics from Antiquity to the Contemporary World*, eds J. H. Arnold and S. Brady (London, 2013), 27; R. W. Connell, *Masculinities* (London, 2018), 195.
38 B. Hollander, *The Psychology of Misconduct, Vice and Crime* (London, 1922), 74.

male interpersonal violence.[39] This trend is also revealed in research conducted on crime across nineteenth-century Germany and France and nineteenth-century England: the growth in polite society values first seen among the elites had trickled down to the 'respectable' working class, and generally there had been a shift away from crimes against the person towards crimes against property.[40] Thus, societies which continued to indulge in violent behaviour were perceived as less civilized, and by extension groups within a society who persisted with violent behaviour were disparaged by the elites. Public displays of male violence in Scotland were predominantly viewed as lower-working-class behaviour by the elites and the 'respectable' working classes, who had all largely eschewed violence.[41] Thus, civilizing male behaviours changed gradually and were learned through emulation. A socio-economic construction of masculinity had evolved differentiating males by social class.

For men in the 'respectable' working classes, providing for a family so that his wife did not have to work was the foundation of manliness. For others, unable or unwilling to emulate 'quieter' elite domestic arrangements, masculinity could be played out through violence in spheres of work and leisure. Here socio-economic constructions of masculinity combined with cultural norms. Feuding among clan chiefs, a thousand years of conflict with its neighbour and emigration across the empire have contributed to Scotland's long-term notoriety for violence – a sense of 'Scottishness' revealed through displays of aggression to assert men's role in society. It has become a behaviour perceived as a national trait, particular to the working classes, and regionalized so that Glaswegian men are especially considered more 'masculine' and therefore more violent than other Scottish males.[42]

Growing up in Glasgow during the early twentieth century, Ralph Glasser described violence as 'intertwined with everyday life', a phenomenon which was accepted with 'fatalism'.[43] Glasgow's notoriety for territorial gang violence is arguably best described in Alexander McArthur's and Kingsley Long's bestselling *No Mean City*, first published in 1935, which fictionalized Glasgow's

---

39 P. Spierenburg, *A History of Murder: Personal Violence in Europe from the Middles Ages to the Present* (Cambridge, 2008).
40 Knepper, *Writing*, 41; Gatrell and Hadden, 'Criminal Statistics', 370 and 377.
41 A. Murdoch and R. B. Sher, 'Literary and Learned Culture', in *People and Society in Scotland, volume 1 1760–1830*, eds T. M. Devine and R. Mitchison (Edinburgh, 1988), 127.
42 L. Abrams and E. Ewan, 'Interrogating Men and Masculinities in Scottish History', in *Nine Centuries of Man: Manhood and Masculinities in Scottish History*, eds L. Abrams and E. Ewan (Edinburgh, 2017), 7; P. Carlen, *Women's Imprisonment: A Study in Social Control* (London, 1983), 39–44, quoted in E. Stanko, *Intimate Intrusions: Women's Experience of Male Violence* (London, 1985), 52; Young, 'Being a Man', 136.
43 R. Glasser, *Growing up in the Gorbals* (London, 1986), 61.

gang culture of the 1920s drawing on McArthur's personal observations while unemployed.[44] They described violence concentrated among working-class communities living in atrocious conditions in the city's dilapidated and densely populated tenements where religious sectarianism could break out into cinemas and dance halls where the classes might mix.[45] Clydeside's men had earned a reputation for tough behaviour during the war when confronting labour disputes and negotiating with government. Thus, these anecdotal experiences suggest that working-class male violence was embedded in everyday life in Glasgow, to a degree not reflected in Scotland's other major cities during this period.[46]

Such hyper-masculine violent behaviours were typical of men employed in heavy industry, which was the focus of male employment for south-west Scotland.[47] On Clydeside and in Glasgow, hard physical work in the shipyards and ancillary workshops was rewarded with hard drinking and frequent fights.[48] In working-class circles, manual work was viewed as manly in comparison to office work, the outward signifiers being rolled-up shirt sleeves with exposed forearms, which publicly emphasized manliness and physical prowess.[49] Thus 'real men' engaged in manual employment and at the end of the week, their masculinity earned further expression through the pay packet.[50] They could finance their drinking, smoking and other leisure pursuits, and being the breadwinner imbued them with a sense of proprietorship at home; for some men handing over money for the housekeeping was a transaction to be repaid with sex.[51] For young, single men, this same transaction might be anticipated when paying for a young woman's evening out at the cinema with an expectation of some degree of sexual contact while escorting her home. Pay-packet masculinity could, therefore, apply to married and single men alike.

Thus, masculinity could be a hegemonic, patriarchal construct manifested through civilized behaviour and non-violent dispute resolution among the elites and 'respectable' working-class men but with a 'hard man' variation particular to certain male groups within the working class. Within this male-dominated

---

44 A. McArthur and H. Kingsley Long, *No Mean City* (London, 1989).
45 A. Davies, *City of Gangs: Glasgow and the Rise of the British Gangster* (London, 2014), 1–2.
46 R. Johnston and A. McIvor, 'Dangerous Work, Hard Men and Broken Bodies: Masculinity in the Clydeside Heavy Industries', *Labour History Review*, 69, no. 2 (August 2004): 138.
47 B. S. Godfrey, C. Emsley and G. Dunstall, 'Do you have Plane-Spotters in New Zealand? Issues in Comparative Crime History at the Turn of Modernity', in *Comparative Histories of Crime*, eds B. Godfrey, C. Emsley and G. Dunstall (London, 2003), 14.
48 Abrams and Ewan, 'Interrogating Men', 1.
49 J. Begiato, 'Between Poise and Power: Embodied Manliness in Eighteenth and Nineteenth Century British Culture', *Transactions of the Royal Historical Society*, 26 (2016): 135.
50 J. Bourke, *Working-Class Cultures in Britain, 1890–1960* (London, 1994), 130.
51 Johnston and McIvor, 'Dangerous Work', 142.

structure, socio-economic factors and class status were integral components affecting a man's self-perception of his type and degree of masculinity; masculinity had become a product learned through socialization.[52] However, in certain contexts, an individual's perception of the need to be seen as masculine, to conform to his peers' concepts of masculinity, could manifest itself in male interpersonal violence and sexual violence against women – a gender power conflict that could transition into a criminal act. In Glasgow in 1930, four men were prosecuted for raping a 29-year-old domestic servant. They had opportunistically pounced on her after dark. The leader asked, 'Are you going to give me a ride?' A male witness testified that instead of going for help, he had 'stayed to watch a bit of fun'. Both perpetrators and witness displayed their perceived superior rights as men to behave without regard for women.[53]

Historiography

Research on male sexual violence is a recent area of scholarship and can be divided into two sections: contemporary publications and the work of more recent historians. Titles in the first group are few. From the late nineteenth century, the government commissioned and published investigations into the condition of the working classes, notably the *First* and *Second Reports of Her Majesty's Commissioners for Inquiring into the Housing of the Working Classes, Scotland* (1885), followed by the *Report of the Royal Commission on the Housing of the Industrial Population of Scotland, Rural and Urban* (1917).[54] Ostensibly designed to collect information concerning population and living densities, types of home, house dimensions and amenities, with the intention to advise on improvements, the investigators also collected testimony, which they believed supported a correlation between overcrowding and deviant behaviour. The 1917 report was investigated and compiled under the chairmanship of Sir Henry Ballantyne with a board entirely comprised of Scottish men. However, by the early post-war years, the government's welfare focus had turned to sexual offences against children, predominantly females. This change of focus was largely the result of female emancipation and enfranchisement. Government legislation

---

52 Connell, *Masculinities*, 22.
53 AD15/30/54, JC14/40; all four men found guilty, sentences between three and five years penal servitude.
54 *First* and *Second Reports of her Majesty's Commissioners for Inquiring into the Housing of the Working Classes, Scotland* (Edinburgh, 1885); *Report of the Royal Commission on the Housing of the Industrial Population of Scotland, Rural and Urban* (Edinburgh, 1917).

provided new platforms for empowered women already debating women's and children's issues. Newly elected female MPs such as Viscountess Astor continued the work of late Victorian female philanthropists from within the 'establishment' by raising the matter in Parliament, and JPs such as Margery Fry, who used her secretaryship of the Howard League for Penal Reform to raise similar issues.[55] As Bingham et al. state, 'offences against (mainly female) children were kept on the agenda ... because they were a focal point for women's politics'. With few other avenues for political exposure in the early days of female enfranchisement, 'moral welfare' as a branch of women's social work was a subject rich with possibilities for women new to politics.[56]

In 1926, the *Departmental Committee on Sexual Offences against Children and Young Persons in Scotland* investigated and reported on the procedure for dealing with cases of sexual abuse and examined possible methods of prevention and care of victims post-trauma; their remit also included recommendations for changes in the law.[57] The committee comprised four male lawyers and three married women, one of whom was a doctor qualified in Edinburgh and Glasgow. Evidenced by the number of qualifications cited after their names, all committee members can be assumed to have been part of the educated middle class. Their report explicitly connected the working classes and overcrowded single-end homes with perceived increases in sexual crime, specifically committed against female children. This was a continuation of late nineteenth-century medical opinion, which 'confined [incest] to the poor and mentally defective'.[58]

However, by the early twentieth century, the acknowledgement of familial sexual abuse had transformed into a broader medical investigation of male sexual violence. Psychiatrist Bernard Hollander examined many aspects of male deviance from drinking and drug-taking to theft and ultimately to violence and 'sexual perverseness'. His work revealed that some men were unable to control their 'passions', offering motives such as 'a superfluity of energy' or epilepsy to explain violent behaviours.[59] Two decades later, the medical inspector of prisons and prisons commissioner William Norwood East expounded his own theories based on observations of incarcerated sexual offenders. He concluded that it was in the psyche of the lower-ordered male to commit sexual violence and extended

---

55 A. Bingham, '"It would be better for the Newspapers to call a Spade a Spade": The British Press and Child Sexual Abuse, c.1918–90', *History Workshop Journal*, issue 88 (2019): 96.
56 A. Bingham, L. Jackson, L. Delap and L. Settle, 'Historical Child Sexual Abuse in England and Wales: The Role of Historians', *History of Education*, 45, no. 4 (2016): 414.
57 *Departmental Committee on Sexual Offences against Children and Young Persons in Scotland*, (Edinburgh, 1926), 3–4, Hansard Cmd 2561.
58 J. L. Herman, *Father-Daughter Incest* (Harvard, 1981), 9.
59 Hollander, *Misconduct*, 83 and 81.

some licence to sexual criminals, who were 'perhaps more liable to be misjudged by prejudice and ignorance' than other criminals.[60] Contemporary investigations had not only constructed theories for the prevalence of sexual crime among working-class males in overcrowded communities but had also formulated hypotheses on motive with a view towards understanding the criminal mind.

Possibly the most socially taboo aspect of sexual violence is incest for which historical oral and written testimony is understandably rare. Most sexual violence cases were prosecuted *in camera* and newspaper reportage was limited and often euphemistic, making identification of incest cases especially difficult.[61] Posthumously, Virginia Woolf published a description of the incestuous actions of her male cousin towards her and her sister at the turn of the century; Ralph Glasser described a friend's alleged encounters in Glasgow with his sister in his autobiography.[62] Woolf, a middle-class author, and Glasser, a working-class boy turned psychologist and economist, described events from opposite ends of the social spectrum. Authors of fiction have also explored incest. In *Sunset Song*, the first volume of Lewis Grassic Gibbon's 1932 semi-autobiographical classic *A Scots Quair*, Gibbon provided a fleeting example of attempted father-daughter incest in a remote Scottish farming community.[63] Freud's work in Austria, which had identified a significant occurrence of familial sexual violence in middle-class homes, was not yet popular in Britain. His argument that incest was 'endemic to the patriarchal family' and included 'respectable family men' would have been unpalatable to the 'gentlemen' being accused.[64] Thus, personal testimony of incest or public discussion is sparse, hidden behind euphemism in newspaper sources or explored at a personal remove through literature.

Anthony Wohl's exploration of incest in the Victorian working-class family attempts to explain incest as either a symptom or the cause of a 'disrupted family'. He argues that incest was a casual, temporary occurrence between younger family members and concluded that 'demographic pressures' resulted in 'forms of urban social and moral pathology', such as infanticide and murder, to which he added incest. His arguments support the contemporary assertion that overcrowding provoked incest.[65] However, overcrowding per se cannot

---

60 W. Norwood East, 'Sexual Offenders – a British View', *The Yale Law Journal*, 55, no. 3 (April 1946), 529; Norwood East wrote widely on sexual offences among all social classes.
61 K. Stevenson, '"These are cases which it is inadvisable to drag into the light of day": disinterring the Crime of Incest in Early Twentieth-Century England', *Crime, History and Societies*, 20, no. 2 (2016): 2.
62 V. Woolf, *Moments of Being* (London, 2002), 33–4; Glasser, *Growing up in the Gorbals*, 132.
63 L. G. Gibbon, *A Scots Quair: Sunset Song* (Edinburgh, 2006), 79 and 112.
64 Herman, *Father-Daughter*, 9.
65 A. Wohl, ed., *The Victorian Family, Structure and Stresses* (New York, 1978), 196–216.

explain incest when so many of Britain's working classes inhabited cramped homes but did not commit, or were not prosecuted for, incest. More reasonably, as Judith Herman's 1970s study of American sexual abuse showed, the causes of incest are complex and include the mother's agency within the home, economic instability, social isolation, poor health and the stresses of caring for large families.[66] Although her study was some forty years after the period studied here, she explored incest within a working-class community and her analysis provides insightful guidance for understanding the narratives contained in Scotland's historical incest prosecutions. Elizabeth Stanko's more general criminological research on male violence against women supports Herman's study. Stanko argues that incest is inherently coercive but not always violent; the coercion exists within the structural positions within the family of the offender and the victim.[67] This explanation is integral to understanding why another person's agency was often sought in order to report a crime and the difficulties victims overcame to reach the police. Both Stanko and Carol Smart comment on the extent of under-reporting of incest and other sexual crimes committed against women and children.[68] Although not working within the same legal system, their explanations of the social and familial obstacles to reporting inform an examination of the Scottish processes of prosecution, from reporting at the police office to an appearance in court.

Incest may be perpetrated by any combination of familial partners and can be consensual or non-consensual. As Scotland's supreme criminal court, the HCJ records contain evidence of three types of incest outside paternal abuse. Firstly, tri-generational incest which remains possibly the least explored incestuous relationship. The normative social construction of grandfathers as caring, often indulgent older members of a family has occluded understanding of their role in incest. As Jean Goodwin et al. reveal, grandfather incest is often viewed as benign. They calculate that tri-generational incest accounts for 10 per cent of all prosecuted incest and argue that fathers who become offending grandfathers is a systemic development.[69] However, in the 1920s in Scotland, the evidence contained in the HCJ records counters both of these arguments.

---

66 Herman, *Father-Daughter*, 45–9, 78.
67 Stanko, *Intimate Intrusions*, 25.
68 C. Smart, 'A History of Ambivalence and Conflict in the Discursive Construction of the "Child Victim" of Sexual Abuse', *Social and Legal Studies*, 8, no. 3 (1999): 391–409.
69 J. Goodwin, L. Cormier and J. Owen, 'Grandfather-Granddaughter Incest: A Tri-generational View', *Child Abuse and Neglect*, 7 (1983): 163–70; it is impossible to know how much more was committed but remained unreported or failed to reach prosecution at some stage of the process.

Secondary sources analysing sibling incest fall largely within the scope of sociology rather than history, and to date, a Scottish historical perspective is missing. Sibling incest in middle-class English homes was neither 'uncommon, nor was it frowned upon', as Roper and Tosh argue, which Kuper supports in his survey of south London's Clapham Set.[70] The HCJ records contain no evidence of middle-class sibling incest and only a small sample of working-class cases, which were all male-initiated assaults, often resulting in pregnancy. Sociologists Tidefors et al. suggest that 'sibling abuse is even more under-reported' than adult-initiated incest, which may account for the very small sample in the HCJ records.[71] Of the cases of uncle-niece incest prosecuted, some were consenting and a subset was non-consanguineous. Under Scots Law at the time, incest by affinity (by marriage) remained a crime, and again, there is a scarcity of literature examining the historical perspective.

The history of interpersonal violence in the late nineteenth and early twentieth centuries in England has caught the attention of numerous scholars, but the field of sexual abuse of non-relations has particularly attracted historians of childhood and women. These researchers have largely concentrated on discrete county and city studies with similar approaches investigating the Scottish experience remaining sporadic and regional. To date, this is the first whole-country survey for Scotland to be undertaken.

Louise Jackson's formative study of Victorian child abuse in London examined both incestuous and extra-familial cases of abuse perpetrated on girls under sixteen years. Jackson examines a slightly earlier period and relies on elite perceptions of working-class sexual conduct to conclude that alcohol could provide mitigation in court, that overcrowding 'often limited the opportunities' for incestuous and non-familial abuse and that girls who revealed sexual knowledge were clearly seen by the authorities as 'depraved and therefore untrustworthy'.[72] She contextualizes the 'socio-economic standing of victims and defendants' and argues that 'gendered notions of sexual morality were intertwined with perceptions of social class', which were particularly important within the juridical sphere.[73] Jackson's data was drawn from the Middlesex Assize records,

---

70 J. Tosh, 'Domesticity and Manliness in the Victorian Middle Class', in *Manful Assertions: masculinities in Britain since 1800*, eds M. Roper and J. Tosh (London, 1991), 44–73; A. Kuper, *Incest and Influence: The Private Life of Boureois England* (Harvard, 2009), 39.
71 I. Tidefors, H. Arvidsson, S. Ingevaldson and M. Larsson, 'Sibling Incest: A Literature Review and a Clinical Study', *Journal of Sexual Aggression*, 16, no. 3 (November 2010): 348.
72 Jackson, *Child Sexual Abuse*.
73 Jackson, *Child Sexual Abuse*, 7; L. Jackson, 'Family, Community and the Regulation of Child Sexual Abuse: London, 1870–1914', in *Childhood in Question: Children, Parents and the State*, eds A. Fletcher and S. Hussey (Manchester, 1999), 139.

which operated under English law. Frustratingly, incest cases are not statistically comparable between England and Scotland because, as contemporaries acknowledged, 'the difference is a matter of classification'. Unlike Scotland where incest has been a crime since 1567, in England it was only classified as a distinct indictment separate from other sexual assaults in 1908. Attempts to compare the two countries would lead, as was recognized shortly after the new legislation became law, to Scotland being 'presented as more criminal than England and Wales'.[74] Further, Jackson's study does not differentiate between individual sexual assault indictments, which also prevents attempts at statistical comparisons. However, her work as well as extensive research by Carol Smart on the experience of childhood sexual abuse in England in the early twentieth century provoke numerous questions concerning reporting methods and the social and patriarchal construction of child victims and perpetrators within the judicial process.[75]

Whereas this English research provides limited opportunities for direct comparisons with Scotland, Roger Davidson's interest in Scottish sexual deviancy, child abuse and the dissemination of venereal disease (VD) in the late nineteenth and early twentieth centuries provides material prosecuted under the same judicial system. Davidson confirms the existence of a 'moral panic' concerning child abuse 'sweeping the Scottish cities' in the 1920s. He explores medical professionals' reliance on nineteenth-century attitudes towards the transmission of VD based on 'cultural meanings of disease, dirt and pollution' and how welfare and judicial responses to this moral panic resulted in legal instructions to prosecute cases with the aggravation of 'communication of VD' at the HCJ, thus increasing the number of trials prosecuted there.[76] However, his interpretation of an increasing reliance by the judicial authorities on forensic science in the prosecution of sexual crime prompts debate; this research of the HCJ sexual violence case files for the 1920s finds that Procurators Fiscal (PF), Scotland's public prosecutors in criminal cases, requested forensic reports in only a small proportion of prosecutions, and Scottish juries seem not to have been overly persuaded by the authority of celebrity forensic physicians.[77] Davidson identifies the difficulties encountered in contemporaries' ability to diagnose VD in a male which correlate with identification of semen on rape victims' clothing;

---

74 'The Difference is a Matter of Classification', *The Scotsman*, 6 March 1926, 8.
75 Smart, 'Ambivalence', 391–409; 'Reconsidering the Recent History of Child Sexual Abuse, 1910-1960', *Journal of Social Policy*, 29, no. 1 (2000): 55–71.
76 R. Davidson, *Illicit and Unnatural Practices: The Law, Sex and Society in Scotland since 1900* (Edinburgh, 2019), 35.
77 Davidson, *Illicit and Unnatural*, 34.

it is clear that in testimonies uncorroborated by eyewitnesses, forensic medicine could be employed to substantiate their claims.

Exploring the victim's experience outside the judicial process, Linda Mahood's and Barbara Littlewood's research on women's and children's welfare organizations, industrial schools and the management of delinquent girls in early twentieth-century Scotland concludes that welfare officials failed to recognize the signs of incestuous abuse preferring to discover non-familial sexual violence.[78] The HCJ records very much support their conclusion. Further, Jeffrey Meek's investigation of Scottish homosexuality post-1918, and its extension into lodging practices in the 1920s, has provided wider insight into problems associated with over-familiarity, trust and sexual abuse of landladies' children in poor communities where many families relied on extra income from lodgers' rent.[79]

Carolyn Conley's Victorian micro study of Kent as well as her writing on violence in historical perspectives provides the connection between north and south of the border. Although her comparative research on the UK's constituent countries is based mainly on homicide records, her observations on violence towards women and children conclude that contemporaries had a 'realization that the residuum might be beyond civilizing'.[80] It was a contemporary awareness that is not borne out in the records which reveal that working-class males of all types – not just those among the most impoverished residuum – could be resistant to compliance with societally and legally imposed expectations.

Female victims could also be 'guilty' of non-compliance with contemporary elite expectations. As Judy Giles explains, 'expressions of sexuality in working-class girls were perceived as transgressive of gender and class boundaries'.[81] Lucy Bland's analysis of four 1920s criminal trials involving 'transgressive flappers' found that 'too much sexual knowledge in a woman, especially an unmarried woman, compromised her respectability'.[82] Thus, working-class young women

---

78 L. Mahood, 'Family Ties: Lady Child-Savers and Girls of the Street, 1850-1925', in *Out of Bounds: Women in Scottish Society 1800-1945*, eds E. Breitenbach and E. Gordon (Edinburgh, 1992), 42–64; L. Mahood, 'Give him a Doing: The Birching of Young Offenders in Scotland', *Canadian Journal of History*, 37 (December 2002): 439–57, and L. Mahood and B. Littlewood, 'The "Vicious" Girl and the "Street-corner" Boy: Sexuality and the Gendered Delinquent in the Scottish Child-Saving Movement, 1850-1940', *Journal of the History of Sexuality*, 4, no. 4 (April 1994): 549–78.
79 J. Meek, 'Boarding and Lodging Practices in Early Twentieth Century Scotland', *Continuity and Change*, 31, no. 1 (2016): 79–100; *Queer Voices in Post-War Scotland* (Basingstoke, 2015).
80 C. Conley, *Certain Other Countries: Homicide, Gender and National Identity in late Nineteenth-Century England, Ireland, Scotland and Wales* (Ohio, 2007), 206.
81 J. Giles, '"Playing Hard to Get": Working-Class Women, Sexuality and Respectability in Britain, 1914-1940', *Women's History Review*, 1, no. 2 (1992): 242.
82 Bland, *Modern Women*, 192 and 194.

who testified using 'knowing' language could be framed as culpable in their sexual assault. Sufficient examples exist in the HCJ records to support this argument, although there is also enough evidence of PFs prosecuting cases in which the young woman cannot be constructed as a 'perfect' victim. The early twentieth-century Scottish experience of sexual violence does not appear to have been wholly 'the perpetrator expressing his masculinity through violence and the establishment enforcing its masculinity through the legal system'.[83] Class and gender bias is evident in the case papers, but it is not visible in jury verdicts.

A criminological approach further helps to understand societal responses to sexual violence. Elizabeth Stanko and Stevi Jackson argue for a 'dominant rape mythology' whereby a victim's behaviour both at the time of the assault and throughout the judicial process may affect a trial's fairness or indeed prevent a case from proceeding to trial. This mythology is important to understanding the PF's guiding impetuses for selection of proceedable cases. It is also applicable to arguments considering the women contained in the 'dark number' who decided not to report an assault because of their personal perceptions of the 'mythology' and the possible reluctance to rely on a patriarchal judiciary to prosecute on their behalf. Stanko's research provides a theoretical exploration of male violence concerning victims of sexual crime, which is relevant here when working-class female lifestyles and working patterns are considered. Unchaperoned and travelling at irregular hours exposed many working-class women to sexually violent predators.[84] Kim Stevenson's research on English sexual consent and judicial attitudes towards sexual violence has provided valuable insight into societal perceptions of those committing incest and rape, the censorship of incest cases in the media and how notions of consent were enshrined in law but not necessarily upheld by it.[85] Her work is complemented by Aileen McColgan's more recent legal examination of sexual history evidence and juridical responses to non-virginal rape victims.[86]

In her insightful work on a mid-nineteenth-century Lancastrian town, Shani D'Cruze reveals that women brave enough to seek legal redress challenged

---

83 G. Greer, BBC Radio 4, *Today*, 20 March 2018.
84 E. Stanko, 'Typical Violence, Normal Precaution: Men, Women and Interpersonal Violence in England, Wales, Scotland and the USA', in *Women, Violence and Social Control*, eds J. Hanmer and M. Maynard (London, 1990), 129.
85 Among other publications, Stanko, *Intimate Intrusions*; Stevenson, '"These are cases"'; 'Ingenuities of the Female Mind: Legal and Public Perceptions of Sexual Violence in Victorian England, 1850-1890', in *Everyday Violence in Britain 1850-1950, Gender and Class*, ed. S. D'Cruze (London, 2000), 89–103.
86 A. McColgan, 'Common Law and the Relevance of Sexual History Evidence', *Oxford Journal of Legal Studies*, 16, no. 2 (1996): 275–307.

potentially biased elite perceptions and that the courts 'enabled working-class women to voice a somewhat different perception of acceptable masculine conduct'. By stepping outside their expected sphere of acquiescence, they disrupted patriarchal assumptions concerning access to female bodies.[87] D'Cruze's study provides a less restrictive assessment of the judicial processes that permitted some cases to appear in court, which may otherwise have been considered not proceedable due to the unsympathetic nature of the victim's character, class and lifestyle. D'Cruze's research supports arguments concerning the PF's potential to 'sift' cases prior to prosecution.

Wider-ranging studies by Joanna Bourke and Martin Wiener have examined early twentieth-century England and Wales and the United States. Bourke's reflections on sexual violence globally and her specific study on rape are instructive for their comprehensive insight. Having surveyed British and American legal and social responses to rape across the late nineteenth and twentieth centuries, she concludes that 'societies characterized by sexual equality, peacefulness and high levels of female economic power tend to have relatively low levels of rape'.[88] As this study suggests in its conclusion, it is possible that concepts of masculinity and maternal domestic and financial agency were causal factors influencing geographical patterns of sexual violence prosecutions. Martin Wiener's detailed exploration of Victorian male violence has concentrated on English murder and spousal and familial violence.[89] While neither's research is directly comparative, their breadth and scope have influenced theoretical considerations of the HCJ Scottish data, and areas of convergence and divergence.

Lastly, an understanding of the changing attitudes and consequent legislation enacted from the middle of the nineteenth century is important in contextualizing the judicial environment prevailing in the 1920s in Scotland. As the elites recognized and restricted their own tendencies to sexual violence, increasingly they feared what the lower orders might be capable of and in consequence organized the law to deter and punish violation of females. Lindsay Farmer traces the progression of sexual offences laws in Scotland from the late seventeenth century, when MacKenzie's 1678 *Law and Customs in Scotland in Matters Criminal* offered 'a separate chapter on rape, following the title on incest, sodomy, and bestiality' but categorized these as 'moral or religious wrongs' rather

---

87 S. D'Cruze, 'Sex, Violence and Local Courts: Working-Class Respectability in a Mid-Nineteenth Century Lancashire Town', *British Journal of Criminology*, 39, no. 1 (1990): 40 and 51.
88 J. Bourke, *Rape: A History from 1860 to the Present* (London, 2010), 436; J. Bourke, *Disgrace: Global Reflections on Sexual Violence* (London, 2022).
89 Wiener, *Men of Blood*.

than as sexual offences. After the Union of 1707, in general Scottish legislation followed English statutes, notably the Offences against the Person Act (1828), which redefined carnal knowledge to require only penetration and not emission to constitute rape. Further legislation between 1861 and 1885 progressively increased the age of the victim through which sexual assault was criminalized, culminating in the 1885 Criminal Law Amendment Act (CLAA), which consolidated previous legislation. Finally, belief that consent was given as a defence in non-penetrative sexual assaults was removed for girls and boys under sixteen years in the 1922 revision of the CLAA.[90] Thus, by the 1920s, a significant body of legislation existed to protect women from unsolicited male sexual advances and underage girls (and minor boys) from sexual assaults to which they may or may not have consented. It is within the chronological confines of this legislative development that most historians of sexual violence have written.

Methodology

Any quantitative and qualitative study of sexual crimes must rely on criminal records. This research examines the records of the HCJ between November 1918 and December 1930.[91] The HCJ records contain court papers, indictment sheets, correspondence between PFs and Crown Counsel (CC), occasional police notes, medical and forensic reports, but most importantly precognition statements. The precognitions contain the alleged victim's description of the assault and her supporters' eyewitness, contextual and corroborative testimonies as well as a wealth of social details concerning working-class living conditions. Thus, 'the precognitions were . . . witting testimony of the crimes being investigated' while providing 'unwitting testimony' on the legal process and the 'society in which they were taken'.[92] As documents recorded for legal purposes by the judicial officers, they cannot be read as a completely unbiased set of records, although to what extent they were mediated also requires consideration. The HCJ papers are complemented by Books of Adjournal and Minute Books,

---

90 L. Farmer, *Making the Modern Criminal Law: Criminalization and Civil Order* (Oxford 2016); *Criminal Law, Tradition and Legal Order: Crime and the Genius of Scots Law 1747 to the Present* (Cambridge, 2005).
91 Originally, it had been hoped to extend to September 1939 to examine the impact of an imminent second war on criminal statistics; however, the project was overwhelmingly well-populated with case studies after the first decade had been collected.
92 R. Shiels, 'The Crown Practice of Precognition in Mid-Victorian Scotland', *Law, Crime and History*, 2 (2015): 31.

both of which summarize trial proceedings and provide jury details and assist reconstruction of the key protagonists and the crime. Where available, trial transcripts have also been consulted.

The indictments collected are incest, rape, attempt to ravish and LLPB between November 1918 and December 1930. Similar case details have been collected every five years from 1885 to 1910 to provide a pre-war comparison. A further survey of HCJ assault records was made to ascertain how many were male-on-female cases and of those which included elements of sexual assault. In total, over 700 case files across all indictments now populate a database of sexual crime. Where a case was indicted under combined charges, for example, rape and LLPB, it has been counted under the higher indictment. Geographical distribution has been collected by loci of the crime rather than the circuit court in which it was heard. Water closets, stairs, buses and railway carriages have all been counted with other interior locations because of their 'closed' environment with walls and doors, while waste ground and streets are counted among exterior locations. A few rapes occurred in parked vehicles, which have been counted as exterior locations because these assaults could have been witnessed by passers-by. Unless the victim's age when assaults began is stated in the records, their age at the date of trial has been used.

Monkkonen and Johnson state that 'all crime rates are of questionable validity' not only because they can only measure 'a fraction of the amount of criminality' but also because across time and jurisdictions, the methods of data collection change and therefore direct comparison is extremely difficult. Thus, this study does not rely heavily on comparative analysis of crime statistics between jurisdictions.[93] Further, Arnold and Brady question the comparability of archive over time: 'are we looking at the same thing?'[94] From a detailed reading of the late nineteenth-century pre-war sample years and the 1920s, the answer in the case of the HCJ records is yes: not only do the precognitions demonstrate the same methodology but also the same judges' and PFs' names appear across the decades. While Peter King argues that 'counting and comparing indictments' is 'extremely limiting', quantification is valuable to understand the 'amount' of crime prosecuted and comparison between the pre-war cases and the 1920s is useful to plot fluctuations in sexual violence by individual indictments.[95] However, by complementing the statistics with qualitative research to include the

---

93   Monkkonen and Johnson, *Civilization of Crime*, 233.
94   Arnold and Brady, eds, *What Is Masculinity?*, 2.
95   P. King, 'Female Offenders, Work and Life-Cycle Change in late Eighteenth-Century London', *Continuity and Change*, 11, issue 1 (1996): 62.

'voices' contained in the HCJ papers, it is possible to delve beyond the numbers to understand the lived experience of both the victim and the accused. Historical investigation of crime has developed so far in recent decades that reliance on one without the other would provide a rather barren argument. However, it is necessary to read 'across the grain' of any archive to understand the social context of the key participants in the legal process.

An uncritical 'respect and a lack of scepticism' towards the data obscures any biases, motives and working methods of those compiling the records. Thus, by subjecting the compilers of criminal statistical and narrative records, such as the precognitions, to contextual scrutiny, it may be possible to discern 'the experience and decisions of a multiplicity of actors in the interactive social process of criminal justice'.[96] Thus, the PF and his team of precognoscers and other associates cannot be assumed, by their background or professional training, to have been part of the elites, although they were directly employed by them and their sympathies may have leaned towards their employers. In precognoscing victims and witnesses to sexual crime, these legal officers may provide 'direct access to the speech of ordinary people . . . who otherwise have no voice'.[97] However, it cannot be assumed that the precognitions contain a verbatim transcript of witnesses' testimonies. Witnesses' wording may have been smoothed to conform to legal English, although the precognitions provide ample examples of what appear to be direct transcription of key phrases and dialect.[98] It is possible that witnesses' testimonies were rehearsed in some way, refining their suitability to support a prosecution. However, as will be explored in the next chapter, from the process for their collection, the speed at which they were collected after a crime was reported and the discipline required of the PF in carrying out his duties, the precognitions are likely to be as close as possible to the witness's spoken words as the historian could expect.

Further, it must be emphasized that the cases examined here are *prosecuted* cases. They may not be typical of the whole amount of sexual crime, but in order to become prosecutions at the HCJ, they satisfied, to a degree or wholly, the legal requirement for corroboration. However, there were several obstacles at which a case might fail to proceed and could disappear among the 'dark number' of unknowable crimes.

---

96   R. M. Morris, 'Lies, Damned Lies and Criminal Statistics: Reinterpreting the Criminal Statistics in England and Wales', *Crime History and Societies*, 5, no. 1 (2001): 116–17, 125.
97   M. A. Crowther, 'The Criminal Precognitions and their Value for the Historian', *Scottish Archives*, 1 (1995): 76.
98   Crowther, 'Criminal Precognitions', 78.

The first obstacles occurred within the judicial process. A case could either be unproceeded with: the system rejected the case; or it could be unproceedable: it had not reached the bar of evidence required to prosecute.[99] Firstly, the police might dismiss a complainer's report without further progress. This type of police decision could be determined by the complainer's reputation as a frequent reporter of non-existent or petty crimes, or on a perceived class bias. The class and ethnicity structure of the Scottish police had changed considerably over the nineteenth century. In Glasgow in 1860, of a total officer cohort of 725, 146 or 20.1 per cent were Irish, 3 were English with one foreign national and the rest were Scottish born. By 1910, the overall number of officers in the city had expanded to 1,613 and the proportion of Irish had decreased to 16.1 per cent, with 42 English and one foreign national. By 1920, the cohort had further expanded to 2,247 with Irish comprising only 11.6 per cent. This trend away from unskilled Irish towards native Scots indicates that police employment had become more professionalized with prospects of a career. This is further supported by police retention. In 1910, 183 constables could boast of having fifteen to twenty years' service; by 1920 that number had increased to 280.[100] Between 1900 and 1905, Highlanders formed a quarter of Glasgow's native police force, but by 1914 and particularly by 1930, increasing numbers of Glasgow's constables were local men recruited locally. The situation was replicated in the Highlands where police had generally always been native Highlanders.[101] Thus, Scottish police constables appear to have been recruited largely from the more 'respectable' working classes within their own communities.[102] If any class bias existed, it may have been assumed rather than inherent. However, the process in Scotland left the police with little discretion whether to dismiss a complaint at its first reporting.[103] They did not possess powers to reject reports of criminal acts without consulting the PF.

Having passed their preliminary notes detailing the victim's and accused's particulars, locus and nature of the crime reported to the PF, it was now his

---

99 Bourke, *Disgrace*, 11.
100 A. L. Goldsmith, 'The Development of the City of Glasgow Police c. 1800-1939', unpublished PhD thesis (University of Strathclyde, 2002), appendices IV, VI and IX. Grant's figures vary slightly, but they illustrate the same trend; Grant, *Thin Blue Line*, 50.
101 N. Davidson, L. Fleming, L. Jackson, D. Smale and R. Sparks, 'Police and Community in Twentieth-Century Scotland: The Uses of Social History', *British Journal of Criminology*, 57 (2016): 27.
102 Glasgow's police force in 1910 was classified as skilled manual 34 per cent and semi-skilled manual 54 per cent, which in 1924–5 were 56 and 30 per cent, respectively; L. A. Jackson with N. Davidson, L. Fleming, D. M. Smale and R. Sparks, *Police and Community in Twentieth-Century Scotland* (Edinburgh, 2020), 220.
103 P. Gordon, *Policing Scotland* (Glasgow, 1980), 124; Shiels, personal emails to author, 7 and 20 November 2019.

duty to investigate promptly to establish the facts and seek corroboration. If corroboration could not be found, the case might fail to reach prosecution at any level of court – it was unproceedable. Thus, 'sifting' of cases at this initial stage of investigation would be chiefly an evidence-based operation rather than one based on possible class biases towards complainers. Consequently, the quantity of cases heard at the HCJ does not include all the sexual crime reported to and preliminarily investigated by the PF. Further, if corroboration was established through witness or expert testimony, CC might still direct a case to a lower court, such as the sheriff or police court, if the evidence could only support a lesser indictment.[104] Thus, the cases considered here had satisfied the PF's inquisitorial duty to gather corroborated and compelling evidence supporting a legally defined crime, which was worthy of prosecution at the HCJ.[105]

However, there remained another unquantifiable amount of crime, which has always been, and remains, invisible to the records: the unknowable amount of crime committed but never reported and suffered in silence. This is what historians term the 'dark number', which the anonymous author of the *Howard Journal* acknowledged in 1926 writing: 'it is difficult to form any precise estimate as to the prevalence of these offences. Probably not more than a third are reported to the police' and fewer still reached prosecution.[106] The women and girls who experienced sexual violence but did not report it have left no record of their suffering. However, the real and perceived obstacles preventing their official complaints may be comparable to those in more recent times.

Firstly, women may have feared that police, who they perceived as part of the 'establishment', would not believe them. When reporting social rape (rape perpetrated by a known acquaintance), young women raped by a non-spousal partner may have been reticent in presenting themselves at a police office for fear of any report becoming a matter of his word against hers.[107] As an unchaperoned working-class girl out late with a boyfriend, she would not

---

104 Archival enquiries have been unable to locate reported crime records, ledgers or similar, which were once held by the police and PF. Thus, reported cases that failed due to lack of evidence, or otherwise, remain invisible.
105 Once remitted to the HCJ for trial, unless the records have been lost in the intervening century, the current NRS catalogue comprises the full list of sexual violence cases heard at the HCJ.
106 Anonymous, 'Sexual Offences against Young Persons', *Howard Journal of Criminal Justice*, 2, no. 1 (1926): 48; also included in the 'dark number' are male-on-male cases of sexual violence, a crime which presents further obstacles to reporting and prosecution because of contemporary attitudes towards same-sex intercourse. These crimes fall outside the scope of this study.
107 Sexual violence within marriage did not constitute a crime in the 1920s. Sexual violence in the context of domestic violence was largely heard at sheriff court as assault and does not form part of this survey.

necessarily have satisfied accepted ideals of femininity.[108] However, as exhaustive research on policing in Glasgow reveals, it was the most intensively policed city in Scotland, making constables more visible and readily accessible to working-class victims.[109] The police may not, after all, have been as universally resented by the working classes as a controlling force. Their protection through street patrols and their long-respected welfare role in society, which distinguished the Scottish police from their English counterparts, may have encouraged perceptions of accessibility which in turn may have prompted victims' willingness to report.[110] This would also account for the preponderance of sexual crimes prosecuted in Glasgow which will be explored in the conclusion.[111] However, for some victims, it must be considered that reporting sexual violence to a Scottish policeman, despite his familiarity and welfare role, was too great a hurdle to overcome. Yet, the fact that some victims did report assaults would indicate that the police were not necessarily an insensitive male or patriarchal force working solely at the behest of the elites, although some could have viewed them as enforcing middle-class values on working-class people.

Secondly, there were obstacles specific to the type of crime being reported, because minor victims of rape had first to understand that a crime had been committed against them and then had to convince a parent or other guardian to seek justice on their behalf. Victims of incest had actively to accuse a relation. In this instance, the web of power, coercion, loyalty and love may have appeared too difficult to escape. Evidence in the HCJ records reveals that some mothers sought medical confirmation of their child's injuries before reporting to the police, indicating their need for elite validation before making an official complaint. Again, here is the fear of rebuttal by the authorities without some form of 'permission' to report having been sought beforehand.

Thirdly, some victims may not have been able to face the indignities of a medical examination. The precognitions reveal that in urban areas, police or casualty surgeons would often conduct a first examination. In rural areas, the local general practitioner more usually attended. Very few female doctors'

---

108 S. S. M. Edwards, 'Provoking Her Own Demise: From Common Assault to Homicide', in *Women, Violence and Social Control*, eds J. Hanmer and M. Maynard (London, 1990), 153.
109 Glasgow 506 population per officer, Edinburgh 537 per officer, Dundee 830 per officer and 888 per officer in Inverness; *Fifty-Fifth annual report of His Majesty's Inspectorate of Constabulary for Scotland, for the year ended 31st December 1912* (London, 1913), Parliamentary Papers, Cmd.6712, 58, 37, 46 and 51, respectively; Jackson et al., *Police and Community*, 54–5.
110 W. W. J. Knox and A. McKinlay, 'Crime, Protest and Policing in Nineteenth Century Scotland', in *A History of Everyday Life in Scotland 1800-1900*, eds T. Griffiths and G. Morton (Edinburgh, 2010), 198, 215–16; R. Storch, 'The Policeman as Domestic Missionary: Urban Discipline and Popular Culture in Northern England 1850–1880', *Journal of Social History*, 4 (1970): 487.
111 Gordon, *Policing Scotland*, 23; D. Donnelly, *The Scottish Police Officer* (Abingdon, 2014), 26.

names are noted in the case papers. In cases involving the youngest minor girls, female attendants were rarely present in a welfare protection role despite the requests of government welfare inspectors and the assertions of women police of their necessity.[112] Lastly, the ordeal may have destroyed a victim's confidence and emotional resources to survive the legal process. However, in the 1920s, the time between making a complaint and possible prosecution was very quick, and once before the HCJ, trials were heard and discharged within a matter of hours.[113] They were not the exhausting affairs conducted for sexual violence prosecutions today. Yet, some women, girls and their families may not have possessed the resources to endure the process.

With the unquantifiable 'dark number' in mind, what can these prosecuted cases of sexual violence tell us? They confirm that not all the women, girls and their supporters reporting to the police perceived them solely as a law-enforcing tool of the elites; for these complainers, the police were accessible. Further, their victim and witness testimonies satisfied the PF's requirement for corroboration, which may have been assisted by medical experts. The description of the crime fulfilled one of the sexual violence indictment definitions, which made them eligible for prosecution in the highest criminal court in Scotland. Because the Scottish legal system was built on the reputation of its long-apprenticed public prosecutors and their adherence to a universal code of conduct, there would appear to be few, and perhaps no, inherent class biases precluding some cases from proceeding to the HCJ. However, it is impossible to dismiss the personal inclinations of individual PFs. With so much time spent in office, building relationships with the crown office and circuit judges, it is possible that PFs might have assumed pejorative views concerning working-class females aligned to those adhered to by their employers. Andrew Dewar Gibb, a practising Scottish lawyer of the period, certainly held judgemental views, believing teenage girls could be readily persuaded to have sex who would later cry rape.[114] Equally, PFs may have held counter values informed through close contact with the working classes. Thus, any 'sifting' by PFs of cases suitable for prosecution based on assumptions of what might be considered acceptable to their superiors is difficult to discern: it may exist and it may not.

Since the HCJ sexual violence papers are certainly not the entirety of male sexual violence perpetrated or reported, they can answer only certain questions,

---

112 *Departmental Committee*, 23; 'Minutes of Evidence of the Committee on the Employment of Women on Police Duties', *Parliamentary Papers*, 1921, Cmd.1133, Q.1955.
113 The HCJ Minute Books reveal several cases being heard before the same jury all in a single day.
114 A. Dewar Gibb, *A Preface to Scots Law* (Edinburgh, 1944), 103.

perhaps only giving an overview of the process and the individuals involved at all levels. With the limitations described in mind, the HCJ papers can be used to evaluate what types of crime were heard at the high court; case details can be employed to test the PF's degree of impartiality in the process; they can aid understanding of the elements of dominant rape mythology – could girls with an 'unsympathetic' character expect a PF's and the jury's empathy and hopefully a conviction? Lastly, the case papers allow an evaluation of the role and authority of forensic evidence in the process when compared to the jury's verdict. The HCJ papers cannot tell us everything we might wish to know about historical male sexual violence, but their close reading provides deep insight into the attitudes of elite groups towards working-class sexual crime and the types of women and families who felt sufficiently outraged to report a crime in the hope, possibly expectation, that it would be dealt with fairly by the judicial system.

The 'invisible' middle classes

Also most probably hidden within Scotland's 'dark number' is the complete absence from the HCJ criminal records of any cases involving middle-class victims and perpetrators of any type of sexual violence. Despite statements given by Glasgow's welfare officers that they had not observed incest outside the slum areas, they did acknowledge that 'it is not confined to any one class of society'.[115] It has been argued that restricted social contacts among middle-class adolescents could produce amorous, if not erotic, intra-familial relationships and siblings could form intimate attachments which went uncensured.[116] Analysis of Victorian family structure supports this argument for middle-class endogamy and further suggests that the Victorian tradition of middle-class families intermarrying through partnerships forged by first cousins was its own form of incest.[117] Virginia Woolf's description of her stepbrother's advances towards her and her sister cannot be an isolated middle-class transgression; H. G. Wells reportedly accused Edith Nesbit's husband of incest with his daughter.[118] The Great War was the watershed after which family sizes decreased and arguably opportunities for incest were restricted.[119] However, cossetted in the family home, it is difficult

---

115 *Departmental Committee*, 35; see also Jackson et al., *Police and Community*, 186.
116 Tosh, 'Domesticity and Manliness', 57.
117 Kuper, *Incest and Influence*, 39.
118 Woolf, *Moments of Being*, 33–4; E. Fitzsimmons, *The Life and Loves of E Nesbit* (London, 2019), 200.
119 Kuper, *Incest and Influence*, 253.

to imagine that the behaviour of the nuclear family had altered significantly in the intervening years. Yet, the HCJ records reveal that there were no prosecuted incest cases of any relational degree among the Scottish middle classes between 1885 and 1930.

The HCJ sexual violence case papers only contain records of working-class men and women. They reveal that working-class men raped and sexually assaulted females of their own class. Middle-class men appear not to have been prosecuted at the HCJ by working-class girls for sexual assault despite anecdotal evidence to the contrary. In her memoirs of life in Buchan in late nineteenth-century north-east Scotland, Christian Watt recalled how the laird's sons 'would try and take on the girls' while they were bed-making, and later she explained that 'some landowner's sons showed polish "to their own ladies"' but maids could end up 'saddled with an illegitimate child to bring up'.[120]

Thus, it would appear middle-class men in Scotland in the 1920s never committed sexual violence against women. However, if committing crime is an essential characteristic of being human, then logically all classes commit crime.[121] However, a combination of perceived sexual morality and socio-economic status could keep the middle classes out of court because they could afford malleable doctors prepared to diagnose 'illness'. If that failed, they might engage good defence counsel able to avoid a trial completely or to persuade the PF to hear the case on a less severe charge at a lower court.[122] If these strategies failed, then a middle-class offender might appear at the HCJ.[123] Therefore, with an absence of middle-class perpetrators from the Scottish HCJ data, either men of this class committed sexual crimes below the threshold of a HCJ prosecution or their activities were redefined as non-criminal; a convenient episode of insanity could be dealt with outside the judicial system. Or any sexual crime committed in the home or within the confines of the elites' geographical enclaves was 'hushed up' in order to preserve decency and the man's reputation, and that of his wider family.

---

120 D. Fraser, *The Christian Watt Papers* (Collieston, 1988), 56–7 and 61.
121 L. A. Knafla, 'Structure, Conjuncture and Event in the Historiography of Modern Criminal Justice History', in *Crime History and Histories of Crime: Studies in Historiography of Crime and Criminal Justice in Modern History*, eds C. Emsley and L. A. Knafla (Westport, 1996), 37.
122 Jackson, *Child Sexual Abuse*, 7; J. Weston, *Medicine, the Penal System and Sexual Crimes in England, 1919-1960s: Diagnosing Deviance* (London, 2018), 88; K. Stevenson, 'Unearthing the Realities of Rape: Utilising Victorian Newspaper Reportage to Fill in the Contextual Gaps', *Liverpool Law Review*, 38 (2007): 416.
123 S. D'Cruze, 'Introduction', in *Everyday Violence in Britain 1850-1950, Gender and Class*, ed. S. D'Cruze (London, 2000), 4.

Largely, the middle classes inhabited comfortable, spacious homes with sufficient outdoor space not to be overcrowded internally or externally, and marital sex could be enjoyed in a separate and private bedroom.[124] In this middle-class scenario, a wife's refusal of her husband's conjugal 'rights' could have led a so-inclined husband to seek sexual relief elsewhere: incestuously among daughters or rapaciously among additional females in the home, such as servants. Whether this occurred or not is impossible to know; HCJ records for incestuous assaults from 'respectable' homes do not exist. Was respectability so highly valued among middle-class families that reporting incest to the police would subvert their pretensions to a more moral lifestyle than their working-class 'inferiors'? Equally, detached professional and upper-middle-class homes placed in the midst of gardens created discrete family 'islands'. Without the overcrowding and lives spilling into the closes experienced in working-class districts, what went on behind middle-class closed doors remained there and no amount of 'curtain twitching' could detect incest or other sexual violence unless the victims sought help. Servants may not have reported assault because they valued their position and income more than their well-being; and they may not have reported incest, if observed, for similar reasons.

Middle-class daughters were chaperoned indoors when male visitors called and on outdoor trips because, since the 'Maiden Tribute of Modern Babylon' scandal in the late nineteenth century concerning prostitution among young girls in London, it was acknowledged that men's sexuality could be a threat to the welfare of middle-class daughters.[125] By the 1920s, middle-class girls had won some freedoms to leave the family home without chaperones, but it was unlikely they ventured into working-class areas. The new department stores and smart cafés frequented by middle-class girls were not located on the streets most frequently noted in the HCJ papers. All classes might rub shoulders in Glasgow's Sauchiehall Street on Saturday evenings at nightclubs and outside picture houses. However, the requirement for virginity and purity was instilled in middle-class females, because signs of immodest behaviour might wreck their marital prospects.[126] Thus, while working-class young people were socially independent at an earlier age, middle-class young women in the post-war period remained largely restricted from unchaperoned access to members of the opposite sex

---

124 L. Hall, 'Impotent Ghosts from No Man's Land, Flappers' Boyfriends, or Crypto-Patriarchs? Men, Sex and Social Change in 1920s Britain', *Social History*, 21, no. 1 (January 1996): 69.
125 D. Gorham, 'The Maiden Tribute of Modern Babylon – Re-examined, Child Prostitution and the Idea of Childhood in Late Victorian England', *Victorian Studies*, 21, no. 3 (Spring, 1978), 356.
126 Giles, '"Playing Hard to Get"', 247.

of any class.[127] Further, the class transgression of a working-class youth raping a middle-class girl was highly unlikely to avoid being prosecuted if reported. Thus, the non-existence of such cross-class prosecutions from the HCJ records suggests either a genuine absence of these crimes or a total absence of middle-class girls prepared to report such transgressions.

Within the home, middle-class wives might have ignored sexual abuse of servants and daughters in return for 'a quiet life' or may even have accepted such behaviour as the norm if they had experienced it at the hands of their own fathers. Without independent income, middle-class women lacked agency in their relationship with their husband-provider. They risked reputation, livelihood and a roof if they reported sexual violence in their homes. Equally, heavily surveilled, abused daughters were unlikely to report violence because they too potentially jeopardized status, marriageability and a home. If middle-class females had the temerity to report domestic sexual violence, the ultimate male alibi could be disbelief: by the perpetrator, the police and the judicial system. Because it was almost never reported, it did not happen.

Scepticism could extend to the medical profession, who were reluctant to recognize sexual abuse in middle-class females because it did not fit with their correlation of depravity and the working classes.[128] Therefore, it might be virtually impossible for a girl or young woman to accuse her own father, uncle or other male in the household and be believed by those with the power to seek justice for her. Thus, the HCJ records indicate that if middle-class Scottish women and girls did report sexual violence, it was unsuccessful in reaching the HCJ, although it might have been dealt with discreetly elsewhere. In 1922, Hollander wrote: 'schoolmasters and clergymen who come in contact with little girls have consulted me from fear of giving way to their evil impulses; while others have come after being discovered to help them in case they get prosecuted'.[129] This is evidence that elite men could avoid prosecution by using the services of a doctor. Thus, it is probable that the middle and upper classes are absent from the HCJ records for sexual violence, not because they did not commit abuse of any kind but because elite men could 'keep their weaknesses out of sight'.[130]

---

127 A. Woollacott, 'Khaki Fever and Its Control: Gender, Class, Age and Sexual Morality on the British Homefront in the First World War', *Journal of Contemporary History*, 29, no. 2 (April 1994): 327.
128 Jackson, *Child Sexual Abuse*, 85–9.
129 Hollander, *Misconduct*, 139.
130 T. C. Smout, *A Century of the Scottish People, 1830-1950* (London, 1986), 138.

Naming and shaming: The ethics of sexual crime research

Access to the HCJ criminal case papers, which was restricted under the UK's 100 years archive closure rules, required special permission from Scotland's Lord President. The complete anonymization of all personal details for victims and panels, specific loci of crimes and witnesses' names was instructed because descendants of victims and perpetrators may still be alive, and in certain cases, they may not be aware they are the product of rape or incest. The Lord President has acted on their behalf as non-consenting, non-active participants in this research.

Disclosing family narratives, which the protagonists may not have wished to divulge, risks breaking their familial and wider societal trust. The deceased subjects of historical research retain their human right to privacy which must be respected.[131] These individuals can no longer consent to their identities being made public, thus the use of their narratives and their 'voices' relies on the researcher's integrity and any ethical committee advising the research. However, by anonymizing their personal details, the individuals contained in this study have become a data source, although this is not incompatible with their empathetic treatment.[132] Nevertheless, the question remains: by anonymizing the victims and perpetrators, is the researcher removing their identity to interpret their suffering and speak on their behalf?[133]

Scholarly argument debating anonymity in modern rape trials remains undecided whether to name victims. If victims are anonymized in press reports this increases the stigma of rape, yet that same stigma necessitates anonymity.[134] The scepticism towards and perceived shame of being a rape victim, which is different from being a victim of most other violent crimes, perpetuates societal attitudes towards rape: it is both disgraceful to be a rapist and to be a victim.[135] Thus, naming historical victims and providing personal details of their lives might help to remove perceived biases concerning the types of women who became victims – so-called 'rape myths' – which in turn could influence modern perceptions. Also, by naming historical victims, their suffering is memorialized

---

131   W. E. Smythe and M. J. Murray, 'Owning the Story: Ethical Considerations in Narrative Research', *Ethics and Behavior*, 10, no. 4 (2000): 313.
132   Smythe and Murray, 'Owning the Story', 317; B. Godfrey, T. Hitchcock and R. Shoemaker, 'The Ethics of Digital Data on Convict Lives', www.digitalpanopticon.org/The_Ethics_of_Digital_Data, accessed October 2022.
133   Smythe and Murray, 'Owning the Story', 324.
134   D. Denno, 'The Privacy Rights of Rape Victims in the Media and the Law: Perspectives on Disclosing Rape Victims' Names', *Fordham Law Review*, 61 (1993): 1116.
135   Denno, 'Privacy Rights', 1124, 1126.

in a way similar to unknown soldiers of the Great War whose names are engraved on the Menin Gate. However, a name alone cannot convey the suffering they endured; it simply recognizes their existence as a victim without context.

In modern news media, until a verdict is returned, the participants in sexual violence trials are prefixed with 'alleged' victim and, less frequently, as 'alleged' perpetrator. To avoid unnecessary repetition, this prefix has been assumed for both parties throughout, which also removes the implication of disbelief in the victim's complaint. All the victims discussed here were assumed to be speaking the truth because the PF decided to prosecute on their behalf. Thus, 'complainer' (equivalent of English law complainant) is used more frequently in the introduction and Chapters 6 and 7 when discussing the judicial processes while elsewhere 'victim' is preferred.

Sexual violence is a predominantly gendered crime, and it would be easy to insinuate bias into any research in this area. Thus, when describing the protagonists and judicial processes in each case, constructing them in a wider contextual and theoretical framework, great care must be taken to avoid injection of authorial biases.[136] The required anonymization of the case studies assists impartial analysis; the personal details and background, and wider lived experience, of the individuals populating the dataset supporting this research could be too painful to know. Making historical victims and perpetrators of sexual violence real by naming them risks injecting subjectivity where absolute objectivity is required. Too much time has passed for them to be heard to set the record straight.

* * *

The book is structured to provide the reader with a detailed introduction to Scots Law and the criminal prosecution process in Chapter 2, after which further chapters are divided into two parts. Part I provides a survey of male sexual violence as experienced in 1920s Scotland. Thus Chapter 3 offers an in-depth analysis of incest, describing the different approaches to familial assault taken by fathers, stepfathers, brothers, uncles and grandfathers. This fills in some part an identified lacuna in historical research on intra-familial abuse in the twentieth century.[137] Because this research has identified a preponderance of non-familial assault perpetrated on minor females, Chapter 4 discusses the 'landscape' of sexual abuse against minors, which is complemented by and compared with

---

136 Smythe and Murray, 'Owning the Story', 325–6.
137 Stevenson, '"These are cases"', 1–2.

the experience of sexual violence of adult women in Chapter 5. By exploring the 'voices' of the victim, and where possible the perpetrators', it is hoped that their previously 'unheard' lived experience of sexual violence can inform our understanding of historical judicial approaches to these crimes. Thus, Part II examines the judicial process from reporting crime to pleading in Chapter 6, while Chapter 7 investigates jury decision-making, the potential impact of female jurors on deliberations and verdicts and judges' sentencing trends. An important theme to emerge in this chapter is the different experience of the Scottish and English judicial systems.

Frustratingly, the records do not provide details of motive or causal factors. Therefore, the concluding Chapter 8 will explore arguments concerning spatial, social and cultural differences in crime distribution across Scotland. It will attempt to offer explanations for the disparity between violence in the urban south-west and rural Highlands and north-east. And finally, it will offer some thoughts on the relevance of historical sexual violence for today's juridical officers: have the dynamics of sexual assault and societal and judicial responses to it changed over the intervening century? What can history teach us if we are to improve prosecutorial outcomes for victims of sexual violence?

2

Scots Criminal Law and the Prosecution Process

Scots Law along with Scotland's church and education system were retained after the Act of Union in 1707. Thus, Scots Law is unique and its legal institutions are different from English law in several features. Scotland has long had a system of public prosecution which was supervised by the Lord Advocate and assisted by the Advocate Depute (AD) and regionally by nine Procurators Fiscal (PF). The Lord Advocate was, and is, the chief legal officer for the Crown. He decided which cases to prosecute and in which courts: whether summarily at police or sheriff courts where charges and sentencing tariffs were lower or under solemn procedure when the charge was sufficiently serious to be heard by a jury at either the sheriff court or High Court of Justiciary (HCJ). Thus, defence counsel could not elect for a jury trial. All solemn prosecutions were heard in the Lord Advocate's name. Arguably, the role of the PF in Scots Law as the public prosecutor provides the greatest distinction from English law. In conjunction with Crown Counsel (CC), which is Scotland's prosecutorial body comprising the Lord Advocate, his Deputes and the Solicitor General, the PF decides whether to proceed with any complaint reported to him and how to proceed.

In 1747 the Heritable Jurisdictions Act was passed which effectively placed the Crown in control of jurisdiction. Thereafter, local justice was centrally organized by the HCJ and the practices of circuit courts were regularized.[1] Further improvements were made in 1868 with the reorganization and standardization of the fiscal service, introducing nine regional PFs appointed by the Lord Advocate.[2] PFs were not legally trained men in the academic, university sense. Often, they began their careers as clerks before training to become solicitors

---

1   L. Farmer, 'Criminal Law', in *A Compendium of Scottish Ethnology, series: Scottish Life and Society*, ed. M. Mulhern (Edinburgh, 2012), 180; B. Levack, 'The Prosecution of Sexual Crimes in Early Eighteenth-Century Scotland', *Scottish Historical Review*, LXXXIX, no. 228 (October 2010): 183.
2   E. R. Keedy, 'Criminal Procedure in Scotland', *Journal of the American Institute of Criminal Law and Criminology*, 3, no. 5 (1912): 740.

before being appointed PF. By the early twentieth century, the appointment of a PF could only be rescinded by the Secretary of State for Scotland, which meant that, effectively, it became an appointment for life. As a result of long service, a PF might build a wealth of local knowledge and become an invaluable source of advice to judges and advocates depute in court.[3]

The process of reaching court began when a complainer (complainant in English law) reported a crime to the police office. Scottish police did not possess discretionary powers to decide which complaints to investigate, therefore all complaints were reported to the PF.[4] On receipt of a complaint, the PF commenced his investigation. In the first instance this comprised taking precognition statements, the Scots form of deposition, from the complainer and witnesses, who, in crimes of sexual violence, could include parents, siblings, neighbours, other community members as well as the arresting and custody policemen involved. Precognitions were not usually taken under oath, although the solemnity of the occasion and respect for the process may have affected those participating in the interview. In order to create a standardized application of the law, since 1868, the PF had been obliged to follow the instructions contained in the *Book of Regulations*.[5] Thus, from whatever region the PF reported to CC, methods of evidence collection and scrutiny of witnesses were expected to meet common standards.

Precognoscing of victims was carried out as soon as possible after a crime was reported.[6] This was usually within a few days as the *Book of Regulations* stipulated that 'no time should be lost in taking a precognition'.[7] In practice as evidenced by the HCJ records for sexual violence cases, this meant complainers and their immediate witnesses were precognosced within forty-eight to seventy-two hours of a complaint first being reported at the police office. When precognoscing a witness, the PF was instructed not 'to make the evidence stronger than can be fully supported in the event of a trial . . . and evidence calculated to bring out the truth should be carefully sought for'.[8] The implication was that when asked in court, a witness should be able to respond to questions with details matching those in their precognition; leading questions from the precognoscer

---

3   Keedy, 'Criminal Procedure', 742.
4   P. Gordon, *Policing Scotland* (Glasgow, 1980), 124.
5   R. S. Shiels, 'The Mid-Victorian Codification of the Practice of Public Prosecution', *The Scottish Historical Review*, 98, supplement 248 (October 2019): 426; the *Book of Regulations* underwent revised editions in 1896 and 1920.
6   *Departmental Committee on Sexual Offences against Young Persons* (1925), Hansard Cmd 2561, 22–3 and 27.
7   Shiels, 'Codification', 419.
8   Shiels, 'Codification', 419.

could result in a witness not recalling later the content of their precognition. Precognitions were usually taken in the PF's chambers, where he personally interviewed the witness or he deputized this to a team of precognoscers, which in the 1920s, as today, could be a solicitor's clerk or a retired police constable. Precognoscers were, thus, not necessarily part of the legally trained elite and were largely employed from a group of trusted individuals with a respect for the responsibility of the role and the requirements of a precognition.[9]

The PF's ability to compile the precognitions and other evidence relied on maintaining good relationships with the local police and their knowledge of the main protagonists, although if a witness demurred to give a precognition when requested by the police, the PF had the power to compel him or her to attend his office to be precognosced.[10] How closely each PF adhered to the code cannot be discerned from the HCJ records. However, homogeneity in question style and composition of precognitions from records compiled by all nine regional PFs in the late nineteenth and early twentieth centuries suggest the code was followed. Equally, the length of service of individual PFs suggests their continued employment was predicated on proper practice; Glasgow's PF in the 1920s, John Drummond Strathern, served into the 1930s.[11]

Throughout the precognition process, the PF sought to establish the details of the case from all parties, while during further investigations he sought corroboration of the essential facts of the crime, a key component of Scots Law. Without corroborating evidence, the PF was unable to pass the case to CC for evaluation. As explained by a team of welfare investigators reporting on sexual crime in the 1920s: 'evidence of one person is insufficient to warrant a conviction upon a criminal charge, and there must be corroboration either by independent testimony or by facts and circumstances'.[12] Thus, witnesses were not precognosced in each other's presence to avoid conflation of one another's testimonies.[13] Where eyewitnesses did not exist – a common circumstance in incest complaints – the PF corroborated the precognitions with reports from medical experts. Where an eyewitness might be another child in cases of assault against minors, precognitions were taken, although the child may not have been

---

9   D. J. Christie and S. R. Moody, *The Work of Precognition Agents in Criminal Cases*, Scottish Executive Central Research Unit (1999), 24.
10 Keedy, 'Criminal Procedure', 742.
11 Strathern's service is evidenced by his signature on all the Glasgow prosecution papers.
12 *Report of the Departmental Committee on Sexual Offences against Children and Young Persons in Scotland*, (Edinburgh, 1926), National Records of Scotland, Cmd. E878/79, 22; see Chapter 6 for further discussion.
13 R. MacGregor Mitchell, *A Practical Treatise on the Criminal Law of Scotland by the late Right Honourable Sir J H A MacDonald*, fourth edition (Edinburgh, 1929), 321.

called to give evidence in court. The PF was expected to precognosce all parties in a case, but in practice he might focus on prosecution precognitions. If the PF had not managed to take exculpatory precognitions, the panel could pay for them to be taken, but they appear to have been only occasionally produced in sexual violence prosecutions. Without exculpatory precognitions, defence counsel did not have supporting evidence to challenge any facts he believed to be irrelevant to the defence, although in practice informal disclosure of prosecution precognitions to defence counsel may have occurred.[14]

Before 1898, the panel or defendant gave a declaration shortly after apprehension, usually before the sheriff or a judge. The panel's declaration included personal details: age, marital status and occupation, and often provided some form of explanation of their crime. For example, in an 1885 incest case, the stepfather explained that he had woken up to find himself in the act of connection with his stepdaughter with whom he usually shared a bed along with his wife, who was currently away from home convalescing with a relation.[15] In a rape case the same year, one of two panels denied raping the victim, although he admitted in his declaration that he had tried to have his 'will of her, but did not manage it'.[16] After the Criminal Evidence Act of 1898, police were allowed to ask questions before they charged a person, but once charged they could not interrogate a prisoner, although he might respond voluntarily to any questions posed; this evidence would be admissible in court. Therefore, after 1898 panels no longer gave a statement before their first court appearance for fear of self-incrimination.[17] From 1898 onwards, the possibility of 'hearing' the panel's 'voice' in sexual violence cases disappears unless they appealed their case, which was only possible after 1926 when the criminal appellate court was established in Scotland. In this instance, the original trial transcript used to judge the appeal has survived, although appeals for sexual violence cases were very rare and therefore transcripts also.

The PF could not be compelled to prosecute if the case could not be sufficiently corroborated or the initial evidence did not support a legally defined crime, or if the accused had sufficient excuse for his actions. In these instances, the PF ordered 'no further proceedings'.[18] However, once a competent and compelling case had been compiled, the precognitions were assembled in a standardized

---

14 R. Shiels email to author, 7 November 2019.
15 AD14/85/13.
16 AD14/85/126.
17 Keedy, 'Criminal Procedure', 743.
18 Mitchell, *Practical Treatise*, 321; Gordon, *Policing Scotland*, 125; these cases are invisible to this study which investigates HCJ prosecuted crimes.

format with an index and any extract convictions relating to the panel's previous charges.[19] They were then presented to the Crown Agent (CA) in Edinburgh, accompanied by the PF's opinion of the case.[20] Thereafter, the case papers were submitted to CC. Officially, CC decided the indictment and the court in which a prosecution would be heard. If the sentencing possibilities for the chosen indictment exceeded two years, automatically the case would be heard in the HCJ.[21] However, in practice, the PF would have already indicated his choice of indictment and court, and from correspondence available in some sexual violence cases, the PF might proceed with a prosecution against CC's advice. Again, the PF's local knowledge gained through long service and his personal proclivities towards certain types of crime could influence a case's progress and possibly its ultimate success.[22]

Once complaints had been received and precognitions taken, any further interviews conducted after the precognitions were presented to the CA were not included, which meant that the case to be tried would be judged on evidence collected as close in time to the event as possible. The next opportunity for witnesses to give evidence was in court. Unless instructed to collect further details by the AD, these precognitions formed the basis for a future prosecution. Occasionally and most often involving children's precognitions, the AD might ask for clarification of facts or meaning and, therefore, a further precognition would be taken and appended to the original.

Sent in 1912 by the American Institute of Criminal Law and Criminology to Scotland to investigate the administration of the Criminal Law, Edwin Keedy reported that the PF's private examination of the witnesses prevented public dissemination of the facts prior to the trial. Keedy also commented on the lack of disclosure of evidence between prosecution and defence counsel and the dearth of newspaper reports prior to a trial which prevented case details becoming known to potential jurors. The lack of news reportage served to downplay the number of sexual violence prosecutions, and the use of euphemistic vocabulary in news reports in the thirty years after the Great War further diverted attention away from the sexual nature of reported cases.[23] Among witnesses, the speed and privacy of gathering precognitions virtually eliminated the potential for

---

19 Shiels, 'Codification', 424.
20 Keedy, 'Criminal Procedure', 746–7; Shiels, 'Codification', 424.
21 Keedy, 'Criminal Procedure', 746–7.
22 Keedy, 'Criminal Procedure', 746–7.
23 Keedy, 'Criminal Procedure', 747; A. Bingham, '"It would be better for the Newspapers to call a Spade a Spade": The British Press and Child Sexual Abuse, c.1918-90', *History Workshop Journal*, issue 88 (2019): 92.

embellishment or re-emphasizing elements of the testimony in response to a precognoscer's reactions, although it did not preclude witnesses in the same community from discussing their testimonies with each other before appearing in court. However, once in court if their testimony diverged from the evidence contained in their precognition, counsel might pose uncomfortable questions to ascertain the truth.

In the 1920s, sexual crimes sufficiently severe to be prosecuted at the HCJ under solemn procedure were indicted as incest, rape, attempt to ravish and the particular Scottish indictment of lewd and libidinous practices and behaviour (LLPB). Incest was 'a crime of carnal intercourse between near relations' and had been an indictable crime in Scotland since the Incest Act of 1567 when it had been punishable by death.[24] Incest was later defined in the *Police Manual* (1910) as a 'crime of intercourse between persons connected by birth, or through affinity through marriage'.[25] The rules defining incestuous relationships followed Leviticus 18:9:17: incest by consanguinity included sex between a man and his sister, daughter, granddaughter and half-sister; incest by affinity could be committed by a man and his uncle's wife, daughter-in-law or brother's wife. The prohibition then extended to include a daughter or granddaughter of a relationship with a woman 'with whom you may have had intercourse'.[26] Crucially, connection had to have taken place, although an attempt to commit incest was also viewed as criminal.[27]

In England and Wales, incest had only been designated a separate crime by the Punishment of Incest Act 1908 and did not include incest by affinity. Incest could only be charged between a man and his daughter, granddaughter, sister, mother and half-sister and did not extend to blood aunts and nieces.[28] The different judicial approaches to incest particularly exercised the PF in 1928 when presented with a case of consensual incest between a Scottish stepfather and stepdaughter which had occurred in England. He wrote to the CA explaining that he could not use evidence of their sexual relations committed elsewhere

---

24 'The Law of Incest in Scotland: Report on a Reference under 3(1)(e) of the Law Commissions Act 1965', *Scottish Law Commission*, No.69 (Edinburgh, December 1981), 1–3.
25 *Police Manual*, fifth edition (Glasgow, 1910), 105.
26 Leviticus 18:9:17, *Holy Bible*, authorized King James edition (Edinburgh, 1952).
27 Mitchell, *Practical Treatise*, 217.
28 I. F. Grant, 'The Law of Incest in Scotland', *Juridical Review*, 26, no. 4 (1914): 438. Speaking in the House of Commons, John Rawlinson MP suggested that passing the 1908 Bill would leave the accused open to blackmail, that half-siblings should not be included, and asked: 'Was there the slightest reason to doubt that the spread of education and of civilising influences was doing away with this evil, and that there was, therefore, less need to deal with the matter so drastically as was proposed by the Bill?' Further he stated that prosecutions for incest in Scotland were 'exceedingly rare'; Hansard, 26 June 1908, fourth series, vol. 191, cc.278–80.

to prove the case in Scotland since south of the border no crime had been committed.[29]

Before 1908, an English court might try incest as rape or attempted rape if non-consent could be established, or as a sexual assault if involving a child or as 'carnal knowledge under the age of consent'.[30] The requirement for non-consent in a pre-1908 English case of incest/rape was the reverse of a Scottish incest complaint in which evidence of non-consent was inherent in the charge: what woman would consent to intercourse with a near relation?[31] In England and Wales even after the 1908 Act became law, very few prosecutions were brought under the indictment with English courts seemingly preferring to use different charges to deal with these crimes.[32] Thus, direct comparison of incest figures for Scotland with England and Wales is impossible because, firstly, incest by affinity cases are included in Scottish figures for the period and would have to be removed from the total count and, secondly, it is impossible to calculate the amount of incest by affinity committed in England and Wales because it was not prosecuted as incest if indeed it was brought to the authorities' attention. Further, the number of consanguineous incest cases in England which may have been prosecuted under a different indictment is impossible to identify in existing records.

Rape was the 'carnal knowledge of a woman forcibly and against her will', and if under the age of twelve years, the charge remained rape even where force was not used, because a child was deemed unable to consent. Penetration, whether full or partial, was essential, although emission was not, and the hymen could remain unruptured. Crucially for adult rape victims, their resistance had to be 'to the utmost', but if the victim was overcome by other physical violence such as being held down by the perpetrator or his fellow assailants, this too was considered rape despite the victim no longer continuing to resist. Resisting but 'after however much distress, at last yielding consent' was different from being prevented from offering resistance and therefore was not considered to be rape.[33]

The requirement for physical resistance depended on the victim's legal age of consent, which had changed during the latter half of the nineteenth century.

---

29 AD15/28/17; PF's letter to Crown Agent, 31 January 1928.
30 K. Stevenson, '"These are cases which it is inadvisable to drag into the light of day": Disinterring the Crime of Incest in Early Twentieth-Century England', *Crime, History & Societies*, 20, no. 2 (2016): 4.
31 B. Levack, 'Prosecution of Sexual Crimes', 189. The HCJ records show that in consensual incest cases where both parties were adults, both individuals were usually prosecuted, although sentencing tended to be more lenient for the female party.
32 A. Bingham, L. Delap, L. Jackson and L. Settle, 'Historical Child Sexual Abuse in England and Wales: The Role of Historians', *History of Education*, 45, no. 4 (2016): 414–15.
33 Mitchell, *Practical Treatise*, 175–6.

Until the Criminal Law Amendment Act 1885 (CLAA), sexual crime against children had not been legally defined as a specific set of indictments. In Victorian England, the sexual assault of a minor could be charged as anything from unlawful carnal knowledge, incest, criminal assault, indecent assault to an 'unnatural act'.[34] However, the CLAA had been the legislature's response to a social outcry against child prostitution in London revealed through the salacious reporting of W. T. Stead in his 'Maiden Tribute of Modern Babylon' for the *Pall Mall Gazette*. A journalist and social reformer, Stead was a passionate campaigner intent on raising the age of consent to protect girls from child prostitution in the capital. His articles describing the procurement of a young girl to be sent to Belgium to be trained before returning to London to commence work as a prostitute provoked public outcry among the middle and upper classes and aided the passage of legislation increasing the age of legal consent to sixteen years.

However, a legal grey area remained for girls aged between thirteen and sixteen years. Sexual violence against girls under thirteen was considered a felony under Section 4 of the CLAA, while 'to unlawfully and carnally know or attempt to have unlawful carnal knowledge of any girl being of or above the age of 13 years and under 16 years' was a misdemeanour.[35] When the CLAA was applied in Scotland, the difference was a sentence of penal servitude the duration of which was to be decided by the judge if the victim was under thirteen years and a sentence of two years' imprisonment if the victim was between thirteen and sixteen years.[36] This difference suggests either a vestige of the previous lower age of consent law or an acknowledgement by the legislature that girls in the thirteen to sixteen years age group could be sufficiently mature, perhaps 'knowing', to participate in sexual intercourse and who might afterwards claim rape. In cases where the female victim was aged over sixteen but lacked mental capacity to consent or suffered 'weakness of mind', she was treated legally as a child.[37] Where the charge was indecent assault, the age of consent remained thirteen years for all minor females until a revision of the CLAA in 1922, which raised the age of consent to sixteen years for all sexual crime indictments.[38]

---

34 C. Smart, 'A History of Ambivalence and Conflict in the Discursive Construction of the "Child Victim" of Sexual Abuse', *Social and Legal Studies*, 8, no. 3 (1999): 393.
35 Criminal Law Amendment Act 1885, 48 & 49 Vict. c.69, sections 4 and 5 (London, 1885). Felony and misdemeanour are English legal terms.
36 A. M. Anderson, *The Criminal Law of Scotland* (Edinburgh, 1892), 97.
37 Mitchell, *Practical Treatise*, 176.
38 *Departmental Committee*, 21.

A further age distinction was employed when the charge was an attempt to ravish. Assault of a girl under twelve years was not an attempt to ravish if it was 'only a seduction of the child to comply with the accused's advances', but the same or similar activities were deemed more serious if 'the accused assaulted a child with intent to ravish', that is, with intent to continue to full rape.[39] Considering this fine distinction, often decided on evidence from a confused minor, an indictment of attempt to ravish was frequently combined with LLPB where victims were minors, thus allowing for a suspected perpetrator to be convicted on a lesser charge if the jury did not consider the evidence sufficient for attempt to ravish or rape. LLPB was defined as 'immoral practices toward young girls and boys, by inducing them to commit indecencies, and thereby debauching their mind', which could include exposing oneself to a child, inducing them to expose themselves and handling each other's private parts.[40] Revisions to the CLAA were made in 1922 and 1928, which affected the age of consent in all categories of sexual crime thus incorporating indecent assault. The 'reasonable cause of belief' clause that allowed an accused to argue that the complainer looked older than sixteen was restricted in the 1922 revision to men aged twenty-three and under on their first charge only. It became known as the 'young man's defence', and it is important to emphasize that it applied to the panel's first *charge* not first *prosecution*; if arrested again for similar behaviour with underage girls, a panel may have already used his one and only plausible excuse.[41]

Once charged on an indictment supported by the precognitions and other evidence, the case was heard at the first diet, or plea hearing, at the sheriff court. This was usually within forty-eight hours of apprehension and could result in the accused being held 'until liberated in due course of law' or until further investigations indicated whether a trial was necessary.[42] The panel was asked to enter his plea and any special defences or pleas in bar of trial, for example, an alibi or a plea of insanity. If the panel pleaded guilty, his case was remitted to the HCJ for sentencing. This took place some days later where his plea was confirmed before a judge, the panel's counsel might enter an argument of mitigation and then the judge passed sentence. If the panel pleaded not guilty, for indictments where sentencing guidance exceeded two years' imprisonment, the case would

---

39 Mitchell, *Practical Treatise*, 164–5.
40 *Police Manual*, 123.
41 The potential impact of these revisions will be explored in Chapter 6.
42 T. B. Smith, 'Bail before Trial: Reflections of a Scottish Lawyer', *University of Pennsylvania Law Review*, 108, no. 3 (January 1960): 316.

proceed to the HCJ for jury trial.[43] This was automatic for indictments of rape and incest.[44]

If the panel pleaded guilty, his agent could ask for bail under the provisions of the Bail (Scotland) Act 1888. However, in sexual violence cases this appears not to have been favoured, and if granted by the sheriff, the PF was the sole law officer with the right to appeal the sheriff's decision. If bail was requested after commitment for trial, it was again at the sheriff's discretion. There is a presumption of innocence in English and Scots Law, which if taken to its extreme would preclude an alleged criminal from arrest. Therefore, when deciding whether bail was appropriate, the sheriff considered both the accused's likelihood of further perpetration of crime, the risk of his fugitation, his ability to intimidate witnesses or tamper with evidence and public safety. This was not a pretrial inquiry but an evaluation of the public interest conducted by the sheriff as judge.[45] In practice in prosecutions for sexual violence, bail was rarely granted. Thus, in 1885 a man accused of rape against a 42-year-old travelling grocer in Elgin was granted bail of £10 but it was later thought he might have absconded to America; while in the same year a 23-year-old married miner in Leven charged with rape of a seventeen-year-old was liberated on bail of £50.[46] Thereafter, because the cases examined here are all drawn from HCJ prosecutions post-1888, any instances of requests for bail were made after commitment for trial.

While the panel was in custody awaiting trial, his defence prepared his case. Since few panels could afford for a set of exculpatory precognitions to be taken, and in some cases prosecution witnesses might not agree to be precognosced by defence counsel, then the Crown would allow the defence to read its precognitions and gave notice of all other productions to be produced in court.[47]

In cases heard under solemn procedure, a jury was required to be selected and sworn in. A Scots jury comprises of fifteen individuals who are empanelled from a list of assize which is broadly drawn from eligible individuals.[48] Five were special jurors with ten common jurors, the formers' status based on the value of their property.[49] Some women became eligible to serve as jurors under the Sex

---

43 Keedy, 'Criminal Procedure', 747.
44 C. Gane, 'The Scottish Jury', *Revue international de droit penal*, 72, no. 1 (2001): 266 and 261.
45 Smith, 'Bail before Trial', 309, 317–18, 320.
46 AD14/85/259 no verdict recorded; AD15/21/154 unanimously convicted on lesser charge of attempt to ravish, nine months' imprisonment.
47 Smith, 'Bail before Trial', 321.
48 1985 SCCR 282, quoted in Gane, 'Scottish Jury', 265. With an odd number of jurors, a Scottish jury can only return a majority verdict, albeit sometimes a majority of one.
49 Keedy, 'Criminal Procedure', 752–3; a special juror had to pay land tax 'upon $500 of valued rent' or pay assessed taxes on the annual rent of property of $150, own land with a rentable value over $100 per year or personal property valued over $1,000.

Disqualification (Removal) Act 1919, but in reality, women did not appear on Scottish juries hearing sexual crimes until early in 1921. Jurors were neither paid nor had their expenses reimbursed, because service was regarded as a civic duty.[50] Male jurors' occupations in the late nineteenth century ranged from distiller to farmer, merchant and innkeeper, while in the 1920s, male jurors fulfilled similar occupations such as clerk, farmer, plumber and fruiterer.[51] Female jurors in the 1920s could be teachers, milliners or married women with no occupation. As late as 1956 in England, Lord Devlin described juries as 'predominantly male, middle-aged, middle-minded, and middle-class'.[52] The position in Scotland in the 1920s appears somewhat different. Working-class tradesmen may not always have constituted a majority, but they were well-represented among the fifteen, levelling the social mix as Keedy had observed in 1912. Jurors' ages were not recorded, but government welfare investigators in 1926 reported that witnesses believed some jurors were too young and uninformed to consider sexual violence cases.[53] From 1919 onwards, to be eligible to serve, men had to be twenty-one years and over, while women had to be thirty or over. Thus, the welfare investigators' comment on youth probably pertained to male jurors, who were perceived to lack life experience and were also the age group often appearing at the HCJ on a sexual violence charge.

Before the jury was sworn in, the prosecutor and defence had the right of peremptory challenge of up to five common and two special jurors; causal challenge was unlimited for both parties. Either type of challenge was rare, as Keedy observed, which he attributed to jurors being intelligent men imbued with the seriousness of their role.[54] The records for the 1920s provide no examples of either form of challenge. Once sworn in, the court clerk read the indictment omitting any of the panel's previous convictions to avoid the possibility of jury bias, although both counsels and the judge were aware of previous convictions through their inclusion in the precognitions. The prosecution's case was heard first, and questioning was based on the precognitions. Once in court, the PF was not allowed to introduce new witnesses who had not been precognosced nor their names provided to the defence.[55] This meant that the court heard the evidence as known when recorded at the earliest point of the investigation – within days,

---

50 Keedy, 'Criminal Procedure', 753.
51 JC11/111 & JC11/118.
52 P. Devlin, *Trial by Jury* (London, 1956), 20.
53 *Departmental Committee*, 27.
54 E. R. Keedy, 'Criminal Procedure in Scotland: Part II', *Journal of the American Institute of Criminal Law and Criminology*, 3, no. 6 (1912–13): 835–6.
55 Keedy, 'Criminal Procedure II', 836–7.

often hours, of an assault – and no new threads of enquiry could be introduced as the case evolved, thus curtailing the more adversarial element of a prosecution. Thus, Scots Law operated on a system of 'proof evaluation' and an investigation to ascertain the truth of the facts presented.[56] Leading questions were disallowed to the prosecution, but in cross-examination prosecution witnesses could be led by defence counsel.[57] Once the prosecution's case and cross-examinations were concluded, the defence called any exculpatory witnesses. It was very unusual for the panel to give a statement once the rules of admissibility changed with the introduction of the Criminal Evidence Act in 1898.

As with English law, after all the evidence was produced, the judge explained any points of law to the jury, who then departed to consider their verdict, their role being to assess whether the prosecution had proven the charge rather than to judge the panel's guilt or innocence.[58] A Scottish jury can select from three possible verdicts: guilty, not guilty and not proven. The first two are universally understood. The third verdict is one of acquittal and can indicate two things: that the jury feels there is insufficient evidence to prove the case beyond reasonable doubt and as a corollary, that the panel may still be guilty but the prosecution has failed to provide compelling evidence to convict.

Since the middle of the nineteenth century, Scottish judges have debated the relevance of a not proven verdict. There is a suggestion of stigma attached – not guilty but don't do it again – as well as a perception that jurors may choose not proven because they are unable to reach a decision.[59] However, returning a verdict of not proven was not an acknowledgement by the jury that it was unable to reach a unanimous or by majority verdict and therefore offered a compromise; not proven is a verdict in itself. It recognizes the panel's innocence until proven guilty and that his guilt has not been sufficiently demonstrated by the prosecution's case to convict, which is different from being declared not guilty, and therefore innocent, of the charge.

Once women were admitted to juries, not proven verdicts became a hotter topic of debate. As one contemporary law officer commented, with mixed juries there was the possibility for doubt to creep in. Considered debate and deliberation

---

56 M. Damaska, 'Criminal Procedure in Scotland and France', *Yale Law School Faculty Scholarship Series*, 1588 (1976): 782; Keedy, 'Criminal Procedure II', 839.
57 Mitchell, *Practical Treatise*, 511.
58 J. Chalmers, F. Leverick and V. E. Munro, 'Beyond Doubt: The Case against "Not Proven"', *Modern Law Review*, 0 (2021): 1–32; I. D. Willock, 'The Origins and Development of the Jury System in Scotland', PhD thesis (Aberdeen, 1963), 353.
59 W. Roughead, 'The Luck of Adelaide Bartlett: A Fireside Tale', *Juridical* Review, 36 (1924): 218 quoted in Chalmers et al., 'Beyond Doubt', 10.

could be supplanted by a desire to relieve their consciences.[60] Also, there was no right of appeal in the HCJ until 1926. Without a criminal appellate court, judges feared that wrongful admission or exclusion of evidence or providing an unfair summing-up could further influence a jury's verdict, making the benefit of the doubt more onerous, leading again to possible not proven verdicts.[61] It was feared that a not proven verdict might allow inexperienced young male or 'squeamish' female jurors to avoid the responsibility of a guilty verdict. However, these notions proved to be contemporary perceptions unsubstantiated by analysis of jury and verdict returns for Scotland in the 1920s.[62]

Once a verdict was reached, the foreman informed the court whether the jury's decision was unanimous or by majority without divulging the exact division, because there was the possibility with a three-way verdict system that a significant majority for any single verdict may not be reached. For example, if six jurors voted guilty and five not guilty and four not proven, if the foreman declared the jurors' votes, there was the possibility that defence counsel could request an acquittal.[63] However, in the 1920s, majority verdicts for sexual offences appear to have been relatively rare and where returned, the court papers seldom record the jury's division, although in 1910 in Perth the division of an all-male jury was divulged as a majority twelve to three verdict in a rape case involving two panels and a girl aged twelve.[64] Keedy also observed the disclosure of the jury's voting as unusual, but when done it could influence the severity or leniency of the judge's sentencing depending on the weight of the division.[65]

In a verdict of not guilty, the panel was automatically dismissed from the bar, and in verdicts of not proven, the sentence was 'assoilzied and dismissed' with the same effect: the panel was free to go and could not be retried for the same offence. Where the verdict was guilty of the most serious charge on the indictment or guilty of a combination of charges as indicted, or infrequently where the jury had decided guilt on a different charge, sentencing followed guidelines established by the legislature. The judge was informed of any previous convictions against the panel, their nature and sentence. If desired, the jury could recommend leniency to the judge which is especially evident in sexual violence cases where the panel was a young, single man. At this point, the panel

60 I. D. Willock, 'The Jury in Scotland', in *Stair Society*, vol. 23 (Edinburgh, 1966), 221; Keedy, 'Criminal Procedure II', 843.
61 *Scottish Law Review*, XXXVIII (1922): 182 – judges here debated the right of appeal in capital cases.
62 See Chapter 7 for analysis.
63 Willock, 'Jury System', 366–7.
64 JC11/116.
65 Keedy, 'Criminal Procedure II', 841.

had no recourse to appeal the judgement or to object to the libel or the evidence led. Thus, when the judge pronounced sentence, it was required to be consistent with the indictment and the law. A child or panel under eighteen years could not be sentenced to death or penal servitude and would therefore be sentenced to a period of imprisonment. In practice though, case studies suggest that penal servitude could be handed down to male panels under eighteen years.[66]

Sentences for statutory crimes, for example, the CLAA 1885, were dictated by the statute and failure to punish accordingly could negate the sentence.[67] However, sentencing for common law sexual violence crimes – rape – followed a pattern of precedent based on the severity of the panel's crime, any previous convictions and, as will be discussed, the personal attitudes of judges towards the crime and the convicted individual. In guilty verdicts for incest, the guidance provided in the Children Act 1908 stipulated a sentence between three and ten years.[68] Thus, unless constrained by statute, the sentencing powers of the HCJ were unlimited and depended on the inclination of individual judges.

* * *

What follows is a discussion and analysis of crimes of incest, rape, attempt to ravish and LLPB prosecuted at the HCJ. These are prosecuted crimes only and therefore crimes tried at lower courts or assaults not reported remain outside the parameters of this research. The former may be a quantifiable number of cases, whereas the latter will always remain unknown, the 'dark number' of unreported crimes. However, with so little oral or written testimony from women of the late nineteenth and early twentieth centuries describing their personal experience of sexual assaults and their outcomes, the HCJ precognition statements provide a valuable and rich primary source revealing the closest insight into these crimes that the historian of crime is likely to achieve.

The precognition statements contain the verbal testimony as noted down by precognoscers in face-to-face interviews very shortly after the alleged crimes were committed. These documents cannot be assumed to be the verbatim transcripts of the victims' or witnesses' actual words, although there are instances in which the testimony appears to have been an authentic transcription. In Aberdeen in 1921, the precognoscer interviewed the four-year-old victim of a rapist. Unlike other interviews of girls of similar age, this one was conducted in the vernacular

---

66 Mitchell, *Practical Treatise*, 569–73.
67 Mitchell, *Practical Treatise*, 572.
68 A. Wohl, 'Sex and the Single Room: Incest among the Victorian Working-Classes', in *The Victorian Family: Structure and Stresses*, ed. A. Wohl (New York, 1978), 210.

because either the child could only speak Gaelic or knew insufficient English to reply fully. Whereas the precognoscer's questions are not included in other precognitions, in this one, the interviewer's questions are noted in English while the child's responses appear to be a direct transcription painstakingly typed out including all the required apostrophes to convey the vernacular.[69] Other precognitions contain childish words for adult anatomy using 'birdie' or 'feather' to describe a man's penis or stating that he used 'the thing he pees with' to assault her. The inclusion of this vocabulary combined with evidence of childishly constructed sentences suggests the precognitions may be closer to the actual words spoken than previously considered.

However, statements taken from older girls and adult women reveal evidence of following a 'script': 'I struggled with all my might', 'I resisted to my utmost' may be straightforward responses to a precognoscer's questions or they may be the answers the victim understood were expected of her, the 'rape script' that she perceived existed to support her complaint and to convince the man in front of her that she had suffered proper rape and additionally had no previous sexual experience. Where previous relationships were admitted, there was usually some effort by the woman to explain that she had not had sex for some time prior to this assault. Resistance, screaming and putting up a fight were not mentioned in precognitions for incest, presumably because to make a complaint of incest required an enormous amount of emotional effort which was recognized by the police and PF when first reported, whereas a rape complaint might be 'his word against her's'.

There is undoubtedly a mediating role played by the precognoscers because they were invariably male and the victims were all female as were most of their eyewitnesses and supporters. There is no indication whether a female welfare officer or policewoman accompanied a child when giving her statement, but considering the lack of involvement from female authority figures in any of the cases prosecuted at the HCJ in the 1920s, it seems unlikely and yet there is no evidence either that a family member might have sat with the child during precognoscing.

There are identifiable omissions in the HCJ records which would otherwise provide insight into elite attitudes towards sexual violence, namely judges' directions to the jury, their deliberations and judges' summings-up. Because these cases were heard behind closed doors, potentially useful newspaper court reports for sexual violence crimes are extremely rare. On 20 December 1921 at

---

69 AD15/21/182.

the HCJ at Glasgow's second court, for a crime involving a mentally impaired woman, an all-male jury found the panel guilty as libelled for which he was sentenced to three years' penal servitude. The court journalist reporting the day after the trial provides no further insight into court proceedings.[70]

Thus, the court records for prosecutions can only provide so much evidence of the experience of sexual violence and judicial and societal attitudes towards the perpetrators and victims. However, the Scottish precognitions go further than most judicial records in providing the details required to reconstruct what happened.

---

70 *Glasgow Herald*, 21 December 1920, 9.

Part I

Intimate violence

3

'Abhominabill vile and fylthie lust of incest'[*]

Incest

The early twentieth-century lawyer Andrew Dewar Gibb acknowledged the long-held acceptance that incest, the 'carnal knowledge between persons who are near of kin', had always been a crime in Scotland.[1] The repugnance felt towards perpetrators of incest is emphasized by Scottish judge Lord Sands, summing up a 1921 incest prosecution: 'incest is a crime for which even a greater abhorrence has been entertained than for rape, and perhaps in Scotland 300 years ago the only proper punishment for such an offence would have been regarded as burning alive'.[2] As social and legal authorities have more recently confirmed, sexual abuse of one's children provokes strong emotional responses because it violates societal universal taboos and damages the moral welfare of the family and the parental responsibility to nurture.[3]

Despite prohibition under Biblical authority and society's abhorrence of this crime, some men have continued to commit incest and it is recognized that much more incest is committed than reported. Testifying in 1925, Scottish female probation officer Dorothea Maitland stated: 'I am afraid there is much more incest than ever comes to the surface'.[4] In England in the same year, Dr Letitia Fairfield, Chief Medical Officer for London, claimed: 'incest is much more common than is imagined. It is not increasing but the full extent of this evil is not

---

[*] 'The Law of Incest in Scotland: Report on a Reference under section (3)(1)(e) of the Law Commissions Act 1965', *Scottish Law Commission*, no. 69 (December 1981): 1.
[1] A. D. Gibb, *Scotland in Eclipse* (London, 1930), 90; *The Law of Incest in Scotland*, Memorandum no.44, Scottish Law Commission (April, 1980), 5.
[2] JC14/36.
[3] J. G. Jones, 'Sexual Abuse of Children: Current Concepts', *American Journal of Diseases of Children*, 136, no. 2 (1982): 142; Scottish Law Commission, *Law of Incest*, 4.
[4] D. Maitland, *Report of the Departmental Committee on Reformatory and Industrial Schools in Scotland, Minutes of Evidence taken before the Young Offenders Committee* (Edinburgh, 1925), NRS, cmd 878/73, Q1408.

yet realized'.⁵ How much incest was committed was incalculable because not all, perhaps very few, cases were prosecuted, but contemporary welfare investigators suspected that it occurred at all levels of society, although they believed it was concentrated among the economically disadvantaged inhabiting poor housing and often exacerbated by alcohol abuse.⁶

Society's attitudes towards incest had become entrenched during the nineteenth century as legislation was introduced gradually raising the age of consent to sixteen years by 1885 with the introduction of the Criminal Law Amendment Act (CLAA). During 1884, the *Royal Commission on the Housing of the Working Classes* took evidence from witnesses around Britain on topics ranging from tenement construction, wages and rents to immorality and incest.⁷ The commission reported overcrowding which precluded privacy and produced shame. Incest was considered 'common' where families ate, lived and slept in a single room.⁸ The late Victorian Fabian, Beatrice Webb, in her autobiography, also spoke of her experiences with working-class girls, who confessed to pregnancies by their fathers and brothers.⁹ But the contemporary correlation between overcrowding, intimate domestic arrangements and incest was not only a British argument; it was also described in late nineteenth- and early twentieth-century Germany by psychologist Iwan Bloch.¹⁰ However, middle-class philanthropic interest constructed incest as only a working-class phenomenon, which presented the elites with a double nightmare: sexual abuse and moral corruption within the sanctity of the family home, where prying eyes could not investigate.¹¹

A father, brother, uncle and/or grandfather are all deemed protectors of the women in their families, with the Biblical restriction that they must not sexually assault any female relation.¹² However, as more recent studies of incest have discovered, by reporting her abuse to another family member or authority

---

5   *Departmental Committee on Sexual Offences against Young Persons* (1925), Hansard Cmd 2561, 15, §18.
6   *Departmental Committee on Sexual Offences against Children and Young Persons in Scotland* (Edinburgh, 1926), 35; J. L. Herman, *Father-Daughter Incest* (Harvard, 1981), 9; Scottish Law Commission, *Law of Incest*, 7.
7   The commission's findings became law in the 1885 Housing of the Working Classes Act; the commission was presided over by the Prince of Wales and fifteen other titled dignitaries.
8   L. A. Jackson, 'Family, Community and the Regulation of Child Sexual Abuse: London 1870-1914', in *Childhood in Question: Children, Parents and the State*, eds A. Fletcher and S. Hussey (Manchester, 1999), 133; L. A. Jackson, *Child Sexual Abuse in Victorian England* (London, 2000), 29.
9   B. Webb, *My Apprenticeship* (New York, 1926), 321, footnote.
10 I. Bloch, *The Sexual Life of our Time* (New York, 1908).
11 A. Wohl, 'Sex and the Single Room: Incest among the Victorian Working Classes', in *The Victorian Family*, ed. A. Wohl (New York, 1978), 201.
12 Leviticus 18:9-17, *Holy Bible*, authorized King James edition (Edinburgh, 1952).

figure, the female victim challenges the right of the men to do as they please in their own home.[13] Thus, as the 1920s Scottish data suggest, the authorities seem to have preferred to prosecute incest when it was reported to them rather than to seek it out in the family home where assaults were difficult to detect or address the societal factors they believed were the cause. Despite being illegal in Scotland since 1567, the complex web of socio-economic and intra-familial relationships involved in cases of incest meant that reporting and bringing a perpetrator to justice presented many hurdles. Summoning the courage to report abuse to a family member or neighbour required the victim to set aside shame or guilt at accusing a once-trusted male relation, to convince those she told of her truthfulness and then to take them all on the judicial journey with her to reach court.[14]

A 1922 Glasgow prosecution illustrates many 'classic' elements of Scottish incest cases during the 1920s, which will be examined in this chapter. A nineteen-year-old whose father had been killed in the war in 1914 had suffered sexual abuse by her new stepfather for over a year. Assaults always occurred when her mother was out at Salvation Army meetings on Sunday evenings and if siblings were at home, the stepfather sent them out on errands while he assaulted her. He threatened his stepdaughter that if she told anyone, she would be sent to prison, and when finally she told her mother, he denied it and accused her grandfather. As punishment for accusing him, the stepfather hit his spouse and stepdaughter after which his wife left him. Only after noticing that her daughter was becoming 'stout' did the mother confront her husband again at which point he confessed. It appears that the grandfather, mother and sister all knew about the stepfather's behaviour but failed to report it until the girl's pregnancy was discovered. When apprehended, again he denied it saying 'this is a surprise to me'. The girl gave birth in the street on the way to the maternity hospital and in her precognition, she clearly states that she had never had or attempted to have connection with another man. A jury of eight men and seven women found the case not proven by a majority.[15] This girl had suffered abuse for a long period; family members were aware but did not or could not intervene; there had been disruption in the family during the war; the mother used an alternative strategy to discipline and shame her husband until the evidence could no longer be denied.[16] If she had not

---

13 Herman, *Father-Daughter*, 129.
14 Jackson, *Child Sexual Abuse*, 48.
15 AD15/22/51, JC14/36.
16 Jackson, 'Family, Community', 135.

reported the crime, it may have remained invisible to the historical record like so many other cases of unreported incest.

From a comprehensive examination of prosecuted incest case records for 1920s Scotland, this chapter will explore who were the perpetrators; which male relations were the predominant offenders; whether incest was an indoor or outdoor crime; who reported incest to the police; and it will describe patterns of incest geographically and trends across the decade. Between November 1918 and December 1930, Scotland's High Court of Justiciary (HCJ) prosecuted 108 cases of incest, which is almost double the number prosecuted between 1885 and 1910.[17] There were undoubtedly cases tried at sheriff court under different charges and reported cases that were unproceedable for whatever reason as well as the 'dark number' of unreported incest assaults. However, it is apparent that these 108 cases had satisfied the Scots Law requirement for corroboration and were deemed sufficiently compelling and convincing for the Procurator Fiscal (PF) and Crown Counsel (CC) to prosecute.

Perpetrators

Of 108 cases tried on HCJ circuit hearings, there were 135 victims, of whom 125 were victims of 98 perpetrators of non-consensual incest.[18] These data suggest that prosecuted incest in Scotland in this decade was largely a single-perpetrator/single-victim crime. As the 1884 Royal Commission and more recent historians' research on sexual crimes in England and Wales have all discovered, the known perpetrators were predominantly working class.[19] Research for the Scottish Law Commission in 1980 also revealed that prosecuted incest is largely perpetrated by working-class relations, although they acknowledged that the survey data contained inherent biases.[20] From the HCJ records, it is clear that all prosecuted perpetrators in Scotland were working-class males; there were no middle- or upper-class panels.

---

17 NRS catalogue lists forty-six cases between 1885 and 1910.
18 Consensual incest cases have been omitted from this figure since there is no violence or intimidation by the male party.
19 M. Wiener, *Men of Blood* (Cambridge, 2004), and C. Conley, *Certain Other Countries: Homicide, Gender and National Identity in late Nineteenth-Century England, Ireland, Scotland and Wales* (Ohio, 2007), investigated nineteenth-century sexual abuse, but since incest was not yet an indictable offence in England and Wales, they did not analyse intra-familial abuse as a separate discussion.
20 Scottish Law Commission, *Law of Incest*, 7.

These men were miners, skilled and unskilled shipyard workers, carters, general labourers, tram conductors, firemen, bricklayers, farm servants or unemployed. The variety of employment illustrates that prosecuted incest was committed by men from all working-class strata and was not confined to a perceived 'under class', a 'residuum beyond civilizing'.[21] Perpetrators ranged in age from eighteen-year-old brothers to grandfathers over seventy. Brothers committing sibling incest were both older teenagers and young men in their twenties. Incestuous step/fathers ranged from over thirty years to men in their fifties.

The victims' testimonies reveal that incest was largely committed by coercion rather than active violence. These were not brutal rapes in the normal understanding of sexual violence but instead were perpetrated using threats, bribes and fears of shaming the entire family if neighbours found out. Where physical violence was employed, it was perpetrated by natural fathers rather than any other male relation. In a 1924 case, a 43-year-old man had been widowed in 1920 leaving him with five daughters and two sons aged between nineteen and three years. The assaults on the oldest daughter began three years later once she was sixteen during which he pinned her to the bed. He was known to drink methylated spirits and to thrash his children so badly that neighbours had intervened, but his abuse was only discovered when the girl stopped menstruating. Having told her father, he administered 'salts' but she consulted her doctor who asked if she had been misbehaving, which she denied. After being taken ill at work and sent home, her father instructed her to tell the doctor the culprit was a young man now in Canada. She was discovered to be six weeks pregnant and the doctor went to the effort of asking at the sawmill where she was employed if any young man had recently left for Canada. No one had and the father was arrested. The girl admitted she had told no one because since the abuse began, the father had 'ceased severely chastising the family'.[22] Another father kicked his sixteen-year-old daughter before having intercourse with her over a period of a year, and he was known to be violent to the rest of the family including the mother, who had attempted to intervene.[23] Generally, the absence of physical violence may be attributed to the emotional relationship between a father and his daughter, and the latter's deference to his authority, which allowing the abuse to continue beyond the first assault may be explained by the victim's fear

---

21 Conley, *Certain Other Countries*, 206.
22 AD15/24/8.
23 AD15/25/33.

of shaming her family, of betraying her mother and general emotional confusion leading to acquiescence.[24]

Victims

Incest with babies does not exist in the records presumably because either it did not occur or, for obvious reasons, went unreported by the victim or other family members. However, among the total of 125 non-consensual incest victims, 75 were girls aged under sixteen years, of whom 70 per cent were aged between thirteen and sixteen years.[25] Thus, most prosecuted incestuous assaults were perpetrated against girls in the legal grey area of not being a child under twelve years but having entered puberty, although not yet of legal majority. These victims were also in an age group potentially with greater resources to complain than younger girls which may have influenced their ability to report and achieve a prosecution.[26] Among young women aged sixteen to twenty-four years, fifty-four were incestuously assaulted (including ten consensual cases, by admission of the female party) – with six adult women victims aged over twenty-four years.

Although case numbers are much lower per year, comparative cases examined between 1885 and 1910 reveal a similar victim age group, with one 1910 case in particular revealing the precarious position of early teenage girls. In an attempt to remove the prosecution's key witness against his client – a 34-year-old carter charged with incest against his 14-year-old daughter – the panel's legal agent wrote to the PF stating that the girl might have been 'over the age of puberty at the time of the alleged crime'. The agent interpreted her pubertal status as somehow implying complicity, which meant she could not be adduced as a witness unless first charged with incest herself and then the Crown accepting her testimony as King's evidence. It was a vain attempt to silence an underage victim who had intermittently suffered her father's abuse which coincided with her mother's frequent hospital stays during pregnancy.[27]

Figures 3.1 and 3.2 reveal two gaps in prosecutions of incest. Firstly, between the Armistice and the end of 1918 (less than two months), when there were no cases tried for any age groups. There was a Winter Assize which sat at Glasgow

---

24 Scottish Law Commission, *Law of Incest*, 34.
25 Unless age when assaults began is stated in the records, the age of the victim at date of trial has been used.
26 See Chapter 2 for discussion of Criminal Law Amendment Act 1885 and differences between felony and misdemeanour charges dependent on the age of the victim.
27 AD15/10/145, JC13/128; letter agent to PF 19 December 1910, six years' penal servitude.

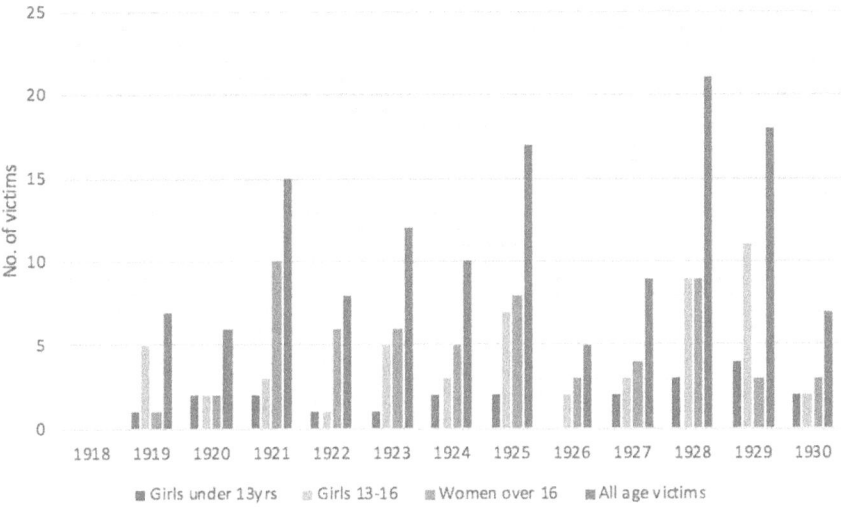

Figure 3.1 Incest: Victims per year by age group.

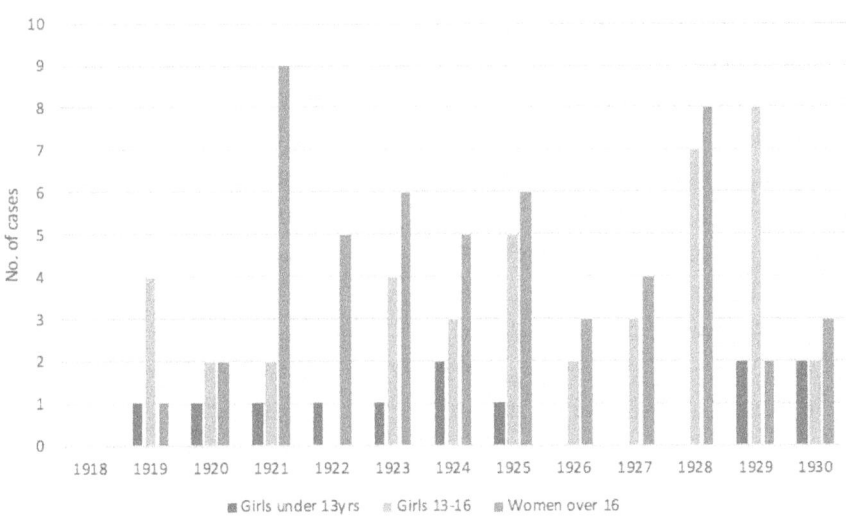

Figure 3.2 Incest: Number of cases per year by age group.

on 26 December 1918, but no incest cases were tried. If the judiciary had intended to delay scheduling incest cases until the new year, there were none heard in January 1919 and only two in February, with a further case heard in April. Given the short time span usual between reporting to the police office and a trial as evidenced in the records, it is likely there was a real gap in incest prosecutions at the end of 1918 extending into early 1919, although this does not mean there was no incest committed or reports made that for some reason were not prosecuted. Secondly, throughout 1926, no cases were heard for girls under thirteen years and there were only three cases for females over sixteen years.

The continued low incidence of cases in 1919 and 1920 may reflect a slow resurgence of the crime as male relations returned to the home after demobilization from early 1919 onwards. However, the indictment sheets for these cases do not cite previous accusations of incestuous assault or war service, making it impossible to explore conclusions regarding demobilization and a resumption of incestuous behaviours. In fact, annual fluctuations in case numbers may be attributable to reluctance or inability to report incest, thus delaying proceedings, as a 1919 case illustrates: a non-serving father had been committing incest with both his daughters since 1917, but it was only discovered and reported after the girls' mother had died and their aunts assumed control of the household.[28] The comparative sample years 1885 to 1910 also experienced low counts, with no year exceeding two cases until three were prosecuted in 1910, and no cases prosecuted at all in 1900. These may be genuinely and inexplicably low years for prosecutions.

The reduction of prosecuted incest during 1926 is also difficult to explain with any certainty. Again, it is possible incest was not committed in the same quantities during this year, or if it did occur, victims may have chosen not to report it, or for some reason, the evidence for cases reported in 1926 failed to convince the PF in a way that cases in other years had. Lower figures of prosecuted incest continued into 1927, while significant increases occurred in 1928 and 1929. However, testing these increases against identifiable periods of economic downturn (post-war economic slump in 1921, industrial action in 1926 and later global recession after 1929) and resulting unemployment do not correlate sufficiently to argue that peaks in incest prosecutions coincided with the impact of economic depression on families. Thus, it appears that cyclical economic pressures were probably not a causal factor in the incidence of incest in Scottish families, which would correspond with research conducted for a South Wales mining community in the 1930s, where economic depression did not result in increased or decreased expressions of masculinity and male-female power relations remained consistent irrespective of financial problems in the home.[29] Furthermore, revisions in 1922 and 1928 to the 1885 CLAA did

---

28 AD15/19/45; pleaded not guilty, four years' penal servitude.
29 N. Penlington, 'Masculinity and Domesticity in 1930s South Wales: Did Unemployment Change the Domestic Division of Labour?', *Twentieth Century British History*, 21, no. 3 (2010): 282.

not affect incest legislation and thus were unlikely to have had an impact on prosecution levels.[30]

Peaks in the number of victims aged thirteen and over in 1921, 1925, 1928 and 1929, as illustrated in Figure 3.1, are explained by step/fathers assaulting multiple girls in one family. In 1925, for example, seventeen victims resulted from twelve cases, in one of which a father assaulted four daughters.[31] Assaults against women over twenty-four years were negligible (six cases), although 50 per cent occurred in a single year, 1925. There were no consensual cases prior to 1922 and, overall, consensual incest remained stable ranging from one to two cases per annum with zero counts in 1925, 1926 and 1929.[32] These figures cannot include reported but unprosecuted cases or the 'dark number' of incestuous assaults remarked upon by Dorothea Maitland, the Scottish female probation officer. These invisible cases assume a deeper hue with incest: a crime committed behind closed doors by an intimate relation, possibly perpetrated over a number of years with familial and reputational damage a consequence if reported.

Typically, many cases appearing at the HCJ contained similar details: the mother was dead or absent, the girl had turned thirteen and she was coerced not to tell. This suggests that absence of a credible adult witness, puberty and secrecy were many panels' modus operandi. Sufficient precognitions across the period indicate this to be the case. In 1885 in Edinburgh, a fifteen-year-old's first experience of her stepfather's abuse occurred after he had delivered his unwell wife to his brother's house to convalesce. He returned home, attempted incest with her older sibling who defied him and then waited for everyone, including two lodgers, to leave before he assaulted her.[33] Three decades later, again in Edinburgh, a thirteen-year-old's father who had been a widower for ten years and was 'much addicted to drink' commenced incest with her after both her grandmothers, who had cared for her since her mother's death, died. Within three weeks, her father slipped into her bed in the kitchen, 'put his hand on her private parts and said, "all other girls do what I am doing to you"'.

---

30 The most significant revision to the 1885 CLAA, made in 1928, extended the period for the victim's counsel to bring a prosecution from nine to twelve months, thus allowing time for improved evidence gathering.

31 The Criminal Statistics for Scotland in 1925 largely corroborate the HCJ data held at the National Records of Scotland. The slight discrepancies in annual total counts may be attributable to some case papers being lost or not catalogued correctly in the intervening century or to errors made when the Statistics were collated.

32 The number of consensual cases averaged one per year, with annual fluctuations increasing to two or decreasing to zero, which might reflect that these were the only cases in those years sufficiently worthy of prosecution. Consensual incest will not be discussed in the same depth as the cases for girls aged thirteen to sixteen years.

33 AD14/85/13.

He had intercourse with her and forbade her to tell anyone. Between 1 April and 20 November 1919, this father had incestuous intercourse with his blood daughter at least four times; on other occasions she evaded him by getting out of bed and sitting on a chair all night. Finally, she went to live with an aunt, whom she told and who in turn informed the police.[34]

It was rare for precognoscers in incest cases to ask whether the girl had offered any resistance or had called for assistance. In contrast, in rape and ravishment cases, these details were always sought out by precognoscers, even from the youngest victims. The absence of these details from the incest precognitions points to the legal authorities' construction of incest as inherently non-consensual and understandably unresisted.

Fathers, stepfathers and ignorance of the law

In this period, Scots Law made no distinction between consanguineous paternity and step-paternity, although this may not have been apparent to everyone in the wider population. What mattered was the power relationship and the child's lack of agency; this bond endured irrespective of consanguinity.[35] A case from 1920 illustrates how the Scottish courts were blind to the difference between blood and step-relations. A widower was accused of incest with the 'lawful daughter of your wife' in 1920. His stepdaughter had been ten when they were bereaved, but once the child turned thirteen, the assaults began and were indicted as incest. Simultaneously, he was accused of attempted incest with his natural five-year-old daughter, both girls' evidence corroborating his drunken activities towards them in the communal bed in their aunt's kitchen. The older girl had suffered full penetrative intercourse; the child could not recall being penetrated, although her older half-sister said she had witnessed it. The jury found him unanimously guilty of incest with both girls.[36]

It might be assumed that a man raised in a community with instinctive and societal prohibition on incest would not assault either a blood daughter or a stepdaughter, although a possible lack of understanding by some stepfathers of the application of incest law to stepdaughters might have led to confusion. Two cases of stepfather incest demonstrate how ignorance of the law could be a first-stage defence. In a 1926 case, the accused's counsel wrote to the PF that the panel,

---

34   AD15/19/37.
35   Herman, *Father-Daughter*, 70.
36   AD15/20/93, JC14/35; seven years' penal servitude.

who had impregnated his seventeen-year-old stepdaughter, had declared that he 'did not have the least idea intercourse with her was a criminal act and the fact that he called at the County Buildings when he heard that a criminal charge was being talked of indicates the state of his mind in the matter'.[37] Likewise, a man in 1928 cautioned by the police with 'incestuous intercourse' with his stepdaughter replied: 'Is that a charge? That is not incest'.[38] Conversely, a case from Arbroath in 1924 of blood father incest with his six-year-old daughter suggests that others in the community recognized his behaviour as incest even if he was undeterred by the law. Neighbours were suspicious of a series of assaults on the child between October 1923 and April 1924 despite the denial of the mother. A male neighbour accused the father openly, threatened to go to the police but instead told the 'gas collector next week and I think he told the chief constable'.[39] Having pleaded not guilty, the jury found the father unanimously guilty. In this case, three strata of society – neighbours, the gas collector and legal authorities – all understood that incestuous intercourse with a young daughter was illegal. However, under the maxim 'ignorantia iuris neminem excusat' (ignorance of the law does not exist), whether the accused understood his behaviour to be criminal or not, it was recognized as criminal by the law, and therefore he had committed a crime.[40]

The number of widows seeking new marriages post-Great War led to stepfathers replacing deceased fathers in many families resulting in numerous half-blood and stepchildren in one home. Research on homicide within the family has revealed that stepchildren in the home can be an aggravation creating tension between new marital partners; the interruption of war could create uncertainty over paternity of younger children who might have been sired during home leave or be the product of a wife's infidelity. Such tensions could result in violence, particularly towards stepchildren.[41] Or as one perpetrator admitted in a 1921 Glasgow case, 'he was only doing it to get at her girls', meaning marriage to his new wife had provided access to her female children. At trial he objected to the relevancy of the charge of incest by affinity.[42] However, the HCJ data reveal that the prosecuted perpetrators of 1920s Scottish incest were predominantly fathers, not stepfathers or other male relations and that the

---

37 AD15/26/4, JC5/17; 51-year-old parent pleaded guilty; twelve months' imprisonment.
38 AD15/28/46, JC26/1928/57; 31-year-old showman traveller; eighteen months' imprisonment.
39 AD15/24/79, JC15/35; unanimously guilty, five years' penal servitude.
40 G. H. Gordon, 'Criminal Responsibility in Scots Law', unpublished PhD thesis (University of Glasgow, 1959), 40; Baron David Hume, *Commentaries on the Law of Scotland, Respecting Trial for Crimes*, 4th edn (Edinburgh, 1844), 26.
41 M. Daly and M. Wilson, *Homicide* (London, 2014), 81.
42 AD15/21/148, JC15/32; eighteen months' imprisonment.

majority of prosecutions were crimes against early teenage girls, aged between thirteen and sixteen years.[43]

Of ninety-eight non-consensual perpetrators of incest, only twenty were stepfathers, compared with fifty-eight natural fathers. Apart from the case already mentioned, the records do not give any further hint of motive or excuse for stepfathers' behaviour. Also, the data do not show a peak of stepfather assaults in the first years of the decade in which a greater number of post-war remarriages were likelier to have occurred; rather there is a steady trend of two to three stepfather cases per annum with no cases in 1919, 1925 and 1930. Census data distinguishing between the total number of natural and stepfathers in the population do not exist, which makes it impossible to ascertain the ratio of incest cases per type of paternity and therefore whether one was proportionally likelier to commit incest than the other.[44] Although the law treated consanguineous incest and incest by affinity in the same manner, because the societal taboo attached to intercourse with a blood relation was greater than with a relation by affinity, it is possible that judicial officers in the 1920s approached consanguineous incest more robustly. However, stepfathers may also have been more successful in preventing their assaults from being reported and therefore reaching a prosecution.

However, the prosecution data suggest that the trend throughout the decade was for fathers to assault their pubescent daughters, and from the number of cases where victims and siblings date the point at which the abuse commenced, the majority of fathers delayed full penetrative incest until the girl's thirteenth birthday. This correlates with similar research conducted on nineteenth-century London where attaining the age of consent corresponded with commencement of sexual assault and with late twentieth-century research from Germany connecting biological maturity to sexual attractiveness to male relations.[45] However, it contradicts Freud's analysis of his Austrian clinic patients, from which he surmised that younger pre-cognizant daughters would have borne the brunt of penetrative incest, fathers selecting them because they would not

---

43 A similar pattern was confirmed by Lord Ackner fifty years later attested from his practice as an English High Court judge; Lord Justice Ackner, 'The Crime of Incest', *Medico-Legal Journal*, 48 (1980): 86.
44 Michael Anderson offers in-depth statistical analysis of single and married men and women for 1911–31, but again it is impossible to ascertain stepparent figures from his data; M. Anderson, *Scotland's Populations from the 1850s to Today* (Oxford, 2018), chapter 11.
45 Jackson, 'Family, Community', 147; H. Maisch, *Incest* (London, 1973), 172–8, quoted in Scottish Law Commission, *Law of Incest*, 33–4.

remember the act in future years or be able to report it within or beyond the family.[46]

Incestuous fathers may have believed that the law became less punitive once a daughter had entered the legal grey area between the ages of thirteen and sixteen, thus providing some rationale for their assaults on pubescent daughters, although there is no narrative evidence from any of the panels or their victims expressly stating this. Daughters below the age of thirteen may not have understood the assaults as criminal and thus failed to report them, or if they did understand the nature of the attacks, they may have lacked the resources to seek help – again, the deferential parental-filial relationship hindering the ability to report a crime. These potential 'dark number' cases may skew the evidence towards what appears to be a trend for pubescent girls to bear the majority of assaults, which may not necessarily be the complete picture. From evidence in a few victims' precognition statements, they believed they were providing a sexual replacement for a deceased, ill or reluctant wife. This is illustrated by two cases: a father in 1919 threatened his thirteen-year-old daughter that if she told anyone he would 'get six months and said he was doing what he did to my mother', her mother having left with another man; and in another case in 1927, a seventeen-year-old daughter explained that her father had said: 'I would have to take the place of my mother and allow him to have connection with me', because her mother had died.[47]

For some step/fathers, incest was committed under the influence of alcohol. Of fifty-eight fathers accused, twenty-nine cases involved drink, six cases noted the father's sobriety at the time of the assault or in general and in twenty-three cases there was no mention of alcohol. Alcohol is and was recognized as relaxing natural inhibitions. Temperance advocates among the elites and working classes connected drink with crime and with domestic violence in particular where the need for 'moral improvement' was especially noted.[48] Yet, the victims' testimonies reveal that not all precognoscers enquired about the involvement of alcohol. Their focus appears to have been to determine what had occurred between parent and daughter, whether there had been witnesses and what the domestic sleeping arrangements were rather than to identify a potentially

---

46   E. Ward, *Father-Daughter Rape* (London, 1988), 104.
47   AD15/19/52, JC15/30; unanimously guilty, five years' penal servitude; AD15/27/88, JC14/39; unanimously not proven, assoilzied and dismissed.
48   T. C. Smout, *A Century of the Scottish People 1830-1950* (London 1986), 138; W. W. Knox, 'The Political and Workplace Culture of the Scottish Working Class, 1832-1914', in *People and Society in Scotland, volume II 1830-1914*, eds W. H. Fraser and R. J. Morris (Edinburgh, 1990), 153.

mitigating factor; incest was incest in law irrespective of whether the accused felt there was an excuse for his behaviour.

Where drink was involved, these cases were not isolated alcohol-induced aberrations. A familiar pattern was weekend assaults coinciding with payday drinking, which occurred over a prolonged period, such as the abuse experienced by twelve- and thirteen-year-old sisters in Glasgow when their stepfather returned home from work having drunk his wages; he appears to have alternated between the girls depending who was home on Friday nights.[49] Other fathers were described as 'habitually drunk' and their attacks did not follow a discernible pattern, while other men were not noted as drinkers yet committed incest with their daughters. It appears that for some step/fathers alcohol was not required to lower their moral guard and that forcing a step/daughter into sex was an active decision without the mitigation of alcoholic confusion.

Active decisions

Apart from a handful of cases where penetrative sex was committed with very young girls, the majority of prosecuted step/fathers began their sexual assaults with inappropriate touching and exploring of the youngest daughters before changing their behaviour to full incestuous sex, with or without emission, at puberty. The predominance of assaults prosecuted against step/fathers apparently waiting for girls to attain puberty suggests premeditation, although it placed step/fathers at risk of making the girl pregnant. A case in 1928 illustrates the premeditation employed by one stepfather; he stopped assaulting his twelve-year-old stepdaughter when she was having a period and restarted his assaults afterwards. He took the girl into the basement and the child told the precognoscer: 'it was always when my mother was upstairs cleaning'. In his last assault, the mother found them in the act, the husband denied it, but later it became apparent the girl was pregnant.[50] Avoidance of pregnancy could be a major concern for step/fathers because it might precipitate discovery. Few perpetrators took prophylactic precautions, although for those who did, contraceptive planning points definitively to acknowledgement of the risk of sex with a step/daughter and strongly suggests premeditation. In a 1921 case, the forensic report discovered large quantities of quinine contained in a cacao butter

---

49 AD15/28/93, JC15/39; unanimously guilty, twelve months' imprisonment.
50 AD15/28/28, JC9/21; pleaded guilty, twenty-one months' imprisonment.

pessary in the girl's person. As Professor Glaister, Scotland's leading forensic physician of the period, explained: 'quinine destroys the vitality of male seed and thus prevents impregnation or conception'.[51] In a case involving a ten-year-old stepdaughter in 1929, the stepfather's assaults began while his wife was in a convalescent home. Once she had returned, he planned his assaults around her absence from the house. The assaults continued over a period of eighteen months and each time he swore the child to secrecy with the threat of a thrashing. His abuse was discovered when the wife found the child on the street one evening. He had struck her for crying during intercourse. The mother took her to the police office, and from there, the case built. His use of soap to lubricate the child indicates further his planning for the assaults.[52]

In all these cases, there was clearly a deliberate decision taken by the step/father, not prompted by the uninhibiting effects of alcohol. The decision to withdraw prior to emission demonstrates their acknowledgement that incest and potential pregnancy with a daughter was a prohibited act. When questioned by the precognoscer, most girls said: 'he did not make me wet', and one daughter explained that her father went to the sink afterwards to ejaculate.[53] However, the number of fathers who did ejaculate and made their daughters pregnant suggests a disregard for the consequences if discovered. Also, some fathers may not have anticipated that their victims would dare to report them. Twenty per cent of fathers indicted for incest got their daughters pregnant, one father making a daughter pregnant twice, while 30 per cent of stepfathers indicted caused pregnancy. There is no correlation between those under the influence of alcohol and those not. The narratives provide no explanation for the greater number of stepfathers disregarding the consequences of their actions and resulting in pregnancy. Further, potential claims of confusion over the legality of intercourse with a stepdaughter provide no explanation either: if it was not incest, then an unconsenting assault with a stepdaughter would have been rape instead.

Illegitimate daughters

For some, alleged confusion surrounding sexual relations between step/fathers and daughters was further compounded by the legal question concerning a girl's legitimacy. Sexual relations with illegitimate blood or stepdaughters

51 AD15/21/148.
52 AD15/29/54, JC14/40; pleaded guilty, four years' penal servitude.
53 AD15/24/40, JC15/35; pleaded guilty, nine months' imprisonment.

were not included in Leviticus. Illegitimacy could be a special defence that, if proved, would force a case to collapse. Stepfathers might be released if the stepdaughter's illegitimacy was proved, but the situation became completely absurd to the layman in cases where the father was the illegitimate girl's natural parent: intercourse with an illegitimate blood daughter was not incest. It might be indicted as rape if non-consensual, although there are no cases recorded.

Before the Legitimation of Children Act 1926, the situation in Scots Law proved confusing even for the judiciary. In 1924, the PF wrote to the Crown Agent (CA) asking if a father whose daughter was born illegitimate yet who had signed the birth register as the father and who later married the mother could be indicted as incest.[54] After the Act, determining a daughter's status required delving into the birth register. In the case in which the stepfather queried whether sex with his stepdaughter was actually a crime, the arresting constable questioned the child's legitimacy. At the time of her birth, her mother and father were unmarried making her a 'bastard', which would have disallowed an incest charge against her stepfather, although it was later proved that her natural parents had eventually married, thus legitimizing her.[55] The distinction was painfully clear for a Glaswegian family in 1930 where the father of a thirteen-year-old was indicted for incest and it was known he had also had 'carnal knowledge' of her older stepsister. Under Scots Law, the charge was incest for both girls until it was revealed the older stepdaughter had been born out of wedlock, thus 'no charge of incest could be brought' because there was no possibility of legitimizing her; the alternative of rape was not considered on the indictment sheet or by the jury. However, the younger blood daughter's case was successful.[56]

In a particularly convoluted 1928 case, a stepfather attempted to prove that his two stepdaughters were actually his blood daughters by a woman who had enjoyed a dalliance with him during a period of absence from her husband and had fallen pregnant during their affair. If he had managed to prove the girls were his natural daughters as a result of the affair, they would have been illegitimate and there would have been no charge of incest to answer. The jury found him unanimously guilty, but the judge gave him only a twelve-month sentence for incest with two girls aged thirteen and twelve, perhaps demonstrating the court's confusion about the girls' status in law.[57]

---

54 AD15/24/15, JC5/16; pleaded guilty, two years' imprisonment.
55 AD15/28/46, JC26/1928/57; unanimously guilty, eighteen months' imprisonment.
56 AD15/30/13, JC5/18; 37-year-old coal carrier, pleaded guilty, four years' penal servitude.
57 AD15/28/93, JC15/35.

Fathers' excuses

When charged with incest, the majority of panels pleaded guilty in the first instance. Among those who pleaded not guilty, some offered an excuse for their behaviour. In one imaginative case in Glasgow in 1920, the accused told the arresting constable: 'I could not get into the kitchen bed because my wife is very stout and required all the room', which explained why he had moved beds but not why he had had intercourse with his fifteen-year-old stepdaughter.[58] Another attempted to impugn the character of his thirteen-year-old daughter, hoping to prove she was 'a person of loose and immoral character and that she has been on terms of improper familiarity with various men'; he even suggested that her grandfather had attempted incestuous connection with her.[59] A father in Blantyre in 1923 justified assaults on his seventeen-year-old daughter as a test of her virginity 'to see if anyone had been there before him'. The girl's pregnant mother had gone to her grandmother's home for her confinement and the father took his wife's absence as his opportunity for incestuous sex; he had not previously assaulted his daughter. The girl's older sister had sought employment as a domestic servant to escape from the family's single-room home, where she shared a bed with her father who had also assaulted her.[60] Fathers ascertaining virginity through incest is now a recognized phenomenon suggesting a tendency towards incest if daughters are suspected of indulging in premarital sex; in this instance the girl admitted sex with a boy who had since emigrated to Canada.[61]

Others blamed their drinking, with one father explaining to the police that 'when drink is in, wits out, and you could not expect anything else, all huddled together in one bunk as we were at the time'; he later pleaded guilty.[62] However, diminished responsibility due to inebriation was a very rare excuse and appears only to have been offered at the police office as a first line of defence. In some cases, a lack of sexual knowledge among daughters helped fathers to continue their activities. Explaining to the precognoscer why she had not reported her pregnancy, one twenty-year-old daughter explained: 'father often told me he was ruptured and could do me no harm', implying he considered himself infertile. She also stated that she did not 'know what his conduct meant' when the

---

58   AD15/20/76; unanimously guilty, twelve months' imprisonment.
59   AD15/20/86; by majority not proven, assoilzied and dismissed.
60   AD15/24/40, JC26/1923/15; prophylactics were used in this case, not guilty, assoilzied and dismissed.
61   R. E. L. Masters, *Patterns of Incest, a Psycho-Social Study of Incest based on Clinical and Historical Data* (New York, 1963), 66 and 81, quoted in Wohl, 'Sex and the Single Room', 205.
62   AD15/21/1, JC9/17; three years' penal servitude.

assaults began shortly after her periods started aged thirteen. The father halted his activities during her pregnancy but recommenced after the birth, when he told her: 'it would prevent my requiring to have to go with young men'.[63] This father had preyed on his daughter's innocence, possibly lying about his physical condition and emphasizing his ownership of her.

Few panels claimed temporary insanity as a special defence, possibly because the automatic sentence for an insanity plea was indefinite incarceration 'at His Majesty's Pleasure'. Also, it did nothing to alleviate the stigma of incest on the family name. However, in cases of chronic insanity, an indefinite custodial sentence could not be avoided. One 1928 case is particularly depressing for the entire family involved. The husband, a sailor, had married his new wife in 1914, who already had two daughters; their liaison produced two more daughters. The abuse included all four girls over a period of three years from 1925 to 1928. The mother excused his general behaviour due to epilepsy, which she believed had been caused by sunstroke during a voyage to India, in addition to several injuries to his head in the course of his work. His epilepsy and consequent amnesia were so profound that during one episode he had tied a rope to the kitchen table, instructed the girls to sit on top and had then lowered himself out of the window. The next day, he recalled nothing and so the mother decided against informing the police, because she blamed his illness. The girls described their sleeping arrangements with mother sharing a bed with the two younger girls and a small brother, while the two older stepdaughters shared with the panel. The mother was also physically abused by her husband, but it was an anonymous letter from a neighbour disclosing their knowledge of what was occurring that ended the family's suffering. Until this point, the mother appears to have attempted to protect her family from stigma and the removal of the father.[64]

Hereditary mental illness in a 1930 case in which a father assaulted his ten-year-old female child also elicited an insanity plea and incarceration. The child's stomach pains alerted the authorities at school who informed the police, suggesting school staff might have been watchful for symptoms of sexual interference among their pupils. The following day, her father drew his unemployment insurance money, left it at the police office and confessed. A personal history of delusions and mental illness combined with the death of his father in a mental asylum, thus hinting at hereditary illness, was sufficient to uphold the insanity plea; he was deemed 'of unsound mind and threatening to

---

63   AD15/22/132, JC5/15; pleaded guilty after further questioning at HCJ, three years' penal servitude.
64   AD15/29/39, JC13/138; incarcerated at His Majesty's Pleasure – one of only three incest cases where 'insanity in bar of trial' was pleaded. All three were upheld with the same sentence.

danger of the lieges'. His war service and wounds were noted by the PF, but no further mention is made in either the case papers or the trial Minute Book.[65] Similarly, in a few other cases where war wounds and service were detailed in family precognitions, they appear to have had no mitigating impact on verdicts.

Cramped living conditions were endemic across working-class districts of Scotland with 60 per cent of the population of Glasgow and Dundee living in single-end and two-roomed houses; the situation was little better elsewhere.[66] The need to share beds to save space as well as for warmth was well attested to in family precognitions, yet one father's elaborate embellishment to allay the fears of his nineteen-year-old daughter who was afraid to sleep alone and who was described by a neighbour as 'weak minded' landed this father with a heavy five-year sentence.[67]

Welfare considerations

Since over half the population of Scotland lived in one- and two-roomed homes sharing with at least one other person, welfare authorities were keen to ameliorate working-class living conditions and to offer moral improvement to their children. They associated overcrowding and lack of privacy, particularly for young girls, with sexual violence.[68] However, there were two approaches to offering assistance: in Edinburgh, the focus of the Royal Scottish Society for Prevention of Cruelty to Children (RSSPCC) was on the neglect of children within the home while other welfare investigators preferred to concentrate on the culpability of strangers rather than admit to domestic sexual abuse.[69] The HCJ records provide only three incest cases involving official welfare bodies, of which only one was detected by school authorities.

A stepfather incest case in 1920 in Glasgow was reported after the welfare officer at the sisters' school heard the younger sibling, aged five, discussing an assault. The family, including the stepfather, shared a bed in the kitchen at the

---

65 AD15/30/52, JC13/138.
66 W. W. Knox, *Industrial Nation: Work, Culture and Society in Scotland, 1800-Present* (Edinburgh, 1999), 192.
67 AD15/21/9, JC9/17.
68 W. W. Knox, 'Urban Housing in Scotland, 1840-1940', chapter 4, www.scran.ac.uk; *Departmental Committee*, 14.
69 C. Kelly, 'Continuity and Change in the History of Scottish Juvenile Justice', *Law, Crime and History*, 1 (2016): 73 and 82; L. Mahood, 'Family Ties: Lady Child-Savers and Girls of the Street, 1850-1925', in *Out of Bounds: Women in Scottish Society 1800-1945*, eds E. Breitenbach and E. Gordon (Edinburgh, 1992), 47–8.

girls' aunt's home, where they had all removed to live when their mother died. The abuse had been going on for seven months when overheard at school.[70] The second incest case was reported anonymously in 1930 in Glasgow, resulting in a detective collecting the child from school to take her to the police station.[71] In the third case already mentioned, the school staff reacted to the child's stomach pains by informing the police, suggesting they suspected sexual interference or possible parental neglect.

None of the cases prosecuted at the HCJ was detected in the home for which there are several possible reasons. Domestic cases detected by welfare officers may have been tried on lower indictments at sheriff courts because the evidence suggested a lesser charge or because the authorities were keen to reduce the dislocating impact of a High Court prosecution on the family or its complete dissolution. Other cases may have collapsed before reaching the HCJ. Also, reporting as much incest as they suspected occurred may have undermined support for their services among elite groups, because it could be construed as evidence that their methods were not working. The authorities, neighbours and often other family members understood the threat incest posed for the well-being of young girls, but, arguably, overconfidence in the correlation between overcrowding and slum conditions and the potential for sexual violence outside the home diverted the 'child-saving' authorities' attention away from scrutiny of the type of men capable of committing urban incest. Among over 100 HCJ prosecutions for incest in the decade from 1920, it might be anticipated that welfare officials' involvement would be more frequent. Yet, their contribution to the detection of incest or their testimony in the case papers is largely and frustratingly absent; there is no definitive answer why they failed to detect or be involved in these cases.

Sibling incest

Recalling his teens in late 1920s Glasgow, Ralph Glasser remembered a conversation with a contemporary who described sibling incest with an older sister. Glasser was shocked, but the friend considered it normal behaviour and insisted: 'ye'll no find a feller who's go' an older sister who's no' been intae 'er'.[72] He attributed sibling incest to close living quarters and bed-sharing and was

---

70 AD15/20/93, JC14/35; 7 years' penal servitude.
71 AD15/30/52, JC13/138; insanity, custody at His Majesty's Pleasure.
72 R. Glasser, *Growing Up in the Gorbals* (London, 1986), 132.

incredulous that Glasser had not done likewise. Social historians have since questioned Glasser's reliability, but writing his memoirs, he remembered this as a credible story. This incident might point to widespread sibling incest in 1920s Scotland, or a single perpetrator misguided about his fellow youths' nocturnal habits.

The HCJ records provide only eight cases of sibling incest for the whole of Scotland between 1918 and 1930, with no more than two cases in any single year and seven years with none, whereas there were three non-consensual cases perpetrated by adult brothers prosecuted in 1910. Thus, in a thirty-year period, Scotland prosecuted just eleven cases of sibling incest compared to only six *reported* cases in England and Wales between 1909 and 1969.[73] Whether families disguised intra-familial assault as indecent assault in order to bring cases before lesser sheriff or police courts is unlikely; any public airing of private family matters might bring disrepute on the family and any hint of incestuous behaviour reported to the police would be referred to the PF who was obliged to prosecute incest at the HCJ. Thus, these eight cases are all that PFs throughout Scotland prosecuted between 1918 and 1930, although they are unlikely to be the entirety of what was reported or perpetrated. Indeed, if Glasser's friend was correct, many cases of incest may have gone unreported as 'harmless' teenage experimentation, possibly not involving violence or coercion. Or Glasser's friend may have been exhibiting teenage bravado, boasting sexual prowess. Later researchers considered sibling incest to be more prevalent than any other form, yet the most reported in the HCJ data was that between step/father and daughter.[74] It is possible that some girls colluded with their brothers in a mutual need for sexual experience; these cases were very unlikely to be reported let alone reach the HCJ. As contemporary welfare officers stated, 'in many cases youths and girls of the age of puberty occupy the same room, and, indeed, the same bed. In such circumstances, some cases of incest are sure to occur'.[75] Others may have suffered abuse in silence, or if they did report it, they were disbelieved. If parents decided to keep quiet, victims were unlikely to be able to pursue a complaint without support or familial corroboration.

However, for these eight cases to reach the HCJ, the victims had overcome possible familial resistance to reporting the crime; the girls' families may have been supportive and outraged by their son's behaviour in the home, and ultimately, the girls' evidence had satisfied the legal requirement for

---

73 Ackner, 'Incest', 86–7.
74 Scottish Law Commission, *Law of Incest*, 8.
75 *Departmental Committee*, 14.

corroboration. All eight girls' precognitions included some variation on 'he made me wet', thus confirming emission. Unsurprisingly, six cases resulted in pregnancy. This would have made a sibling assault difficult to hide, although families may have found other means of concealing an incestuous pregnancy, for example, accusing the girl's boyfriend and seeking their marriage or sending her away until the baby was born and could possibly be adopted. In a 1921 case, having successfully hidden her pregnancy caused by an abusive brother, the incest was only discovered when the 21-year-old victim attended the police office to make funeral arrangements, the baby having died at six weeks old.[76] Therefore, this small sample of cases is potentially the exception.

All the male siblings were in their late teens and twenties. Assaulted sisters ranged in age from fourteen to thirty-two years. Possibly, brothers may have acted in the belief that their sisters would not report the assault or that their parents would disregard the matter. Unlike step/fathers, some of whom took contraceptive precautions, the number of pregnancies caused by brothers was possibly due to inexperience or a lack of concern for the consequences of their behaviour, or they were less able or willing to purchase contraceptives. However, following a similar modus operandi to paternal incest, these brothers committed their assaults while the female was alone in the home, visiting the outside lavatory, on the stair or in the backcourt. Further, every female was instructed not to tell, suggesting brothers comprehended the prohibition on incest.

In 1921 in Edinburgh, a 26-year-old woman reported her brother's incestuous assault after a single incident. She was residing with an older brother and his wife when they took in another brother, who had been discharged from the army with a 'crippled' arm and was unemployed. His sister was assisting him financially. In September, their sister-in-law went into hospital, and when their married brother was out of the house, her crippled brother attacked her. The attack was not unprecedented, as he had attempted to interfere with her three years previously. She did not mention the latest assault to her sister-in-law because of her 'delicate health', nor to her married brother because 'he had tried to interfere with me in the past' when she was fifteen years old.[77] The distinction here is that the previous attempt by the older brother may have been considered a teenage experiment and the girl was younger and possibly less able to report the crime,

---

76   AD15/21/4, JC5/14; pleaded guilty at second diet, three years' penal servitude.
77   AD15/21/11, JC9/17; pleaded guilty, three years' penal servitude.

whereas this assault had occurred between adults, was brutal, premeditated and resulted in pregnancy.

Where a brother had suffered horribly during the war, sibling sympathy may have delayed a sister reporting the crime. In Glasgow in 1919, a war-widowed sister with three children who had written to her brother throughout his four years as a prisoner of war in Germany offered him lodgings against their mother's wishes. She reported that her brother was drinking heavily, and despite erecting a single bed for him and squeezing her three children into her own bed, he used force to have intercourse with her. This occurred on four occasions over two months, resulting in pregnancy. When she informed him of her condition, he threatened her and their mother with a razor if she told anyone. Brother, sister and children then went away until his desertion from the army forced her to return to Glasgow, where she gave birth. Her mother's new husband reported the crime to the police. When both parties were charged, the brother said: 'If it's true, they can't do anything to me, they can only make me pay'. His application for bail was refused, although the sister's was granted, and in prison awaiting trial, the brother told the medical officer he wished he 'were dead because he had committed a horrible crime'. He had attempted to hang himself before the prison warder spotted him and removed 'all utensils' from his cell. Sister and brother were sentenced to six and twelve months imprisonment, respectively, indicating that the court considered the sister was also culpable.[78] Again, this man's actions were premeditated and violent, and the razor threat and his confession indicate his awareness of his criminal actions, although no allowance appears to have been made for possible wartime post-traumatic stress.

In two cases, there had been a history of previous assaults against the victim, one having been sent to a convent as a young child to avoid her brother's attentions.[79] In the case of a fourteen-year-old victim of an eighteen-year-old unemployed brother (the youngest perpetrator), the circumstances suggest this was not experimentation; he ejaculated and told her not to inform their mother. His repeated assaults always occurred while their mother was out, father in hospital or in the seclusion of the stair lavatory.[80] Thus, prosecuted cases of sibling incest appear not to have been the result of night-time experiments in crowded beds, the possible number of which cannot be calculated. In five of the eight cases, the male was unemployed, and it is possible that he committed

---

78 AD15/19/36, JC26/1919/86.
79 AD15/25/28, JC14/38; twelve months' imprisonment.
80 AD15/28/67, JC13/137; pleaded guilty, six months' imprisonment.

the act out of frustration and feelings of emasculation. However, historians investigating working-class male behaviour suggest that men did not impose their masculinity on their womenfolk to a greater extent during periods of unemployment; instead, male-female power relations continued much the same.[81]

Eight cases are a small survey from which to derive absolute conclusions. However, the case details suggest that prosecuted sibling incest was premeditated and often repeated over a lengthy period and shares similarities with research conducted on abuse in Scotland's industrial schools: two sisters sharing a bed with a drunken father and older brother, mother dead and after frequent assaults, the sixteen-year-old girl fell pregnant.[82] All eight cases of sibling incest resulted in guilty verdicts, which suggests that the PF considered the evidence sufficiently robust to be confident of a conviction and explains why this handful of possibly exceptional cases reached the HCJ in the first place when so many others may not have.

Sons and mothers

The circumstances of filial incest are varied. There are only three cases in the HCJ data and each perpetrator was aged thirty or over, drunk at the time of the assault and in two cases so was the mother. However, unlike step/father and sibling assaults, filial attacks were opportunistic single events, possibly provoked by the uninhibiting effects of alcohol. The juries convicted all three panels.[83] In the third case, there is a twist: the 39-year-old panel pleaded guilty at the first diet at the sheriff court in Edinburgh, but on hearing he was to be remitted to the HCJ for sentencing, he attempted to alter his plea, presumably because if he were going to the HCJ anyway, he could chance his luck before a jury which might find him innocent. They did not and he received three years' penal servitude for assaulting his sober and 'industrious and hard-working' mother.[84]

81 Penlington, 'Masculinity and Domesticity', 282 and 299; J. Bourke, *Working-Class Cultures in Britain 1800-1960* (London, 1994), 130–1. The recording of the panel's employment status may have been simply a routine court exercise.
82 L. Mahood and B. Littlewood, 'The "Vicious Girl" and the "Street Corner Boy": Sexuality and the Gendered Delinquent in the Scottish Child-Saving Movement 1850-1940', *Journal of the History of Sexuality*, 4 (1994): 569.
83 AD15/24/78, JC15/35; by majority guilty, three years' penal servitude; AD15/25/45, JC13/136; unanimously guilty, three years' penal servitude.
84 AD15/26/18, JC9/20.

Grandfathers and granddaughters

There are three cases of interwar tri-generational incest between grandfathers and granddaughters resulting in five victims. These girls were younger than victims of sibling incest but similar in age to those assaulted by step/fathers. Prolongation of assaults, absence of maternal protection and discovery followed patterns for sibling and step/father incest. In a case involving two step-granddaughters aged ten and eleven years, the assaults continued over a protracted period. Their mother was dead and they were living with their grandparents until their father's remarriage. The grandmother suspected her husband of misconduct, but when questioned, the girls lied at first to protect him.[85] In another case, the assaults became known when the sixteen-year-old granddaughter fell pregnant. When confronted, her grandfather declared: 'there'd not be a disgrace if we'd only keep our mouths shut'.[86] In the final case, the grandfather assaulted his granddaughter aged between twelve and sixteen and her friend over an extended period.[87]

Modern studies of tri-generational incest in the United States reveal that grandfathers usually had a history of incestuous abuse with daughters before moving onto granddaughters.[88] However, the indictment sheets for the Scottish cases do not include any previous charges of a sexual nature, which they would even if those cases had been prosecuted at a lower court. It has been suggested that older molesters do so to compensate for old-age impotence.[89] Yet, the Scottish cases, each perpetrated over a period of time, do not suggest any inadequacy of function. Likewise, alcohol was not mentioned in the precognitions and employment status does not appear to have influenced the grandfathers' actions. However, the grandfather who made his victim pregnant attempted to excuse his behaviour, saying: 'I did not think I would do her any harm, I thought I was past that twenty years ago'. He was seventy-eight.[90]

---

85 AD15/25/24, JC14/38; unanimously guilty, four years' penal servitude.
86 AD15/26/34, JC9/20; three months' imprisonment.
87 JC26/1929/75; sentence unrecorded.
88 J. Goodwin, L. Cormier and J. Owen, 'Grandfather-Granddaughter Incest: A Tri-Generational View', *Child Abuse and Neglect,* 7 (1983): 163.
89 Goodwin, Cormier and Owen, 'Grandfather-Granddaughter Incest', 164.
90 AD15/26/34, JC9/20.

Uncles and nieces

Consanguineous uncle/niece incest provides eleven cases, of which five were non-consenting, and exhibits similar patterns to sibling incest: the victims were usually over sixteen years, pregnancy occurred in eight cases (five being non-consensual) and the crime was committed over a period of time.[91] Alcohol was often a factor and the crime occurred indoors, except for one case where the panel was of 'rather weak intellect' and the girl aged nineteen was deformed and of 'weak and facile mind'. A neighbour stated they were 'a strange, distant family'; she confused the uncle as the family's eldest son.[92] Unusually for uncle/niece incest, this example appears to have been one of opportunity on a single occasion, the uncle assaulting his niece on their way home from the cinema, which resulted in pregnancy; otherwise, he may have remained undiscovered. The other cases were, like paternal and sibling incest, intentionally perpetrated while other adults were out of the home.

The few uncle/niece by affinity cases were all consensual and all except one involved women above sixteen years. If it had not been for the strict interpretation of Leviticus, these cases would not have been considered criminal, except one involving a fifteen-year-old which otherwise might have been indicted as rape or under CLAA 1885. In a rare comment from the bench, it is clear that attitudes towards incest by affinity were changing in the 1920s, which may explain their rarity in the records. When summing up a case in 1928 involving a 41-year-old shepherd and his 25-year-old niece with whom he had had a child and both of whom claimed ignorance of their crime, the jury having found them both unanimously guilty, Lord Fleming confirmed the indictment was correct as incest, then promptly admonished and dismissed them. Sitting with him, Lord Salvesen, who in 1921 had questioned the appropriateness of a charge of incest in a similar case but had been forced to accept the indictment then, was now forced to uphold the precedent seven years later.[93]

Preventing detection

In the HCJ data, victims reported that step/fathers required their silence, except in the few witnessed cases. However, despite coercion in the form of threats of

---

91 Consanguineous and affinity uncle/niece incest were treated equally under the Scots Law irrespective of consent.
92 AD15/28/32, JC5/18; the girl had suffered childhood rickets and was three feet tall, pleaded guilty, nine months' imprisonment.
93 JC26/1928/91, JC34/1/90, JC14/40.

physical violence and monetary bribes from some perpetrators, committing the act behind closed doors could not always contain the secret within the family. A younger girl sworn to secrecy, especially as the victim of paternal incest, often told the precognoscer that she was afraid to tell her mother for fear of her father's retribution; instead, she confided in an older sister, a neighbour or an aunt. Contemporary welfare investigators reported that when seeking corroborative evidence from a wife, women were often reticent to give evidence against a husband unless the victims were her own children.[94] However, a mother could not always be relied upon to report abuse. In the case of a seven-year-old victim in 1924, the family's sleeping arrangements comprised a bed and a 'crib' in the kitchen. When she shared a bed with her parents, the child recalled her mother telling her father 'to leave me [daughter] alone' at night, but she did not understand why her mother said this. Despite his wife's willing complicity, or coerced connivance, in the crime, a neighbour finally reported the panel to the police: the family shouted a lot because the wife and mother was deaf and they could be heard through the walls; she was also pregnant throughout the period cited for abuse.[95] This intervention follows similar patterns identified in Scottish homicide when neighbours would only intervene if noise levels exceeded accepted norms and extreme violence was suspected.[96]

Despite awareness in communities of the potential for severe sentences for incest, it appears not to have deterred fathers intent on incestuous behaviour, who might use 'a conspiracy of secrecy' to conceal their activities when authority over their daughters and wife failed. Hiding their abuse from a wife required daughters' silence, which could be interpreted by contemporary welfare authorities as complicity.[97] Similarly, male siblings forbade their sisters to tell anyone and in uncle/niece non-consensual incest, again, the male sought to enforce silence with instructions and threats not to divulge their secret. Further, fathers often offered bribes to prevent detection, which emphasizes their cognizance of the possible penalties. However, despite the delay in reporting caused by such threats and bribes, the fact that PFs prosecuted these crimes suggests that corroboration of evidence outweighed considerations of any consenting participation.[98]

---

94 *Departmental Committee*, 12; a wife could give narrative evidence but her testimony was inadmissible in court.
95 AD15/24/79.
96 A. Brown, 'Social History of Scottish Homicide, 1836-1869', unpublished thesis (University of Leicester, 2015), 24.
97 Herman, *Father-Daughter*, 40 and 163; Jackson, 'Family, Community', 143.
98 Legal attitudes to consent will be discussed in Chapter 6.

Mother's whereabouts

The mother's absence was usually crucial to the commission, and sometimes the detection, of incest, especially in paternal and sibling cases. Most precognitions reveal that she had either left home, was in hospital or, in the greatest number of cases, was dead, all of which meant the girl had no natural protector in the home, although in some cases there were resident older sisters. In a 1920 case, their mother had died three years previously leaving a thirteen-year-old daughter and the youngest victim, her five-year-old half-sister, by their mother's new husband. After six months of abuse, the child confided in a female neighbour that her daddy was interfering with her; the neighbour's husband then reported it to the police.[99] Writing in 1946, prisons commissioner Norwood East noted that 'incest was much more prevalent in the age group 40 to 50 years' which he thought indicated 'many were widowers with daughters living at home'.[100] Where the mother was alive and still resident, equal numbers reported they were either unaware of the abuse or were aware but had not witnessed it. In a 1929 case already discussed, the mother was afraid of her husband's violent epileptic fits and drunkenness and only reported the abuse of her four daughters when a neighbour wrote anonymously threatening to do so.[101] In cases where the mother remained unaware, the revelation of a daughter's pregnancy provoked her to report the abuse, often first to a doctor who advised her to go to the police. Abuse in one family had commenced when an outbreak of diphtheria forced a change in sleeping arrangements. The father had abused all three girls over an extended period which began before the war, but the youngest child's tears and the seventeen-year-old middle girl's pregnancy meant secrecy was no longer an option; they had to tell their 51-year-old mother.[102] In other cases, often the girl could not bear to upset her mother and instead reported the crime either to a friendly neighbour or directly to the police. Only older victims took the latter route.

Where maternal absence was temporary, assaults were planned when the mother and usually the rest of the family were shopping, at work or visiting. One father was caught in the act with their thirteen-year-old daughter when his wife returned from shopping. The girl admitted the abuse had been occurring

---

99 AD15/20/93, JC14/35; unanimously guilty, seven years' penal servitude.
100 W. Norwood East, 'Sexual Offenders' – a British View', *The Yale Law Journal*, 3, no. 55 (April 1946): 544.
101 AD15/29/39.
102 AD15/21/176, JC11/119; unanimously guilty, ten years' penal servitude.

for at least six months, during which time the mother had been unaware. She took her immediately to the police.[103] Another father disturbed in bed with his twelve-year-old daughter by his seventeen-year-old daughter, who returned home unexpectedly, had not only told the younger girl that 'you're the only one I've got, are you going to let me do it?', but when discovered told the older girl his 'brain was turned', that he would get five years if reported and he would cut his throat. Previously witnessed sleeping on the lavatory stair to avoid her husband's brutality, their mother was currently in hospital, so the older girl told a female neighbour who took them to the police.[104] Two especially harrowing cases, one in 1921 and a second in 1924, might reasonably be read to suggest a correlation between mothers incapacitated by illness and the commencement of incest by fathers.[105] In the latter case, incest began in May 1922 when the girl's mother fell ill. The mother slept in the kitchen bed, and the victim shared a bed with her stepfather and a sister. It is possible the mother was unaware of the abuse, but the night she died and was laid out in her coffin in the kitchen, the stepfather assaulted the fourteen-year-old, again threatening her if she told the aunt who was coming to collect the children.[106] In the earlier case, the mother lay dying in the kitchen bed while her husband assaulted her fourteen-year-old daughter, which continued after her death. A younger sister confided in a neighbour, who found an excuse to get the girl alone to question her and thereafter reported it.[107]

In cases of non-consenting consanguineous and affinity uncle/niece incest, again pregnancy was the main catalyst for disclosure.[108] Usually, the mother reported the crime, although occasionally fathers were involved. In 1923 after three assaults in a single month, a fifteen-year-old girl became pregnant. Her mother questioned her, which resulted in the family visiting the uncle who at first denied it, then breaking down crying, he confessed. The mother threatened to inform his wife and he tried to excuse his conduct saying he had been drunk at the time. The girl interjected that that was true only for the first assault. Present throughout the altercation, the father and the accused's brother went for the police immediately.[109]

In research conducted in the 1970s in a predominantly Roman Catholic, poor community in the United States, it was found that in homes where the mother

103 AD15/21/39, JC26/1921/185; pleaded guilty, five years' penal servitude.
104 AD15/28/75, JC15/39; pleaded guilty, twenty-one months' imprisonment.
105 Herman, *Father-Daughter*, 43 and 45.
106 AD15/24/12, JC5/16; pleaded guilty, twelve months' imprisonment.
107 AD15/21/85, JC13/133; by a majority not proven, assoilzied and dismissed.
108 AD15/19/44, JC15/30; uncle with twelve-year-old blood niece; unanimously not proven, assoilzied and dismissed.
109 AD15/23/51; not proven, assoilzied and dismissed.

is strong incest is not tolerated and may even be non-existent. However, where mothers lacked agency in their home and family, they might tolerate various forms of abuse including incestuous sexual assault. Also, financially dependent and socially isolated mothers who might be ill and caring for large and young families were less able to challenge their husbands.[110] In Scotland in the 1920s, the case testimonies suggest that where mothers were aware of the abuse, they were reluctant to report it. This does not mean that they were in collusion with the abusers or that they were failing in their maternal role; simply put, they existed in a family dynamic that prevented them from taking control of their circumstances and protecting their children.[111] Their descriptions of their family situation correspond with those in the US survey. None of the precognosced mothers was noted as working mothers, making them likely to be financially dependent on the male head of the household and potentially subject to his coercive behaviour. Also, most of the families were large, with the ages of children ranging from babies to adults at work; many mothers suffered poor health. However, these mothers were not socially isolated; they lived in close-knit communities with neighbours watching each other and willing to intervene if asked.

Social historians of the late nineteenth and early twentieth centuries and sociologists of later periods investigating reasons not to report intra-familial violence have highlighted the risk of removal of the breadwinner from the household as a forceful disincentive to disclosure: reporting jeopardized both the marriage and household income.[112] Wives who reported abuse and then became reluctant to proceed with a case could have been warning the husband that she had agency if he persisted with the assaults. If reporting to the police alone were intended to warn an incestuous father to desist, families may have withdrawn their complaint before prosecution, which makes the cases prosecuted at the HCJ potentially different from those contained in the 'dark number'. In the HCJ prosecutions, wives and other family members not only reported male relations to the police but also gave precognitions supporting their complaints. Even if reported by another family member, if the mother was still alive, in every case she gave a precognition statement, and none intimated any reluctance to do so.

---

110 Herman, *Father-Daughter*, 47 and 78.
111 W. Leeming, 'New Taboo? Some Observations on the Late Arrival of Changes to the Law of Incest in Scotland', *International Journal of the Sociology of Law*, 24 (1996): 328.
112 R. E. Dobash and R. P. Dobash, 'The Nature and Antecedents of Violent Events', *British Journal of Criminology*, 24, no. 3 (July 1984): 269–88; Herman, *Father-Daughter*, 132.

Either the mothers in these cases possessed power or, possibly, circumstances had progressed beyond the warning stage.

Ethnicity

In cases where the accused had an obvious ethnic origin, these were Irish, German or Italian families. Many surnames appear to have an Irish derivation, but without confirmation from the case papers, it cannot be assumed that the family was Irish by birth, descent or through one spousal partner. However, the Irish in Scotland, particularly Catholics, were often considered a low class of immigrants. As the contemporary lawyer and anti-Irish xenophobe Andrew Dewar Gibb wrote: 'wheresoever dirty acts of sexual baseness are committed, there you will find the Irishman in Scotland'.[113] Research into early twentieth-century working-class cultures has revealed that Irish criminals were five times more likely to be sent to prison than their English contemporaries, and that figure increased tenfold for Scotland.[114] Yet, in Scottish cases where ethnicity is apparent, the records provide no judicial comment on the perpetrator's behaviour nor any Irish traits. In a 1926 case identified as Irish, a landlady described the assaulted victim, who had assumed her deceased mother's position in the home, as 'dirty, a slatternly girl who neglects her household duties, does nothing during the day'.[115] The landlady's comment was aimed at the twenty-year-old victim's inability to maintain domestic standards, not at the family's ethnicity. The father's eighteen-month sentence was comparable with non-Irish perpetrators of equivalent crimes. The available evidence suggests that the legal process may have been blind to the popular perception of the 'filthiness' of the Irish.

A single case in 1928 involved a German national, resident in Aberdeen since 1901, who was accused of assaulting his eighteen- and nineteen-year-old daughters. Their uncle and mother had become suspicious of the abuse, and during the final assault, the uncle observed them through a window before informing a neighbour who informed the police. They arrived in time to find them in the act. In a police telegram, the accused was described as a 'ship chandlers canvasser' soliciting German trawlers for work and acting as interpreter, as well as being 'a whining, snivelling creature and as his conduct indicates a person of low moral character'. The PF described their living conditions in two rooms as

---

113 Gibb, *Scotland in Eclipse*, 55.
114 Bourke, *Working-Class Cultures*, 204.
115 AD15/26/69, JC15/37; unanimously guilty, eighteen months' imprisonment.

'poorly furnished and filthy'. The actual words used are not inherently racist or anti-German, although they convey a negative sentiment against a man lacking a good moral character and ability to support his family. In court, the panel pleaded guilty, then tried to withdraw his plea but with no one available to speak for the accused, the Advocate Depute refused.[116]

The Italian case involved a consenting consanguineous uncle and niece, and the papers contained no pejorative comment from witnesses or legal officials. Besides a three-month sentence for both parties, the prosecution moved for expulsion of the male party from the UK under the Aliens Order Act 1920.[117]

* * *

Conclusion

Cases prosecuted at the HCJ may have been exceptional and not indicative of cases hidden in the 'dark number', which not only failed to proceed beyond the PF's office but also went totally unreported. As the National Society for the Prevention of Cruelty to Children's (NSPCC) General Booth remarked in 1890: 'If so many [fathers] were brought to justice, how many [girls] were there of whom the world never heard in any shape or form?'[118] Occasionally the difference between the number of cases reported to the police and those proceeded against can be discovered from contemporary reports. The *Criminal Statistics for Scotland* 1925 noted twenty-five cases reported to the police and sixteen prosecuted at the HCJ; for reasons unlikely ever to be established, nine cases were not proceedable.[119] Beyond this, the actual numbers of incestuous assaults are a matter of conjecture. Attempts in the United States in the 1970s to extrapolate numbers of incestuously abused women across the population from surveys of middle-class women failed to recognize that the demographic group surveyed was less likely to experience abuse than economically disadvantaged and otherwise stressed women.[120] They conservatively estimated that around one million American women might have experienced incestuous assault while

---

116 AD15/28/14, JC26/1928/39, JC9/21; five years' penal servitude.
117 AD15/23/12, JC5/16.
118 W. Booth, *In Darkest England and the Way Out* (London, 1890), 102. Booth recognized the incidence of incest among London's poor but termed it 'unnatural sins'.
119 *Criminal Statistics for Scotland: Statistics relating to Police Apprehensions, Criminal Proceedings, and Reformatory and Industrial Schools, for the year 1925* (Edinburgh, 1925), 22.
120 Herman, *Father-Daughter*, 14.

over 75 per cent of incidents were never discovered.[121] Thus, there is a consensus among researchers that incest is not only the most stigmatized crime of sexual violence but also the most underreported.[122] Complex family relationships, shame and even possible acknowledgement of a father's rights over his children meant bringing an incest case was extremely brave and not necessarily a route to removing the problem from the home.[123] Whether incest was common in Scotland in the 1920s – or any other country – is impossible to say, but evidence adduced from more recent victim studies indicates it was far more prevalent than the HCJ records suggest.

However, what those records can tell us is that in prosecuted cases, judicial authorities were relatively uninterested in the mitigation of alcohol to provoke abuse and that perpetrators could not claim ignorance of the law, since their requirement for secrecy and silence demonstrates they were cognizant of the penalties. Paternal incest had, and has, no excuses. Absent or sexually reluctant wives cannot be blamed for a father's interference with his step/daughters unless the notion that a father 'owns' the females in his family is accepted.[124] In these prosecuted cases, clearly that concept, if at any point acknowledged, had been properly rejected by the time the females in the family reached the police office.

Contemporaries attempted to explain incest among the lower classes as a fundamental flaw in the people's moral standards exacerbated by overcrowding and lack of privacy. The HCJ records reveal that when prosecuted, incest had taken place predominantly in bedrooms, shared kitchen beds and even stair lavatories, often in Scotland's most densely populated urban centres. However, why one father living in such conditions committed incest when a neighbour in similar circumstances did not and why one daughter managed to report an assault when another may have decided not to remain unfathomable questions that rely on an understanding of the psyche of individual perpetrators and the fears obstructing their victims from reporting every incidence of abuse.

---

121 D. Finkelhor, *Sexually Victimized Children* (New York, 1981), 88 quoted in Herman, *Father*-Daughter, 14; E. Stanko, *Intimate Intrusions: Women's Experience of Male Violence* (London, 1985), 25.
122 Jackson, 'Family, Community', 139.
123 C. Smart, 'Reconsidering the Recent History of Child Sexual Abuse 1910-1960', *Journal of Social Policy*, 29, no. 1 (2000): 64.
124 Herman, *Father-Daughter*, 49.

4

'Outrages against little girls'*

Sexual violence against girls under sixteen years

The 1920s was a turbulent decade of post-war economic depression and unemployment, gender tensions, fears of violence and concerns regarding recently enfranchised men and women. However, the fears expressed by contemporary authors were largely impressionistic and not necessarily evidence based. They conveyed a two-tier threat: class antagonism felt by elite groups towards the working classes and a gender-based threat that women were not safe in a masculinized society. However, the High Court of Justiciary (HCJ) records of prosecuted cases of rape, attempt to ravish and lewd and libidinous practices and behaviour (LLPB) reveal that the threat of sexual violence was not just directed at adult women; younger females appear to have been almost equally as likely to be victims. Therefore, this chapter investigates sexual violence committed against non-familial minors – girls under sixteen years – in an attempt to ascertain, firstly, whether incidences of sexual crime escalated in the post-war years in comparison with pre-war levels; secondly, whether sexual violence in the 1920s could be interpreted as a response to the war; and, thirdly, whether child sexual abuse was simply a feature of everyday life in Scotland. The richness of the HCJ records allows analysis of who committed crime against whom; the victims' ages; the degree of acquaintance between victim and perpetrator and its potential impact on the type of sexual violence committed; and how these crimes became known to the authorities.

All the prosecuted cases of sexual assault against minors were reported on their behalf; where minor males were among the victims in a group indictment, which were extremely few, their supporters were not the main protagonists reporting the crime. The scarcity of prosecutions of assaults perpetrated on minor males corresponds with other late nineteenth- and twentieth-century

---

* P. Gibbs, *Now It Can Be Told* (South Carolina, 2015), 167.

research, which argues that young boys were not considered part of the sexual abuse experience.[1] The relative invisibility of minor boys in the HCJ records may be explained by the contemporary distinction between 'vicious girls' and 'street corner boys', the former possessing a degree of sexual delinquency while the latter were considered relatively benign.[2]

In the late Victorian period, ideas concerning childhood were increasingly constructed through both social attitudes and legislation and were predominantly focused on young females. Girls' sexuality, protection of their virginity and innocence can be traced through age of consent legislation. Starting in 1875, the age of consent increased from twelve to thirteen years before reaching sixteen years in 1885 with the Criminal Law Amendment Act (CLAA), which created a legal distinction: sex with females under thirteen years attracted a more severe sentence than for having unlawful sex with girls in the grey area between thirteen and sixteen years.[3] Thus, the agency of sexually mature girls aged thirteen to sixteen to consent to sex was judicially removed. Arguably, the legislation aimed to control and correct female adolescent sexual behaviour while also protecting the youngest girls from sexual abuse.[4] Archival evidence of child sexual violence is further clouded by the use of euphemism and imprecise language both in legal records and newspaper reportage, thus confounding historical analysis of a complete amount of abuse against minors of both sexes. It has also created barriers for ascertaining the severity of what exactly occurred between perpetrator and victim.[5]

These emerging concepts of childhood combined with class hierarchies further confounded opinions towards sexually assaulted minor girls, complicating attitudes towards child culpability. A middle-class girl's behaviour was assumed to be different from that expected of a working-class girl, who shared intimate living space with brothers and fathers and lacked basic privacies. Inherent in the working-class child's experience was the insinuation that she

1 C. Smart, 'A History of Ambivalence and Conflict in the Discursive Construction of the "Child Victim" of Sexual Abuse', *Social and Legal Studies*, 8, no. 3 (1999): 394. Sexual assault of minor boys may have been discharged under 'sodomy' laws or not seen as criminal to the same extent or as dangerous to contemporary concepts of feminine dignity.
2 L. Mahood and B. Littlewood, 'The "Vicious Girl" and the "Street Corner Boy": Sexuality and the Gendered Delinquent in the Scottish Child-Saving Movement 1850-1940', *Journal of the History of Sexuality*, 4 (1994): 549–79.
3 A. M. Anderson, *The Criminal Law of Scotland* (Edinburgh, 1892), 97.
4 L. T. Hedler Ferreira and M. Grasten, 'Law's Lolita Paradox: Translating "childhood" in Statutory Rape Jurisprudence', *Review as Australian Feminist Law*, 47, no. 2 (2022): 7–8; L. Jackson, 'Sexual Assault, Criminal Justice and Policing since the 1880s', www.historyandpolicy.org, access August 2022.
5 B. Coldrey, 'The Sexual Abuse of Children: The Historical Perspective', *Studies: An Irish Quarterly Review*, 85, no. 340 (Winter 1996): 371.

may have been to blame for any attack against her. Writing in 1944, Professor of Law at Glasgow University Andrew Dewar Gibb certainly expressed long-held pejorative attitudes towards girls aged thirteen to sixteen and the extent to which they had been 'knowing' accomplices to the crimes committed against them.[6] Even a 1926 government report on sexual offences freely stated that 'offences against young children are the true "assault" cases – those against older children are very frequently with consent, and, although statutory offences, they are not assaults in the popular sense.'[7] Despite the changes in the law enacted in the 1885 CLAA, elite men perceived lower-working-class girls of less value than their own daughters and the problem of sexual abuse of minor girls by all classes of male persisted, although the precise amount was unquantifiable.[8] In Victorian Glasgow, individuals from all classes were involved in sexual abuse with underage children as the theatrical newspaper columnist 'Roving Jack' reported. He described an 'Old Party connected with the law' preferring his female conquests to be under eighteen years old.[9] By 1922, the CLAA had been revised. The most significant changes for minor females in the new CLAA were the elapse of time between commission of a crime and prosecution, which was increased from six to nine months and allowed more time for a complainer to report a crime and for evidence to be collected, and removal of the active consent clause, which no longer provided a defence to anyone perpetrating non-penetrative sexual assault on minor boys or girls.[10]

For the period 1910–14, the *Criminal Statistics for Scotland* reported for *all age* groups an average of sixty-four rapes, attempts to ravish and LLPB per year, which decreased to thirty-four per year during the war years 1914–19. This constitutes an average of five and three prosecutions per month, respectively.[11] Frustratingly, the *Criminal Statistics* does not provide age-group differentiation. In Scotland in the twelve years from November 1918 to December 1930, there were an average of twenty-eight prosecutions per annum for sexual violence

---

6   A. D. Gibb, *A Preface to Scots Law* (Edinburgh, 1944), 103.
7   *Departmental Committee on Sexual Offences against Children and Young Persons in Scotland* (Edinburgh, 1926), 11.
8   D. Gorham, 'The Maiden Tribute of Modern Babylon: Re-examined, Child Prostitution and the Idea of Childhood in Late Victorian England', *Victorian Studies*, 21, no. 3 (Spring, 1978): 365.
9   T. Cheadle, 'Music Hall, "Mashers" and the "Unco Guid": Competing Masculinities in Victorian Glasgow', quoting from 'Notes by Roving Jack', 9 January, 13 March, 15 May and 2 October 1886, in *Nine Centuries of Man: Manhood and Masculinities in Scottish History*, eds L. Abrams and E. Ewan (Edinburgh, 2017), 237.
10 L. Farmer, *Making the Modern Criminal Law: Criminalization and Civil Order* (Oxford 2016), 276.
11 *Criminal Statistics for Scotland: Statistics Relating to Police Apprehensions, Criminal Proceedings, and Reformatory and Industrial Schools, for the year 1925* (Edinburgh, 1925), 20.

against minor females. By comparison, this constitutes two prosecutions per month nationwide for crimes perpetrated against girls under sixteen years.

Perpetrators

The prosecuted crime data for 1920s Scotland reveal rape, ravish and LLPB as crimes committed by the working classes against children of their own class. Similar to those perpetrating incest, the accused were employed in a range of activities, both skilled and unskilled, and very few cases recorded details of the panel's war service. This may have been because panels had not served or that judicial officers were blind to military service as mitigation in sexual offences or simply that precognoscers did not consider it worthy of note. Of these possibilities, the total absence of requests by defence counsel for mitigation of sentence based on military service in the HCJ Minute Books suggests that it was not worth asking.

Of 101 rape cases tried at the HCJ between November 1918 and December 1930, forty-seven cases were perpetrated on girls under sixteen years, which produced seventy-five underage victims. Only in one case were multiple panels indicted (see Figure 4.1). Prosecuted rape of minors appears to have been a single-perpetrator crime, often against a single child but frequently perpetrated against multiple victims.

One hundred cases of attempt to ravish, in the same date range, produced 110 victims and in none of the cases were multiple panels indicted (see Figure 4.2).[12] Thus, attempt to ravish appears to have been largely a single-perpetrator-single-victim crime, though in one case in 1921 there were six victims.[13] Only eight attempts to ravish cases were also charged as rape, which suggests that the evidence was sufficient to persuade the Procurator Fiscal (PF) to prosecute in the hope of securing a conviction on the more serious charge and if unsuccessful, then the jury might consider attempt to ravish from the same evidence. However, twenty-eight rape cases were combined with the lesser charge of LLPB, indecent assault or assault. This suggests again that the evidence collected in the child's precognitions and medical reports indicated rape to the PF, but in court a child's

---

12 From the 1880s, the phrase 'assault with intent to ravish' was indicted, although by the 1920s 'attempt to ravish' was printed on the front of the indictment sheets. The HCJ data for attempt to ravish total 108 cases, 8 of which were indicted with the higher charge of rape. They have been counted as rape for this survey.
13 JC26/1921/183.

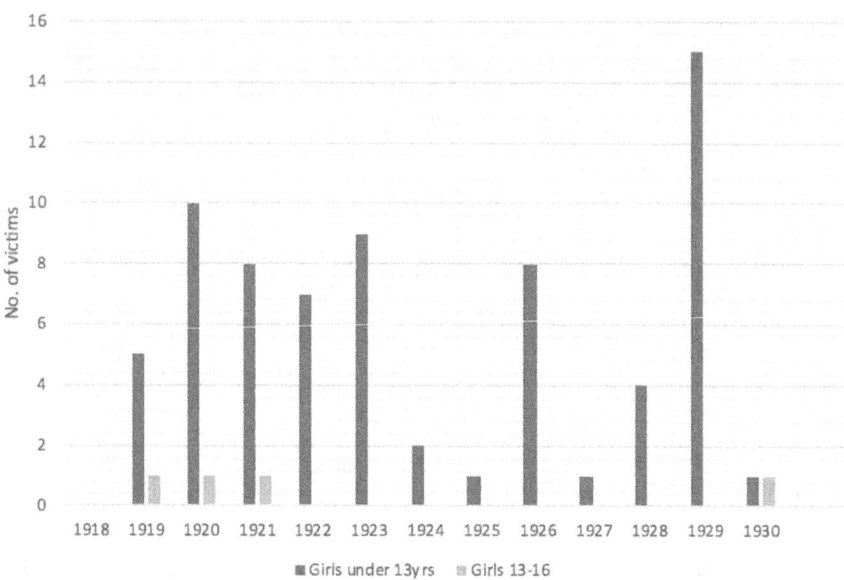

Figure 4.1 Rape: Minors by age group.

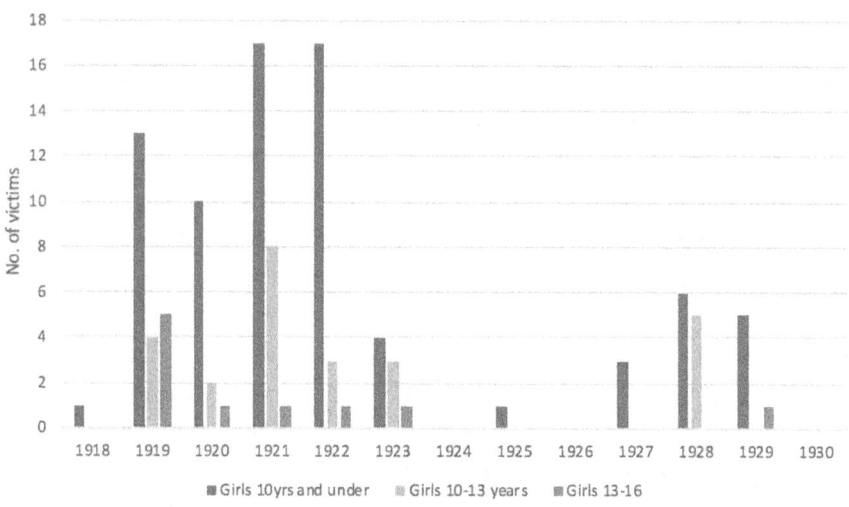

Figure 4.2 Attempt to Ravish: Underage victims by age group.

testimony may not have been as convincing to a jury, leaving them with the difficult decision of acquitting entirely or returning a guilty verdict on the LLPB charge.

Figure 4.3 reveals that LLPB was a sexual violence indictment used for minors, because of a total of 294 victims from 114 cases, 290 victims were under

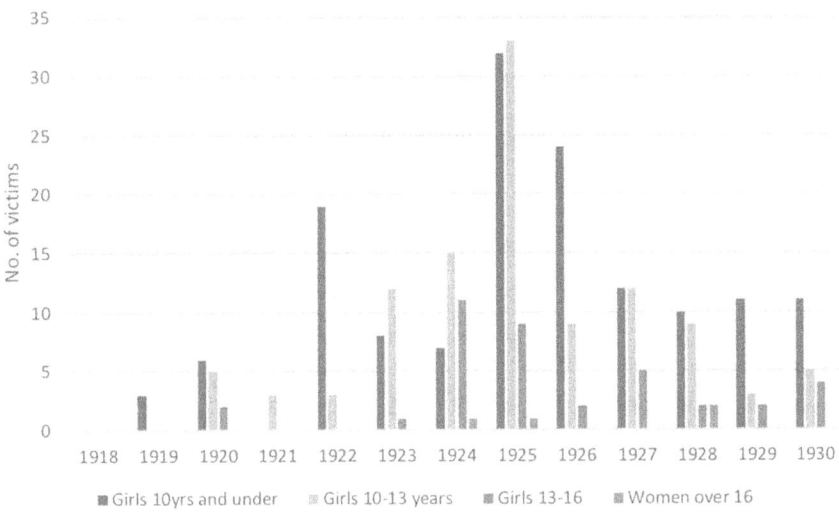

Figure 4.3 Lewd and libidinous practices and behaviour: All age victims by age group.

sixteen years. The difficulty of corroboration with underage victims may have led PFs to indict on the lower charge because of the quality of evidence offered by young girls. LLPB involved intimate handling without penetration, the details of which could be extremely difficult for a precogniscer to determine, and corroboration, unless witnessed, could be even more difficult to establish since forensic evidence was largely unavailable. As already suggested, the low number of cases combining indictments of rape with LLPB indicates that in the majority of either rape or LLPB cases, Crown Counsel (CC) was sufficiently sure of the accuracy of the single charge indicted or presumptive of a jury's response based on the available evidence.[14] Where a charge of LLPB was combined with attempt to ravish, this indicates that only a non-penetrative assault had occurred or could be corroborated, even if something more violent had actually occurred. The inclusion of attempt to ravish indicates that the evidence suggested intent to continue to full rape, which a charge of LLPB alone did not cover, but again the combined charge was an attempt by the judiciary to secure a guilty verdict if the more serious charge proved unconvincing to the jury. Cases with less injurious physical and sexual characteristics, such as indecent assault, were ineligible for prosecution at the HCJ and would have been heard at a lesser summary court.

Similar practice of combining indictments was used in the last decades of the nineteenth century. In a case in Stirling in 1885, a seventeen-year-old young

---

14   See Chapter 6 for a fuller discussion of corroboration and multiple indictments.

miner was accused of 'rape or assault with intent to ravish' by a fifteen-year-old farm servant. The evidence persuaded the PF to indict on rape, but in this case the less serious charge and its concomitant lower sentence led the panel to plead guilty on the assault charge only requesting removal of 'the aggravation of intent to ravish'; he was sentenced to four months' imprisonment.[15] Of a total of twenty-five rape prosecutions in 1885, eight cases involved minor females and all of them were indicted as rape combined with either LLPB or indecent assault. However, the small number of rapes against minors prosecuted in 1890, 1895, 1900, 1905 and 1910 relied on a single rape indictment. A close reading of the precognition statements for these cases does not reveal any differences in the quality of the evidence that would explain why the single indictment was charged and not a combined charge with another less serious sexual offence.

For cases of rape and attempt to ravish prosecuted in the 1920s, the perpetrators can be divided into two age groups: older men ranging up to seventy years and those under twenty-four years. Older perpetrators were noted as both married or single, employed or unemployed. Those employed were mainly unskilled or semi-skilled workers such as miners, labourers and motor drivers. Males under twenty-four years account for 27 per cent of cases. The youngest perpetrators appear to have raped the youngest girls, always girls under thirteen years and sometimes as young as three and four. However, there do not appear to be situational patterns in their behaviour or reasons evident from the court papers for their choice of victim. For example, a 1919 Mossend case involved a seventeen-year-old who lodged with a family and raped their eleven-year-old girl. He instructed her five-year-old sister to walk ahead of them, which she refused thus providing corroborating evidence, while he raped the older child under a railway bridge before continuing to the cinema. The girls' precognitions did not describe any previous abuse from him, which may indicate this was a first assault or they may have failed to recognize previous advances from him as sexual. The PF noted that the accused was 'quite beyond his father's control' and had been in lodgings for six months. His mother was dead and he kept 'undesirable companions', none of which provided mitigation for his behaviour.[16] A Partick case the following year committed by a boy too young to undergo Borstal training was perpetrated on a three-year-old girl while he was left alone with her in a neighbour's house.[17] In 1923, a seventeen-year-old was charged with rape of a seven-year-old child in a Glasgow park while her friend stood waiting. He refused to

---

15   AD14/81/1, JC26/1885/292, JC4/82.
16   AD15/19/2, JC5/13; pleaded guilty, three years' penal servitude.
17   AD15/20/74, JC14/34; pleaded guilty, nine months' imprisonment.

plead guilty to the entire charge, although he conceded guilt to the lesser charge of LLPB, which the PF accepted.[18] These young rapists were employed as chauffeurs/drivers and labourers; others declared themselves 'idle'. No record of possible motive exists in the case papers.

In 1929, the only rape case committed by multiple panels involved three boys who were all aged seventeen and recently unemployed; their victim was thirteen. Importantly, the Glasgow casualty surgeon described her as 'fairly well-grown for her age', potentially a pejorative comment which afforded leeway for their guilty plea to attempt to ravish, because the boys could have mistaken her for someone more mature and above the age of consent and her behaviour as flirtatious.[19] This case is an anomaly in the records and suggests an instance of young men 'tomfooling' with a girl they believed to be much older, which also suggests male entitlement to female bodies as a learned masculine behaviour. Neither excuses their criminal actions.

For all indictments, the panels' relationship to their victims indicates that these assaults were generally not stranger rape; a degree of acquaintance existed and possibly trust between the perpetrators and their victims. Panels were neighbours, lodgers, local shop owners and men recognized around the community. For example, in 1926 in Govan, a 23-year-old raped and assaulted seven girls under thirteen years. They all lived in the same neighbourhood and knew him.[20] An older male in 1927 in Glasgow coerced his former landlady's eleven-year-old to go on a tram ride to his home, where he explained that his wife was out. He sent the girl's five-year-old sister for chocolate while he committed rape in private.[21] Descriptions of physical violence are absent from these precognitions, suggesting that, because of their established relationship, the men did not need to employ force to restrain their victims or the perpetrator's superior strength was sufficient to overpower a child victim.

Only six rape cases against minors were perpetrated by strangers. A 1919 case involved a 39-year-old soldier, who was still in uniform having returned home to Barrhead a few days previously. He raped two sisters aged seven and six in a lane. He was unknown to them. However, the police knew of him for general assault offences prior to the war and one sergeant added that it was 'not the first occasion on which he has been suspected of interfering with young girls';

18 AD15/23/59, JC15/34; six months' imprisonment.
19 JC26/1929/34, JC15/40; unanimously guilty of attempt to ravish, nine months' imprisonment each.
20 JC26/1926/54, JC13/137; pleaded guilty, seven years' penal servitude.
21 AD15/27/87, JC14/39; by majority guilty, three years' penal servitude.

his previous seven convictions dated from 1903 to two in 1914.[22] Another case in Fife in 1920 involved an ex-soldier newly residing in a lodging house. The owner's six-year-old daughter lived there and had followed the man when he went to play cards. Later, he took her for a walk. A miner witnessed the rape and assisted the child home.[23] In the handful of cases of stranger rape, the perpetrator tended to be older and chose to assault very young girls. The tradition of child deference to adults in the 1920s may have facilitated these assaults, because they also did not need to use physical violence to perpetrate their crimes.

Victims

The seventy-five minor victims of rape fall into three age groups: forty-three were under ten years, twenty-eight were aged ten to twelve years; and four were aged between thirteen and sixteen. The increase in the number of rape victims in 1929 (see Figure 4.1) is attributable to two cases of multiple assaults.[24] Of 110 victims of attempt to ravish, 102 were under thirteen years, making this an indictment used for assaults against the youngest members of society, with most cases appearing between 1918 and 1922, after which the annual case load dropped significantly. Among LLPB victims, 50 per cent were under ten years, with a significant and sustained increase in the use of this indictment from 1922 onwards with a notable spike in 1925.[25] Thus, the data reveal that predominantly, the more serious indictments of sexual crime against minors were prosecuted in the earlier part of the 1920s and significantly, the victims were under thirteen years. For girls aged thirteen to sixteen, notions of consent become more difficult to defend – had she consented in some manner to some degree? – especially if the girl appeared more mature than her real age as already illustrated in a multiple assault case. However, these are prosecuted crimes and therefore CC possessed sufficient evidence to indict irrespective of the girl's appearance and the PF considered the case proceedable because he believed her non-consent was established. However, it may be that cases where the victim's

---

22 AD15/19/49, JC14/34; no jury listed, ten years' penal servitude.
23 AD15/20/19, JC9/16; pleaded guilty, seven years' penal servitude.
24 AD15/29/43, JC13/138; five victims, unanimously guilty, five years' penal servitude; AD15/29/59, JC15/40; six victims, pleaded guilty at second diet to lesser charge of LLPB, three years' penal servitude.
25 The decline in ravish prosecutions and possible consequent increase in LLPB cases will be discussed in Chapter 6.

complicity could be insinuated were unproceedable and therefore become part of the 'dark number'.

Questions posed by precognoscers cover similar material both before and after the war. Specific questions ascertaining whether the perpetrator was in uniform or known to have served might have been a response by judicial officers to middle-class fears of brutalized soldiers as described by commentators such as Philip Gibbs and Cicely Hamilton, but there is no evidence in the HCJ papers. It is possible – but how likely? – that victims of ex-soldiers declined to report them out of some misguided respect for their service, or that ex-servicemen did not commit brutal crimes on their return. Also, the young age of some perpetrators of rape and attempt to ravish later in the 1920s precludes them from having served in the Great War. However, precognoscers' questions concerning working-class living conditions suggest they were seeking evidence, which correlated with contemporary welfare investigators' ideas of other sources of sexual danger within working-class communities.

Life on the streets

Repeatedly, the precognitions describe young girls running late-night errands around working-class areas, particularly in Glasgow and Edinburgh. In February in 1919 in Glasgow, a seven-year-old was raped on vacant ground on her way home from buying salt for her mother after dark.[26] Another girl aged eleven had been sent for chips at 10.15 pm in Shettleston, Glasgow; she was raped on vacant ground on her way to the shop. Afterwards, the attacker said: 'don't tell anyone, go for your chips', but he had been seen. On her way home, a neighbour found her crying and told her to tell her mother.[27] Similarly, tenement living arrangements required young girls to use the close or stair lavatory at night, which is where one seven-year-old in Wishaw was raped before bedtime in 1920 by a stranger lurking in the dark.[28] Other girls were lured away from their playmates in the closes and scraps of vacant land in their neighbourhood by men known to them.

Working-class families did not have the resources to cosset their children at home, which meant they gained their independence at an earlier age than their

---

26   AD15/19/49; as previous.
27   AD15/19/86, JC13/132; unanimously guilty of lesser charge of attempt to ravish, six months' imprisonment.
28   AD15/20/91, JC14/34; unanimously guilty, five years' penal servitude.

upper- and middle-class counterparts.[29] Also, due to chronic overcrowding, working-class families by necessity lived their lives on their neighbourhood streets where they found leisure and entertainment.[30] Parents lacked the economic resources and time to chaperone or entertain their families indoors. Inadvertently, this left their children vulnerable to prowling males intent on sexual crime.

Cohort victims

In cases of multiple victims or 'cohort victims', the rape data reveal significant trends. Apart from one perpetrator, all the men were middle-aged, for example: a 40-year-old married ice cream shop-owner; a 70-year-old known in the community; a 49-year-old married lodger; and a 58-year-old unemployed widower and neighbour. Their position in the community may have allowed them to carry out their crimes with four or more girls over extended periods before being discovered. Generally, the girls were nine years old and above, although the seventy-year-old panel also raped a six- and seven-year-old. All of them committed their crimes indoors: in their own homes, in adjacent outbuildings and, in the case of the lodger, in the family home and the common stair. These men had won access to the girls by acquaintance and possibly trust, and this may have facilitated their repeated assaults. Their crimes were not opportunistic, as is illustrated in 1929 in the case of the 58-year-old widower. Dismissed as a storekeeper in 1925 for drunkenness, he had since been idle on parish relief. The girls knew him as 'Granda D****', a nickname perhaps implying affection. The girls were assaulted in his hen shed out of sight of his adult daughter who lived with him. He bribed them with pennies and they returned frequently over the course of January 1927 to October 1928.[31]

The youngest perpetrator of cohort rape was a 23-year-old male. In 1926, he attacked seven girls, the most of all the cohort rapists. Rather than discovery in a close-knit community, the records suggest he was able to 'groom' a group of girls because of their proximity. They all lived on the same street in Govan, and from the case details, it appears they shared the same tenement, perhaps even the same stair.[32] Because five of them were under nine years old and it appears

29 Gorham, 'Maiden Tribute', 372.
30 Mahood and Littlewood, 'The "Vicious Girls"', 554.
31 AD15/29/59; as previous.
32 JC26/1926/54; as previous.

that none of them was assaulted in the company of another, he may have hoped that if discovered, their individual evidence would be uncorroborated and easily refuted. However, the PF charged him with multiple indictments of rape, LLPB and contravention of CLAA 1885 and its 1922 revision for crimes carried out over a year. This strategy negated any possibility of a jury acquitting him entirely on any permutation of the charges and victims.[33] A similar multiple indictment strategy is illustrated by the 'Granda D****' case: he pleaded guilty on the lesser alternative charges of LLPB and CLAA offered for each victim, thus avoiding a rape verdict. His three-year sentence probably reflected the number of victims and assaults rather than the seriousness of the charge to which he eventually pleaded.[34]

Whether any of these cases could be defined as paedophilia is difficult to ascertain at this distance. In the late nineteenth and early twentieth centuries, the concept of the 'sexual psychopath' or paedophile was limited, and despite concern about their presence in the community, their behaviour was not yet medicalized in Scotland.[35] In the United States, in the first decade of the twentieth century, psychiatric research was further advanced in its medical approach to sexual offences and offenders' behaviour was being viewed as 'psycho-pathological' by the courts. In 1925, American psychiatrist John Holland Cassity described 'pedophilia' as 'the most flagrant and indefensible act in the whole category of sexual atrocities', a disease which only when it reached a 'criminal climax' was noted by psychologists.[36] The cohort victims' case papers do not use the label 'paedophilia', which was a novel term in the 1920s, or attribute any mental derangement to the perpetrators, so that the married ice cream shopkeeper who raped four girls aged nine to fourteen was not noted as mentally ill, neither was the seventy-year-old in 1923 charged with rape of four girls under eleven years.[37] However, the ice cream vendor preyed on girls from the poorhouse and, among other convictions, had previous indictments for contraventions of the Children Act 1908 in 1911 and 1919.[38] In a 1920 Perthshire ravish case, the panel had attacked a girl aged eight and had previous convictions between 1910 and 1913 for charges ranging from LLPB to attempted rape, all of underage victims.[39]

33   Use of multiple indictments is discussed in Chapter 6.
34   AD15/29/59.
35   V. Bates, '"Not an exact Science": Medical Approaches to Age and Sexual Offences in England, 1850-1914', PhD thesis (University of Exeter, 2012), 22.
36   J. H. Cassity, 'Psychological Considerations of Pedophilia', *The Psychoanalytic Review*, 14 (1927): 189–90.
37   AD15/21/163 and AD15/23/74, respectively.
38   AD15/21/163.
39   JC26/1920/14; pleaded guilty, five years' penal servitude.

Drawing conclusions about these men from a modern perspective would be wrong; some may have been paedophiles in the modern sense, while others took repeated opportunistic sex with young girls. From these case papers, if doctors were beginning to correlate sexual offences against minors with mental illness as it was understood at the time, it appears either they found nothing suggesting it or they were not instructed to report on the panels' mental condition. Considering the other, often peripheral, medical observations contained in their reports, such as a panel's recent passing of urine or the condition of a child's underwear, it is unlikely that doctors would have failed to notice and comment on a panel's mental state. The most famous forensic physician of the period Professor John Glaister of Glasgow University recognized that some of his colleagues saw every 'barbarous and abominable crime' as the 'operations of insane persons', and that the number of criminals who could claim insanity was very small.[40]

Numerous cases of LLPB indicate that girls returned to their assaulter repeatedly, and one 1925 Glasgow case also suggests the girls taunted their attacker. Charged with indecent exposure and LLPB, in the first instance eight girls aged eight to fourteen claimed that this perpetrator had exposed himself frequently to them at his window between June and July. Between July and August, one eight-year-old and two ten-year-olds in the group visited his house several times where he handled them intimately.[41] This begs two questions: had the girls heard their parents discussing a known 'flasher' in the community and were curious to see what he did? Did the older girls cajole the youngest three into visiting him to discover what might happen next? A further 1920 Glasgow case offers similar details, with four eight- and nine-year-olds repeatedly visiting two brothers in their shop, where the men exposed themselves and attempted to ravish the girls. A doctor found no evidence of assault and the brothers' counsel proffered an insanity defence, a rare event.[42] Were the children teasing two known 'simpletons' whose actions escalated beyond their intentions? Whatever the girls' motives in both cases, they were sufficiently shocked by the outcome to report it to their parents, who may have already suspected the men of sexual interest in young girls.

The number of repeated assaults of single and cohort victims in the data reveals that when reported, the girls were informing their parents what *had been happening* to them over time, not what *had occurred* earlier that day. By not

---

40   J. Glaister, *A Textbook of Medical Jurisprudence and Toxicology* (Edinburgh, 1915), 551.
41   JC26/1925/86, JC14/38; first diet pleaded not guilty, second diet pleaded guilty as libelled, three years' penal servitude.
42   JC26/1920/120, JC9/17; remanded under the Mental Deficiency Act 1913.

reporting on the first occurrence, were these children unaware that the assaults were wrong? Or were they already inured at a young age to sexual violence as an everyday hazard of working-class life? After all, the assaults occurred on tenement stairs, in close lavatories and hen sheds, which, although private loci for intimate abuse with children, were unable to mask screams or cries if the assault physically hurt, which 'many reported it did. Or perhaps these children did not expect to be believed if they informed their guardians? It is also possible that a panel's threats sufficiently deterred them from reporting. The HCJ records do not provide the answers in these specific cases and cannot explain more generally how some incidents of sexual assault went unreported. It is clear, however, that in these prosecuted examples, once the parents were made aware of the assaults, they reported them to the police and the evidence they provided supported a prosecution.

The dual role of Scottish police as maintainers of law and order as well as providers of welfare may have made reporting sexual abuse of children an obvious response for these families. Police were responsible for sanitation, street lighting and clean water, and as already seen in an incest case, a newborn's funeral might be arranged at the police office.[43] Once a report was made, the police were bound to inform the PF which removed mediation of reporting; they were not invested in the prosecution process neither instigating nor conducting investigations. They received complaints, wrote up the particulars and passed their documents to the PF for his consideration. Unless as occurred in Glasgow, the PF might appoint a police officer as his depute, who had powers to decide cases to be heard at the police courts.[44] It is possible that some parents' complaints were prosecuted in this manner. However, of the cases prosecuted at the HCJ, none contains identifiable extract previous sexual offences which might have been heard at police courts. Of those with previous sexual offences listed, their cases had all been heard at sheriff court before escalating their activities to warrant a HCJ prosecution.

The data also suggest that perpetrators avoided victims aged thirteen to sixteen in contrast to incest where the majority of victims of prosecuted crimes were pubertal. From the perpetrator's perspective, the decision to attack very young females may have been to avoid pregnancy and consequent discovery.

---

43 W. W. J. Knox and A. McKinlay, 'Crime, Protest and Policing in Nineteenth Century Scotland', in *A History of Everyday Life in Scotland 1800--1900*, eds T. Griffiths and G. Morton (Edinburgh, 2010), 216–17.
44 L. A. Jackson with N. Davidson, L. Fleming, D. M. Smale and R. Sparks, *Police and Community in Twentieth-Century Scotland* (Edinburgh, 2020), 29–30.

Further, older girls may have been readier to report an assault and their testimony may have been easier to corroborate or had a higher credibility among the police and legal authorities. Despite the acknowledged 'knowingness' of teenage girls which might make their complaints unproceedable, the evidence for similarly aged incest victims would contradict this. Or simply, men with a personal predilection to have sex with minors favoured very young girls. Writing of his early twentieth-century experiences as a prisons' commissioner, Norwood East recognized that 'senile sexuality, deprived of an adult victim or accomplice sometimes expresses itself by indecent assaults upon willing and unwilling children'.[45] This observation would include the middle-aged assaulters described earlier. Norwood East went on to explain: 'the sexual object of the typical heterosexual exhibitionist is fairly well fixed' – a stranger, possibly other girls present – and 'her age must be fairly constant'.[46] This is suggested in the 1925 'window flasher' case.

The most serious indictment – rape – returned the fewest number of cohort victims, with the data here emphasizing younger, single girls, presumably because a rapist's activities would require any other girls in the group to wait their turn. Fundamentally, the process of getting to court relied on the strength of the child's word against an adult male's and absence of culpability on her part. After all, 'knowing' girls might be partially responsible for the lapse in otherwise good behaviour by adult males.[47]

'Fantasies of little girls'

From the victim's perspective, she may have lacked the resources to report an assault or potentially she was too young to have understood the particulars of the sexual act, which would have delayed reporting to her mother, sister or other guardian.[48] Further, once the child had communicated the details of any interference, it might not necessarily have resulted in an immediate or coherent description of what had occurred. As psychological research in the 1950s acknowledged, an assaulted child is confused by conflicting feelings of hurt and

---

45   W. Norwood East, 'Sexual Offenders – A British View', *The Yale Law Journal*, 55, no. 3 (April 1946): 543.
46   Norwood East, 'Sexual Offenders', 547.
47   Smart, 'Ambivalence', 399.
48   The sub-title is taken from *Conference of the Educational Association* (1921), quoted in R. Graves and A. Hodge, *The Long Weekend: A Social History of Great Britain 1918–1939* (London, 1995), 104.

culpability, and they may not be able to articulate their physical and emotional turmoil.[49]

Testing the veracity of a very young child's experience occurred in the first instance in the home, where the mother had to be convinced of the assault. From the HCJ records, this was usually achieved by physical inspection rather than verbally. In a 1928 case, a six-year-old in Glasgow was found weeping; she had been raped by an unmarried nineteen-year-old male in the park. Her mother collected her and once home, the child managed to describe how he had 'put his feather against my feather'. The mother found no injuries but decided to attend the doctor's surgery. He confirmed she was uninjured, although later the mother presented her child at the police office; clearly, she was concerned that something had happened to her daughter despite the lack of visible injuries. Forensic medical opinion concluded that the child had experienced 'some degree of penetration', with her hymen most probably ruptured at the time.[50] In another Glasgow case in 1920, a three-year-old had been raped by her next-door neighbour. Noticing at bath times the girl's genitals were sore, the mother powdered them before realizing the true nature of her injuries, confirmed by questioning the child.[51] In both cases, neither girl volunteered their information without their mothers' constituting the framework for the testimony. The HCJ data contain several similar cases, in which a mother recognized the symptoms of a child's molested genitalia, which may indicate their awareness of sexual assault in the community. How they learned to look for such molestation is a matter of supposition but may have been through personal experience or advice transferred through generations of women.

For cases involving very young girls, maternal agency was critical to reporting an offence, the lack of which is illustrated by a Glaswegian case in 1920. Raped by a neighbour 'three stairs up', an eight-year-old ran to her mother who was drunk in bed. Instead of taking the child to the police or doctor, the mother confronted the accused, a married man, with whom she had been drinking earlier in the afternoon. Blood on the child's underclothes was insufficient to convince the mother, who stated she had 'never heard of him interfering with any child until 5th April', the date of the rape. The mother's interpretation of the perpetrator's character outweighed the child's testimony until corroborated by adult female

---

49   E. M. Litin, M. E. Griffin and A. M. Johnson, 'Parental Influence in Unusual Sexual Behavior in Children', *The Psychoanalytic Quarterly*, 25 (1956): 38.
50   AD15/28/73, JC15/39; first diet pleaded not guilty, second diet pleaded to indecent assault only, eighteen months' imprisonment.
51   AD15/20/74, JC14/34; pleaded guilty second diet, nine months' imprisonment.

neighbours, who had heard the accused's bed creaking and had witnessed the child leaving his home.[52] Again, suspicion of a man's potential for sexual offence had led to the neighbours' conclusion.

Families or neighbours reporting sexual assault on behalf of underage females had first to convince the authorities that their complaint was worth pursuing. Research conducted on the Middlesex Assize in the late nineteenth century concluded that reports were evaluated on the basis of gender, class, age and the child's reputation or that of her family; evidence of sexual innocence and 'knowingness' was sought in deposition statements.[53] This study encompassed a largely urban population in London where attitudes towards working-class girls' precocity were arguably at their most vociferous. Whereas the HCJ cases cover an urban and rural nation. The uniformity maintained in Scotland across all the regional PFs' offices potentially excluded an individual PF's personal attitudes towards complainers of sexual abuse. Questions posed by the precognoscers on precocity, consent and culpability may have inferred personal attitudes or followed the PF's guidance towards violated girls. However, once presented by the PF to CC, the precognitions and other case papers were considered by lawyers removed from the local circumstances without personal knowledge of the protagonists involved. Thus, if a PF held pejorative or other opinions about sexual violence victims, the upper level of the judiciary might play a homogenizing role. Importantly, because of the Scots Law requirement for corroboration, contemporaries acknowledged that with many cases 'there is little or no chance of getting any evidence sufficient to convict' because the deed was perpetrated in privacy. Welfare officers reported that from statistics gathered in Glasgow in 1924, 'out of 262 cases of indecency' reported to the PF, 41 per cent, or 109 cases, did not proceed.[54]

The potential impact of a PF's personal inclinations was further removed because sections 29 and 30 of the Children Act, 1908, did not apply to Scotland. In England, a child's deposition could be presented in lieu of her appearance in court, but in Scotland it was compulsory for child victims to testify in person.[55] Potentially, this removed a PF's disinclination to proceed with a case if he queried the victim's credibility and reliability or if she appeared 'unsympathetic'. He could present the case to CC based on the evidence alone because if CC

52 AD15/20/92, JC14/35; unanimously guilty, seven years' penal servitude.
53 L. A. Jackson, 'The Child's Word in Court: Cases of Sexual Abuse in London 1870-1914', in *Gender and Crime in Modern Europe*, eds C. Usborne and M. Arnot (London, 2001), 222.
54 *Departmental Committee*, 12.
55 *Departmental Committee*, 18 and 22.

agreed to support a prosecution, the complainer had to appear in court. Thus, the complexities of evidence evaluation and a victim's 'character' weighed against a jury's verdict were removed. And where corroboration existed, irrespective of a complainer's unsympathetic character, it appears the PF and CC proceeded as illustrated by a 1920 case involving an eight-year-old girl. She had experienced previous assaults by other men and now accused a neighbour of rape in his home. The PF considered an alternative explanation for the child's injuries: 'the girl's damaged private parts may be from sliding down a stair with brass knobs' and he noted the panel's previous good character compared with the child's bad name. However, the examining doctor reported the injury was caused by 'the male organ' and with this corroboration the case proceeded. An all-male jury returned a unanimously guilty verdict of indecent assault, not the single charge of rape as indicted. This is possibly because of limited understanding of the continued presence of the child's uninjured hymen post-assault, although there were seminal stains and blood on her clothing, all of which had convinced the PF and CC to proceed to a jury trial.[56]

Establishing a child's previous unadulterated state produced another challenge: if unblemished, she should not be sufficiently informed to describe the crime, which meant she might be unable to offer convincing evidence.[57] The frequent use of euphemism in the girls' precognitions helped to substantiate their claim to innocence. 'Feather', 'birdie' or 'the thing he pees with' were common terms for a penis, followed by descriptions of where the attacker may have placed it: 'on my birdie', 'between my legs'. The latter was especially confounding when determining an indictment of rape or LLPB because it could imply non-penetrative assault. Such inconclusive language might lead a PF to use personal interpretation of a child's testimony. In a 1919 case, Glasgow's PF emphasized that it was the girl's word against the accused's but added that the girl's tame accusation of 'he only put his hand up her skirt' was 'amply accounted for by her natural diffidence in speaking of such a subject'. He felt able to conclude this because the girl had reported 'the whole story to the police within an hour of the occurrence'.[58] CC agreed with the PF's interpretation and advised him to prosecute, despite the girl's restrained description of the assault. Young children may have been 'given to fantasies' and misinterpretations of adult advances, but when reports of sexual assault were made speedily, this appears to have convinced PFs and CC of truth-

---

56 AD15/20/125, JC14/35; eighteen months' imprisonment with hard labour.
57 Jackson, 'Child's Word', 223.
58 AD15/19/86, JC13/132; unanimously guilty of lesser indictment ravish; six months' imprisonment.

telling, because it reduced the opportunity for concoction of a child's fantasy, potentially embellished by a mother's leading questions.[59]

With girls aged thirteen to sixteen, establishing their non-culpability and lack of consent in an assault was paramount to prosecution. In 1885, the CLAA had established a girl's age of consent at sixteen years. However, in the decades afterwards, the debate continued concerning 'vicious girls' of all ages: characterized as sexually curious girls and teenagers who might cry rape to entrap unwitting men. The law was absolute on the age of consent, but discourse concerning a female's reputation, amount of resistance offered and possible consent continued. In some of the HCJ cases it could be inferred that some girls in the thirteen- to sixteen-year-old grey area had been 'culpable' to an extent. There is evidence that as late as 1918, government ministers were comfortable saying: 'juries will not convict where consent is favoured and the girl is of indifferent character'.[60] In 1926, welfare investigators in Scotland recognized that older girls might be culpable to a degree 'because an incipient sex instinct has been stimulated'.[61] Consequently, 1920s Scottish precognoscers often asked even the youngest victims if they had prior sexual experience. Little girls responded that this was the 'only time someone has done dirty things to me' and 'no one has ever interfered with me before'.[62] Similar circumstances existed in the 1880s with only some girls being asked if they had been 'meddled with' before.[63] The fact that not all very young girls were asked may indicate regional or individual precognoscer differences as well as approaches to testimony-gathering influenced by the complainer's presentation.

Girls of all ages described their screams and crying, but only older girls were questioned further on the degree of resistance they had offered. Resistance confirmed that an assault had been perpetrated 'against her will'. Yet, if resistance indicated non-consent, did its absence imply consent or reflect a victim's fear of further injury? The medical profession's position was informed by Professor Glaister who advised medical students in 1915 that 'so long as a woman is in complete possession of her senses, it does not require great physical strength to deny entrance to her body' and where rape was accomplished, he suggested 'either that she had become physically worn out and incapable of further resistance'

59 Graves and Hodge, *Long Weekend*, 104. The correlation of speedy reporting of sexual assault with veracity of the accusation continues to be an established 'rape myth'.
60 National Archives, HO361664/91027, quoted in K. Stevenson, 'Not Just the Ideas of a Few Enthusiasts: Early Twentieth Century Legal Activism and Reformation of the Age of Sexual Consent', *Cultural and Social History*, 14, no. 2 (2017): 231.
61 *Departmental Committee*, 13.
62 AD15/26/78 and AD15/27/87.
63 AD14/85/194.

or had lost consciousness or 'that marked disproportion in strength has been present on the side of her assailant'. The latter surely covered the majority of cases.[64]

The age of consent at sixteen years was clearly enshrined in the CLAA 1885, yet continued questioning of teenage girls suggests judicial uncertainty: under sixteens were legally minors but were also potentially 'knowing'. Escaping from her assailant once after her screams alerted a neighbour, a twelve-year-old girl in Thurso in 1921 described how his threat to shoot her had forced her final acquiescence. Despite corroborative witness testimony and the forensic report confirming 'there had certainly been partial penetration and possible complete penetration', the jury found the case not proven. Evidence proffered by the panel's sister-in-law may have undermined the case. She described the child 'following the accused to the stable', asking him for pennies and advised him to 'give her a good slap' to stop her pestering.[65] As Norwood East observed: 'the element of seduction may even emanate from the victim who then proceeds to the rank of an accomplice', and once puberty arrived 'interference with girls under age is hardly to be considered as abnormal if the girl is sexually mature, consenting and conceals her true age'.[66] The HCJ precognitions for the older cohort of girls particularly reflect the continuing requirement for resistance and unblemished character despite changes in the law forty years earlier.

'Mental defectives'

Similar inconsistencies with the law appear in cases involving adult female 'mental defectives' aged over sixteen years who were legally treated the same as girls aged thirteen to sixteen under section 5 of the 1885 CLAA.[67] Sexual assault against 'any female idiot or imbecile woman or girl' even where 'there is only weakness of mind' was a 'misdemeanour' attracting a sentence 'not exceeding two years'.[68] However, testing these women's mental incapacity was pivotal to understanding their ability to consent. The HCJ records provide six rape cases of mentally impaired females and one of LLPB. The latter case involved a nine-

---

64   Glaister, *Medical Jurisprudence*, 499.
65   AD15/21/162, JC15/32; assoilzied and dismissed.
66   Norwood East, 'Sexual Offenders', 530 and 554.
67   A contemporary phrase used to describe individuals with impaired mental faculties.
68   *Criminal Law Amendment Act 1885*, 48 and 49 Vict. c.69 s.5, 44–5; R. Macgregor Mitchell, *A Practical Treatise on the Criminal Law of Scotland by the Late Right Honourable Sir J H A MacDonald*, fourth edition (Edinburgh, 1929), 176.

year-old child who had suffered 'infantile paralysis' or polio, leaving her mentally defective. The jury returned a majority not proven verdict.[69] In the remaining six adult cases, capacity to consent and the panels' prior knowledge of her disability were weighty factors even if the woman had solicited sex.

In 1922 in Perth, an 'imbecile' 21-year-old's father found her locked in a pigsty, where her attacker had left her the night before. The father took the case to the sheriff court where the panel's counsel declared: 'it's not a crime to have intercourse with a female', which prompted the PF to seek the Advocate Depute's advice, who counselled that 'rape can still be the charge even if no violence was used and if the woman is mentally and physically incapable of resistance'. The accused insisted that she 'knew quite well what she asked'. The case proceeded to the HCJ where medical evidence confirmed she was no longer *virgo intacta* and her mental capacity was that of a fourteen-year-old; the panel was sentenced to three years' penal servitude.[70] However, two Highland cases were less successful despite strong evidence of the women's incapacity.

In 1919 at the Inverness Assize, the mother of an 'imbecile' young woman accused a uniformed soldier in his twenties of rape. The case hinged on the panel's knowledge of the condition of this twenty-year-old with Down's syndrome. The mother's eyewitness account of the attack in a field and medical evidence confirmed rape, yet an all-male jury found the panel not guilty.[71] In this instance, the panel's recent war service may have provided mitigation, not because he had served his country but because having been away for four years, he could not be expected to remember her mental condition despite its visible physical characteristics. In a 1920 Dunoon case involving the rape of a twenty-year-old imbecile woman, mental capacity to consent and pregnancy appear to have caused confusion. Despite the PF writing to the Crown Agent that 'the case evidence is as much against the accused as in his favour', the case proceeded perhaps because the young woman's mother and doctor provided compelling evidence that the accused knew of her mental condition. However, the complainer confessed to sex with the panel on several occasions which may have led the jury to understand she had capacity to consent, while her pregnancy and stillbirth placed suspicion on the family, who were thought to be seeking financial compensation.[72] Yet a Dumfries case in 1920 involving a 30-year-old woman and 65-year-old perpetrator resulted in a unanimously guilty verdict.

69　JC26/1927/19, JC13/137; assoilzied and dismissed.
70　AD15/22/57, JC13/134; majority guilty verdict.
71　AD15/19/114, JC11/118; case papers state 'Mongolian idiot'.
72　AD15/20/48, JC13/132; unanimously not guilty, assoilzied and dismissed.

The woman had no previous history of associating with men and had been assaulted in her own bed. The doctor examining both parties reported that the panel confessed: 'I was larking with her and she with me, . . . she was as keen for doing it as I was'. He stated he was unaware of her mental condition. However, her declared innocence and his previous convictions for 'assault and mischief' resulted in a three-year sentence.[73]

In all these cases, the women were not expected to offer resistance, but the verdicts suggest they were required to be virgins and not solicit sexual gratification.[74] Even in the case of a sixteen-year-old farm servant considered 'little more than a child', her two alleged rapists were unanimously acquitted as not proven. She had lost her virginity aged fifteen, and it appears the men on the farm had passed her round among themselves.[75] Despite clause 5 of the CLAA, it appears that if an imbecile woman's behaviour could imply loose morals and therefore an invitation to sex, juries were reluctant to convict, even when supported by strong medical evidence.

Scene of the crime

Unlike incest, which was predominantly an indoor crime, non-familial sexual assault of minors was committed equally indoors as outdoors in houses, water closets and outbuildings, or under bridges, in parks and on vacant land, and the youngest victims often suffered the most repeated assaults without resort to physical violence. These features are also all evident in the late nineteenth-century HCJ records as well as research conducted on New York.[76] Generally, when committed indoors, the case was one of repeated assaults over time, implying planning, enticement and coercion.

Outdoor assaults tended to be single occurrences and opportunistic – the lodger who raped his landlady's daughter under the railway bridge did so on one occasion, as did a panel in 1919, who assaulted a child going for salt, on vacant land.[77] The precognitions describe working-class children playing in courts and

---

73   AD15/20/120, JC14/35.
74   Glaister gave four signs of virginity: intact hymen, 'normal condition of the fourchette & posterior commissure', narrow vagina with 'rugose walls' and darkened nipples. Glaister, *Medical Jurisprudence*, 483.
75   AD15/22/91, JC12/55.
76   K. J. Taylor, 'Venereal Disease in Nineteenth-Century Children', *Journal of Psychohistory*, 12, no. 4 (1985): 458.
77   AD15/19/2 and AD15/19/86, respectively.

closes, and wasteland, always in close proximity to home, suggesting that sexual assault of young girls was a closely local crime. Children were not abducted or lured any distance and assailants were local men seemingly acting spontaneously. However, unlike many incest cases where family members occupied the same room or even bed, whether indoors or outdoors, men perpetrating sexual assaults against minors did so in complete privacy, suggesting their appreciation of the illegality of their activities. Where a second child was involved, she was often instructed to keep watch for potential witnesses or despatched to buy sweets.

However, despite a perpetrator's best efforts, he might be observed and again, a 1928 Glasgow case suggests women were watchful for aberrant male behaviour in their vicinity. Looking out of her bedroom window, a neighbour stated she saw a man enter the park with two girls. Seeing one girl leave, she became suspicious as she saw him carry the remaining child 'through a gap in the hedge'. By the time she reached him, he was doing up his trousers and the girl emerged pulling up her knickers.[78]

Motives

Their choice of unobserved loci and desire to keep their activities secret suggest that perpetrators recognized their behaviour as illegal. However, the real motive as might have been explained by the panels is difficult to comprehend in either contemporary terms or framed by modern understanding. The HCJ records for underage assaults only note an insanity defence in two attempts to ravish cases, both of which were upheld.[79] Defence counsel may have advised against an insanity plea due to the unpredictable duration of incarceration at 'His Majesty's Pleasure' and as seen with incest cases, physicians were likely to have commented on a panel's mental state even if he did not elect to benefit from it. The case papers contain very few medical reports where mental condition was assessed but was dismissed before reaching court.[80] As explored earlier, the legal

---

78 AD15/28/73, JC15/39; pleaded guilty to indecent assault, three months' imprisonment. Louise Jackson found contemporary anxieties were provoked by assaults on children by 'park perverts' in nineteenth-century London; however, there are insufficient similar cases prosecuted at the HCJ to ascertain whether this was a real problem in Scotland; L. A. Jackson, 'Women Professionals and the Regulation of Violence in Inter-War Britain', in *Everyday Violence in Britain 1850-1950: Gender and* Class, ed. S. D'Cruze (Harlow, 2000), 130.
79 JC26/1919/7 and JC26/1928/77; at His Majesty's Pleasure.
80 An insanity plea may have been avoided if a doctor agreed to treat a panel as a medical patient, which would make the case invisible in these records.

and medical authorities in this period did not readily correlate the capacity to sexually assault children with a psychological illness.

While older abusers may have been playing out some senile fantasy once adult women were no longer attracted to them, among younger panels, as contemporary psychologist Bernard Hollander suggested, 'a superfluity of energy for which they get no outlet, as when confined to the house or office' may have been the motive.[81] However, the HCJ data reveal no correlation between periods of widespread unemployment or sedentary types of employment, such as office errand boy, and increases in prosecution of serious sexual assaults.

Domestic arrangements might provide an opportunity for those inclined towards sexual assault of young girls where long-term lodgers, who shared bedrooms with children, could gain their trust and connive to rape them clandestinely without their parents' knowledge. This was the situation in a Greenock case in 1929 involving four girls and a boy under twelve.[82] The mother's precognition described 'a heavy smell' frequently in their crowded two-room house with kitchen, where the lodger shared a bedroom with two of the children. Initially, her husband 'was of opinion that [the lodger] was suffering from a running wound, war service', but on inspection of one child's underwear, his suspicions were aroused. The abuse had occurred over seven months.[83]

Discussing males of all ages, Norwood East noted that sexual crime increased with 'the lengthening days and the better weather allow[ing] opportunistic crimes to take place in quiet woods and parks'.[84] He claimed open-air sexual crime was perpetrated on strangers, but again the prosecuted case records contradict this near-contemporary perception. Sexual crime was rarely perpetrated on complete strangers if they were minors and was not necessarily a summer or outdoor crime. However, his further comments on unmarried men and alcohol deserve exploration.

Norwood East observed that 'sexual criminality is committed to a large extent by unmarried people'.[85] Where the perpetrators were in their twenties and older, and where the court records noted marital status, the HCJ data show an even number of married and unmarried panels. Being single in itself is insufficient motive to rape small girls, but when restricted access to sex is

---

81 Norwood East, 'Sexual Offenders', 543 and 535; he also commented that 'an enlarged prostate gland' could often be the cause 'in elderly men', an observation not grounded in medical fact; B. Hollander, *The Psychology of Misconduct, Vice and Crime* (London, 1922), 83–4.
82 N. Penlington, 'Masculinity and Domesticity in 1930s South Wales: Did Unemployment Change the Domestic Division of Labour?', *Twentieth Century British History*, 21, no. 3 (2010): 288–9.
83 AD15/29/43, JC13/138; unanimously guilty on six charges, five years' penal servitude.
84 Norwood East, 'Sexual Offenders', 532.
85 Norwood East, 'Sexual Offenders', 532.

considered, some perpetrators may have taken a 'moral holiday' in order to satisfy their sexual tension.[86] None of the sexual crimes against minors involved physical violence beyond the act of violation. The assault was unequal in that one party was subordinate in age, strength and social position to the other. This may explain why some adult men felt able to seek sex from underage females in a patriarchally subjugated society spilling onto the streets to find space for recreation.[87] Further, the legal minimum marriageable age for girls remained twelve years until the Marriage Act 1929, which raised the age limit to sixteen for both sexes.[88] Was rape of girls as young as twelve not considered a serious crime by perpetrators who desired a 'subordinate/superordinate' relationship, since the girl was eligible to marry? It may have assuaged a perpetrator's guilty conscience and allowed him to complete the act without compunction, because if she became pregnant, he could propose to hide the assault. Additionally, the number of older unmarried men accused of rape and ravish may have chosen younger victims because they could not criticize poor performance, as Norwood East described them: 'the constitutional psychic inferior group of psychopathic personalities [who] commit offences to overcome their feelings of inferiority'. He continued by excusing them as 'not necessarily sexual perverts in the narrow sense'.[89]

Where alcohol was mentioned in the HCJ papers, it appears mostly in cases of habitual and repeated abuse and usually by lodgers in the home, rather than in one-off opportunistic outdoor crimes. Thus, alcohol-induced disinhibition does not appear to be a prime reason for sexual 'mistakes' with minors. Glaister's position on inebriation was that 'the condition of drunkenness *per se*' did not answer a charge completely but 'may be a mitigating factor'. He acknowledged the lack of medical understanding of responsibility when drunk but held the personal opinion that 'in the bulk of cases of drunkenness, responsibility for actions cannot be removed', because 'drunkenness is but a relative term'.[90] As one of Scotland's leading medical jurisprudence authorities, his opinion undoubtedly influenced judicial approaches to inebriation and culpability.

From his observations of prison inmates during the 1930s and early 1940s Norwood East also attributed some sexual offences to 'emotional excitement'

---

86 S. Jackson, 'The Social Context of Rape: Sexual Scripts and Motivation', *Women's Studies International Quarterly*, 1 (1978): 36.
87 Jackson, 'Social Context', 37.
88 *Age of Marriage Act (Scotland) 1929*, 19 Geo 5, clause 1.1.
89 Norwood East, 'Sexual Offenders', 540; such theories attempting to explain the motive for sexual assault of minors can only inform the historian's reading of the legal case papers; they cannot suggest the motive.
90 Glaister, *Medical Jurisprudence*, 587–9.

induced by the 'fear of detection' enabling 'a release of sexual tension' and thus alleviating depression.[91] Again, of the few cases which remark on the mental health of perpetrators, there is no comment on this rationale for assaults. However, it remains possible that perpetrators did commit their crimes due to mental ill health. In a lecture at the London School of Economics during the 1930s, German criminologist Hermann Mannheim reflected that 'a considerable rise in *sexual offences* [sic] since the last War ... have been a consequence of increased mental instability due to the War', a comment supported by 'similar increases ... noticeable through Europe after 1919'.[92] While the official statistics for the 1920s corroborate an increase in *prosecuted* sexual offences in the immediate post-war years, the HCJ records do not suggest a causative correlation with war trauma. Where war service is mentioned in the precognitions, it is not repeated in court in the Books of Adjournal or Minute Books as mitigating evidence. For example, the 1919 Glasgow case of the girl sent to buy salt stated the perpetrator was a soldier, but the charge transcribed into the Minute Book failed to mention it.[93]

In 1926, Scottish welfare officers speculated that some men assaulted children because 'it costs them little or nothing' and there was a reduced risk of contracting venereal disease from a child. As men potentially operating under a different moral code, they may not have considered sexual molestation as harmful to the child.[94] They suggested also that the girls' unwitting behaviour might have provoked their assailant. They advised that after dark, 'children should not be allowed out on the streets' and that 'little girls should wear closed knickerbockers and dresses of sufficient length'. They concluded: 'it should be obvious that this is a necessary precaution' and that parents should warn their children.[95] However, in cramped homes where entertainment spilled onto the streets, it was almost impossible for parents to enforce this and, ultimately, the blame did not lie with any child or her attire. Thus, without the panels' 'voice', it is impossible to ascertain their motives, although the privacy they sought during the assault suggests they understood the criminal nature of their behaviour. Except in one case of a six-year-old girl whose younger brother came to the door of the house where a neighbour was raping her; the perpetrator allowed him to stay. He gave the boy a book to occupy him while he continued. This panel appeared not to consider disclosure a threat from either child, unless his penny

91   Norwood East, 'Sexual Offenders', 541 and 542–3.
92   H. Mannheim, *Social Aspects of Crime in England between the Wars* (London, 1940), 122.
93   AD15/19/49, JC14/34.
94   A. P. Fiske and T. S. Rai, *Virtuous Violence* (Cambridge, 2015), 178.
95   *Departmental Committee*, 15.

bribes given to the girl are considered. By offering her a half penny each time, he was able to repeat his assaults while buying the child's silence. On this last occasion, the girl's tears on her return home alerted her mother. The child was clearly unaware of the nature of the abuse because the precognoscer managed to ascertain how the panel had hurt her using 'something from his trousers'.[96]

Maintaining silence

Perpetrators were able to keep their crimes secret for extended periods through bribery and coercion. As with incest, threats of physical violence if the children told their parents were frequent in all types of non-familial abuse, and occasionally small monetary rewards were offered to buy silence or to tempt a repeat visit. The perpetrator may have viewed the assault as transactional sex, although the child is unlikely to have comprehended the gift of sweets or a penny as anything different from recompense for running an errand and parents clearly considered this as bribery once they were informed. Where perpetrators chose a particular girl from among a group of friends, another child was posted as lookout, or if two children were out alone, often one was bribed to remove her from the scene. In these circumstances, the perpetrator manipulated the situation to achieve his goal and although not necessarily always a totally premeditated assault – some perpetrators appear not to have planned on whom, where and when to pounce – the modus operandi suggests a degree of forethought. However, there is no discernible pattern identifying why they chose a particular girl from a group or who to bribe.

Research on Victorian London shows that penny bribes were often believed by the perpetrator to 'settle the matter'.[97] One Scottish case from 1885 could be interpreted in this way. The ten-year-old victim had been babysitting her sister's infant when a neighbour assaulted her in her sister's home. Afterwards she refused his offer of a ha'penny, so instead he placed the coin in the baby's fist. Later the child bought apples with it. Having also compelled her to silence, the assailant's insistence on paying his victim may be read as having recompensed her. Three days later when her mother discovered the child's injuries, she immediately sent her husband for the police.[98] Her interpretation of the penny bribe clearly

---

96   AD15/22/72, JC14/36; pleaded guilty, three years' penal servitude.
97   L. A. Jackson, *Child Sexual Abuse in Victorian England* (London, 2000), 117.
98   AD14/85/208, JC13/114; pleaded guilty to assault with intent to ravish, eighteen months' imprisonment.

rejected any notion of recompense. Further, the nineteenth-century London research discovered cases where parents had been bribed to dissuade them from reporting an assault. However, the HCJ records for 1885–1930 do not include any similar instances except one case involving a child's grandparents. Having raped their granddaughter, their lodger offered 'to sign a paper promising £1 per week' as maintenance for her.[99] It is possible that these grandparents adhered to an older way of settling child molestation that was anomalous by the 1920s.

However, if bribing parents no longer held any efficacy, bribing victims and their friends proves unambiguously that perpetrators acknowledged their behaviour was wrong and possibly criminal. And returning home with sweets or pennies alerted suspicious mothers to potential abuse.[100]

Parent power

For incest cases, the absence of the mother, either temporarily or permanently, permitted male relations to perpetrate their crimes without the victim's foremost protector being available to witness, prevent or report the assault. However, with rape, ravish and LLPB cases, while the mother's existence could not prevent assaults committed outside the home, her presence was pivotal to detection and reporting, since the majority of non-familial assault victims had living mothers and she was usually the first person to be suspicious or informed. There is only one instance of a father discovering abuse, although some others became involved later when reporting the crime. In this 1928 Glasgow case, the assault occurred during the mother's absence in hospital, which may or may not have been coincidental. At bedtime, the father, a 49-year-old marine fireman, spotted discharge on his daughter's sheets. He called for a female neighbour who advised taking the child to the police, which he did.[101] This is the only case of a father coping with the entire process. In the few cases where fathers were involved at a later point, they assumed control only of the final stage – taking the child to the police. In his contemporary observations, Bernard Hollander explained that 'there is no father who does not feel he would shoot the seducer of his daughter

---

99 AD15/23/10, JC5/16; pleaded guilty, four years' penal servitude with recommendation for deportation.
100 L. A. Jackson, 'Family, Community and the Regulation of Child Sexual Abuse, London 1870-1914', in *Childhood in Question: Children, Parents and the State*, eds A. Fletcher and S. Hussey (Manchester, 1999), 136.
101 AD15/28/47.

on the spot', yet the Scottish evidence reveals no examples of fathers taking the law into their own hands prior to seeking police assistance.[102]

Any suggestion that parents falsely complained, presenting ill-kempt daughters at the police office to report a rape in the possible hope of either removing a troublesome neighbour or for financial gain, is not evident in the HCJ case papers.[103] If any families did employ this tactic, then the PF would have been unable to corroborate their complaint or might have revealed their motive during his investigations, thereby stopping proceedings. In most cases, mothers did not report to the police without first checking for evidence themselves, which suggests they understood that they needed to be sure in order to be heard. For younger victims, typically a mother's agency in the legal process began at bath-time, when physical injuries were discovered. Attendance at the police office was also often preceded by a visit to the family doctor who referred them to the police. Checking with a medical expert illustrates the mothers' requirement for official corroboration prior to lodging a complaint.

Occasionally, an intermediary informed the mother, as in the earlier case of the woman watching from her bedroom overlooking the park. Collective supervision of children was typical of working-class districts and included disciplining children, reporting behaviour to parents or simply assisting an assaulted child.[104] Sometimes women in the street or playmates found a child returning home upset and took her to her mother. Where a schoolteacher or inspector was involved, the matter was taken directly to the police and parents were informed afterwards. Two rape cases in 1920 involved the school. One occurred in Glasgow, in which a female police constable questioned the eight-year-old girl at school after an anonymous report of truancy and repeated abuse by a neighbour. In her precognition, the child admitted to subsequent assaults by two other men.[105] The second case, in Fort William, involved three girls overheard gossiping by their headmistress. She reported the incident to the police 'to stop the girls from telling their companions how to get money from immoral acts'. She had not reported the incident to protect the abused girls but in order to prevent the debauchery of more pupils.[106] Cases of indecent assault

---

102 Hollander, *Misconduct*, 74.
103 Mahood and Littlewood, 'The "Vicious Girls"', 574.
104 E. Ross, '"Not the Sort that Would Sit on the Doorstep": Respectability in Pre-World-War I London Neighborhoods', *International Labor and Working Class History*, 27 (Spring 1985): 49.
105 AD15/20/125, JC14/35; indicted as sole charge of rape, unanimously guilty of indecent assault, eighteen months' imprisonment.
106 AD15/20/157, JC11/118; unanimously guilty, five years' penal servitude.

discovered by welfare authorities would have been heard at sheriff or police court, but it is noteworthy that so few more serious rapes, attempts to ravish and LLPB were either not detected or not reported by them.

Interestingly, very few precognitions mentioned a mother's suspicions prior to the final assault which had provoked recourse to the law. However, the time between a child complaining of being sore, a mother's discovery of assault and police assistance was usually a single day. These families did not delay in their recourse to the police once they knew their child had been sexually assaulted; but this does not account for families who decided to bathe their child, put her to bed and, if possible, forget about it. As contemporary welfare officers averred:

> We had evidence that many cases of indecent assault are not reported to the police. This arises from the disinclination of the parents to subject their child to the ordeal of a public trial, with the possible result of fixing the matter more definitely in the child's mind.[107]

Research on rape prosecutions between 1918 and 1970 in England and Wales found that cases were rare and mainly involved adult women complainers, whereas the Scottish records for the 1920s show an almost equal number of underage rape prosecutions as adult prosecutions.[108] However, the Scottish records do coincide with trends in England and Wales where cases involving girls under sixteen were more likely to be prosecuted on a lesser charge, presumably because it would be easier to secure a conviction.[109] In the LLPB records, 290 out of 294 victims were under sixteen years, with LLPB often combined with charges of attempt to ravish or contravention of CLAA 1885 and latterly the 1922 revision. The multiple charge of LLPB with attempt to ravish disappeared after 1923, but while it continued in use and where the jury found the panel guilty, the lesser charge was often preferred. Thus, despite the details recorded by the precognoscer that mothers believed their children had been raped, often the PF and CC decided the evidence required a lesser indictment or group of charges, and the jury might alter that decision further in its verdict.

---

107 *Departmental Committee*, 14.
108 L. A. Jackson, 'Child Sexual Abuse in England and Wales: Prosecution and Prevalence 1918-1970', 2, http://www.historyandpolicy.org/policy-papers/rss_2.0, accessed October 2022; the whole number of assaults – prosecuted, reported only and unreported – may reflect a different balance.
109 Jackson, 'Prosecution and Prevalence', 2.

Recidivism

A PF's long service accumulating local knowledge was particularly useful in cases of suspected repeat offences. In an age of handwritten ledgers and typed forms, in numerous cases, the PF relied on locally filed paperwork and memory, while in cases involving a panel from further afield or an itinerant, regional police offices provided evidence. Panels who kept their sexual recidivism below the bar of a HCJ trial are invisible to this study, but of those prosecuted at the HCJ, many panels had previous non-sexual convictions listed on their indictment sheets, for example, assault or breach of the peace heard at sheriff or police courts. However, there are almost no sexual reoffenders among the HCJ rape, ravish or LLPB cases. As welfare officers acknowledged, 'officially . . . only 10 per cent of convicted sexual offenders against children and young persons have a previous conviction for the same class of offence'; they also remarked that repeated offending was least likely in the more serious sexual indictments. These observations are supported by the HCJ records.[110] Where repeat sexual offences are listed, the previous charges are not of the same severity as the current prosecution.

For example, in 1912, then aged thirty-three, a panel was tried for assault (unknown if sexual) at Edinburgh Sheriff Court, receiving twenty-one days' imprisonment. By 1913, he had progressed to attempt to ravish plus the previous conviction now heard at Edinburgh High Court, for which he was sentenced to four years' penal servitude. He reappeared in 1927 charged with ravish and LLPB plus his previous convictions, but the current charges were found by a majority not proven.[111] Sentencing for his 1913 crime compares with others in the 1920s with previous convictions, who had escalated their behaviour, but the verdict in 1927 could not have been influenced by his previous convictions because previous offences were not disclosed to the jury; they were only available to prosecution and defence counsel and the judge.[112] In another case, a married shoemaker was charged with rape of a nine-year-old during spring 1921 in Ayr. He pleaded guilty receiving eighteen months' imprisonment. In April the previous year, he had been found guilty of LLPB with three girls under thirteen years but had obviously not served the entire eighteen months sentenced for

---

110 *Departmental Committee*, 18.
111 JC26/1927/28, JC9/20; assoilzied and dismissed.
112 In her Victorian study of rape, Conley found similar evidence where a labourer with previous convictions (including a ten-year sentence for rape) received only three months for his latest assault on a young child; C. Conley, 'Rape and Justice in Victorian England', *Victorian Studies*, 29, no. 4 (Summer 1986): 530.

that offence. In comparison with other crimes with previous convictions, the 1921 sentence is quite lenient even when his guilty plea is considered, but by 1927 he had reoffended against three girls under thirteen. He was charged with LLPB and went down for three years' penal servitude.[113] If the 1927 offence had been his first, this would have been a harsh sentence in comparison with others for similar offences. But in this instance, the judge's sentence may reflect contemporary attitudes to repeat offending, although it may also indicate inconsistency of sentencing.

* * *

Conclusion

When compared with the analysis of incest in Scotland in the 1920s, the commission and prosecution of rape, ravish and LLPB differ in several aspects. Firstly, these non-familial sexual crimes are not predominantly committed indoors. Secondly, the existence of a mother provided no protection to young girls; they were all potential victims and perpetrators do not appear to have selected them because they lacked maternal protection. Thirdly, in these prosecuted cases, mothers' recourse to the law was immediate on their discovery of evidence of sexual abuse, either via a doctor or directly to the police. Most significantly, whereas prosecuted incest was usually perpetrated against pubertal girls, prosecuted non-familial assaults were largely committed against underage females and often against the youngest children, especially when the offence was indicted as LLPB.[114]

These cases suggest that sexual criminals assaulted their neighbours' children, young girls who knew them and whose trust they could win. The evidence does not indicate whether panels sought out a certain type of girl, but it does suggest that accessibility was a factor as well as age, which could hinder collection of corroborating evidence. These were the premeditated crimes. However, the records show there were also a comparable number of opportunistic assaults. These records suggest strongly that returning soldiers were probably not the culprits. The number of teenage males charged also repudiates Mannheim's

---

113 AD15/21/10, JC26/1927/86 and JC14/39.
114 The HCJ records may not be representative of reported but unprosecuted non-familial sexual violence. It is doubtful whether verifiable, narrative sources for such cases still exist, which might reveal similar trends.

contention that bringing such cases to court gave 'undue prominence . . . to an incident which is better forgotten' since so many cases involving teenage perpetrators appeared at the HCJ.[115] It has been argued that panels refused to speak and therefore they were acquitted due to lack of evidence; however, this also is not apparent from the HCJ sexual violence records.[116] Without trial transcripts providing some access to the panel's voice, the trial Minute Books always recorded the panel's confirmation of his plea; they detail lists of prosecution and exculpatory witnesses and note if defence counsel requested mitigation of sentence after the verdict was returned. None of the HCJ sexual crime cases collapsed because the panel refused to cooperate at this late stage, most likely because where he pleaded not guilty, he was at pains to prove his innocence, even if he knew he was not.

There appears to be no correlation between unemployment and sexual offending, or the reverse in periods of economic boom when men may have viewed themselves in the ascendancy displaying their masculinity through sexual conquests. Neither does there appear to be connection between alcohol and reduced inhibitions; alcohol was neither accepted as catalyst nor mitigation.

Comparative analysis of late nineteenth- and early twentieth-century Scottish HCJ prosecution records reveals little difference in the types of crimes committed against underage girls and how they were committed. However, the numbers of prosecutions on behalf of minor females constitute a considerably lower proportion of overall sexual assault prosecutions. Why? Journalist and campaigner W. T. Stead compared the new age of consent legislation, the 1885 CLAA, to game laws: no one ate a fish out of season, therefore do not seduce girls still going through, or who have not yet reached, puberty.[117] For anyone subscribing to the *Pall Mall Gazette* or knowledgeable about game laws, the warning was clear. However, working-class Scotsmen, predominantly in Glasgow where the greatest number of cases was prosecuted, may not have had contact with either. However, they did enjoy the services of the longest existing paid police force in the country. Glasgow police's dual roles of law and order combined with welfare may have made them more accessible to working-class families thus increasing the number of reports received and converted into prosecutions. Post-war, considering inflammatory suggestions of brutalized soldiers returning to commit sexual crime, the authorities may have taken a more serious approach to sexual offenders, again affecting the report-to-

---

115 Mannheim, *Social Aspects*, 81.
116 J. G. Kellas, *Modern Scotland* (London, 1980), 81.
117 W. T. Stead, 'Close Time for Girls', *Pall Mall Gazette*, 8 July 1885, 3.

prosecution rate as families realized the authorities were prepared to listen. Or are the lower proportions of sexual abuse of young female children in the late nineteenth century attributable to families who suffered the abuse of their children in silence? Whereas post-war, mothers, sisters and female neighbours had gained agency and were prepared to use it?

How much sexual crime went unreported by parents is impossible to ascertain, even if crimes heard at lesser courts were included. However, from the perspective of the parents of the young daughters who complained, they believed they had been raped, ravished or otherwise indecently assaulted and felt compelled to seek retribution. Research on child victims in the 1920s and 1930s concluded that the authorities hoped children would forget what had happened; otherwise, there was a risk they might be perceived as 'vicious girls'.[118] Some parents may have hushed up an assault and never spoke of it again. However, in the case of girls and women over sixteen years, they might speak up for themselves.

---

118 Smart, 'Ambivalence', 404.

5

'Vice and virtue'*

Sexual violence against women over sixteen years

The rape of women by men is a human behaviour that has affected all societies over time to a greater or lesser extent. How it is viewed, the degree of fear it engenders in women and how victims and (largely) male-dominated judiciaries respond are socially constructed across time and place.[1] There has always been a relatively low number of prosecutions per head of female population and an even lower number of convictions. This trend tells us more about the difficulties in bringing a successful prosecution than it does about who rapes whom, where and how.

Before attitudes towards women in society began to change in the early nineteenth century and before legislation increased the age of consent to reflect notions of childhood extending into mid-adolescence, females were considered an adjunct of the patriarch in their family. A wife and daughters were the property of the husband and father and, in their absence, of the eldest son and brother. Thus, a rape prosecution was conducted by the male on behalf of his female 'property' who might no longer be as publicly valuable to him, either as a sullied wife or a non-virginal daughter of marriageable age. Although societal attitudes towards sexual violence recognized rape as a heinous crime, discourse surrounding rape continued to describe it as a rare event, difficult to prove and essentially a crime provoked by natural tendencies.[2] As women gained greater agency and legal commentators considered female consent, or its absence, to be pivotal to complaints of sexual violence, slowly women began to report rape for themselves.

---

*   Traditional English.
1   M. N. Christoffersen, K. Soothill and B. Francis, 'Who Is Most a Risk of Becoming a Convicted Rapist? The Likelihood of a Rape Conviction among the 1966 Birth Cohort in Denmark', *Journal of Scandinavian Studies in Criminology and Crime Prevention*, 6 (2005): 42.
2   L. Olsson, '"Violence that's wicked for a man to use": Sex, Gender and Violence in the Eighteenth Century', in *Interpreting Sexual Violence, 1660-1800*, ed. A. Greenfield (Abingdon, 2016), 141.

However, increasing female social, economic and legal autonomy was inseparable from male anxiety surrounding female identity and importantly women's sexuality; consent and fear of false accusation from 'irrational' women fuelled debate.[3] By the late nineteenth century, the Criminal Law Amendment Act of 1885 (CLAA) had raised the age of consent to sixteen and a common law charge of rape could be brought on penetration only without the need to prove emission. And yet, proving that one had not consented to sex, had struggled with all one's might and had screamed and kicked to exhaustion were still unofficial 'scripts' in a rape case that could be judged both in the pretrial evidence and in court. Thus, attempting to test developments in female ascendancy since the late nineteenth century against actual rape prosecution statistics to ascertain whether the former influenced the latter is almost impossible.[4]

In the late nineteenth and extending into the early twentieth century, young working-class women were considered by elite groups as precocious, predatory, often infected with venereal disease, likely to become illegitimately pregnant and poor parents.[5] Yet, oral testimony from women who experienced the 1920s first-hand discussed there being a lot of sex, although it was 'discreet' and 'a private thing' but not initiated by 'nice girls'.[6] The correspondence between Marie Stopes, author of *Married Love*, and her readers has revealed that sex with fiancées or long-term girlfriends was often a spontaneous single event rather than customary.[7] Thus, working-class premarital sex was contested as frequent, not indulged in by respectable girls or at best a momentary lapse, but the point at which solicited and unsolicited sex became unconsenting sex – rape – raises important questions about societal attitudes to the vulnerability of females.

Sexual assault cases brought by adult females and their supporters at the High Court of Justiciary (HCJ) can be divided into two groups: social rape in which a degree of acquaintance existed between the perpetrator and victim and stranger rape where both parties were unknown to one another.[8] Examination

---

3   J. Randolph, 'Rape and Resistance: Women and Consent in Seventeenth-Century English Legal and Political Thought', *Journal of British Studies*, 39, no. 2 (April 2000): 172–9.
4   V. A. C. Gatrell, B. Lenman and G. Parker, *Crime and the Law: The Social History of Crime in Western Europe since 1500* (London, 1980), 289.
5   L. A. Jackson, 'Girls and Delinquency', in *Women, Crime and Justice in England since 1660*, eds S. D'Cruze and L. A. Jackson (Basingstoke, 2009), 143.
6   J. Giles, '"Playing Hard to get": Working-Class Women, Sexuality and Respectability in Britain, 1918-1940', *Women's History Review*, 1, no. 2 (1992): 250–1.
7   L. A. Hall, 'Impotent Ghosts from No Man's Lane, Flappers' Boyfriends, or Crypto-patriarchs? Men, Sex and Social Change in 1920s Britain', *Social History*, 21, no. 1 (January 1996): 59; M. Stopes, *Married Love* (London, 1918).
8   The distinction between social and stranger sexual assault is an established division as evidenced by *The London Rape Review: A Review of Cases from 2016*, Mayor's Office for Policing and Crime

of the details contained in the precognition statements and other court papers allows analysis of the class structure of sexual violence and contemporary attitudes towards consent and culpability. For all age groups, the legal definition of rape constituted 'the carnal knowledge of a woman forcibly and against her will' with penetration to any extent and with or without emission. Attempt to ravish was the intent to 'have connection' and was an aggravation of the general indictment of assault.[9] Lewd and libidinous practices and behaviour (LLPB) was rarely indicted for adult females, presumably because adult victims could provide sufficient details for Crown Counsel (CC) to prefer a rape charge and also because the 'intimate handling' that was the mainstay of an LLPB charge was deemed resistible behaviour by a grown woman.

The evidence

Unlike sexual assault of minors, 77 per cent of adult rapes were committed outdoors. Glasgow accounted for 32 per cent of all adult rape prosecutions, while Dundee, Fife and the Highlands provide figures between 6 and 11 per cent; Edinburgh was at the top end of that range, although two-thirds of rapes heard at the HCJ in the capital were committed in outlying rural locations. Urban centres, predominantly in southern counties, accounted for 38 per cent of the total number of assaults. Therefore, in the 1920s in Scotland, rape could be experienced by any adult female, although from the prosecuted crime records, the possibility appears to have been greater for urban women and most prevalent in and around Glasgow.

The situation is somewhat different towards the end of the nineteenth century. In 1885, there were seventeen rape cases brought by adult women which were tried on assize around the country reflecting a wider geographical distribution of prosecutions beyond the three southern centres of Edinburgh, Glasgow and Dundee. Thereafter, the number of rape prosecutions in the late nineteenth and early twentieth centuries decreased significantly and annual prosecutions were mostly in single figures, although the geographic distribution began to concentrate in Glasgow (Figure 5.1).

(July 2019). For this study, 'social rape' is further divided into social rape between individuals who properly knew one another and acquaintance rape between individuals more distantly acquainted.
9 R. Macgregor Mitchell, *A Practical Treatise on the Criminal Law of Scotland by the late Right Honourable Sir J H A MacDonald*, fourth edition (Edinburgh, 1929), 175 and 164.

'Vice and Virtue'   123

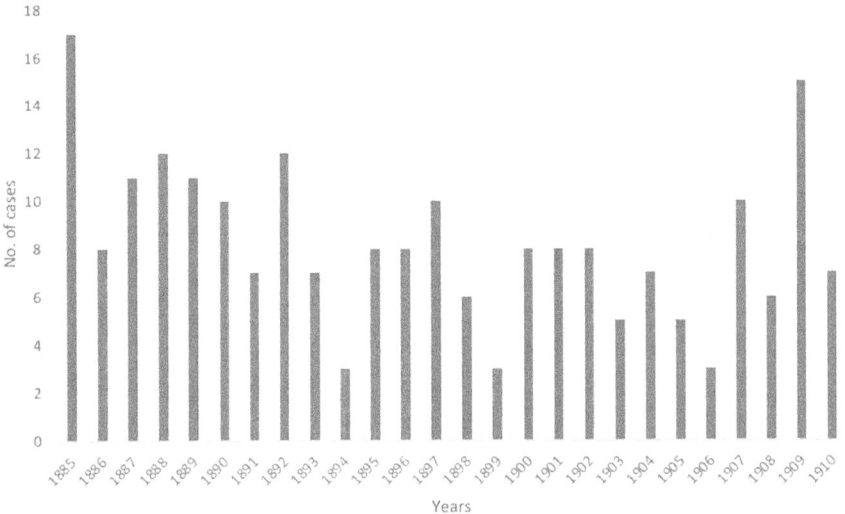

Figure 5.1 Rape: Adult victims over sixteen years annual counts 1885–1910.

By 1910, six out of a total of seven cases of adult rapes were prosecuted at the HCJ in Glasgow.[10] After the Great War, the trend in adult female rape prosecutions follows a pre-war pattern with three cases prosecuted in 1919, twelve in 1920 and eleven in 1921 before a decline to seven in 1922. By the end of the decade, annual rape prosecutions for adult females were one and five, respectively (see Figure 5.2).

There does not appear to have been an immediate post-war increase in rape prosecutions and as with rapes of minors, a possible delay in rape prosecutions towards the end of the hostilities is not evidenced by the records: the first adult rape case to be prosecuted at the HCJ in 1919 had been committed in July and was tried almost exactly a month later.[11] Any assaults not meeting the bar for a rape prosecution would have been heard at lower courts, thus not appearing in the HCJ records, but holding trials at lower courts would appear an illogical response if the elites were, in any way, responding to substantiated post-war fears of working-class violence. Further, the increased case load for 1920 and 1921 cannot be considered a post-war 'backlog', because for almost all adult rape prosecutions only two months elapsed between the date of the rape and

---

10 The five-year average to 1914 for rape of *all* age groups was 18 cases per year, with the five years to 1919 averaging nine cases annually; *Criminal Statistics: Statistics Relating to Police Apprehensions, Criminal Proceedings, and Reformatory and Industrial Schools, for the year 1925* (Edinburgh, 1925), 20.
11 AD15/19/128.

Figure 5.2 Rape: Adult victims over sixteen years annual counts 1918–1930.

the trial; for example, a rape committed on 22 November 1919 was tried on 27 January 1920.[12] Once reported, a rape case had to be heard within six months of commission under the terms of the CLAA and seemingly during the 1920s, the HCJ proceeded to trial safely within that time frame; no cases exceeded a three-month elapse between report and trial.[13] Since none of the adult cases prosecuted at the HCJ took longer than twelve weeks to bring to trial, they were clearly supported by compelling and corroborated evidence, whereas the Procurator Fiscal (PF) may have investigated other cases over a longer period in order to gather proceedable evidence but which fell down for some reason before the six-month and, after revisions to the CLAA in 1922, the nine-month deadline.

Across the decade, the precognitions reveal similar questioning strategies suggesting that the requirements for evidence collection and attitude towards rape victims did not change over the period. Questions concerning degree of struggle, evidence of emission and previous sexual history were common in the post-war precognitions and similar to those from late nineteenth-century prosecutions. As with underage victims, questions pertaining to military service of the accused are not evident in the 1920s testimonies; either the authorities were not as interested in correlations between soldiers and violence as social commentators intimated or there was no evidence that returning soldiers were more rapacious. However, perceptions of vulnerability to crime can be

---

12 AD15/20/136.
13 L. Farmer, *Making the Modern Criminal Law: Criminalization and Civil Order* (Oxford, 2016), 276.

affected by demographic changes which may be especially pertinent in post-war Scotland, where the media had reported huge male losses during four years of hostilities. Thus, exploring the demographic gender division is necessary to better understand sexual violence crime statistics.[14]

In 1911, there were 93.9 males per hundred females in Scotland in the age group fifteen to forty-nine, which had decreased to 90.3 by 1921.[15] The difference between 1911 and 1921 suggests men would have experienced slightly less competition for available females in the early part of the 1920s. If attracting a partner were easier, presumably there would be less impetus to seek non-consensual sex and consequently fewer rape prosecutions. Gender ratios did not recover within the decade, continuing at 90.5 males per hundred females until 1931, making it unlikely that post-war demographics had an impact on increases in sexual violence prosecutions between 1920 and 1922.[16]

Asked to reflect on his perception of crime during 1919, Sir Nevil Macready, chief commissioner of the Metropolitan Police, explained that due to 'modern methods of publicity', the situation was no worse than after the Crimean War, when he understood previous increases in violent crime had been experienced, and 'what was happening now was that directly a crime occurred a great deal more than usual was made of it'.[17] Macready acknowledged a perceived increase in crime, which he attributed to the media. The statistics for Scotland published in 1925 and collected annually for the previous five years reveal for *all* crimes against the person the average number of cases per year between 1910 and 1914 was 4,427 which fell to an average of 2,362 cases between 1914 and 1919, followed by totals of 3,201 in 1921, 2,646 in 1922 and continued static for the remainder of the reporting period.[18] These figures for *all* crimes against the person do not replicate the sexual violence spikes seen in 1920 and 1921; seemingly they are anomalous and also are not explained by socio-economic events in these years. Declining industrial activity and subsequent unemployment was repeated in the latter part of the decade without a concomitant increase in sexual violence prosecutions.

---

14 E. Monkkonen, 'New Standards for Historical Homicide Research', *Crime, History and Societies*, 5, no. 2 (2001): 12.
15 M. Flinn, ed., *Scottish Population History from the 17th Century to the 1930s* (Cambridge, 1977), 318.
16 A longer time series may reveal similar or possibly random variations.
17 'Crime Wave Reported to be Sweeping over the Country at the Present Time', *Manchester Guardian*, 24 January 1920.
18 *Criminal Statistics*, 18.

Perpetrators and victims

The evidence for Scotland in the 1920s reveals a picture of working-class men sexually assaulting working-class young women who shared similar backgrounds and often worked alongside one another; essentially 'Mr. Average rape[d] Ms. Average'.[19] Between November 1918 and December 1930, fifty-four rape prosecutions named fifty-seven adult victims and seventy-three panels were charged (sixteen cases involved multiple rapists). In twenty-eight cases, the panel and victim(s) knew each other to some extent. Where ages for the accused were available, in general the panels were a similar age to the victim(s), although there are three cases committed indoors in 1921, 1927 and 1930 where the victims were widows over seventy. In these cases, the widows opened their doors to the men, but only one woman knew her attacker. In two of these cases, the accused had taken alcohol and one woman had been drinking with her attacker prior to the assault.[20] These cases appear anomalous in the records, which without notes from the juries' deliberations become impossible to understand in their societal context.

Panels ranged in age from sixteen years to men in their forties. There is no discernible pattern of unmarried younger men committing rape in the earlier part of the decade when they might have been in competition with 'war heroes' for available single women.[21] In fact, in a 1920 Highland case, the twenty-year-old panel was just old enough to have enlisted but not to have seen active service. He had only been married a few weeks when he was charged with rape of an unmarried eighteen-year-old.[22] Unlike incest and rape/ravish of children, 77 per cent of adult rapes were committed outdoors: in fields, on pathways and in urban closes. Similar loci also appear in late nineteenth-century adult rape prosecutions, and the modus operandi of perpetrators indicates these were opportunistic crimes, although not necessarily completely un-premeditated. Some precognitions provide evidence that men, individually or in groups, lay in wait to attack a female, such as the sixteen-year-old being escorted home by her dance partner in 1924 when they were approached by three men. All male

---

19 S. Jackson, 'The Social Context of Rape: Sexual Scripts and Motivation', *Women's Studies International Quarterly*, 1 (1978): 28–9.
20 AD15/21/175A; unanimously not proven, assoilzied and dismissed; AD15/30/19; pleaded guilty, five years' penal servitude.
21 A. Woollacott, 'Khaki Fever and Its Control: Gender, Class, Age and Sexual Morality on the British Homefront in the First World War', *Journal of Contemporary History*, 29, no. 2 (April 1994): 326 and 342.
22 AD15/20/119; not guilty, assoilzied and dismissed.

parties were of a similar age ranging from nineteen to twenty-one years and were unmarried, but only the dance partner had consenting access to the girl. She stated that they told her partner 'to buzz off, it's her we want'. Their collective instruction to her partner suggests pre-planning, although their choice of victim was opportunistic. A jury of six men and nine women found them unanimously guilty but convicted on a lower charge of assault with intent to ravish.[23] Of the ten cases where the panel and victim knew each other properly, the assaults appear to have been spontaneous, occurring usually when a young couple were walking home from an entertainment late in the evening. Although time of day is rarely noted, from the statements given by the victim and witnesses, most rapes occurred after dark.

Descriptions reveal the panels to be average men in the community.[24] They were miners, painters, ironworkers, farm servants and an apprentice riveter. Men appearing in the 1920s HCJ cases were no different from their peers or from panels prosecuted between 1885 and 1910. Where noted, panels in the 1920s were either employed or unemployed, although cases involving unemployed panels offer no correlation between periods of economic depression in 1926 and 1928 onwards and a rise in sexual violence. Indeed, one rape case in 1926 and three in 1928 are particularly low annual counts. The panels were all working class, and the precognitions contain no special features regarding the case; only one of the accused attempted an insanity defence and none of the exculpatory witnesses mentioned epilepsy or other mental debilitation as mitigation. The panels were all nominally average, unremarkable working-class men.

Between 1885 and 1930, there are no middle-class rapists or victims in any of the rape prosecutions. In this period, most middle-class young women would have been escorted whenever they were outdoors and it has been argued that 'unprotected' working-class lifestyles invited opportunistic assaults whereas women living 'protected' or chaperoned lives were less likely to become victims of sexual violence.[25] Middle-class women's daily routines separated them spatially from working-class milieux; shopping streets and restaurants were segregated by class which might be supervised by the local police.[26] Thus, working-class men appear not to have transgressed visible and invisible middle-class boundaries,

---

23 AD15/24/42, JC13/135; six to fifteen months' imprisonment each.
24 Jackson, 'Social Context', 28.
25 E. Stanko, 'Typical Violence, Normal Precaution: Men, Women and Interpersonal Violence in England, Wales, Scotland and the USA', in *Women, Violence and Social Control*, eds J. Hanmer and M. Maynard (London, 1990), 132.
26 J. Carter-Wood, 'Self-Policing and Policing the Self: Violence, Protection and the Civilizing Bargain in Britain', *Crime, Histoire & Societies*, 7, no. 1 (2003): 113.

making rape and ravishment a same-class crime perpetrated in working-class districts.[27] Their absence from the HCJ records does not mean that middle-class men did not commit rape or that middle-class women were not victims, but it suggests that prosecuted cases fitted an elite concept of victim and perpetrator profiles of working-class 'loose' women and aggressive men.

Social rape

It is an accepted fact of sexual violence that most perpetrators and victims knew (and know) each other to some extent prior to the assault, that men have been (and are) considered to 'need' sex and that women can be seductive. Where need intersects with perception of seductiveness – that a girlfriend 'wants it' – it can result in unconsenting sexual violence.[28] Social rape between individuals who knew one another comprised 20 per cent of adult rapes in the HCJ records and all the victims were aged between sixteen and twenty-three: a young woman who was walking home late from the cinema with a friend when a previous family lodger approached them and raped one; a couple had danced together and accompanying the twenty-year-old domestic servant home at 4.00 am, the man threw her to the ground and tried to have intercourse shouting, 'Ye bugger, I'll have what I want'; or a girl who rejected her dance partner's offer to walk her home, so he knocked her down, raped her and afterwards when she threatened to tell her parents, he said, 'I'm not worrying my word is as good as yours'.[29]

The ultimate violence of the assault – penetration – appears to have been a key factor promoting these cases beyond courting behaviour to rape prosecutions. In a 1928 case heard in Edinburgh, a 22-year-old farm servant assaulted a 17-year-old dairymaid. She had asked him to lift a heavy milk can. Afterwards, he put his arm round her waist and under her clothes; she struggled to avoid him and that was it until two weeks later when the same happened, but the accused took it

---

27 See Introduction for discussion of middle-class sexual violence.
28 A. P. Fiske and R. S. Rai, *Virtuous Violence* (Cambridge, 2015), 170; J. Bourke, *Rape: A History from 1860 to the Present* (London, 2010), 43.
29 AD15/21/135 no forensic evidence reported for penetration and no seminal stains on either parties' clothing, although the victim clearly recalled his ejaculation, unanimously not proven, assoilzied and dismissed; AD15/21/44 doctor confirmed 'hymen disappeared' although would have expected to 'see greater injury to the parts' given the victim's testimony of 'deep penetration' which he confirmed despite no physical evidence, possibly because the girl was considered of 'irreproachable character' and the panel was a 'drunken worthless fellow', pleaded guilty, five years' penal servitude; AD15/23/79 doctor's opinion that there had been 'recent connection' and confirmed recent rupture of hymen and bruising, jury of eight women and seven men found him unanimously guilty, two years in Borstal.

further and raped her in the barn. In her precognition, the woman stated that 'if he'd not done anything more to me, I probably would have said nothing at all', but outrage at being forced into full intercourse appears to have provoked her report to her employer and ultimately the police.[30] Refusing a man who thinks she may be willing can be constructed as the female exerting agency in the face of male assumed dominance, thus cases of social rape may be constructed as a gender power struggle won by forcible intercourse.[31] This is especially pertinent when the value of premarital female chastity is considered. Women were required to remain 'pure' protecting their virginity while exhibiting reluctance to participate in premarital sex even if they desired it, whereas men were eager for sex using persuasion to overcome the woman's reluctance.[32] When reluctance proved to be a total rejection of his advances, violence could ensue.

In all the prosecuted social rape cases, the woman's unchaperoned presence with a lone man could be read as a 'sexual script': a signal of her availability and sexual invitation to the male party.[33] In some cases after the rape, the woman allowed the man to continue to walk her home as occurred in a case in Dundee in 1930. Having gone for a motorbike ride with her attacker, after the assault, the young woman rode home with him 'because I did not want to walk by myself'. Despite medical confirmation of penetration and human blood on the accused's clothing, the jury found the panel not guilty. Described as a 'well-built, healthy and well developed 5ft 4in' woman, one doctor asserted that 'given the physique of both parties, we are inclined to the view that resistance on the part of the girl could not have been very strenuous'; thus the absence of scratches and bruises suffered during resistance was construed as consent to sex.[34] Combined with her continued presence afterwards with her assailant on the motorbike, the jury's verdict might appear reasonable and to confirm her consent to sex. Yet despite walking home with their attackers after the assault, these women did not shrug it off as over-eager courtship. They risked their reputations by reporting their assaults as rape. This contradicts the 'sexual script': simply agreeing to be alone with a male did not, in these victims' eyes, equate to sexual availability, with or without reluctance and resistance. By reporting their assaults, these complainers understood their experience as criminal sexual violence distinct from other

---

30 AD15/28/25, JC5/18; unanimously guilty of indecent assault, six months' imprisonment.
31 Fiske and Rai, *Virtuous Violence*, 170.
32 E. Stanko, *Intimate Intrusions: Women's Experience of Male Violence* (London, 1985), 4; Giles, '"Playing Hard"', 252.
33 S. D'Cruze, 'Sex, Violence and Local Courts: Working-Class Respectability in a Mid-nineteenth Century Lancashire Town', *British Journal of Criminology*, 39, no. 1 (1990): 46.
34 AD15/30/108, JC11/121; unanimously not guilty, assoilzied and dismissed.

forms of 'everyday' violence against women. Equally, all of the prosecuted social rapes were reported immediately before any of the victims could suspect they were pregnant, which suggests they were not revengeful rape charges to cover premarital pregnancy or a marriage refusal.

From the PF's perspective, the victims' testimonies and doctors' reports, however inconclusive, provided sufficient corroboration on which to proceed. The case papers do not contain any pejorative comment on the possibility of these cases being working-class courtships gone too far, although cases in which this may have been the PF's opinion were unlikely to proceed to the HCJ, although they might have been prosecuted on a lower charge elsewhere. Equally, premarital non-consensual sex is not visible in the records where it resulted in marriage because marriage itself would have legitimized any sexual violence between the spouses. Further, the Registrar General's Annual Review for Scotland in 1921 revealed that marriage rates had not fluctuated significantly for either males or females between 1911 and 1920, suggesting that young women had not hastened into post-war marriages to gain spousal protection in a society perceived as sexually violent.

Acquaintance rape

The HCJ records contain eighteen rapes in which the women knew their assailant by acquaintance. In one case in 1920, returning home drunk, it appears the perpetrator could not recall where he lived in B*** Street, Glasgow. Known as 'the terror of the neighbourhood', he attempted sex with one 37-year-old before moving to another property where he slipped into bed with a woman and her husband and tried again. Eventually, he found a third victim, an older widow living alone and raped her before assaulting two police constables who came to her assistance. Two doctors disagreed on the forensic evidence for semen in the widow's person, and the panel pleaded not guilty to a combined indictment of indecent assault, rape, assault and previous charges.[35] It is probable that the PF and CC proceeded despite conflicting doctors' reports because the precognition evidence clearly identified the same man committing a similar crime in close proximity, although no victim or her supporters witnessed another's assault. Hence the multiple charges on the indictment sheet which made it almost impossible for him to be found not guilty of all the charges against all three

---

35 AD15/20/73, JC14/34; unanimously guilty, five years' penal servitude.

women. Of the other cases of rape by a single perpetrator-acquaintance, the victims ranged in age from seventeen to twenty-nine. All the victims were unmarried, making this also a crime against younger, unprotected women. A 1922 Glasgow case exemplifies this. Two servants aged twenty-one were walking home together when a man, known to one of them by sight, approached them. He caught hold of one, but she yelled out that she was a married woman and he was to leave her alone. Instead, he attacked the unmarried woman, suggesting that this assailant respected spousal ownership of another man's wife.[36]

Because of their degree of acquaintance, victims were easily able to identify their attackers. These perpetrators made no attempt to hide their identity, and in some cases, they conversed with their victims during the assault, usually making threats or casting aspersions on their chastity. As with sexual assaults against minors, these men may have believed they acted with impunity but had not reckoned on the moral strength of the women they outraged. The 1920s were a period of economic and social emancipation for women; they rode the wave of female participation in the war effort, which had given them entrance to previously inaccessible work, information and behaviour and which may also have influenced their attitude to male violence. In this atmosphere, it is possible that judicial authorities were more prepared to listen to women bringing rape charges, or, more likely, the women themselves felt able to make accusations and potentially possessed the physical and emotional resources to endure a prosecution. However, in cases of stranger rape, the perpetrator was less easily identified. Firstly, because the victim could not provide a name or identify his associates in order to find him; and secondly, a complete stranger to the victim was likely to be just as unfamiliar to the police, most of whom possessed a comprehensive knowledge of their communities.

Stranger rape

Rapes by strangers totalled nineteen cases (35 per cent), perpetrated by individuals and multiple assailants (discussed under 'group rape'). Again, the victims were women under thirty with only one aged thirty-four and they were unprotected being unmarried or widowed. For example, in 1921, a widowed 27-year-old postwoman was raped by a vagrant in Ayr while on her rounds in a rural area and a seventeen-year-old dressmaker in East Wemyss, who while

---

36 AD15/22/71, JC15/33; unanimously not guilty, assoilzied and dismissed.

waiting for a tram home, was raped on the beach by a man who 'smelled of liquor'.[37] All of the single-perpetrator stranger rapes were committed outdoors, usually a field, path or other unobserved space. These men were opportunists seizing the moment to attack a lone, unprotected female. The precognition evidence does not suggest premeditation. Unknown to the victim, with no witnesses, these perpetrators probably anticipated no reprisals. However, the women reported the crime, mostly very quickly, emphasizing the degree of their moral outrage and perception that the police would respond. To confirm their stories, they were always medically examined.

Medical examinations were rudimentary, only able to determine presence of human blood and semen but not to whom they belonged, and doctors proffered personal opinions in many instances. When examining the postwoman, the doctor stated:

> Her manner of story-telling impressed me to her truthfulness. . . . I am of the opinion that he could have forced his will without leaving injuries. . . . She is of rather poor physique and of nervous temperament, and her resistance in consequence might be of a character that would not call for brutal measures on his part.[38]

Professor Glaister added that he 'could not find seminal fluid on her clothes or vaginal swab'. The postwoman's petite stature, her semi-professional status and an assault by a stranger from out of town combined with a doctor's and Professor Glaister's personal opinions that she lacked the capacity to resist completed the 'dominant rape mythology': she was a respectable widow supporting a small child having lost her husband in the war and a neighbour confirmed that 'I would not believe any suggestion that she had consented to be interfered with by a man' and therefore her story was genuine.[39]

However, in a 1920 case from Rothesay, the circumstances failed to convince the jury. An eighteen-year-old home help claimed to have been raped in a public park by a man, who had sent her sister away in order to get her alone. The medical evidence found her 'vulva inflamed but no other marks', although there was forensic evidence of semen and the victim confirmed he had 'made me wet'. The doctor helpfully added 'appearances did not convey to me the impression that this girl had been habituated to coitus' and again Glaister waded in with

---

37 AD15/21/137, JC13/134; jury of six women and nine men, by a small majority, found him guilty, five years' penal servitude; AD15/21/154, JC11/118; unanimously guilty of attempt to rape, nine months' imprisonment.
38 AD15/21/137.
39 AD15/21/137.

his definitive opinion: 'vaginal fluid shows recent sexual connection'. The PF's investigation had collected corroborating evidence thus permitting him to prosecute. However, some element of the girl's story or appearance in court may have been unconvincing, because the all-male jury found the panel not guilty.[40] Unlike the respectable postwoman outraged by a social inferior, this young woman was of comparable age and class to her attacker; it took place in a public park on her way home from a night out with her sister and possibly, as far as the jury was concerned, these circumstances weighed against her.

In four cases of stranger rape, the same man assaulted multiple victims. In Perth in 1920, a domestic servant aged nineteen and clerkess aged twenty-two were assaulted by a stranger on a public road. He threatened to kill the younger one, while the other he silenced by putting his hand over her mouth. Both women struggled hard, screamed and the younger one left nail marks on his face, but neither witnessed the other's assault and there were no other witnesses. Charged with assault with intent to ravish, indecent exposure and rape, he pleaded guilty to assault only of one woman and indecent assault of the other. Their doctor found the 22-year-old clerkess of 'below average build' therefore lacking 'average physical strength' and she had considerable scratches to her face and was swollen and bruised, her 'maidenhead was rent asunder' and when the police were sent for, the constable called her 'a lady'. The younger domestic servant had been heard screaming by a nearby gardener who had intercepted her and believed her appearance supported her story. Throughout the afternoon and evening before his crime became common knowledge and before he was arrested, the vagrant had been spotted around the village and surrounding countryside indecently exposing himself.[41] The medical assessment and social status of one woman combined with corroboration from the younger victim supported a prosecution. As an unknown in the community, this panel fulfilled the societally received 'script' for a rapist: strangers committed rape. Once convicted, his recidivism earned him eight years' penal servitude.

Another case already discussed involved three women on the same Glasgow tenement stair. Again, there were no common witnesses to the assaults, which was also the case with a 1922 Edinburgh crime involving two women: a farmer's wife aged 58 and 40-year-old married schoolteacher raped by a 28-year-old unmarried coal miner with no previous complaints against him. The former told her husband and son what had happened but only reported the crime officially

---

40 AD15/20/119, JC14/35; assoilzied and dismissed.
41 AD15/20/85, JC13/132; pleaded guilty second diet, previous conviction five years for attempt to ravish in Salisbury.

when she heard that the younger schoolteacher had gone directly to the police.[42] Married and possessing social status, these women were believable both in the police office and when giving their precognitions.

In all these cases, despite the lack of eyewitness corroboration, cumulative accounts and medical evidence against the panels convinced the PF to prosecute and the juries to convict. The women's testimony was credible because it substantiated the rape myth that rape is committed by strangers.[43] However, as with assaults committed by strangers against minors, stranger rape of adult women constitutes a relatively small portion of the total number of sexual violence prosecutions.[44]

Group rape

For purposes of historical accuracy, rape by multiple perpetrators cannot be assumed to be the same as modern concepts of 'gang' rape. In 1920s Scotland, these were *group* rapes and were mostly premeditated yet opportunistic because they were perpetrated by a group of men lying in wait for a suitable victim, and they occurred on a single occasion. Recent scholarship on multiple perpetrator rape (MPR) identifies sociocultural attitudes towards women as key to group rape incidents: hyper-masculinity and a sense of sexual entitlement combined with gender hierarchy and dominance over women, in the right circumstances, could provoke MPR. Participation in group rape for some individuals was found not necessarily to be sexual but instead provided self-validation, a sense of belonging and proved the individual's masculinity to his peers. Modern perpetrators were mostly adolescents and men in their early twenties from poor backgrounds with generally low educational standards. Some older men with similar traits were charged. The research also identified the need for a leader to initiate the event, an individual who participated rather than stood back giving orders and who possessed social hierarchy above the group.[45]

Sixteen group rapes (30 per cent of total adult rapes) prosecuted at the HCJ correlate with late nineteenth-century research in Kent which found that 25 per

---

42 AD15/22/130, JC5/15; pleaded guilty, seven years' penal servitude.
43 Age of Consent podcast, episode 4, https://www.narrativematters.scot/the-age-of-consent-podcast.
44 Stranger rape is also infrequently reported in modern rape statistics; *London Rape Review*, 20.
45 T. da Silva, J. Woodhams and L. Harkins, 'Multiple Perpetrator Rape: A Critical Review of Existing Explanatory Theories', *Aggression and Behavior*, 25 (2015): 151–3.

cent of complainants (English law) were victims of group rape.[46] From the 1920s HCJ cases, five were by acquaintance, one was social and the remaining ten were perpetrated by strangers. In only one case was the involvement of alcohol noted in the case papers, and in all cases, whether there were three or four or only two perpetrators, a leader was apparent from the testimonies of the women. The young female victims were either walking home from work or entertainment alone, or accompanied by a boyfriend, who was dismissed by the perpetrators or failed to intervene; as one young man stated: 'he was too afraid to go to her assistance'.[47] Where the panels' ages were available in the case papers, they were mostly adolescents and men in their early twenties. This corresponds with recent research which suggests that MPR participants are experimenting with sex at a stage when their masculine and sexual identity is being formed.[48] The majority of group rapes were perpetrated outdoors, although one case in 1923 committed indoors reflects the ultra-masculine attitude some group rapists displayed.

A domestic servant aged sixteen was raped at her place of work by three of the farm's outdoor servants, all aged under twenty years. They pushed her into a bedroom where she claimed she fought 'sore all the time', and having locked the door, one of the attackers said, 'stick it in, it's what she's d**** sair needing'. They were disturbed by a female visitor, who told one of the rapists to get off the girl. He replied that 'he would when he was ready' and another accused told her 'it was all for fun'. After which the farmer's widow, aged fifty-six, returned home and was told, 'clear out you old b**** and I'll be after you'. The teenage men's reported words and refusal to stop when discovered reveal male attitudes towards the 'use' of their victim and disrespect for the authority of the women. Despite witnesses and medical evidence that attributed blood on the woman's knickers coming from the nose of one of the attackers and considerable bruising around her genitals, the jury of nine women and six men found the panels unanimously guilty of the lesser indictment of indecent assault.[49] In another group rape on a farm in Strathaven in 1919, this time without witnesses, aspersions cast on the girl's character exceeded those in her favour. Fellow farm workers accused her of 'talking dirty' and one recalled that she had heard the girl's mother discussing financial recompense of £100–£200, which would 'set them up in a farm' if she accused the young men of rape. Precognosced a second time, the young

---

46   C. Conley, *The Unwritten Law: Criminal Justice in Victorian Kent* (Oxford, 1991), 85.
47   AD15/22/91.
48   Da Silva, Woodhams and Harkins, 'Multiple Perpetrator Rape', 151.
49   AD15/23/76, JC11/119; six months each; the doctor found 'no marks of violence on her body' which may have persuaded the jury to convict on the lesser charge.

woman admitted to having had regular sex with another man at the farm over an extended period and the examining physician could find no evidence of assault but did form the opinion that she was 'a girl who had frequent connection with males'. All of which was probably instrumental in the three panels being unanimously found not guilty.[50] Yet, the PF and CC had decided to prosecute suggesting they did not view this girl's case as a false accusation.

Work on sexual violence in Victorian England indicates that employers knew about sexual assaults by male employees on female employees while they were away from the property, which may explain the verdict in the first case earlier.[51] Despite rejecting the authority of the two witnesses, the jury appears to have accepted some degree of licence in the antics of young men working far from home with available young women, all of whom were unsupervised. However, in group attacks committed by strangers, the court's response reflected societal outrage. The details of an assault involving three men aged twenty-three to twenty-six are particularly nasty, involving physical violence beyond the sexual assault. The woman was raped by one man at least twice while another threatened, 'when I'm finished with her, I'll toss her over the f***ing dyke, go get a f***ing razor and cut her f***ing throat'. Medical evidence confirmed that she was not a virgin, prompting the PF to ask the court to 'stretch leniency to sentence'. However, the shocking nature of the attack, which elicited a four-year excuse from further duty for the jury, resulted in long sentences. The panels appealed the verdict on the basis of inconsistencies in the woman's testimony, which the appellate judge disregarded: 'she described [the ordeal] "like a nightmare", such experience would explain her inaccuracies and she did identify *** and *** at ID parade'.[52] Similarly, the rape of a 23-year-old in Rutherglen in 1930 while walking home with her boyfriend ended in seven-year sentences for her three rapists.[53]

In all these group rapes, the panels displayed arrogant attitudes towards their victims and female witnesses; they acted in combination, although with a leader in each case initiating the assault by his own participation. Without the panels' 'voices', it is impossible to understand their individual motives and whether or not they participated because of a desire to belong to the group. However, the snippets of conversation recalled during the assaults suggest hypermasculinity and a sense of male entitlement to sex. In one case, an accused rapist turned

50 AD15/19/85, JC14/34.
51 D. Gorham, 'The Maiden Tribute of Modern Babylon – Re-examined, Child Prostitution and the Idea of Childhood in Late Victorian England', *Victorian Studies*, 21, no. 3 (Spring, 1978): 377.
52 JC26/1928/103, JC15/39, JC34/1/55; seven years' penal servitude each.
53 JC26/1930/21, JC13/138.

to one of his group and was reported to say, 'are you aware *** is my sister and I'm not happy she's out so late', implying that the two young women who were without chaperones had broken some unwritten rule of male dominance of the streets after dark.[54] These cases may simply have been more compelling and violent than others which passed across the PF's desk. However, the increased severity in sentencing in cases prosecuted towards the end of the decade suggests that judges were increasingly intolerant of group rapists.

The victim in one of the group rapes was a prostitute. Providing evidence of rape rather than 'workplace injury' is especially difficult for sex workers and was particularly so in the 1920s with elite attitudes such as those expressed by contemporary psychiatrist Bernard Hollander, who wrote: 'they adopt the life from choice, and remain in it from choice.... The inebriate, poverty-stricken prostitute is not ashamed either'.[55] In this instance, the victim appears to have had little choice how to sustain herself; she may have been inebriate and she was certainly poverty-stricken, but ashamed, probably not since she reported the assault and admitted her profession. The case may be an anomaly among others reported by prostitutes that did not proceed, but it reveals elements of increasing sympathy towards violated women who lived irregular lives, especially when the jury composition in this case of four women and eleven men is considered. They found the two panels unanimously guilty of rape. Four married women, a managing director, assurance manager, teacher, cheese merchant, plumber, jeweller, clerk, cashier and stationer (a jury of thirteen) all agreed that this woman's lifestyle did not discount the violence done to her.[56]

The thirty-year-old woman stated she was a 'potato lifter', working on farms with no fixed abode supplementing slack periods with prostitution. One night in 1922 in Glasgow, a man invited her for a drink; she had several but stated that she was sufficiently sober when they parted. On her way home at 9.00 pm, five or six men insulted her, then they all attacked her during which she was 'kicked on the face and went quite silly', but she remembered struggling and screaming until she was exhausted. A passing cyclist, who heard and saw the attack, went for assistance. Two constables later reported that 'she was completely overpowered so we cannot say if she was struggling'. She was taken to Glasgow's Central Police Office where she was examined and found to be in 'a deeply comatose state from alcohol' and unsurprisingly no longer *virgo intacta*. The physician could find

---

54 AD15/20/34, JC5/14; by majority not proven, assoilzied and dismissed.
55 B. Hollander, *Psychology of Misconduct, Vice & Crime* (London, 1922), 131–2.
56 JC14/36; the case papers do not explain why the jury composition listed four women and eleven men but only gave thirteen occupations.

'no evidence of ill-usage to her genitals', although the bruises to her face and thighs deserved a fortnight's convalescence in hospital. The men were arrested on the spot and at the police office one stated: 'that'll be Barlinnie for me this time', implying not only a prison sentence but also previous assaults.[57] Despite eyewitness corroboration not least from two constables, both men pleaded not guilty. Did they assume her profession and inebriated state would negate her testimony and corroboration from reputable witnesses?

As a single case it reveals little about the wider experience of abused prostitutes; however, it does support research suggesting that the use of prostitutes for extramarital sex or premarital experimentation was increasingly disparaged post-war.[58] From the PF to CC, and jury to judge, the decision to prosecute, to convict and the severity of sentence indicates intolerance of sexually violent men no matter who their victim. Both panels went down for seven years' penal servitude.

Rape with murder

Often considered the most prevalent form of rape primarily because of salacious news reporting, there was only one rape-homicide case prosecuted in the 1920s in Scotland. This 1926 case involved a male hospital attendant and a nurse, both employed at a Greenock mental hospital and who were reported to have 'been keeping company' before having a 'difference'. The morning after a works picnic, the nurse's violated body was discovered; she had also suffered a head injury. The accused had returned to the hospital to complete his night shift but hearing of the discovery, he absconded and was later apprehended with blood-stained clothing in his room. He was charged with rape and murder and pleaded a special defence of insanity at the time of commission, being 'in such a condition of mental abnormality as not to be fully responsible for his actions'. The PF had anticipated as much in a note to the Solicitor General that the defence would 'go for mental abnormality in the hope of reducing [the charge] to culpable homicide'. He added, 'this modern plea has unfortunately not been made a special plea' and suggested 'sadism may be cited'. The post-mortem confirmed death 'due to shock following the outraging and wounding and bruising to the head'. The PF sought medical opinion on the panel's mental state while awaiting trial which described a 22-year-old man, 5 feet 7 inches tall who was 'fit and healthy',

---

57   AD15/22/73, JC14/36.
58   Hall, 'Impotent Ghosts', 59.

although in court various psychiatric specialists were engaged to offer evidence for both sides. Prosecution denied any insanity and pushed for a murder verdict while the defence team argued he was 'insane and irresponsible' at the time of the crime and that he suffered 'impulsive insanity and sadism' – he had set out to do the nurse harm and then rape her, not rape first which could be construed as sexual satisfaction followed by murder to cover up the evidence. The trial took a lengthy four days to hear evidence from eyewitnesses, exculpatory character witnesses and forensic opinions and unusually for a rape trial normally heard behind closed doors, the *Glasgow Herald* reported every detail. The nurse was described as 'a strong girl only overcome by force', and the judge Lord Ormidale said that the jury had taken 'a merciful view' of the panel's acts. On the final day of the trial, there were crowds massed in Jail Square hoping for a glimpse of the panel as he was taken away. The jury did not acquit him as not guilty nor with a verdict of not proven, nor as guilty as libelled. Instead, they believed the defence argument in preference to the prosecution's case because they returned a guilty verdict on the lesser charge of rape with culpable homicide for which he was sentenced to a particularly lengthy fifteen years' penal servitude. As an indication of how distressing the evidence had been, Professor Glaister had attended to a female juror on the first day of the trial and at the end, all jurors were excused further service for three years.[59]

Comparative research conducted on UK juries and crime in the mid- to late nineteenth century argues that Scottish courts were particularly lenient in rape homicides and that many accused were 'acquitted outright'. This UK-wide research covers the period to 1885.[60] Between 1885 and 1930, there were three other rape-homicide cases heard at the HCJ in Scotland. Two cases were prosecuted in 1890 and one in 1905. In the first 1890 case, the panel was found not guilty of both rape and murder, despite the existence of a dead body.[61] A verdict of not proven would have indicated the evidence could not support a guilty verdict 'beyond reasonable doubt', but an outright not guilty verdict was definite: the jury did not believe he had murdered the victim and as far as forensic evidence of the time could prove, he had not raped her either. In the other 1890 case, two men were charged with robbery, assault, rape and murder. The victims were a woman and a murdered man. The evidence on the rape and

---

59 AD15/26/81, JC15/37; *Glasgow Herald*, 19 October 1926, 5, 20 October, 7, 21 October, 3, 22 October, 7.
60 C. Conley, *Certain Other Countries: Homicide, Gender and National Identity in Late Nineteenth Century England, Ireland, Scotland and Wales* (Ohio, 2007), 36. Conley's research conducted in the 1980s stopped at 1885 because of the 100 years access rule.
61 JC26/1890/112, AD14/90/71.

murder counts against one panel was found not proven. The other panel was found guilty on all counts and was sentenced to twenty years' penal servitude instead of capital punishment. His sentence was more lenient than it might have been, but it was no acquittal.[62] In the 1905 rape-homicide prosecution, the South African panel was convicted and executed three weeks after his trial; there was clearly no leniency in his case.[63] These cases suggest that juries in Scotland behaved differently from research on the earlier period and were not necessarily reluctant to convict even if the punishment was doom.

Consent, culpability and class distinctions

For any working-class victim of sexual assault to bring a convincing case, she had first to overcome her own apprehensions as well as elite male attitudes towards the impropriety of lower-class females. In the aftermath of an assault, how the victim made sense of what had occurred could cloud her understanding of consent, particularly when assaulted by a boyfriend: had she given him any signals indicating she was available and willing? When had the acceptable intimacies of courtship become sexual violence? Was it an assault? The women whose testimonies are recorded in the HCJ case papers had no doubt about what had happened, because they reported their assaults as crimes, but convincing elite males in the judiciary could be an insurmountable hurdle. In 1921, Glasgow's PF wrote, 'I did not find her attitude as being at all consistent with the charge of rape' after a woman complained of being dragged from back court to back court, robbed and raped both vaginally and anally which was witnessed by a passing constable. The PF could not understand why she would go 'from street to street' with her assailants 'without much complaint', yet she confirmed she was shouting and screaming 'but no one heard me'. The Advocate Depute (AD) wrote on the indictment sheet: 'on the precognitions submitted a conviction unlikely and is scarcely justified'. This woman's potential credibility in court was balanced against her truthfulness. In a society where chastity was equated with honesty and thus credibility, was she worth believing?[64] In the end, the PF thought so because he proceeded to trial, although ultimately the AD proved to be correct.[65]

62 JC26/1890/15, AD14/90/135.
63 JC26/1905/6, AD15/05/112.
64 Age of Consent podcast, episodes 1 and 3, https://www.narrativematters.scot/the-age-of-consent-podcast.
65 AD15/21/75, JC13/133; both panels found unanimously not guilty on charge of robbery and by a majority not proven on the combined charge of rape and indecent assault, assoilzied and dismissed.

For the PF to bring a prosecution, as well as corroboration, he had also to determine whether non-consent had been clearly established, which in the earlier case was questionable because the woman's sister-in-law attested that the complainer 'often drinks to excess and brings different men home, they always leave her at the door'. Thus, when assessing the veracity of sexual violence against adult females, precognoscers interrogated the complainers about the most intimate details of the assault, asking repeatedly about consent, self-defence, penetration and emission and the victim's previous sexual experience. In the earlier case, conclusive medical evidence may have convinced the PF to prosecute, but in court, her ability to consent when inebriated and her degree of resistance were questioned.

Despite the rules on evidence-gathering contained in the *Book of Regulations*, it cannot be ruled out that the PF and precognoscers, or examining doctors, allowed their personal views to influence their judgement.[66] Contemporary author Robert Graves recalled the 'careless twenties' as a period of 'shameless abandon' in which a woman allowed 'her partner a near-sexual closeness of embrace', coupled with 'immodest dress and coiffure and her profane looseness of language'. Women also smoked and entered public houses.[67] The woman assaulted earlier had gone into several pubs looking for her husband and taken a drink in each. To elite groups, this could be construed as reckless behaviour which the working classes could also indulge in cafes, clubs, picture houses and dance halls.[68] However, working-class young women were not the only females enjoying these entertainments. Narrative histories describe certain privileged middle- and upper-class women indulging in the perceived sexual excesses of the 'Roaring Twenties', but they did not end up prosecuting rape charges.[69] If rape occurred – and surely it must have – among the more privileged classes, it was dealt with differently and discreetly.

Very few cases prosecuted at the HCJ contain obvious social comment on the working-class victims confronting judicial officers. As prosecuted cases, they must all have passed the test for compelling and corroborated evidence irrespective of facts – previous sexual experience, illegitimate pregnancies

---

66 Bland's examination of the trials of four 1920s women details smoking, new fashions and bobbed hair as indicators by the prosecution to the jury of the woman's 'modernity' and by association immorality. However, the HCJ papers do not include any of these descriptive details; L. Bland, *Modern Women on Trial: Sexual Transgression in the Age of the Flapper* (Manchester, 2013).
67 R. Graves and A. Hodge, *The Long Weekend: A Social History of Great Britain 1918-1939* (London, 1995), 17, 42–3.
68 Jackson, 'Girls and Delinquency', 150.
69 A. de Courcy, *The Viceroy's Daughters: The Lives of the Curzon Sisters* (London, 2000); S. Evans, *Queen Bees: Six Brilliant and Extraordinary Society Hostesses between the Wars* (London, 2016).

– that might have counted against a complainer in court. As research on Victorian newspaper reportage reveals, what was reported tended to emphasize accepted stereotypes of a rape victim and despite the evidence given in court, a complainer's 'character' – her demeanour, dress and behaviour – could turn against her.[70] However, by combining precognition evidence with the jury's verdict, insight into 'silent' societal comment can be glimpsed. A particularly illustrative case comes from Elgin in 1927.

In her precognition, the 34-year-old complainer admitted she had had an illegitimate baby in 1919 and another in 1924. She was collecting sticks in the wood when a stranger caught her by the throat and threw her to the ground. She claimed she screamed and struggled and managed once to get to her knees, but the assailant put his hand over her mouth and threatened to kill her. He hit her in the mouth and knocked her false teeth inwards nearly choking her. During the ten-minute struggle, he asked if she were married and she replied 'yes', hoping to deter him. She crossed her legs to prevent him, but despite fighting as hard as she could, she could not stop him. She confessed that when he said he would kill her, she relaxed her struggles. Her precognition concludes: 'I have not had traffic with any man since my last child in 1924. I did not consent to [him] having connection with me, he did it by force. I fought as long as I could'. She did not recall if emission had occurred and the examining physician found no violence to her genitals or other bodily injuries. In his opinion, 'assault with intent to carnal knowledge against her will may or may not have taken place, [and] the lightness of her injuries shows she did not resist the act to the utmost of her ability'. A jury of seven women and eight men found the panel unanimously not guilty, even failing to convict on a lesser charge.[71] As Scots Law in the period stated, 'fears for her life if she resist further' was an acceptable reason for ceasing to resist, although if a woman gives up 'after however much distress' and 'at last yield consent' it was not rape.[72] The PF had considered her story sufficiently credible to proceed, but in court her previous 'immoral' sexual conduct, her admission that she succumbed once threatened with greater violence and her inability to confirm emission all counted against her. Did the jury consider the doctor's comment on her less-than-total resistance – an opinion beyond his medical expertise – had insinuated she had finally consented?

70 K. Stevenson, 'Unearthing the Realities of Rape: Utilising Victorian Newspaper Reportage to Fill in the Contextual Gaps', *Liverpool Law Review*, 38 (2007): 421.
71 AD15/27/94, JC11/120; assoilzied and dismissed.
72 Mitchell, *Practical Treatise*, 175–6.

Consent

Paramount to every case was consent: was connection achieved 'against her will'? Clearly, all these prosecuted cases exist because the complainers were able to persuade the PF that consent had been withheld. However, none of the rape case precognitions include a statement from the complainer that she had said 'no' at any point, and from the wording of their testimonies, it does not appear they were asked if they had said 'no'. Instead, the absence of consent was tested through evidence of screaming and crying out and injuries that suggested vigorous resistance which met the judicial and medical benchmark for sufficient struggle.[73] Scots Law stated that it was rape 'if physical resistance be overcome by whatever means' including being held down.[74] In the preceding Elgin case, reducing her resistance after being threatened with death meant she had not sustained anything more than 'light' injuries as the doctor described them, and the jury was not satisfied that she had fought to her utmost ability.

It might be expected that establishing consent would be most difficult in cases of social rape in which the victim had agreed to entertainment and walking home with a partner, but in 50 per cent of these cases, panels were found guilty, suggesting confirmation of absence of consent and belief by the jury that the victim had resisted as much as possible. Supporting the complainer's statement, the examining doctor might add helpful details, such as 'her injuries and present state are consistent with that story, and also with the averment that she never had connection with a man previously'.[75] In a group social rape in 1920 where two men assaulted one female, both pleaded not guilty. It is a reasonable reading of the case that they hoped their version of events would outweigh hers: not only had they possessed greater physical strength when committing the crime but now they had the vocal advantage too. However, the medical examination verified her injuries as consistent with being restrained and confirmed 'rupture of a virginal hymen'.[76] Medical jurisprudence at the time included 'an intact hymen' at the top of the list of proofs of virginity and confirmed that the 'slightest' penetration, even where 'the usual signs of virginity are not interfered with', constituted rape.[77] In this case, the physician's confirmation of injuries and

---

73 K. Barclay, 'From Rape to Marriage: Questions of Consent in Eighteenth-Century Britain', in *Interpreting Sexual Violence, 1660-1800*, ed. A. Greenfield (Abingdon, 2016), 39.
74 Mitchell, *Practical Treatise*, 175.
75 AD15/21/192.
76 AD15/20/126, JC14/35; unanimously guilty, five years' penal servitude each.
77 J. Glaister, *A Textbook of Medical Jurisprudence and Toxicology* (Edinburgh, 1915), 480 and 483.

prior virginity compensated for the victim's dearth of detail on her degree of resistance and the perpetrators' word against hers.

In all types of rape, an 'unblemished' character, corroborated by acquaintances, assisted cases where consent was questioned and there was an absence of visible injuries which would have supported testimony of resistance. In 1920 in Fife, a sixteen-year-old confessed she had not scratched or screamed because '[her attacker] said it would get her a bad name'. However, she had done 'everything she could to prevent him'. The PF was doubtful of a conviction and described the girl as 'well developed and muscular' who 'should have offered considerable resistance if free', but she had not been because the assailant had pinned her hands across her chest. Unable to scratch or hit her assailant, all she could have done was scream, but she did not wish others to misinterpret her situation if they came to her assistance. With no witness to the assault, a friend confirmed: 'I would not call her a flighty or a larky girl, we might speak to chaps but it was usually someone we knew'. If consent could be assumed because a victim had not exhausted all avenues of resistance and attempts to get help despite offering reasons why, then there was little other option for the jury except to return a verdict of guilty on the lesser charge of assault, not originally indicted.[78]

Victim culpability

From the precognitions, these women clearly fall into the 'unprotected' category. They were out foraging for wood, walking home from work or entertainment unchaperoned or with a boyfriend, or were employed in a predominantly male and unsupervised environment such as a farm. This was their normal life and none of their statements express concern about fear of violence in their circumstances. Young women walked home together for company, chaperoning and probably some protection after dark, but it is impossible to know if that was because of fear of assault and theft or fear of sexual violence. Equally, if rape were highly possible for two young women walking home at night, then sensible working-class girls would be unlikely to travel alone or even in pairs for fear of being overpowered and assaulted, unless they had no alternative. Yet, these young women who reported assaults chose to enjoy entertainments after dark and walk home, which suggests that being assaulted was either extremely unfortunate or most other young women abused after a dance kept quiet.

---

78   AD15/20/155, JC11/118; unanimously guilty of assault, four months' imprisonment.

It has been suggested that working-class street violence was a preoccupation of the elites, those with the least experience of interpersonal violence, and that women who walked the streets at night were not considered genteel and feminine. When combined with men's supposed unscrupulous attitude towards consent, the working-class complainers of rape had to surmount class prejudices to convince the legal authorities of their authenticity and overcome elite prejudices towards women whose appearance and behaviour might not coincide with elite ideas of appropriate models of femininity.[79]

In a 1927 Glasgow assault case, a fifteen-year-old girl was slashed across the face with a razor by her ex-boyfriend, a twenty-year-old apprentice fitter, while walking home from work. He assaulted her because she had rejected him. Defence counsel described how they had been accustomed to meeting a few times every week, but she had told him they were finished. He found a razor on a vacant piece of land and intended to show it to her to frighten her. It was her 'attitude towards him' when they met on the stair of their tenement block that had made him lose his temper and slash her. In the sheriff court, the sheriff admonished the panel but also partially blamed the complainer, who because of 'her coquettish manner had aroused the jealousy of the accused'. A combination of unsupervised courtship and overt female seductiveness had led to the victim's disfigurement. If the panel had not pleaded guilty and had his case remitted to the HCJ for sentencing, the sheriff would have given summary judgement based on the evidence and his sole interpretation of the case. However, at the HCJ, the judge described the panel as 'cowardly' to have disfigured a young woman for life for a crime 'absolutely without justification'. This young woman did not comply with the sheriff's vision of 'respectable' femininity and given the sheriff court's sentencing powers, the panel might have received a much shorter sentence, if any. However, the High Court judge declared he 'would not be doing his duty unless he sentenced the accused to a term of penal servitude'. He got three years.[80]

In another Glasgow rape case involving two girls, the fifty-year-old arresting policeman expressed pejorative opinion about their behaviour, saying: 'it is a well-known fact in Larkhall that anyone doing anything like this with these girls, got what they wanted'.[81] However, women police also recognized that girls

---

79 J. C. Wood, 'Criminal Violence in Modern Britain', *History Compass*, 4, no. 1 (2006): 81; L. A. Jackson, 'Women Professionals and the Regulation of Violence in Inter-War Britain', in *Everyday Violence in Britain 1850-1950*, ed. S. D'Cruze (Harlow, 2000), 129; D'Cruze, 'Sex, Violence and Local Courts', 50; S. S. M. Edwards, 'Provoking Her Own Demise: From Common Assault to Homicide', in *Women, Violence and Social Control*, eds J. Hanmer and M. Maynard (London, 1990), 153.
80 JC26/1927/49; *Glasgow Herald*, 11 November 1927, 9.
81 AD15/22/71, JC15/33; unanimously not guilty, assoilzied and dismissed.

might get 'into trouble in the streets' and that there was a requirement to police, to detect and 'bring to justice the cowardly class of criminal who prey on girls and women'.[82] Thus class, lifestyle choices and physical inability, which could be misconstrued as lack of sufficient resistance, combined with elite prejudices were possible challenges confronting working-class adult victims of sexual violence. As one victim stated, she had not cried out for fear of being mistaken for consenting to sex. How many women kept quiet throughout an assault and also failed to report the event afterwards preferring to keep their reputation intact?[83] Yet, despite the risk of reputational damage and these obstacles, at least fifty-seven women in 1920s Scotland decided not to remain silent.

The precognitions do not provide personal comment from the complainer or her supporters explaining wider reasons for bringing the case or how they viewed their prospects of successful prosecution. Yet, it is inherent in the act of complaining that they expected to be heard to some extent. Adult complainers under thirty regularly employed the agency of another to report an assault; this was most usually a mother or female employer. Even the 27-year-old semi-professional postwoman informed the postmaster, seeking his confirmation of her right to complain. It might be anticipated that older women with an established good reputation and who had matured beyond the teenage 'flighty' age would be likelier to expect redress and would report directly to the police. However, women aged sixty and above informed neighbours first who called the police and it is only among women in the thirty to sixty age range who informed the police themselves, although still some told husbands and employers beforehand. Similar to cases involving minors, only a few adult assaults were discovered by the police directly in response to cries for help.[84]

The details provided in their precognitions suggest these women understood the crime committed against them was rape. Their use of another's agency helped to legitimize their claim. In the eighteenth century, a complaint might form part of an informal negotiation forcing settlement out of court because complainers considered the judiciary as an elite structure.[85] By the 1920s, an

---

82 'Minutes of Evidence of the Committee on the Employment of Women on Police Duties', *Parliamentary Papers*, 1921, Cmd.1133, Q.2008; Jackson, 'Women Professionals', 127.
83 Stanko, *Intimate Intrusions*, 17.
84 This does not necessarily imply the police actively chose not to seek sexual offenders on the streets; after all so many adult rapes occurred in isolated locations. However, given their detection of murders in progress during the 1920s (separate HCJ records researched), another crime unlikely to be committed in the open, the failure of police to detect rape in progress appears poor in comparison.
85 J. Gammon, 'Researching Sexual Violence, 1660-1800: A Critical Analysis', in *Interpreting Sexual Violence, 1660-1800*, ed. A Greenfield (Abingdon, 2016), 19.

organized police force and recognized process of legal redress was available to everyone and once the process began it was out of their hands. Yet, seeking another's approval to report a crime suggests continued reluctance to report.[86]

Mitigation and motive

Panels' motives are not recorded in the HCJ papers, but contemporary psychiatrist Hollander acknowledged that 'once social inhibitions are removed, man drops only too readily into his natural role of woman-hunter'.[87] However, the 'unbuttoning effects of drink' appear to have provided no mitigation in any of the HCJ cases. Glaister's guidance to the forensic medical profession was that 'drunkenness cannot be pleaded as an excuse for crime' unless its influence produced insanity. Therefore, 'it is purely a legal question how far such a man would be responsible for an act' and doctors could only attest to the degree of inebriation while recognizing that alcohol affected men differently.[88] Only ten cases recorded whether the perpetrator was drunk or sober, and two examples in 1921 suggest that being drunk and insensible to one's actions, or sober and completely aware, might not influence the verdict. In one case, the victim stated her attacker was sober, therefore *compos mentis* of his actions; he received a seven-year sentence. Whereas in a group rape in which at least one party was declared 'obviously drunk', both panels received ten years' penal servitude.[89] The severity of sentencing does not reflect any difference in attitude towards drunken or sober rapists.

If alcohol could not explain a panel's actions, the precognitions offer evidence that some panels considered they had a right to sex with an acquaintance or even a stranger. As already noted in one case, when disturbed by a visitor to the farmhouse, the attacker refused to halt his activities. Others used language such as 'Ye bugger I'll have what I want' or 'I didn't get what I f***ing wanted to' before raping the victim a second time.[90] In social rape cases, there may have been some confusion concerning how intimate a boyfriend was allowed to be; provocative dress and being unchaperoned might signal availability. Thus, a sexual assault could be interpreted as an act of revenge on a woman who had rejected his advances but whose behaviour had been read as willing. Or was he acting out his frustration

---

86   C. Conley, 'Sexual Violence in Historical Perspective', in *Oxford Handbook of Gender, Sex and Crime*, eds R. Gartner and B. McCarthy (Oxford, 2014), 197.
87   Hollander, Misconduct, 129.
88   D'Cruze, 'Sex, Violence and Local Courts', 49; Glaister, Medical Jurisprudence, 587–9.
89   AD15/21/189 and AD15/21/52.
90   AD15/21/44 and AD15/28/103.

at his misinterpretation of her behaviour?[91] Equally, 'pay-packet rape' may have been the causal provocation for some social rapes. Men controlled the household finances through their pay packet; how much housekeeping they handed over to their wife gave them ultimate power over all members of the family and had the potential to be coercive in the marital bed eliciting sex in return for more money.[92] In a society where young men learned from their fathers and colleagues in the workplace, spending one's wages on entertainment for a girlfriend may have included the assumption that she would be sexually appreciative.

Even an across-the-grain reading of the precognition statements does not provide any real rationalization for the panels' behaviour. The dearth of soldier panels or mention of military service suggests that the judiciary was disinclined to view service as a mitigating factor, although it has been argued that being a non-combatant in a society in which returning soldiers were heroes might have produced particular sexual anxieties.[93] If these resulted in rape, they are not evident in the HCJ records. Group rape has been explained as 'dehumanization and moral disengagement' between perpetrators and their victim and that MPR fulfils a need to belong to a masculine group.[94] However, none of the case papers for group rapes confirm the group's cohesion as friends prior to the attack or as work colleagues. Group rape may be interpreted as a form of male bonding in a confused and gender-competitive post-war society, but that does not explain cases prosecuted between 1885 and 1910. It does not explain why three men in their twenties in 1885 in rural Culross raped a 47-year-old woman visiting a sick friend in the evening except that one of them said: 'if that's no' a whore she should not be out of her house at this time of night'. Neither does it explain the actions of another three men in Edinburgh who climbed through the windows of a tenement to perpetrate rape on a woman they had already abused in the street.[95] However, a case from Glasgow demonstrates the judiciary's attitude towards group rape by 1930: culpability was 'corporate'; no matter whether a panel actually did the raping, by his presence he was culpable.[96]

---

91 Jackson, 'Social Context', 33; Fiske and Rai, *Virtuous Violence*, 168.
92 R. Johnston and A. McIvor, 'Dangerous Work, Hard Men and Broken Bodies: Masculinity in the Clydeside Heavy Industries', *Labour History Review*, 69, no. 2 (August 2004): 142 and 139.
93 C. M. Tylee, 'Maleness Run Riot: The Great War and Women's Resistance to Militarism', *Women's Studies International Forum*, 11, no. 3 (1988): 204.
94 Fiske and Rai, *Virtuous Violence*, 169.
95 AD14/85/265, JC11/111; second diet pleaded guilty to assault only, severally sentenced to six and twelve months' imprisonment; AD14/85/11, JC4/82; two panels received fifteen months, one received five years' penal servitude.
96 JC34/1/81, JC34/1/82 and JC13/138.

Conversely, the speed of apprehension of reported perpetrators may offer a possible explanation of motive: 'rampant masculinity'. Apart from one case involving a fifteen-year-old female whose employer gave her a letter to take home to her mother when she next visited, a fortnight later, all of the panels were arrested on the night of the attack or very shortly thereafter. This was possible because constables on the beat knew their community and they received clear descriptions from complainers. The immediacy of investigation and precognoscing further aided apprehension of malcontents. However, whether known to their victim or complete strangers, on the whole men prosecuted for rape lived in close proximity to their victims and none of them attempted to abscond between the event and arrest.[97] They appear to have been unafraid of the consequences, and in one group rape involving three men, having assaulted a domestic servant aged twenty, they lit her bicycle lamps and walked her back to her employer's house.[98] Combined with their comments recorded in the HCJ papers, these men seem to have considered their victims 'fair game', especially the unmarried ones. Modern young sexual assault offenders in prisons have described this behaviour as 'doing masculinity'.[99] The possibility remains that the perpetrators of sexual offences ranging from LLPB to rape in the 1920s did not consider their acts as criminal, which raises alarming questions about male attitudes to women in Scottish society in the early twentieth century.

Recidivism

There are only six cases among the HCJ records for sexual assaults against adult females where previous convictions 'inferring personal violence' are noted and all of these are stranger rapes. This suggests that social rapes were one-off assaults as explored earlier, while recidivist stranger rapes might be wilful repeat violence, committed by men who may have developed a modus operandi of raping in districts where they were unknown to the authorities or selecting victims who would not recognize them. However, only six prosecuted cases in a decade do not support elite fears of stranger rape and endemic working-class depravity, and in Glasgow where most of the sexual violence against all age groups was prosecuted,

---

97 Cases in which the perpetrator could not be found and apprehended could not be prosecuted, thus the HCJ records which reveal patterns of proximity of assailant and victim, and lack of absconding, may not be the fullest picture.
98 AD15/22/58, JC13/134; three years' penal servitude each.
99 C. Holligan and R. Deuchar, 'What Does It Mean to be a Man? Psychosocial Undercurrents in the Voices of Incarcerated (violent) Scottish Teenage Offenders', *Criminology & Criminal Justice*, 15, no. 3 (2015): 367.

the *Glasgow Herald* rarely contains news reports of the police seeking an absconder. Either recidivist raping did not occur in any great amount or few young women wished to publicize their predicament to the wider public through newspaper notices. Their assaults might be added to the 'dark number'.

* * *

Conclusion

Hollander believed that most women were capable of self-defence, 'and even when their indiscretion delivers them up to the mercy of a man' a woman 'who is not herself excited' might escape, but he balanced his opinion with recognition that 'social custom is repressive of sexual indulgence in woman'.[100] The details contained in the precognitions suggest that precognoscers were at pains to determine the circumstances surrounding each sexual assault they investigated and whether the complainer had indeed defended herself to the utmost and what type of 'character' she was. Hollander also states: 'rape of women is very rare indeed'.[101] Between 1885 and 1910, there were 220 rapes of women aged over sixteen years prosecuted at the HCJ in Scotland or an average of 8.8 cases annually. Between November 1918 and December 1930 there were fifty-four cases prosecuted or an average of 4.5 cases annually. Both date ranges suggest that rape of adult women was sporadic. However, if the unquantifiable 'dark number' of unreported and reported-but-not-prosecuted cases is added, then the incidence of rape is probably more worrying in both periods. The HCJ records cannot answer the pressing questions to explain the differences: were more rapes committed in the nineteenth century? Had the willingness of women to report declined in the 1920s? Was the judiciary tougher on complainers post-war thus did not prosecute as many complaints?

However, precognitions and case papers do indicate that working-class women were victims of sexual violence from average working-class men. They were unable to avoid male contact because of their lifestyles and working patterns. Seeking validation through another's agency before reporting assaults also suggests that victims perceived a 'dominant mythology' among elite males concerning the supposed depravity of working-class women's behaviour and their lack of credibility.

100 Hollander, *Misconduct,* 130 and 129.
101 Hollander, *Misconduct,* 130.

If sexual aggression is associated with power which between the genders manifests as sexual power, in a period of societal reconstruction, men with a predisposition to sexual violence may have indulged their inclination with less compunction.[102] However, the prosecuted crime records suggest that the limited increases of the early 1920s did not continue into the later part of the decade when further societal disruptions were experienced, nor did they exceed many annual counts in the late 1880s and early 1890s. If some form of post-war gender conflict – a moral panic – as perceived by Hamilton, Gibbs and others did indeed exist, there is no evidence from these records that it made an impact on the Scottish authorities. Neither an increase in prosecutions nor in the length of sentences is discernible from the records, suggesting that any potential moral panic did not prompt changes to the judiciary's behaviour.[103] Therefore, despite the absence of explanations for individual rapist's actions or for a complainer's motivation to report, annual fluctuations in the number of sexual assault prosecutions depend on specific circumstances: the perpetrator chose to assault his victim; she chose to report it and the judiciary decided that the case was sufficiently compelling and corroborated to proceed. Thus, the fear of violent sexual crime remains a societal construct in lieu of *actual* crime, neither of which are supported by the HCJ prosecution statistics.[104]

However, whether committed as incest or rape, ravishment or LLPB against females of all ages, the HCJ records suggest that in a patriarchal society, some men felt free to take sex where they pleased, and that sexual violence of all types was prosecuted at a much higher concentration in industrial south-west Scotland. This geographical distribution may be a true reflection of crimes surfacing from 'the dark number' or, as will be explored in the Conclusion, it may be attributable to social, spatial and cultural explanations specific to Glasgow making it 'some mean city'.

---

102 Fiske and Rai, *Virtuous Violence*, 169.
103 P. King, 'Moral Panics and Violent Street Crime 1750-2000', in *Comparative Histories of Crime*, eds B. Godfrey, C. Emsley and G. Dunstall (Cullompton, 2003), 69.
104 Jackson, 'Social Context', 29.

Part II

Recourse to the law

6

Getting to court

Pretrial processes

Sexual violence has a long history of invisibility in official records. The main reason for this absence is the victim's reluctance to report sexual assault. She may risk reputational damage, be disbelieved, suffer further indignities during evidence collection, or simply she might not wish to relive the experience in the minute detail required for a victim statement or court appearance. Therefore, of the prosecutions for incest, rape, ravish and lewd and libidinous practices and behaviour (LLPB), which were heard before the High Court of Justiciary (HCJ) in Scotland in the 1920s, the individuals and families bringing these cases were either exceptional people or the details of the case were sufficiently remarkable and corroborated to convince the judicial authorities to proceed. Since all the cases of sexual assault tried at the HCJ were perpetrated on and by working-class individuals, the victims may also have had to overcome elite groups' perceived prejudices towards working-class behaviour to receive justice. Victims had first to approach the police, who many may have regarded as interlopers in their communities and as instruments of elite authority.[1] Further, some individuals among the legal authorities believed the law had been skewed too far in favour of the female victim, jibing that 'it is better that a hundred innocent men should be convicted than that the body of one young girl should be indecently tampered with'.[2] Thus complainers reporting sexual crimes did so probably against great odds, because their allegations challenged male hegemony in all strata of society.

Research on child sexual abuse in late Victorian England found that 99 per cent of defendants were male and 93 per cent of victims were female.[3] The HCJ records for the 1920s present direct parallels: 100 per cent of defendants in Scotland were male with no female defendants and boy victims appear only

---

1   P. Knepper, *Writing the History of Crime* (London, 2017), 134.
2   Editorial, *Law Journal*, 1926, 61–97, quoted in C. Smart, 'Reconsidering the Recent History of Child Sexual Abuse 1910-1960', *Journal of Social Policy*, 29, no. 1 (2000): 55.
3   L. A. Jackson, *Child Sexual Abuse in Victorian England* (London, 2000), 4.

in a very few cases of LLPB.⁴ Thus, in an overwhelmingly male-dominated society, understanding the victim's route to court – reporting, policing, judicial construction of the victim and her evidence – combined with examination of the process of selecting indictments, pleading and plea bargaining allows us to ascertain whether the Scottish judicial system in the 1920s had developed sufficiently so that a working-class child, young girl or woman could hope to be heard fairly at every stage of the process.

Who reports sexual crime?

Normally, anyone against whom a crime has been committed has recourse to the law, either immediately or within a designated time frame. However, in some communities, approaching the police for help has not always been an obvious choice. In the mid-nineteenth century, police forces were introduced and expanded across Great Britain. While it has been argued that the police were inserted into communities to monitor the political temper of the masses, the working classes' experience of policing was interference in their social lives, from drinking to gambling and enjoying leisure time on the streets.⁵ However, the longevity of the police in Scotland, especially in Glasgow which was the country's first police force, alongside their dual role of policing and welfare, appears to have produced a different experience in some communities.⁶

Individuals reticent about approaching the police would not appear in the records, but from the number of women who called on the police within hours of a sexual assault, it appears that some working-class communities did not delay in reporting this particular species of crime. Not only did the women themselves and mothers report to the police office, but the precognitions offer numerous instances of groups of female neighbours advising a mother to go to the police. There is no evidence in these prosecuted cases that they were reluctant to report because it might result in intensified policing of their community or ostracism of a family who reported because they were violating

---

4   Sodomy and male-on-male sexual assaults fall outside the scope of this thesis. Assaults by females either did not occur during the period under review or were prosecuted at a lower court.
5   R. Storch, 'The Plague of Blue Locusts: Police Reform and Popular Resistance in Northern England, 1840-1857', *International Review of Social History*, 20, issue 1 (April 1975): 64 and 66.
6   L. A. Jackson with N. Davidson, L. Fleming, D. M. Smale and R. Sparks, *Police and Community in Twentieth-Century Scotland* (Edinburgh, 2020), 16.

unwritten codes of working-class behaviour.[7] Glasgow was Scotland's most densely policed city in the 1920s, with one policeman for every 499 citizens and police offices readily found in all the city's wards. With increasing numbers of police serving for longer, constables lived among and knew the communities they policed.[8] Thus, the parents, relations or victims themselves may have felt entitled to police protection and sought redress for sexual violence crimes by swift reporting.

In cases of minor rape, mothers appear not to have delayed informing the police once they had detected sexual violence against their young children. Similarly, the HCJ records suggest that adult females bringing a complaint understood immediately that a crime had been perpetrated against them but hesitated in many instances to report it personally without seeking the validation of a parent or an employer. With incest, girls relied on neighbours, aunts or older sisters to act as their advocate in the absence of mothers. These are prosecuted cases and the trends they reveal may not be representative of the method of reporting employed by women and families whose assaults did not proceed to the HCJ. However, these records reveal a correlation between speed of reporting and proceeding to prosecution.

Clearly, the HCJ records cannot provide evidence of cases in which victims were so reluctant to report the crime they decided against it. Policewoman Edith Tancred recounted that 'an experienced police woman has told me that quite 50 per cent' of cases failed to reach court because victims were asked to give their evidence to a room full of men, which often they refused to do, thus 'the case collapses and the man escapes punishment'.[9] There is some narrative evidence in incest complainers' precognitions of reticence to report a father because of fears of violent physical retribution, but eventually they summoned the courage to do so. Thus, it appears that the individuals, whose allegations of sexual assault progressed to a prosecution, believed the judicial system would achieve some form of justice for them. In fact, one 1922 case illustrates how far a father would go to seek redress. His twenty-year old daughter had been pulled from her bicycle by three men and then raped. Having reported the assault, sometime later her employer, a judge in an Indian district, asked her father if he would 'like it hushed up', suggesting also that the young woman

---

7   J. Bourke, *Rape: A History from 1860 to the Present* (London, 2010), 16.
8   A. L. Goldsmith, 'The Development of the City of Glasgow Police c. 1800-1939', unpublished PhD thesis (University of Strathclyde, 2002), appendices IV and IX.
9   'Minutes of Evidence of the Committee on the Employment of Women on Police Duties', *Parliamentary Papers*, 1921, Cmd.1133, Q.1955.

had changed her mind. He admitted he was keen to return to his position in India and wanted nothing more to do with the matter. The father rejected his approach, although after questioning his daughter again and learning she was now reluctant to pursue things further, he insisted because he wanted 'justice for what the men did to her'.[10] However, it is impossible to understand how many other cases commenced investigations which later failed, because either the Procurator Fiscal (PF) decided not to proceed or the complainer withdrew her accusation.[11]

Without evidence in the HCJ prosecutions papers of complainers being persuaded to let the investigation continue or of the PF instructing families to comply with their original complaint, it is reasonable to assume that the types of people reporting sexual violence anticipated that the judicial system would accept their complaint and allow the process to run its course, as far as possible. The records cannot tell us, and there are unlikely to be sources to explain, how far the victims expected their case to proceed or how much of the process they understood before they lodged their complaint.

From the cases which proceeded, there is no common link connecting a specific type of woman who reported sexual violence, neither by social or employment status nor geographic location. Whether it was a semi-professional post-mistress from Ayr, a mother of a three-year-old on an Aberdeenshire farm, a group-raped prostitute in Glasgow or a 29-year-old domestic servant assaulted in Maryhill.[12] From all walks of working-class life women sought legal redress for what they understood immediately to be a crime. The precognitions contain no evidence that they considered the potential opprobrium reporting an assault could attract for them or their families. The police surgeons, who first examined the complainers in privacy, did not comment on reticence to give an initial statement or resistance to physical examination, or any need to persuade women and girls to continue with their complaint. Considering the perceived biases stacked against any woman complaining of sexual assault, for some complainers, indignation, familial and community support and sufficiently strong and corroborated evidence could succeed in getting cases heard at the HCJ.[13]

---

10 AD15/22/58, JC13/134; unanimously guilty, three years' penal servitude each.
11 Data on reported but unproceeded cases is a recent statistical collection point, collated to support report-to-conviction conversion rates, which will be discussed in Chapter 8.
12 AD15/21/137, AD15/21/182, AD15/22/73 and AD15/30/54, respectively.
13 Bourke, *Rape*, 394.

Reporting incest

Between 1885 and 1909, forty-two incest cases were heard at the HCJ or 1.75 per annum.[14] In 1910, five incest cases were prosecuted with an average of nine incest trials heard per year between November 1918 and December 1930 (total 108 cases). Despite the emotional difficulties inherent in reporting incest, these figures suggest a rising trend, which may reflect a real increase in incidents and/or reports from which to draw proceedable cases. Many of the complainers described repeated assaults over a long period with cases in the earlier years of the 1920s often commencing before or during the war. This rising trend may in fact reveal that families reporting incest on behalf of a relation felt more able to do so post-war. However, without quantification of the 'dark number' of incestuous assaults, it is impossible to understand whether the incidence of incest had increased in real numbers after the war. Either more mothers complained and had sufficient evidence to support a prosecution or PFs were more sensitive to this particular crime placing more cases before Crown Counsel (CC) who concurred.

Reporting minor rape

When reporting rape or ravishment of minors, the evidence further suggests that some working-class families willingly approached the police if their child had been outraged. As evidenced by their precognitions, the guardians of seventy-five minors (47 of a total 101 rape cases) did not hesitate before sending for a policeman or visiting the police office in person once sexual assault had been detected by them. However, since all the cases heard at the HCJ were reported immediately, it is possible that cases where initial hesitation was later overcome were less likely to proceed to prosecution because hesitation might indicate an initial lack of belief in the child by her guardians. Again, families whose complaints proceeded to the HCJ may have been the exception and their prompt action may have contributed to their success in reaching the HCJ. These families had confidence in the police and judicial authorities to prosecute their

---

14   C. Conley, *Certain Other Countries: Homicide, Gender and National Identity in Late Nineteenth Century England, Ireland, Scotland and Wales* (Ohio, 2007), 179, calculated 1.8 incest cases per year between 1867 and 1892.

complaints; if they had little hope of justice, then it is unlikely they would have reported the crime.[15]

Based on the father's occupation, there is no obvious correlation between the family's social status and readiness to report sexual crime. A fifteen-year-old daughter of a Moray labourer was raped in 1919. The father described a visit from the accused, who apologized for the assault since he 'only had his hand up her clothes' and threatened to make the father 'pay for it' if he reported the event; he did so anyway.[16] In Barrhead the same year, a carter's wife discovered the rape of her seven-year-old when she found blood on the child's knickers; she reported it to the police.[17] These men were unskilled, although the skilled coachbuilder stepfather of a twelve-year-old rape victim from Thurso in 1921 could be categorized as 'artisan' working class.[18] The HCJ records show that fathers rarely reported the sexual assault of their young daughters, but among the wives and other female relations of 'upper' working-class families, it might be expected that police assistance would be more readily sought in the belief that the authorities existed for their protection. Thus, occupation, social status and readiness to inform the police do not form any obvious correlation in the HCJ records.

The prosecuted rapes of minors were largely committed in the poorest districts of Glasgow, where density of police and proximity of police offices were higher. But again, if the poorest citizens were shy of approaching the police, there is evidence in the HCJ papers that it was not a class-wide predicament. Despite their lack of detection of minor rapes while on the beat, a denser police presence may have encouraged the inhabitants of these specific districts to report sexual violence. Reporting of less serious crimes such as theft and physical assault may not have followed similar patterns because reporting could promote increased police surveillance, but where sexual violence is concerned and the 'dark number' aside, there is a possibility that these poorest communities may not have been so dislocated from police assistance. In the 1920s, Glasgow employed the most female police. Although unremarked in the HCJ papers, possibly their feminine presence at the police office and during precognoscing may have encouraged families to report sexual crime and thus may account for the number of crimes

---

15 E. Stanko, 'Typical Violence, Normal Precaution: Men, Women and Interpersonal Violence in England and Wales, Scotland and the USA', in *Women, Violence and Social Control*, eds J. Hanmer and M. Maynard (London, 1990), 122.
16 AD15/19/125, JC11/118; pleaded guilty to a lesser indictment, three months' imprisonment.
17 AD15/19/49, JC14/34; pleaded guilty to attempt to ravish with previous charges for similar assaults from summer 1914, 10 years' penal servitude.
18 AD15/21/162, JC11/118; unanimously not guilty, assoilzied and dismissed.

prosecuted in the city compared with other Scottish urban centres where female police were extremely rare.[19]

Reporting adult rape

An exhaustive survey of late nineteenth-century male violence suggests that the number of prosecutions can be no real indication of the true incidence of rape.[20] Thus, the 'dark number' is particularly poignant in cases of rape of adult females where the sympathies attached to a violated child could be replaced by elite biases. Some adult complainers reported rape, while many may have considered it simply too difficult, because of the prospect of reporting to male police with consequent perceptions of stigma and shame. However, of the cases tried at the HCJ, these women had not only reported rape but also succeeded against all the societal and patriarchal hurdles of 1920s society and lingering preconceptions from the late nineteenth century about the sexual morality of working-class women. By reporting assaults, these women disrupted and challenged patriarchal assumptions concerning male conduct and access to female bodies.[21]

From the nineteenth century into the 1920s, and arguably far beyond, the impediments to seeking justice for adult rape victims included low social position, poverty, absence of a protector, need to keep her job and fear of the public ordeal of proceeding with a prosecution.[22] All the complainers in the HCJ cases were working-class; many lived in the most impoverished districts of Glasgow; most lacked a protector at the time of commission; and some may have feared losing their employment, thus deciding against reporting. But for each of the cases heard at the HCJ, the victim did possess a protector in the form of the person she informed first of the assault and who supported her at least as far as providing a convincing precognition. Despite pre-war elite, patriarchal prejudices sustaining into the post-war period as evidenced by some of the legal comments contained in the case papers and the nature of questioning during precognoscing, there is a greater amount of comment describing young girls as 'respectable' who

19 There were thirty-seven women police in Scotland by 1939; Jackson et al., *Police and Community*, 175; the evidence given to the 'Committee on the Employment of Women on Police Duties' by female welfare officers and police must be read cautiously; they may have had an agenda to convince the authorities that the employment of women officers was beneficial to policing.
20 M. Wiener, *Men of Blood: Violence, Manliness and Criminal Justice in Victorian England* (Cambridge, 2006), 78.
21 S. D'Cruze, 'Sex, Violence and Local Courts: Working-Class Respectability in a Mid-nineteenth Century Lancashire Town', *British Journal of Criminology*, 39, no. 1 (1990): 40 and 51.
22 Wiener, *Men of Blood*, 79.

had not been previously known to 'go with young men'. Whether these young women evaluated the hurdles they faced before reporting an assault or hoped that the PF's commentary on them to CC would be favourable, in each case they overcame social and judicial obstacles in favour of naming, shaming and seeking punishment against those they accused. Like families reporting incest and assaults against children, there were no defining characteristics inclining these women to be particularly litigious. Fundamentally, they were sufficiently outraged and well-supported to step onto the first rung of the ladder towards judicial retribution.

Police justice or rough justice?

In nineteenth-century Scotland, it has been recognized that there was a disconnect between elite attitudes to orderly behaviour and how the working classes lived.[23] Most police court business stemmed from urban working-class low-level crime brought to them by the most vulnerable in the community, although in Glasgow where a police superintendent might act as fiscal depute with witnesses also drawn from among the police, some considered the system unfair.[24] However, while slang used by working-class communities against the police – 'blue bottles', 'black locusts' – revealed antagonisms towards their presence in the most heavily policed communities, from 1890 onwards it appears that relations improved particularly concerning crimes of theft and violence.[25] The Scottish police's dual role of maintaining law and providing welfare distinguished them from English police who were seen as imposing middle-class values in working-class districts.[26] Additionally, working-class communities may have invoked the power of the police to enforce their own codes of conduct, so while families may have regarded the 'black locusts' suspiciously, when faced with crime personally,

---

23   W. W. J. Knox and A. McKinlay, 'Crime, Protest and Policing in Nineteenth Century Scotland', in *A History of Everyday Life in Scotland 1800-1900*, ed. T. Griffiths and G. Morton (Edinburgh, 2010), 198.
24   D. Barrie and S. Broomhall, 'Public Men, Private Interests: The Origins, Structure and Practice of Police Courts in Scotland, c.1800-1833', *Continuity and Change*, 27, no. 1 (2012): 110; Jackson et al., *Police and Community*, 29–30.
25   Knox and McKinlay, 'Crime, Protest and Policing', 217.
26   Knox and McKinlay, 'Crime, Protest and Policing', 215 and 216; see Introduction for discussion of the welfare role of Scottish police; R. Storch, 'The Policeman as Domestic Missionary: Urban Discipline and Popular Culture in Northern England 1850-1880', *Journal of Social History*, 4 (1970): 481–509.

they may have employed immediate and expectant appeals to the police because their own, intra-community ethical codes had been transgressed.[27]

However, nuanced differences in police practices existed between the Highlands and Glasgow in the early twentieth century. Rural communities viewed their police as 'insiders' recruited from among them, men who lived in village police houses which often offered other social services. Whereas Glasgow's police had largely been recruited from outside the city in the last decades of the nineteenth and early years of the twentieth century, although post-war that trend was changing and recruits were increasingly local. However, a police career could last decades and so many more experienced Glasgow police had not grown up alongside the families they policed.[28] In the Highlands, familiarity with local men fulfilling policing roles may have made them more approachable to the communities among whom they lived and therefore, per head of population, a greater number of sexual violence assault reports and prosecutions might be anticipated. Yet, the Highlands' continued reliance on 'rough justice' may explain the absence of a significant sexual violence caseload.

With landlords who once supplied justice within the immediate community now absent and police offices sparsely distributed and distant from the remotest villages, communities may have taken the law into their own hands meting out punishment to sexual violence perpetrators, thus obviating the need for police intervention. In Glasgow in the late nineteenth century, there is evidence that wife beaters who went too far and known child molesters could expect justice to be dispensed by neighbours and the victim's family.[29] With the Highland population's access to police further removed and therefore slower than in urban areas, there is no reason to suppose that Highland communities refrained from exercising intra-community justice to some extent in lieu of police assistance for such emotive crimes.

Because rough justice is invariably invisible in official archives, occurrences may only be identified by an intimate and close reading of the records. A curious cluster of LLBP cases tried between December 1921 and October 1922 in Glasgow may contain an example of urban rough justice. The victims were all girls under thirteen years. The HCJ case papers treat the assaults as individual crimes, but it is interesting that they are all listed within a defined, deprived area of Glasgow. None of the assaults were detected by the police, thus frequent reporting from a small locus on this occasion did not result in increased surveillance by the

---

27 Jackson, *Child Sexual Abuse*, 36.
28 Jackson et al., *Police and Community*, 54–7.
29 Knox and McKinlay, 'Crime, Protest and Policing', 220.

authorities. However, it may also be an instance of parents reacting litigiously to an 'outbreak' of sexual violence, which they had dealt with until now through intra-community measures or rough justice. It is more than coincidence that a number of crimes, which had been ongoing for some time before the first arrest, were indicted under the same charge within a limited geographical space and time frame.

A late nineteenth-century study on sexual violence reveals another facet when specifically reporting incest: girls may have sought police assistance in a last attempt to stop long-term familial assaults from a father whose abuse had exceeded the capabilities of the family's and the neighbourhood's own disciplining measures.[30] Because it was a crime perpetrated almost totally in private, cases contained in the HCJ records were not detected by the police and they were very rarely reported by welfare officers, but assaults were often heard through thin walls and known about by neighbours as evidenced in some precognitions.[31] Hidden within the 'dark number' may be cases where community justice was meted out, because the intense scrutiny of working-class sexual crime carried out for the 1926 report of the *Departmental Committee on Sexual Offences against Children and Young Persons in Scotland* did not result in intensified policing of sexual crimes in areas which the committee identified as significant loci. Incest cases in the HCJ records are those reported to, not detected by, the police.

The police detected only one case of incest which was prompted by a concerned member of the public. In 1921 in Aberdeen, a widower and his nineteen-year-old daughter were discovered in bed together by the local sergeant, who had been informed by another girl's father that his daughter was staying out late at this address. When precognosced, the daughter explained that 'I do not think I was doing any harm by my father having connection with me' and she admitted to having had sex with another man who called at the house while her father watched.[32] In this instance, it is unlikely the girl would have reported a sexual assault against her father because she did not perceive his actions as criminal, and the police had not detected the crime without assistance from a member of the public concerned for his own daughter. There is only one other police-

30 Jackson, *Child Sexual Abuse*, 50.
31 B. Weinberger, *The Best Police in the World* (Cambridge, 1995), 135; V. A. C. Gatrell and T. B. Hadden, 'Criminal Statistics and their Interpretation', in *Nineteenth Century Society: Essays in the Use of Quantitative Methods for the Study of Social Data*, ed. E. A. Wrigley (Cambridge, 1972), 353 and 362, for discussion of deficiencies in criminal statistics and their impact on consistency of policing and local practice.
32 AD15/21/9, JC9/17; five years' penal servitude; interestingly charged under 1908 Children Act and not Scottish Incest Act 1567.

detected rape case, and therefore, reporting sexual violence does not appear to have provoked extra police surveillance and it is not apparent from the HCJ records that the police actively sought out sexual crime on their daily and nightly beats. It is possible that the police waited for reports of sexual crime to come to them because from experience they knew they would, since most prosecuted rapes, ravishments and LLBP assaults involved young girls with outraged parents. Actively seeking out sexual violence may have created a strong impression of police surveillance among communities who would not tolerate an everyday police presence and therefore the non-detection of sexual violence may not necessarily have been a failure to police; rather, it may have been their only effective modus operandi.

There is no evidence among the HCJ cases of 'rough justice' by outraged parents or other relations and neighbours taking matters into their own hands prior to reporting to the police. If rapists of young children experienced rough justice, then the perpetrators of that summary justice did not follow it up by reporting to the police, at least among cases that proceeded to the HCJ. And recipients of rough justice are unlikely to have reported it because they would have been forced to divulge the true reason behind it. If rough justice as retribution for sexual crime occurred, it appears to have been sufficiently violent to satisfy the perpetrators that suitable punishment had been delivered. Thus, rough justice is invisible to official records either because it satisfied the requirement for punishment or it did not happen, which is unlikely given anecdotal evidence of relations and neighbours meting out violence in instances of spousal abuse, when a husband was considered to have exceeded an acceptable level of spousal chastisement.[33]

Convincing the Procurator Fiscal

From police and witness precognitions, it is impossible to determine whether people reporting a sexual crime understood the process and the possibility of rejection at any stage. All that can be ascertained is their desire for justice because they did not withdraw their accusation at some point earlier than the HCJ trial. In the Scottish legal system, the PF is the public prosecutor responsible for investigating all reported crimes. It was the police's duty to report every complaint they received to the PF, who would instruct precognoscers and

---

33 Conley, *Certain Other Countries*, 124–61.

doctors to gather precognitions and medical evidence to establish whether a crime had been committed and to corroborate the details. Once collected, the PF presented the case to CC for his opinion whether and on what indictment to prosecute. In the HCJ case papers, this exchange was frequently a handwritten note from the Lord Advocate or Advocate Depute (AD) replying to the PF on his original correspondence. In which court a case was heard depended on the indictment, thus indecent exposure could be dealt with in police courts, but all the indictments investigated here appeared at the sheriff court for first diet (plea hearing) and, thereafter if pleaded guilty, were remitted to the HCJ for sentencing; if pleaded not guilty, automatically they were sent to the HCJ for a jury trial.

The working practices of the police and judicial rules imposed on the PF suggest that 'sifting' of proceedable cases may not have happened in great numbers. Initially, the PF would draw on his possible knowledge of the complainer and accused, employing on-the-job experience to evaluate a complaint. Clearly, cases in which the PF and CC decided there was little point in proceeding are not among the prosecuted cases. However, there is sufficient correspondence between the PF and CC debating a case's individual merit to suggest strongly that the PF often overruled CC's advice and proceeded to prosecute. This is especially interesting when the complainer had not been a virgin prior to the assault, had a poor reputation and testified that she had stopped screaming and struggling at some point during her ordeal. The PF had not 'sifted' these cases because they might appear 'unsympathetic' before a jury.[34]

Two cases illustrate the potential positive impact of the PF's 'dominant mythology' on the success of a complaint proceeding not only from police office to the PF but also beyond to court. In 1921, the PF solicited a higher legal opinion in a letter to the AD. The case involved a group rape of a 27-year-old married woman in Glasgow witnessed by two constables who intervened once they had confirmed the nature of the activity in a secluded close. The PF 'did not regard her attitude as being at all consistent with the charge of rape' to which the AD replied writing directly on the draft indictment sheet: 'AD believes on the precognitions submitted a conviction unlikely and is scarcely justified'. Despite this opinion and his own doubts, the PF proceeded.[35] Why, if he were using his experience to 'sift' potentially unsuccessful cases? In a 1922 Perth case, the PF disregarded the negative personal 'dominant mythology' of the Solicitor General,

---

34   E. Stanko, *Intimate Intrusions: Women's Experience of Male Violence* (London, 1985), 104.
35   AD15/21/75, JC13/133; unanimously not proven, assoilzied and dismissed.

who had already stated that he was disinclined to see the evidence 'justifying a charge of rape, the woman was not a virgin, no marks or bruises, she walked with the men afterwards'. Both he and the AD believed sexual relations would be proved 'but not rape and that the case is one for no pro' (not proven). However, the PF's opinion that 'it is hardly feasible that the girl would consent to all three having connection with her one after the other which is what they stated, and she emphatically denies' prevailed. He overruled the Solicitor General and proceeded.[36] If the police were more likely to forward only 'ideal rapes' to the PF based on their own perceptions of a victim of sexual violence and only those which conformed to the 'dominant mythology' stood a chance in court, then there is evidence among the HCJ cases which refutes this for Scotland in the 1920s.[37]

As the investigators of the 1926 sexual offences report acknowledged, the process of reporting to the police, precognoscing for the PF and appearing in court for women and girls of all ages was 'distressing and injurious'. Since the entire process was conducted by men, they recommended more female examiners to procure evidence that complainers were reluctant to recount to male officers. Their argument was similar to that advanced by policewomen in 1921 giving evidence on their duties.[38] The ordeal was likely to dissuade false or malicious allegations.[39]

On whatever grounds a reported case failed to proceed, the common factor in the cases in the HCJ data is that the PF's personal and legal parameters had been met or exceeded, and competent and compelling and corroborated evidence had been collected.[40] Guided by the rules contained in the *Book of Regulations*, that corpus of evidence was constructed from the PF's personal assessments of the precognition statements and forensic reports and potentially also his personal attitude towards sexual crime. A survey of eighteenth-century Essex property crime records reveals that if even slight changes in the attitudes and decisions

---

36 AD15/22/57, JC13/134; unanimously guilty, three years' penal servitude each.
37 A. McColgan, 'Common Law and the Relevance of Sexual History Evidence', *Oxford Journal of Legal Studies*, 16, no. 2 (1996): 279.
38 *Departmental Committee on Sexual Offences against Children and Young Persons in Scotland* (Edinburgh, 1926), 23 – 'but an experienced judge took the view that, while precognition by women might make matters easier for the children, there was no reason to suppose that it would secure better evidence'.
39 Bourke, *Rape*, 326.
40 Key in Scots Law, corroboration appears, however, to have had an elastic application. For example, in a 1925 Govan rape case, a two years and ten-month-old toddler was precognosced to corroborate the evidence of two four-year-olds and their mothers; and in a 1922 case involving rape of a five-year-old, the PF noted: 'There is ample corroboration of C***'s story without her having been seen with accused'. Her father, grandmother and her deceased mother's niece provided anecdotal corroboration, but there were no eyewitnesses; AD15/25/65 and AD15/22/50, respectively.

of police and prosecutors who controlled the evidence-gathering process could influence indictment rates easily, then changing trends in recorded – and in this case prosecuted – crime must rely on a better understanding of decision-making patterns.[41] In 1920s Scotland despite the homogenizing influence of the *Book of Regulations* on the processes of the procurator-fiscal service across the country and through time, there is the possibility that a PF's personal attitude had an impact on prosecutions.

Constructing the victim from above

In the HCJ incest prosecutions, neither the PF nor CC made any pejorative comments concerning the complainers or their families in their correspondence. Members of elite groups were unlikely to express negative opinions about these girls because of inherent sympathy and abhorrence of the depravity of the crime and because eradicating incest among the lower orders had been a society-wide aim for decades. As Glasgow's PF wrote in 1920 in a case involving a thirteen-year-old stepdaughter and her five-year-old half-sister:

> It is perhaps unfortunate that the girl P*** when spoken to by Mrs D*** denied that accused had interfered indecently with her but she explains she was ashamed to admit what he had done. She is a girl of good appearance and should impress a Jury.[42]

Not only was the PF sympathetic to her reluctance to report, but he looked favourably on her physical appearance. There was nothing about her to which a jury could take offence.

There are also occasional notes in rape cases from the PF revealing his personal opinion such as Inverness's PF who in 1919 described a rape victim, aged between fifteen and sixteen years, as 'a respectable girl with good character'.[43] However, close reading of other cases illustrates how the PF might interpret a case while working his way towards a prosecution. For example, in a rape case from Paisley in 1921, the PF commented that the seventeen-year-old married complainer had changed her story from no penetration during the first assault,

---

41 P. King, *Crime, Justice and Discretion in England, 1740-1820* (Oxford, 2000), 12. Further research is required on individual twentieth-century PFs to ascertain how and why they made certain decisions. An initial subject would be John Drummond Strathern, PF for Glasgow into the 1930s.
42 AD15/20/93, JC14/35; note from PF, unanimously guilty on both counts, seven years' penal servitude.
43 AD15/19/125; letter PF to Crown Agent 17 September 1919.

'because her knickers were still on', to a version which included penetration on the first, second and third assaults by her landlady's brother-in-law. The PF thought the first assault 'unlikely with her knickers in the way' but considered her 'a simple young woman' and proceeded after her alteration to her evidence.[44] In a group rape of a fifteen-year-old domestic servant on an Aberdeenshire farm, the PF noted: 'the girl seems truthful but she is contradicted by all the farm servants who appear to be utterly unreliable but I cannot get anything more out of them'. By his personal assessment, the PF judged the girl to be truthful despite contradictory evidence from her colleagues. Unfortunately, the records do not reveal whether the PF's personal interpretation of the girl's testimony or her behaviour during the assault determined his decision to prosecute. She had told her attackers she was only fifteen hoping they would stop because she was a minor, but they said they 'did not care if she were 14'. Confronted by one assailant aged twenty-one and another over sixteen years old, she had used her understanding of the age of consent to try to stop their assault.[45]

Where personal connection existed, the PF could be particularly sympathetic, as in a 1928 case in Ayr concerning a nineteen-year-old housemaid. The PF knew the girl's 'people' whom he considered 'most respectable and her brother is a chauffeur to a personal friend of mine'. Not only had there been an eyewitness who had intervened to pull the assailant off the girl, but the examining physician considered 'her injuries showed considerable resistance on her part, and considerable violence on his part'. She had robustly resisted, had screamed 'at the pitch of my voice' but, although emission was unnecessary for a charge of rape, the girl had not been able to confirm whether the accused had 'made me wet'. Without a court transcript extant, it is the only element of the case which might explain why the jury disagreed with the decision to indict on assault and rape and returned a verdict of only attempted rape.[46]

Unlike other forms of interpersonal violence, in sexual assaults the presumption of truth-telling by the complainer, irrespective of forensic medical evidence, is not always apparent.[47] Not only is she judged on appearance, family background and employment, but her previous sexual history may also inform judicial opinion. If a complainer was not dissuaded from reporting an assault because of her own perception of how previous sexual experience may look, it

---

44 AD15/21/140, JC13/134; jury of seven women and 8 men returned verdict of guilty of assault and attempt to ravish, four years' penal servitude.
45 AD15/21/183, JC11/119; jury of five women and ten men returned verdict of unanimously not proven.
46 AD15/28/97, JC15/39; letter PF to Crown Agent 14 April 1928, fifteen months' imprisonment.
47 McColgan, 'Sexual History Evidence', 277.

could affect whether the judiciary decided to proceed. If it did prosecute, then in court sexual history evidence would have been revealed to the jury because it had been precognosced and was usually a good defence. Recent studies on jury responses have revealed that juries can be 'profoundly unwilling' to return a guilty verdict if evidence of sexual history is permitted in court.[48] It is an increasing area of debate, but in 1920s Scotland, not only was previous sexual experience provided in the precognitions, but it would be repeated in court and attested to by an examining physician. Yet, numerous examples exist in the HCJ papers where girls admitted at precognition to sexual relations with other boys and illegitimate pregnancies, which did not preclude them, in the PF's opinion, from the possibility of a successful prosecution.

A case involving an eight-year-old who repeatedly returned to her abuser, who played truant from school and had caused the education authorities to complain and had previously behaved indecently with local boys, did not deter Glasgow's PF from prosecuting. The child had visited the panel on 'numerous occasions between 1 June and 1 October 1920' when he had put his 'hand between my legs' and had put her on her back on the kitchen table, penetrated her and had ejaculated. He only assaulted her when his landlady was out, and if she brought a friend with her, he would go into 'the back room, shut the door for 10 minutes and then come back out'. The witness suspected that 'he was doing something wrong to C*** because he was not giving her that money for nothing'; the victim had received pocket money in return for her compliance. The landlady's husband attested to the girl being 'a bit wild' and 'running about with boys', and a forensic examination revealed her to have 'marked anaemia' and to be in a poor condition, although there was no semen on her body or clothing. Despite the financial transaction between the two parties which funded the girl's participation in Highland dancing competitions, the PF prosecuted. He might have indicted on a charge of attempt to ravish considering the lack of forensic evidence and the girl's behaviour. Instead, he prosecuted on the sole charge of rape which was based on only the child's testimony of penetration. The jury disagreed. Although they believed sexual violence had occurred, they returned a unanimous verdict of the lesser charge of indecent assault.[49]

Similar decisions by PFs are apparent from the HCJ records between 1885 and 1910. Admittedly they are few, but these cases in which character and previous sexual history are stacked against the complainer suggest that the PF's personal

---

48 McColgan, 'Sexual History Evidence', 286; further discussion in modern context in Chapter 8.
49 AD15/20/125, JC14/35; eighteen months with hard labour.

interpretations of the victim and her evidence could run counter to historical and contemporary perceptions of elite attitudes.

As revealed by the precognitions, prosecution witness testimonies were largely supportive but might also contain defamatory details. While specific comments within the precognitions do not reveal intra-community tensions and rivalries, they do suggest anxieties surrounding child protection from molestation.[50] The woman watching from the window as a man escorted two young girls into the park in Glasgow and the number of cases in which mothers, in particular, described suspicion of a lodger's behaviour in the staircase lavatories over a number of weeks are especially visible among the LLPB case papers. They suggest general female watchfulness for aberrant male behaviour. However, protection of young women who would often travel to work before sunrise and to entertainment after dark was not so easily surveilled by the community. Therefore, their precognitions contained greater detail concerning their personal behaviour.

In 1915, Professor John Glaister, Glasgow's famous professor of medical jurisprudence, was able to advise medical students that in the absence of marks upon the complainer's body, 'a healthy scepticism as to the truth of her statements' should be employed unless of course there was proof she had fainted or been drugged.[51] Glaister's contemporary and rival in Edinburgh Henry Littlejohn advised his students that where a woman was 'able to twist her body', it would render 'the introduction of the penis extremely difficult, even in women used to coitus, and much more so in a virgin'.[52] Thus, despite developments in the law since the mid-nineteenth century, precognoscers continued to ask complainers: was she overpowered or held down so that she could not struggle sufficiently to injure her assailant or escape? Why did she not scream to her utmost to summon help? Degree of struggle, whether she considered herself to be deflowered ('he had carnal connection with me') and if ejaculation had occurred ('he made me wet') were vital elements in adult complainers' reports. Whether the underlying presumption that rape of a virgin could be especially difficult to perpetrate was upheld by all, some or none of the precognoscers will never be understood, but in asking about a complainer's previous sexual experience, a precognoscer was clearly ascertaining a detail which could be used to construct a victim as either a virgin and possibly also a liar or a loose young woman who may have invited her assailant's attentions.

50 M. Gaskill, *Crime and Mentalities in Early Modern England* (Cambridge, 2000), 24.
51 J. Glaister, *A Textbook of Medical Jurisprudence and Toxicology* (Edinburgh, 1915), 482.
52 S. Smith, *Forensic Medicine: A Text-Book for Students and Practitioners* (London, 1925), 221.

In cases of child sexual violence, the precognitions concentrated more on penetration, emission and pain, rather than a child's resistance, which was futile against an adult male. These questions could be asked repeatedly until the precognoscer achieved self-corroborated truth and clarity, because often a child's language was euphemistic, which required reiterated clarification. 'Birdie' was often used throughout the precognitions to indicate a penis, or 'he put his thing into me and made me wet with yellow stuff' described penetration and ejaculation.[53] These details satisfied the requirement for a structured and coded narrative to present in court. However, if a child appeared too 'knowing' or used adult language to describe body parts or the assault itself, this might imply a lack of sexual innocence.[54] In the HCJ papers, the words 'penis', 'semen' and 'intercourse' are largely absent from the testimonies of minors, which suggests these children fitted the accepted construction of a child victim.

Conversely, excessive modesty in an older girl could also cause concern because she might be hiding the truth having learned the required 'script' to disguise her knowledge of the sexual act. However, there is tangible indignation in most of the precognitions; these young women felt they had a genuine grievance irrespective of their choice of vocabulary describing their ordeal. The uniformity of the precognition statements across different PF regions suggests that precognoscers – retired and active police constables, welfare officers or PF's clerks – did not allow any personally harboured class prejudices or received ideas concerning working-class victims of sexual violence to dilute the veracity of a complainer's precognition. Precognoscing of different groups of women by age and occupation reveals a distinctly similar nationwide approach to statement-taking.

Research on nineteenth-century English depositions and verdicts reveals that courts were more interested in the intercourse element of an assault, but conviction was likelier if a rape had been excessively physically injurious.[55] The Scottish HCJ cases for adult complainers reveal that precognoscers always ascertained both the sexual details and the amount of physical violence used in an assault, which were verified, or not, by subsequent medical examination. Further, the amount of physical violence does not appear to have taken

---

53 AD15/26/78, JC15/37; an interesting case in which the AD believed *de recenti* evidence, hearsay, had been elicited from the victim's mother concerning the accused's gonorrhoea, which she thought confirmed his guilt. The jury returned a unanimous verdict of not proven, assoilzied and dismissed.
54 Jackson, *Child Sexual Abuse*, 29 and 94.
55 D'Cruze, 'Sex, Violence and Local Courts', 51; C. Conley, 'Sexual Violence in Historical Perspective', in *Oxford Handbook of Gender, Sex and Crime,* eds R. Gartner and B. McCarthy (Oxford, 2014), 196.

precedence over the sexual component. Many of the rape cases, especially social rapes, offered scant details of physical injury elsewhere on the body. Thus, in cases concerning older girls and women, precognoscers appear to have concentrated on ascertaining degree of penetration and verbal confirmation of emission, strength of resistance as well as details of previous sexual experience. The answers to these questions created a judicial construction of the victim as she would appear to a jury. Despite research for England indicating the contrary, in the Scottish context often girls and women with unappealing 'characters' could hope to have their complaints prosecuted.

Constructing the victim from below

Witnesses and other contributors to the precognitions sometimes offered unhelpful details such as comment on a teenage girl's inability to maintain household standards for her widowed father, although where exculpatory precognitions were gathered, more serious pejorative tactics might be employed by defence counsel. Exculpatory precognitions are rare among the HCJ papers probably because the panels were all working-class men and could not afford for them to be taken, yet they provide glimpses into societal tensions in working-class communities. Research conducted on interwar childcare discovered that facial expressions and a child's dress might indicate potential delinquency, as well as the child's family background, and possible heredity, environment and intelligence factors.[56] Some of the precognitions suggest that neighbours were prepared to judge a victim using similar criteria. A 1923 Glasgow case is particularly illustrative of defence counsel's use of exculpatory witnesses to defend his client. The accused, aged seventy, was indicted on five charges of rape and LLPB against four girls ranging in age from six to eleven years. Four days before the trial, the panel's solicitor informed the PF that he intended to 'attack the character of' three of the girls. In exculpation, one female witness asserted that she 'always thought S... a respectable decent man'. Another added that 'he does a lot of good work with youngsters' at the Orange Lodge and a reverend avowed that he 'found him clean of speech and very proper in conduct'. Defaming the girls, an adult witness accused one seven-year-old victim of taking her own five-year-old daughter 'to the waste land and interfering with her with

---

56 D. Thom, 'Wishes, Anxieties, Play and Gestures: Child Guidance in Inter-war England', in *In the Name of the Child: Health and Welfare 1880-1940*, ed. R. Cooter (London, 1992), 202–3.

a boy', adding that the victim's own mother complained about her too because 'every time she goes out she comes back with her knickers down'. Others had 'heard the gossip about the girls'. Despite the weight of testimony against the girls and in support of the panel, the case proceeded on a combined charge of lewd practices and rape. The physician reported that at least three of the complainers had been 'interfered with, but improbable that complete penetration took place', which presumably informed the jury's verdict of not guilty by majority on charges involving two girls and unanimously not guilty on charges involving the two youngest girls.[57]

Widows and spinsters

Being an older, unmarried victim of sexual assault or a non-virginal widow could either attract the authorities' sympathy or given their preoccupation with younger girls at risk of debauchery, these women's lower social value might see their cases given less credence. There are thirteen cases of rape reported by widows and spinsters that proceeded to court. Two from 1922 illustrate how 'rape scripts' may have affected these 'unprotected' women. Walking home from work, a forty-year-old widowed teacher was violently and sexually assaulted on a farm road in daylight. She stated that her assailant failed to have connection with her. Earlier, the accused had attacked a 58-year-old farmer's wife on the same track. He succeeded in full rape before she walked home where she informed her husband and son. She did not report the attack until after she had heard of the teacher's complaint. The accused, an unmarried miner aged twenty-eight, pleaded guilty.[58] The teacher was a respectable professional, and walking home alone could not be constructed as suggestive of an 'unprotected' lifestyle. Despite the teacher's confirmation of the absence of penetration and emission, corroboration by the farmer's wife of her assault made the case proceedable. Whether the farmer's wife's complaint alone would have persuaded the PF is unknowable. The other 1922 case involved a thirty-year-old prostitute spinster attacked by two men in Glasgow. The decision to proceed suggests a lack of patriarchal bias against her because of her profession.[59] A widowed postwoman's case in 1921 reflects similar sympathies to the assault on the schoolteacher: her semi-professional status may have eclipsed Professor Glaister's outdated

---

57 AD15/23/74, JC15/34; assoilzied and dismissed.
58 AD15/22/130, JC5/15; seven years' penal servitude.
59 AD15/22/73, JC14/36; seven years' penal servitude each.

comment: 'the description by the woman could not have taken place without marks on her body, but they were only slight after the struggle'.[60]

'Against her will'

In the sixteenth century, consent was assumed if a woman had not sustained sufficient injuries during an assault to justify a claim of resistance or had submitted through fear.[61] These concepts requiring proof of non-consent proved especially difficult to eradicate from the judicial mindset, although movement towards a more sympathetic consideration of the frozen panic that rape might cause began in the mid-nineteenth century in the case of *R v Sweenie* (1858). While one judge upheld that 'the element of violence has always been essential', his colleagues, including Scotland's Lord President, declared that 'the force essential for the crime of rape is relative to the resistance offered, and where there is not resistance to overcome, it is not necessary to prove use of force'. Yet twenty years later, while Edward Cox, publisher of the *Law Times*, acknowledged that 'the wrong done to the victim is enormous', he argued that unless drink or drugs were involved, or multiple attackers, it was the man's word against the woman's, because 'actual rape is so nearly impossible that it should be accepted only on the most conclusive evidence'. Cox also adhered to the notion that 'no' was not necessarily an absolute refusal and that intent to rape had to be established; otherwise, the jury should return 'attempted rape' only.[62] However, the Lord President's prescient and obverse argument was inherent in any case where fear of physical violence and blind terror at the audacity of the assault existed: a woman would not offer resistance, which therefore did not imply consent. By the 1920s, the situation appears to have improved somewhat, although rarely in adult cases was the complainer's and assailant's dimorphism acknowledged: sheer physical size, weight and strength of a man intent on sexual intercourse meant, in theory, that any woman was rapeable.[63]

There are no instances from the responses in the precognitions where it might be inferred that the direct question asked was: did you say no? Instead, the range of answers of a positive and frequently negative nature to questions ascertaining resistance, shouting for help and previous sexual history suggests that the PF

---

60 AD15/21/137, JC13/134; by small majority found guilty; five years' penal servitude.
61 Conley, 'Sexual Violence in Historical Perspective', 193.
62 *R v Sweenie* (1858), 8 Cox CC 223; E. W. Cox, *Principles of Punishment* (London, 1877), 81–4.
63 A. Greenfield, *Interpreting Sexual Violence, 1660-1800* (Abingdon, 2016), 10.

had wide licence to use his personal and professional evaluation of whether the assault had been against the complainer's will. Even when medical reports or child-related institutions, such as schools, or indeed CC offered conflicting or contradictory opinion, cases proceeded. The credibility of a victim's complaint was constructed in terms of her precognition statement, those of witnesses for both sides and a character portrait with which the PF might sympathize. Because the records surveyed for this study are prosecuted crime only, the judicial attitude towards the panels becomes irrelevant. The panel must be presumed innocent, and it was the judiciary's professional duty to set aside any self-held patriarchal attitudes towards him and his conduct. Their keen interest lay in ascertaining whether consent had been given or extracted from the complainer and to assist them, the PF sought medical opinion.

Seeking sperm – forensic medicine and medical jurisprudence

Sexual assaults, most particularly those involving penetration, are the only indictments for which a complainer's physical injuries are crucial to the veracity of her statement; inside and out her body becomes the evidence.[64] In the 1920s, forensic medicine remained relatively unsophisticated by modern standards, although the PF and CC often drew on forensic opinion to corroborate a case. Since 1828, the legal requirement for proof of seminal emission in sexual violence trials had been removed. Without this requirement, it has been argued, rape cases became easier to prosecute because the victim no longer belonged to a husband or father; instead, she had become a victim of violence.[65] Evidence of penetration combined with bodily injuries satisfied the requirement for proof of violence. However, haphazard detection of sexual penetration and medical reluctance to diagnose it in young children had resulted in variable credibility given to medical evidence in court. A child's intact hymen often guided a doctor to form the opinion she had not been raped and in adult females, inflamed genitalia were sought as proof of penetration. However, the 1828 legislation and further medical legal debate in 1843 that only proof of penetration was required and the hymen could remain unruptured did not take hold quickly. Proof of emission, penetration and often a torn hymen remained key factors in proving a

---

64 G. Greer, *On Rape* (London, 2018), 43.
65 M. Wiener, 'The Victorian Criminalization of Men', in *Men and Violence: Gender, Honor, and Rituals in Modern Europe and America*, ed. P. Spierenburg (Ohio, 1998), 206.

sexual violence case into the 1920s.[66] By this time, both prosecution and defence counsel were eager to use the latest forensic methods to enhance the authority of their arguments.

Forensic medicine tests for human blood and sperm were far from definitive. The precipitin test to distinguish human from other mammalian blood was a recent innovation and could only determine that. Tests for human sperm could microscopically detect individual spermatozoa, but they could not attribute ownership. Forensic authority had established that 'the discovery of one distinct and entire spermatozoon is quite sufficient to justify a medical opinion of the spermatic nature of the stain' and where the presence of sperm was established, the forensic physician was at liberty to conclude that rape had occurred.[67] However, judicial officers were alert to the limitations of this relatively new science: Glasgow's PF had already questioned the guilt of a sex offender based on his suffering from gonorrhoea. Detection of blood and semen on bodies, clothes and at the scene of the crime remained inconclusive of guilt.[68] Into the 1920s forensic medicine remained open to the individual doctor's interpretation and personal reaction to the victim.[69] Often an equivocal opinion resulted because the physician either could not come to a firm conclusion on the evidence presented or possibly because of fear of professional reputational damage if defence counsel proved him wrong. In 1920 in a Glasgow rape case involving a three-year-old, despite discovering that her 'vulva was red, labiae swollen, hymen swollen and signs of injury at its edges', the casualty surgeon concluded: 'I am of the opinion that a foreign body has caused the condition of the hymen, but I am not able to state whether it was caused by a finger or by a penis'.[70] Frequently, doctors added that injury might have been caused by 'a blunt instrument', which further removed them from offering an absolute opinion, and where a woman had had previous sexual intercourse, a forensic examination could not offer conclusive evidence of recent rape.[71] However, the immediacy of doctors' examinations and reports suggests that their findings were not constructed to

---

66   *The Medical Times*, 8 (1843): 48; Jackson, *Child Sexual Abuse*, 74–5.
67   F. Taylor, *Principles and Practices of Medical Jurisprudence*, 461, quoted in N. E. Duvall, 'Forensic Medicine in Scotland, 1914-39', unpublished PhD thesis (University of Manchester, 2013), 82.
68   R. Davidson, *Illicit and Unnatural Practices: The Law, Sex and Society in Scotland since 1900* (Edinburgh, 2019), 99.
69   Jackson, *Child Sexual Abuse*, 85.
70   AD15/20/74; in this period rape included only penetration of the vagina or anus by the penis. Today's definition includes all orifices and penetration by the penis, digit or any foreign object.
71   S. Robertson, 'Signs, Marks and Private Parts: Doctors, Legal Discourses and Evidence of Rape in the United States, 1823-1930', *Journal of the History of Sexuality*, 8, no. 3 (January 1998): 375–6, 381.

conform to judicial decisions.[72] In Scotland, general practitioners' and casualty surgeons' handwritten first reports were included loose among the case papers with a typed-up verbatim version included in the precognition bundles. Unless, during a medical examination when noting particulars by hand, physicians anticipated their judicial reception, the collation of the case papers suggests doctors' reports were not adapted for presentation in court. What had been written during the examination is what was repeated under oath.[73] In the case noted earlier, the physician was either at a loss to ascertain the penetrative instrument given the methods of examination at his disposal or he did not wish to give a definitive opinion, which might damage his, his patient's or the panel's reputation. Whatever the reason, and the HCJ papers give no further indication, his response was professionally inconclusive.

In 1885 in a rape case of a 26-year-old mother of an illegitimate child, after describing scratches to the victim's windpipe, the examining physician discovered 'some discharge was seeping from the vagina which closely resembled male seminal fluid'; he did not take swabs to be sent to Professor Littlejohn, Glaister's Edinburgh rival.[74] In another case the same year, the doctor examined the victim's genitalia and was unable to say whether 'the connection was forcible', although he observed 'the girl was large for her age'.[75] The PFs involved in these 1885 rape cases did not request laboratory tests and neither did the physicians send samples of their own volition. By 1895, one doctor examined 'some stains [which] looked like dried semen' but 'the microscope did not confirm this'. He was frustrated that elapse of time between the assault and his examination was 'too long to obtain accurate results'. In this instance, the assault had occurred on 6 May and the doctor's examination took place five days later.[76]

By the 1920s, the process had speeded up considerably and all sexual violence case papers included either a GP's or a police surgeon's examination report which had been conducted on the same day or the day following the assault. A forensic report was included if the PF had requested one and was dated some days later once laboratory tests had been conducted. For the indictment of rape, 58 per cent of cases relied on a GP's report alone, with 31 per cent of cases including a forensic report as supporting, sometimes superseding, evidence. However, it was often the case that medical reports were not always the deciding factor

---

72 S. Robertson, 'What's Law Got To Do With It? Legal Records and Sexual Histories', *Journal of the History of Sexuality*, 14, no. 1/2 (2005): 176.
73 Duvall, 'Forensic Medicine in Scotland', 255.
74 AD14/85/11.
75 AD14/85/22.
76 AD14/95/42.

persuading the PF to proceed. Reports could be inconsistent, offering more than medical opinion – GPs were the worst for narrative nuance – and the remotest rural surgeries appear to have been either too far from laboratories to use their services or had not been instructed to incur the expense. In Fife in 1920, a GP reported:

> How she could be taken 25 yards from the path and no marks of violence show on her wrists I cannot explain. . . . From her story, her general condition, and what I saw, I am of the opinion that it has been a case of rape.[77]

His notes reveal only a cursory external assessment of the sixteen-year-old's appearance and no forensic testing.[78] The same year, another GP initially seemed to display a lack of basic knowledge, reporting in a case involving a 65-year-old in Glasgow that 'I found sticky white stuff in F. . .'s vagina'. Samples sent for testing were inconclusive for semen.[79] In a group rape of an adult woman in 1923, the GP's medical expertise permitted him the opinion that 'it does not appear to have been fear which prevented her from making strenuous resistance, otherwise she would not have been able to judge whether two of her alleged attackers did not succeed in having connection with her'. He found it difficult 'to say definitely in cases of women who have borne children whether they have been raped' which adhered to Glaister's guidance and he did 'not consider it necessary to take a swab' because there was 'no discharge visible'.[80] Evidently, a varied approach to what constituted reliable medical opinion existed. In cases where GPs and police or casualty surgeons submitted separate reports, usually they revealed similar opinions, although at times they were diametrically opposed. The GP's report in a 1928 Edinburgh case confirmed that 'connection had taken place and loss of virginity resulted as evidenced by raw and bleeding remains of the hymen'. However, the police surgeon had been able to 'insert two fingers', thus concluding the seventeen-year-old had not been *virgo intacta* for some time.[81] Glaister did not consider the presence or absence of the hymen a definitive factor in deciding rape or virginity, although he did assert that 'recent rupture' to the hymen 'would signify the forcible introduction of an instrument of some kind'.[82]

---

77 AD15/20/155.
78 AD15/20/155.
79 AD15/20/73.
80 AD15/23/86; Glaister, *Medical Jurisprudence*, 482.
81 AD15/28/25.
82 Glaister, *Medical Jurisprudence*, 484.

Similar conflicts occurred when an expert forensic report had been requested. In a 1930 Glasgow case, the GP reported that 'emission of semen had taken place' before sending the swab for analysis. Once tested, the swabs 'showed no signs of seminal fluid. No evidence in her knickers either', although on his physical examination of the woman a few days later, the forensic physician confirmed penetration had occurred because her 'hymen was completely torn'. Despite the conflict between the forensic evidence and medical opinion, the case proceeded, although the lack of seminal evidence may have been the deciding factor because the jury of eight men and seven women returned a not guilty verdict.[83] Professor Glaister's more authoritative manner also produced results. In a 1920 rape case involving two sixteen-year-olds, Glaister found 'unequivocal evidence of seminal fluid in the form of complete spermatozoa'. The accused attempted to plea bargain offering to admit guilt to indecent assault with one victim and attempt to ravish with the other, but the GP's addition of one victim's 'maidenhead being rent asunder' helped convict this rapist who was sentenced to eight years' penal servitude. It was a particularly harsh sentence, but he also possessed a previous similar conviction served in Salisbury.[84] However, Glaister could also provide bafflingly non-medical reports such as 'there was semen emitted . . . from a male person'.[85]

The inability of GP or expert forensic analysis to determine whose sperm was present on the victim was clearly infuriating for some PFs, as one commented in 1926: 'there is no corroborating evidence that he is the man to do it apart from he has gonorrhoea', which had been diagnosed in the child.[86] Thus, however authoritatively forensic evidence was presented, it could achieve nothing more conclusive than stating that a female might have had sex and the accused identified by her might be the culprit. Some contemporaries recognized this deficiency. Government investigators reporting on sexual abuse acknowledged that 'an inexperienced doctor, coupling a few doubtful symptoms with a plausible story, may assume interference or assault, when, in fact, there has been neither'.[87] In the earlier 1926 case, the GP and a female doctor offering a second opinion both concluded there had been partial penetration of 'the external vulva' which followed Glaister's advice that 'the slightest penetration of the penis within the

---

83 AD15/30/77.
84 AD15/20/85.
85 AD15/20/119.
86 AD15/26/78.
87 *Departmental Committee*, 25.

vulva is sufficient' for a rape offence, but in this instance the jury disagreed and acquitted the panel on a verdict of not proven.[88]

However, reports relying on the latest forensic methods in the 1920s appear to have raised the judicial expectations of medical evidence, especially when famous names were engaged as expert witnesses. The HCJ records reveal peaks in forensic reporting in 1920–1, which tailed off towards the end of the decade. These rises coincided with increases in rape and ravish prosecutions involving girls under sixteen, and particularly in 1921 for children under ten years. These cases are sufficiently geographically distributed around Scotland that the preference for forensic reporting in these years cannot be attributed to the personal decisions of individual PFs. However, judicial officers may have reacted to the upsurge in reported sexual violence among the most vulnerable girls by encouraging the commissioning of more forensic reports in these years. With weaker precognitions from young victims, medical corroboration would at least have allowed a PF to prosecute even if eventually the jury disagreed with the evidence.

Indictments and pleas

When choosing which indictment to cite, the PFs, in consultation with CC, based their decision on the descriptions of the severity of the crime, medical and forensic evidence, but probably most importantly, their assessment of the likelihood of winning on any of the indictments available to them: rape, attempt to ravish or LLPB.[89] Arguably, in cases involving younger girls in which evidence might not be conclusive for rape, a lesser charge could be used in order to secure a conviction, although this could occlude the seriousness of the alleged offence and would earn a shorter sentence.[90] This strategy may have been used

---

88   AD16/26/78, JC15/37; one of only three cases to contain reports from female doctors all reporting on girls under twelve years. Glaister's authoritative work was not as helpful as contemporary physicians may have hoped. At one point, he instructed that the condition of the hymen alone was no clear indication of rape and that other physical evidence such as bruises and blood would be required, while a few pages later, he wrote that absence of visible signs of penetration or other injuries did not necessarily mean that rape had not occurred; Glaister, *Medical Jurisprudence*, 480, 482, 485.
89   As a separate crime involving a relation, incest was not open to interpretation by degree of assault. In fact, 'attempted incest' appears not to have been used at all in the 1920s at the HCJ, possibly because bringing a charge of incest was hard enough, and 'attempted incest' harder still, to report and prove, let alone prosecute.
90   L. A. Jackson, 'Child Sexual Abuse in England and Wales: Prosecution and Prevalence 1918-1970', 2, http://www.historyandpolicy.org/policy-papers/rss_2.0, accessed October 2022.

in 1920s Scotland because 290 victims of the lesser indictment of LLPB out of a total of 294 were aged below sixteen years. However, a 1919 attempt to ravish case indicates that in some instances, the PF was prepared to select a higher indictment than LLPB despite inconclusive evidence. In this case from Fife, a 49-year-old boiler fireman was indicted for attempt to ravish a 9-year-old. The medical report noted: 'no fresh marks of violence on any part of the body except redness scarcely noticeable on the labia. Vagina normal and hymen unruptured', which suggested no visible attempt at penetration, and there was some semen on her left knee. Without witnesses to the assault, the panel's previous convictions of a similar nature between 1916 and 1918 may have influenced the choice of indictment. However, these would not have been disclosed to the jury, yet in court, the child's young age and absence of conclusive medical opinion did not deter the jury from a unanimously guilty verdict.[91]

Similarly, LLPB cases were by definition all non-penetrative. They required proximity or actual touching of the panel's hands or penis to the girl's genitalia. In a Glasgow case involving six girls in 1925, the doctor's examinations proved negative with 'no bruising or injury to the private parts'. At the second diet, the AD accepted the accused's guilty plea to indecent assault only, a charge below LLPB.[92] The descriptions of assault in this and the 1919 attempt to ravish case appear remarkably similar, and this LLPB case with multiple victims potentially offered more corroboration. However, some detail in this case did not attract the higher attempt to ravish charge for one or more of the girls. Thus, for non-penetrative charges in general, PFs appear to have selected the indictment based on the quality of the evidence rather than indicting only to win at some level. This is further supported by the number of minor rape cases heard at the HCJ. Of 101 rape prosecutions, 47 involved minor females. Again, if a child was unable to name the crime committed against her or confirm penetration, the PF would have been better advised to prosecute elsewhere or on a lower indictment. However, the number of rape prosecutions on behalf of minor females suggests that if an indictment of rape was justified by the supporting evidence, and often young girls gave questionable statements, then a rape charge was entered. The number of minor rapes prosecuted at the HCJ suggests that the judiciary sought the correct level of redress for the crime it understood to have been perpetrated.

Judicial rationale for decision-making is not complete in the case papers and often inexplicably – but sufficiently frequently – the prosecution's narrative

91 JC26/1919/14; eight years; penal servitude; this is a severe sentence for a non-penetrative offence, possibly inflated because of the panel's recidivism.
92 JC26/1925/25, JC14/38; eighteen months' imprisonment.

evidence outweighed the combined evidence of professional medical opinion and exculpatory testimony – a reversal of the modern value placed on evidence. These prosecutions for rape of minors are not necessarily representative of a larger number of complaints presented to the PF which proved unproceedable for some reason. However, the high proportion of offences against minors of the total number of rape prosecutions is sufficiently significant to suggest that in Scotland if the quality of evidence supported the charge, then PFs and CC did not shy away from prosecuting on the higher indictment. And if the evidence indicated only LLPB, then the lower charge was used.

The absence of adult females in LLPB cases suggests that confirmation of penetration was vital to a sexual offence charge, presumably because it was expected that women could describe the crime fully and would also resist, therefore preventing an 'attempt' or unwanted intimate handling. Without penetration, the charge would be assault heard at a lower court. As MacDonald, Scotland's legal authority, explained, if the girl was older than twelve, a charge of indecent assault was 'not generally applicable', although if she were between twelve and sixteen years, the Criminal Law Amendment Act of 1885 (CLAA) and its 1922 revision could be used but only if indecency beyond physical assault was testified.[93] However, the judiciary might use a multiple indictment if it were convinced of some form of indecent assault. Thus, all of the adult female attempt to ravish cases were combined with either LLPB or assault, and often child rape cases were combined with LLPB if the evidence did not point clearly to the single charge.

Multiple indictments

Since 1837, Scots Law had allowed the combining of lesser charges with indictments such as rape in an attempt to secure a conviction on one but hopefully the most serious of the charges indicted.[94] The use of multiple indictments acknowledged judicial evaluation of the evidence as supporting the higher charge while also recognizing the possibility that, for some reason, the jury might disagree. The jury could convict on the higher charge, one of the lesser indictments or not at all. However, by including several charges on the indictment sheet, it was incumbent

---

93 R. MacGregor Mitchell, *A Practical Treatise on the Criminal Law of Scotland by the Late Right Honourable Sir J H A MacDonald*, fourth edition (Edinburgh, 1929), 220–1.
94 L. Farmer, *Making the Modern Criminal Law: Criminalization and Civil Order* (Oxford, 2016), 273.

on the panel to convince the jury he was innocent on *all* charges in order to be acquitted, whereas the prosecution only required the jury to return a guilty verdict on one count to secure a conviction. It was a legal strategy that would win a custodial sentence of some duration thus removing the perpetrator from his community. The policy also sent a direct message to the 'offending classes' that toleration was not an option. If protecting a panel from undue publicity in especially gruesome or emotive cases was a consideration, the PF would have requested the case be prosecuted in a non-domiciled assize, but only one case – a Highland adult rape – was heard outside its home circuit, further emphasizing judicial attitudes towards potential offenders.

Pleading

If a panel pleaded guilty at the sheriff court first diet, his case was remitted to the HCJ for sentencing because the sheriff could not hand down sentences exceeding two years. If the panel pleaded not guilty, the case went to the HCJ for a full hearing, where several cases might be heard in a single day.[95] It might be anticipated that a greater number of not guilty pleas would be entered in sexual violence cases perpetrated against the youngest girls, because their evidence might be considered insufficiently compelling and corroborated; after all the complainer's only witnesses might have been her playmates. However, irrespective of the age of the alleged victim, 78 per cent of panels charged with rape in the 1920s pleaded not guilty. In a 1920 rape case in Glasgow involving a three-year-old victim, the perpetrator was young enough to be considered for Borstal if convicted and thus was possibly especially keen to retain his freedom. When attempting to ascertain penetration and thus a charge of rape, this child's evidence included the ambiguous statement: 'he took his "tittie" out, he pees with, and put it against my bum and then on to my "scadda"'. On arrest, the panel told the constable 'I did it', but by the first diet he had decided, or been advised, to plead not guilty. Therefore, the case proceeded to the HCJ, where he adhered to his plea. However, in front of the jury and before witness examinations commenced, he was reinterrogated and admitted guilt.[96]

---

95 Lindsay Farmer comments that in the early twentieth century, cases were tried much faster, thus persuading panels to plead guilty in this period was not an attempt by the judiciary or defence counsel to dispose of as many cases as possible during an Assize; personal comment to author.
96 AD15/20/74, JC14/34; nine months' imprisonment; sentence reflected his age and eventual admission of guilt.

However, in the majority of cases where panels pleaded not guilty at the first diet, most adhered to their original plea even when confronted with the intimidation of a jury. The panel pleaded guilty at the first diet in only thirteen rape cases (not including guilty pleas at second diet before or during jury trial), which involved victims aged between six and seventy-two years. None of these cases contained especially convincing evidence or compelling forensic reports to suggest a reason for pleading guilty at the first opportunity; genuine remorse may have been the only reason. In group rapes, where panels could corroborate their evidence against that of their lone victim, all panels entered a not guilty plea at the first and second diets.

On the lesser charge of LLPB, which attracted shorter sentences, and potentially shorter still if the panel pleaded guilty, similar patterns emerge. Irrespective of how young the victims were, and virtually all LLPB victims were children, panels mainly pleaded not guilty at both diets. Probably they hoped to be acquitted because the child's evidence might be inconclusive and there would be little medical evidence to support a charge of intimate handling. Where they changed their plea at the second diet, they attempted to plea bargain by admitting guilt to parts of the charge in return for the AD removing other charges on the indictment.

Plea bargaining

The welfare investigators of the 1926 report noted that 'not infrequently a modified plea is accepted by the prosecutor', which prevented the full facts of a case being examined in court and they considered it to be 'a mere gambler's throw on the part of the accused to escape the more severe penalty under the major charge'.[97] The earlier case involving the three-year-old and the boy young enough for Borstal could be read as defence counsel advising the panel to change his plea at the last minute in the hope of a shorter sentence. Counsel's view of the jury's mood, how they might receive the panel and the judge's reputation may all have influenced his advice.

Also, counsel might negotiate for a lesser indictment or ask for certain parts of a multiple indictment to be erased in return for a guilty plea to the less serious elements, as occurred in 1924 in a case involving a 37-year-old Glasgow widower. He was indicted for rape of a nine-year-old child and communicating venereal

---

97 *Departmental Committee*, 29.

disease (VD) to her. At the first diet, he pleaded not guilty, but at the second diet, he was prepared to admit guilt only if the words 'and did ravish her' (rape) were removed from the charge sheet. The AD accepted his plea on the revised indictment, which effectively meant the panel was convicted of attempt to rape only with the aggravation of VD.[98] In another case in 1920, the panel offered to plead guilty to indecent assault on an original indictment of assault with intent to ravish, indecent exposure, rape and previous similar convictions. However, Glaister's forensic report and the physician's medical report on the two victims led the panel to further negotiations. He was now prepared to plead guilty to assault on one woman but not indecent exposure and assault with intent to ravish on the other woman because 'he did not succeed in getting his private member into the girl and that her injuries were caused by his hands'. The physician refused to revise his first report in line with the panel's new confession, because he believed only 'a well-developed member or similar object' could have caused that kind of injury, and Glaister commented on the amount of blood. Unable to reduce the charges against him, the panel changed his tune once more and pleaded not guilty at both diets.[99] In two cases, the panels took umbrage at the accusation of anal sex. One pleaded guilty at the first diet having succeeded in having the words 'attempting to penetrate the hinder part of the woman's body' removed from the indictment (the victim was seventy-two), and the other pleaded guilty at the second diet after 'insert your finger into her anus, and did insert your private member into her anus' was removed.[100] Plainly, the stigma of anal sex and possible connotations of homosexuality were feared more than a prison sentence.

In all cases of plea bargaining where the plea was accepted, the panel avoided a jury trial at which there was the risk of jury members questioning the higher indictments still visible on the original charge sheet. When the plea bargain was rejected, a jury trial was inevitable on the original charge/s. Plea bargaining on multiple indictments gave defence counsel room to manoeuvre and as the 1926 report investigators had remarked, if accepted, the more gruesome details of a case went unheard. Having received a shorter sentence, a potential rapist would be released more quickly back into the community.[101]

98 AD15/24/47, JC15/34; three years' penal servitude. The number of sexual violence cases involving the aggravation of VD was inflated by a direct instruction in 1910 from Scottish law officers to 'penalise offenders who communicated VD to young girls as a consequence of rape' and to send cases to the HCJ rather than sheriff court. This was in response to 'the moral panic sweeping the Scottish cities'; the policy sustained into the 1930s; Davidson, *Illicit and Unnatural Practices*, 33.
99 AD15/20/85, JC13/132; PF's letters to CC 18 May and 28 May 1920; eight years' penal servitude.
100 AD15/30/19, JC5/18, AD15/29/65, JC5/40; five years' penal servitude each.
101 An unfathomable negotiation on an indictment of rape, LLPB, Contravention of Criminal Law Amendment Act 1885 section 4 and 1922 section 4 (1) perpetrated on seven girls under thirteen

There appears to be no correlation between plea bargaining and the age of the victim or details of a difficult character, which corresponds with a similar lack of correlation between not guilty pleas and the youngest girls. Thus, it appears that attempts to negotiate to reduce indictments were not based on age, the assumption of unconvincing corroboration or an unsympathetic victim. Instead, negotiations were a legal tactic to see if the panel could 'get off lightly'. And those which took place at the second diet before the AD, judge and jury may cautiously be read as a response to what defence counsel observed as he entered the courtroom with his client.

A gap in indictments

The graphs for indictments of rape, ravish and LLPB reveal an interesting trend. The number of cases for both rape and ravish are at their highest from 1919 to 1922; thereafter they decrease significantly with troughs appearing for both indictments around 1926. However, the number of LLPB cases began to increase from 1923 onwards, peaking in 1925 before decreasing to pre-1923 levels from 1928. Coinciding with these trends was the introduction of a revised CLAA in 1922 with a further revision in 1928. The 1922 revision contained an important amendment: by raising the age of consent to sixteen years for *all* sexual violence charges now including indecent assault, the defence that an underage person may have consented was completely removed. Thus, anyone under sixteen years, whether they had consented to or indeed instigated sexual intercourse, was now considered a victim of sexual misconduct by the person with whom they had had sex, forcibly or otherwise. By capturing indecent assault within the statutory age of consent, a clear message was sent to anyone intent on sexual violence: if they complained, all children were now protected by the law (Figure 6.1).

A further revision stated 'that reasonable cause of belief that a girl was over 16 was not a defence unless the man was 23 or under'; this became known as 'the young man's defence'.[102] Previously, any man could claim a girl under sixteen years had consented or that he *thought* she was older, but from 1922 onwards, 'the young man's defence' would only apply to panels close in age to their victims

---

      years listing eight separate charges, occurred in 1926. The panel pleaded guilty to all charges except the second alternative to charge 5, which meant that he pleaded guilty to unlawful carnal knowledge if they agreed to remove the alternative of LLPB with the same girl; JC26/1926/54.
102 Farmer, *Making the Criminal Law*, 276, footnote 69; also *Scots Law Times*, 7 October 1922, 93.

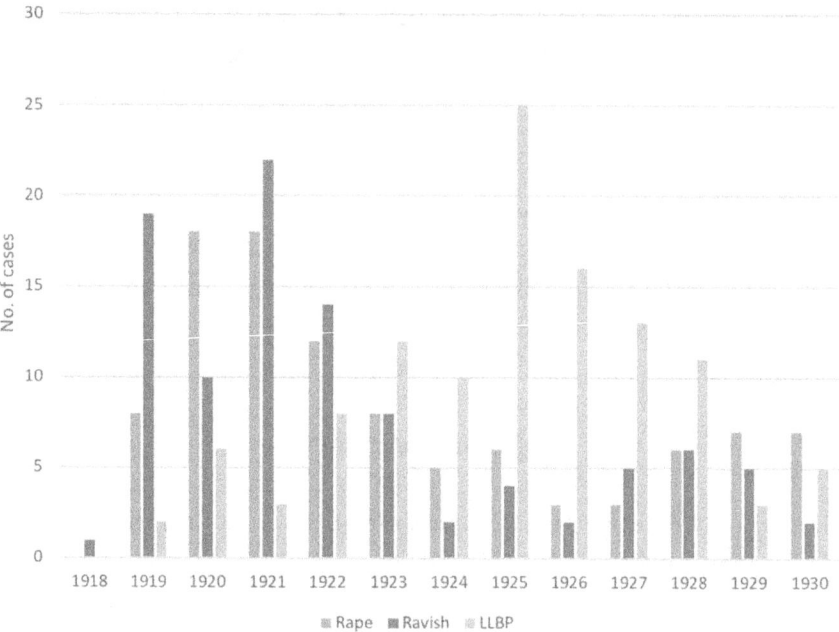

Figure 6.1 Non-familial indictments, total cases per year.

and only on a first indictment, not on first conviction.[103] This reinforced the message that it was a criminal offence to have intercourse with all girls under sixteen years and suggested that the responsibility lay with young men to enquire about a girl's age before any sexual activity.[104] Government investigators of sexual violence noted that this clause continued to attract 'a great deal of criticism' and was now 'the subject of a full discussion in Parliament'.[105] Clearly, elements of the legal profession were dissatisfied with the 1922 revision, and as contemporary criminologist Hermann Mannheim argued, prosecutors might now favour a higher court over police courts or Courts of Summary Jurisdiction where indecent assault would usually be charged as a common assault; in Mannheim's view, this practice would result in an unnecessary inflation of sexual assault statistics.[106]

---

103 A. M. Anderson, *The Criminal Law of Scotland* (Edinburgh, 1892), 97; *The Criminal Law Amendment Act with Introduction, Notes and Index* (London, 1885), 48 and 49 Vict. Cap. 69, 25 and 44.
104 L. Radzinowicz, *Sexual Offences: A Report of the Cambridge Department of Criminal Science* (London, 1957), 423.
105 *Departmental Committee*, 20. Before 1922, a man could claim a girl under sixteen years had consented or that he thought she was older; see Smart, 'Reconsidering the Recent History', 60.
106 H. Mannheim, *Social Aspects of Crime in England between the Wars* (London, 1940), 64.

In Scotland, the increase in LLPB cases in 1925 may represent a slow response to the 1922 legislation with PFs indicting on a lower charge while the wider legal debate concluded or it may have been in response, as reported in 1926, to

> instructions [which] were lately issued by the Lord Advocate that all cases of indecent assault on children involving indecency, or of indecent practices towards children, other than charges involving indecent exposure of the person, should be tried at either Sheriff Court or in the High Court.[107]

This action by the Lord Advocate could have affected the HCJ caseload from 1925 onwards, but figures did not sustain throughout the remainder of the decade, so either this instruction was quickly revoked or it did not have an impact on the number of LLPB cases appearing at HCJ.

Since ravish and LLPB required very similar non-penetrative evidence, reliance on ravish in favour of LLPB at a time when 'to ravish' was becoming an outmoded term may have been reduced. Certainly, the number of ravish cases did not recover their pre-1923 levels after 1925, although it is unlikely that this crime, mostly involving girls under sixteen, ceased. Equally, the number of cases including 'Criminal Law Amendment Act section 5' did not increase; CLAA was very rarely indicted without being combined with LLPB or rape.[108] Thus, the statutory charge had not replaced the common law non-penetrative indictments. However, where the evidence supported it, rape would always be the alternative. Thus, rape statistics would have been largely unaffected by the 1922 amendment. However, if LLPB were selected in preference to a rape indictment after 1922 where the panel's age was twenty-three years and under and the girl was approximately sixteen years, this might reduce the number of rape prosecutions while increasing LLPB cases.

In none of the cases heard during the 1920s, in which the panels and victims were close in age and might satisfy the criteria for the 1922 CLAA revision, was the 'young man's defence' requested or evidence provided for the PF and CC to consider it a reasonable defence. Glaister offers a possible explanation. Quoting Lord McLaren, he advised his students:

> It is not enough to establish this defence that from the appearance of the girl she might be believed to be above sixteen. No defence can be founded upon impressions formed from the appearance of the girl, if such a defence could be entertained, it would nullify the Statute altogether.

---

107 *Departmental Committee*, 18.
108 CLAA 1885 was more usually combined with LLPB and/or sodomy in cases involving underage same-sex assaults.

because a panel had only to say he thought a girl was over sixteen to reduce the charge or sentence. Glaister continued to tell his readership that it was a well-known fact to medics that girls between thirteen and sixteen 'might well be mistaken for a more advanced age', thus implying that men, possibly young men in particular, were being prosecuted on a matter of *legal* consent where possibly *actual* consent had been given by the girl.[109] Thus, the 1922 CLAA revision appears to have acknowledged the 'mistakes' young men could make, even if it appears not to have been used or prosecuted. Thus, the HCJ cases suggest that the indictment chosen by the PF and CC best described the alleged events.

Further, it must be emphasized that of 294 victims of LLPB, 290 were under sixteen years of whom 252 were under thirteen years and therefore panels were sufficiently distant in age from that of their very young victims. There would have been no possibility of using 'the young man's defence' in these cases. The victims' youth would also preclude an argument that broken promises or attempts to cover premarital pregnancies caused the increased in LLPB cases. The permissible age of marriage was raised to sixteen in 1929, which might have resulted in a greater number of LLPB and 'social rape' cases from girls no longer able to disguise a pregnancy with marriage. However, this legal change not only came in four years after the peak in LLPB prosecutions, but victims of LLPB were insufficiently close to marriageable age to affect the data.

The increase in the age of consent for indecent assault may have captured more cases under an LLPB indictment at the HCJ, when previously indecent assault had been heard at the sheriff court. However, if this were the cause of the unusually high number of LLPB cases heard in 1925, the increase would be expected to have remained high for the remainder of the decade because the age of consent was not reduced thereafter. Thus, the sudden increase in 1925 in LLPB cases may simply be a genuine increase for that year only, a phenomenon not influenced by individual PF and CC decisions, judicial instructions or statutory revisions. However, the HCJ records clearly show a preponderance of sexual crimes prosecuted in the Glasgow Assizes, which will be explored in the Conclusion.

* * *

---

109 Glaister, *Medical Jurisprudence*, 481.

Conclusion

The HCJ prosecuted cases suggest that some working-class complainers felt able to approach the police for help when they or their daughters had experienced sexual assault and that they did so immediately after discovery of the crime. The records reveal that often the PF proceeded on the evidence frequently against CC and forensic opinion. Even when the victim was very young and offered questionable testimony, the number of cases heard as rape rather than a more winnable lower indictment suggests that the quality of evidence guided the choice of indictment. The number of not guilty pleas suggests that panels either did not consider themselves guilty or they anticipated that the male-dominated judicial system would favour them. Frustratingly, without the memoirs of the regional PFs, the panels' statements or a wider selection of testimony from working-class victims who declined to report sexual violence, analysis drawn from the HCJ records may only be representative of the individuals and behaviours that succeeded to court. Here societal attitudes towards sexual violence offenders and complainers played out in jury verdicts.

7

Behind closed doors
Judicial processes

Much debate surrounds the question whether the law reacts to social pressures, such as by listening to the public mood on issues regarding criminal sentencing, or if society is influenced by judicial developments, thus the public complies with changes in, for example, age of consent legislation. However, once a criminal prosecution reaches court, what ensues is a combination of both social and judicial responses: the jury represents the people and their perceptions of crime, criminals and victims; the prosecutor is tasked with prosecuting the case while the judge interprets the law for the jury and ensures it is adhered to. What happens in court, particularly in the most vicious crimes, attracts public and media interest keen to participate vicariously in the salacity and spectacle. However, in the 1920s in Scotland, sexual violence prosecutions were heard 'behind closed doors'. Neither public nor journalists were allowed to attend and detailed newspaper reportage was extremely rare; the rape and murder of a Greenock nurse was an exception which warranted four days' coverage and concentrated mostly on the murder details.[1] Thus, cases such as the rape of a 25-year-old servant in Glasgow by three assailants were not reported.[2] The assailants in this case fitted the 'rape myth' that sexual violence on the streets was committed by strangers. If any case might be expected to allow reporters, it would be trials such as this one, but it did not warrant even a listing in the day's newspaper court reports.

Understandably, cases involving child complainers were afforded special protection. After the 1908 Children Act, their cases were heard at a different time from others and those allowed to attend were limited to 'members and other officers of the Court, and the parties to, and other persons directly

---

1 *Glasgow Herald*, 19–22 October 1926.
2 AD15/25/55.

concerned in the case'; this excluded the public.³ The exclusion of newspaper reporters became a bone of contention. In England, the famous judge Mr Justice McCardie argued that 'the publicity of proceedings was an essential element in their usefulness' because publicity was a warning to the reading public of the personal consequences of child sexual abuse as well as raising awareness of a crime many found too distasteful to contemplate.⁴ However, in Scotland, it was felt journalists should not be admitted when the evidence was of 'such a character that its publication is undesirable in the public interest'.⁵ Despite a provision in the Criminal Law Amendment Act 1922 (CLAA) for newspaper reporters to be allowed to attend, reporting on sexual violence prosecutions was in the gift of the presiding judge and few relented during the interwar years.⁶ Invariably the High Court of Justiciary (HCJ) Minute Books record judges' directions for cases to be heard *in camera* whether they involved children or adult women. Thus, the narrative of sexual violence trials is limited to the court proceedings noted in the Minute Books and Books of Adjournal, combined with a detailed examination of jury composition, their verdicts and sentencing patterns. This analysis is essential to understand how the law worked alongside elite perceptions of sexual violence perpetrators; their personal reactions to the alleged victims of incest, rape and lewd and libidinous practices and behaviour (LLPB); the juries' credibility of the evidence; and, ultimately, how the judicial authorities responded to the verdict of 'fifteen men [and women] good and true'.⁷

The new portias

A Scottish jury comprised fifteen men until the Sex Disqualification (Removal) Act 1919, after which some women were eligible for jury duty. Before and

---

3   *Scots Law Times*, 23 May 1908, 15.
4   A. Lentin, *Mr Justice McCardie 1869-1930* (Newcastle-upon-Tyne, 2016), 40.
5   *Scots Law Times*, 23 May 1908, 15. Kim Stevenson's research reveals that in England reporting of child sexual abuse was 'episodic and fatalistic' as 'an inevitable feature of society', while reporting incest was prohibited; K. Stevenson, '"These are cases which it is inadvisable to drag into the light of day": Disinterring the Crime of Incest in Early Twentieth-Century England', *Crime, History and Societies*, 20, no. 2 (2016): 2.
6   M. A. Crowther and B. White, *On Soul and Conscience: The Medical Expert and Crime, 150 Years of Forensic Medicine in Glasgow* (Aberdeen, 1988), 51; they also argue that this absence in news reportage creates the impression that sexual violence only became an issue in the late twentieth century once reporters were allowed in court.
7   By tradition, the division of a Scottish jury's fifteen-man verdict was not disclosed. With three verdicts possible in Scots Law, if the divisions were close, it could provoke long debates (and from 1926 potential appeals); C. Gane, 'The Scottish Jury', *Revue international de droit penal*, 72, no. 1 (2001): 266.

after the Act, male jurors' occupations ranged widely from hotel-keeper to hatter, farmer or slater and coal merchant.[8] Women jurors' marital status was described in the court records by the use of 'Miss' or 'Mrs', a titular feature not used for male jurors, and after 1924, court officials began recording female occupations such as teacher, musician, baker or artist. Throughout the decade, the HCJ records reveal that no female jurors were employed in unskilled occupations. The first female Scottish jurors appeared in sexual violence trials from early 1921, although women did not form a majority jury in rape cases until 1922, with a jury division of eight to seven.[9] In 1923, where juries were listed, majority female juries sat on 25 per cent of rape cases which increased to 66 per cent in 1925. Further female majority juries appeared once in both 1928 and 1930. Women formed a majority of eight to seven in incest indictments slightly earlier with a case in 1921 involving a fourteen-year-old girl and her stepfather.[10]

Women appeared on juries later in Scotland than in England and Wales, although they appear not to have experienced the levels of prejudice women reportedly faced there.[11] Peremptory challenge, judicial orders for single sex juries and persuading women to excuse themselves were frequent tactics employed to remove women from English courts.[12] Contemporary observer Robert Graves described similar behaviour when 'a judge would cough warningly' to alert a female juror to his disinclination towards her continued presence.[13] However, it appears that in Scotland, women were more readily assimilated into the judicial process and such discouragements are not noted in the Minute Books, except in two cases in which defence counsel requested an all-male jury. These both occurred at the Inverness Assize on 7 February and 29 March 1921, and both cases appeared before Lord MacKenzie. The first involved an Italian national aged forty, accused of the rape of four girls aged nine to thirteen, and the second concerned a twelve-year-old girl raped by a twenty-year-old motor driver. Lord MacKenzie refused both requests. The eventual juries' gender divisions are not

---

8   JC11/118 and JC13/136.
9   JC14/36.
10 AD15/21/106, JC13/133; majority not proven; assoilzied and dismissed.
11 S. Anwar, P. Bayer and R. Hjalmarsson, 'A Jury of Her Peers: The Impact of the First Female Jurors on Criminal Convictions', *National Bureau of Economic Research Working Paper* No.21960 (2016), 15.
12 For full analysis of women on English juries see K. Crosby, 'Keeping Women Off the Jury in 1920s England and Wales', *Legal Studies*, 37, issue 4 (2017): 1–23.
13 R. Graves and A. Hodges, *The Long Weekend: A Social History of Great Britain 1918-1939* (London, 1995), 46.

recorded.[14] It is possible that defence counsel requested an all-male jury in the hope of a sympathetic judge not yet accustomed to women jurors. However, the refusal of both requests by the same judge suggests Lord MacKenzie's lack of sympathy, and the absence of further requests for all-male juries from any circuit indicates they were a ploy rapidly abandoned. Similarly, peremptory challenges are not evident in the HCJ records.[15]

Also, women jurors do not appear to have declined to serve on sexual violence cases, which in England provided an excuse to summon fewer women because they might be selective about the cases they would attend.[16] The Scottish lists of assizes included many women called for jury service across the country, and only the arbitrary balloting system of pulling names from a hat disallowed them from serving. It is impossible to ascertain from the HCJ records if women were actively welcomed onto Scottish juries, but evidently, the jury experience in Scotland differed from its English counterpart. However, throughout the 1920s, fewer Scottish women served than men as evidenced by the gender composition of juries. This is attributable to probability: with fewer women eligible to serve, an all-female or majority female jury was less likely.[17] Equally, a single all-male jury in 1922 may also be the chance result of the ballot. In this case, there was no defence counsel request recorded for an all-male jury and the details were not especially distasteful compared to others on which women sat.[18] Whereas all-male juries persisted throughout the 1920s in sodomy trials, suggesting that judicial sensitivities existed for homosexual prosecutions.

The 1919 Act also permitted women to stand as Members of Parliament. Being in political office allowed women to focus on and promote family issues and welfare.[19] Consequently, their potential as jurors on cases involving sexual abuse of children was realized.[20] It was assumed their experience as mothers, wives and carers would affect their verdict. The HCJ records suggest otherwise.

---

14 AD15/21/163, JC11/118; unanimously guilty, two years' penal servitude; AD15/21/162, JC11/118; unanimously not proven.
15 Mr Justice McCardie 'expressed his disapproval of such misuse of the right of challenge and called for it to be ended' having witnessed three women jurors replaced seemingly on defence counsel's prejudice; Lentin, *McCardie*, 78.
16 Crosby, 'Keeping Women Off', 17.
17 Crosby, 'Keeping Women Off', 13.
18 AD15/22/58, JC131/134; group rape by three men of twenty-year-old domestic servant; unanimously guilty, three years' penal servitude.
19 A. Bingham, L. Delap, L. A. Jackson and L. Settle, 'Historical Child Sexual Abuse in England and Wales: The Role of Historians', *History of Education*, 45, no. 4 (2006): 413.
20 Crosby, 'Keeping Women Off', 6.

Jury debates

Without newspaper reports of a judge's summing-up or trial transcripts in appeal cases, the judge's directions on points of law or his personal evaluation of a case are unavailable.[21] Since judicial direction must have taken place, it is reasonable to assume that, as prisons commissioner Norwood East explained, 'the disputants address themselves to facts related to similar experience in the lives of their fellows'.[22] Thus, jurors relied on personal experience to inform their debate and decisions. However, in sexual violence cases, most jurors probably had little to support their discussions except moral abhorrence, potentially further influenced by class biases.

Female jurors were present on almost all HCJ sexual violence cases from 1921, which refutes the notion that female complainers were not judged from a female perspective but from a man's.[23] An alleged victim's evidence and her 'performance' in court were not judged solely from a male standpoint, despite the possible class differences between female jurors and complainers. However, the courtroom scrutiny of a sexual violence victim probably surpassed that of any other complainer of other crimes, whereas the presumption of an accused's innocence applies in any criminal case, although in sexual violence trials, societal damage to the perpetrator's reputation accompanied any conviction.[24] Even if defence counsel relied on the collusion of men on the jury to see the complainer as culpable in some respect, this was balanced by the presence of women jurors, whose sympathies would have been solicited by prosecution counsel.

Research conducted on sexual crime in Victorian England revealed that crimes not involving brutal violence perpetrated by a stranger would be assumed to be a matter of seduction and both parties might be to blame.[25] However, analysis of jury composition and verdict in HCJ sexual violence cases in the 1920s suggests that the evidence was tried impartially, without gender or class biases. Contemporary legal researchers confirmed that Scots Law operated

---

21 J. Bourke, 'Police Surgeons and Victims of Rape: Cultures of Harm and Care', *Social History of Medicine*, 31, no. 4 (2018): 720.
22 W. Norwood East, 'Sexual Offenders – A British View', *The Yale Law Journal*, 55, no. 3 (April 1946): 529.
23 E. Stanko, *Intimate Intrusions: Women's Experience of Male Violence* (London, 1985), 92.
24 Stanko, *Intimate Intrusions*, 84.
25 C. Conley, 'Rape and Justice in Victorian England', *Victorian Studies*, 29, no. 4 (Summer 1986): 536.

under a system of proof evaluation.[26] A Scottish criminal trial was 'not a contest between opposing counsel' but a thorough investigation of the truth of the facts, which had been collected as close in time to the actual crime by experienced officials, with no new threads of enquiry permitted.[27]

Verdicts – incest

Of 108 incest cases, 45 per cent of offenders pleaded guilty, thus not requiring a jury; 36 per cent of cases returned a conviction, including three disposed of on a plea of insanity, and 18 per cent of jury-heard cases were acquitted, including not proven verdicts. There is no noticeable trend connecting an incest guilty plea to age, number of victims or duration over which assaults were perpetrated. For example, in 1924, panels pleaded guilty to incest with two 21-year-old nieces; daughters aged 6, 11, 19 and 36; and a stepdaughter aged 14.[28]

In incest cases when panels pleaded not guilty, thus requiring a jury to sit, the records suggest that including women on the jury did not result consistently in verdicts aligning with their perceived maternal inclinations. In 1921, of twelve incest cases, seven pleaded guilty. Of the remaining five cases, the jury is recorded in three. One was a female majority jury of eight to seven for which the verdict was a majority not proven; one was a jury division of six women to nine men returning a verdict of unanimously not proven; and the last was a jury division of five to ten men with a verdict of unanimously guilty.[29] For all three cases, the medical evidence recorded the girls' hymens were absent or perforated, and all doctors were of the opinion that 'considerable' intercourse had occurred. The victims were daughters and stepdaughters, ranging in age from thirteen to twenty years. The not proven verdicts were returned for the cases including stepdaughters only, which might reflect the jury's attitude towards incest with a non-blood daughter being a lesser crime, until records for another year are examined (Figure 7.1).

In 1927, of seven cases, one pleaded insanity and six were heard by a jury, returning three guilty and three not proven verdicts. The guilty verdicts were

---

26 M. Damaska, 'Criminal Procedure in Scotland and France', *Yale Law School Faculty Scholarship Series*, 1588 (1976): 782.
27 E. R. Keedy, 'Criminal Procedure in Scotland II', *Journal of the American Institute for Criminal Law and Criminology*, 3, no. 6 (1913): 839; R. S. Shiels, 'The Mid-Victorian Codification of the Practice of Public Prosecution', *The Scottish Historical Review*, 98, supplement 248 (October 2019): 436.
28 AD15/24/64, AD15/24/33, AD15/24/79, AD15/25/15, AD15/24/52, AD15/24/8 and AD15/24/12.
29 AD15/21/85, JC13/133; AD15/21/164, JC11/118; and AD15/21/176, JC11/119.

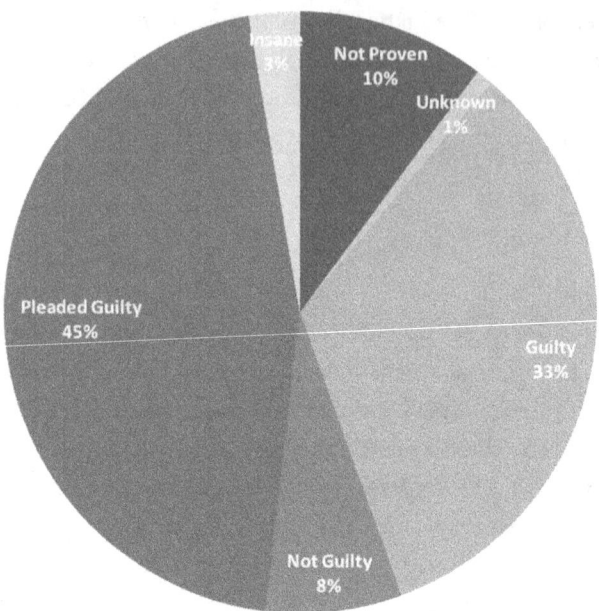

Figure 7.1 Incest verdicts: All age groups.

decided by two majority female juries and one with a division of six women to nine men, in cases involving a daughter, stepdaughter and a consensual niece. The not proven verdicts returned by majority male juries were for cases involving daughters aged fourteen and seventeen and a stepdaughter aged seventeen.[30] There does not appear to be any bias towards stepdaughters in this year, which is further emphasized by two not proven verdicts given in 1928, both of which included blood daughters under sixteen years.[31] Also, there appears to be no correlation between low numbers of women on juries and not guilty verdicts, where overly persuasive male jurors may have held sway. For instance, in 1925 a jury of four women to eleven men heard a case involving a 30-year-old panel accused of incest with his 71-year-old mother. Despite a lack of medical reports and the mother's alcoholic stupor at the time of the incident, the majority male jury returned a unanimously guilty verdict.[32] Further, two cases in 1928 with juries comprising three women to twelve men returned very different verdicts. In

---

30 AD15/27/51, JC14/39; because the alleged incest had occurred without witnesses, the jury may have decided on the lesser alternative indictment offered of indecent assault against this man's fourteen-year-old daughter, twelve months' imprisonment; AD15/27/54, JC14/39; and AD15/27/88, JC14/39.
31 AD15/28/24, JC5/18; and AD15/28/100, JC15/39.
32 AD15/25/45, JC13/136; three years' penal servitude.

one case, a sixteen-year-old aunt had been made pregnant by her eighteen-year-old nephew. The case was consensual, but the jury returned a unanimously guilty verdict.[33] In the second case, a 33-year-old brother was alleged to have made his 39-year-old sister pregnant; the jury found him unanimously not guilty.[34] Male jurors do not appear to have imposed possible previous judicial experience or their masculine 'superior' knowledge on women new to jury service, and the range of outcomes suggests a rigorous and detailed debate behind closed doors. For example, in Aberdeen in 1925, a fifty-year-old marine engineer was accused of incest with daughters aged twenty-four, eighteen, seventeen and thirteen. Of seven charges against the panel, the jury returned majority guilty verdicts on four and found the remaining three not proven, demonstrating that they were unconvinced by the two youngest daughters' evidence, despite its corroboration of their elder siblings' statements.[35]

In a 1927 case involving a fourteen-year-old girl indicted as 'incest or indecent assault', the jury of four women and eleven men returned a verdict which is open to interpretation. The girl had suffered her father's molestation since she was seven; it had previously remained at the 'interfering' stage but had escalated to rape on seven or eight occasions in the past year. The examining physician confirmed his findings as 'consistent with frequent penetration'. By a majority, the jury found incest not proven preferring instead the charge of indecent assault, which only indicted the panel as having 'place[d] your private member in contact with her private parts'.[36] The jury had decided the evidence did not support the charge of incest but was sufficient to prove beyond reasonable doubt the second non-penetrative charge, a crime much more difficult to prove. This appears illogical considering the doctor's confirmation of penetration. Therefore, was the jury using their voice to prevent an escalation of sexual violence in this home while also removing the stigma of an incest conviction from the family's reputation? It is possible that wishing to avoid further damage to a family's cohesion, juries might employ a strategic verdict. However, familial humiliation required no such judicial consideration in rape cases where families and adult women bringing a rape charge may have already jettisoned their reputations in return for seeking legal redress.

33 AD15/28/102, JC12/56; four months' imprisonment.
34 AD15/28/51, JC14/40.
35 JC26/1925/105, JC15/36; seven years' penal servitude.
36 AD15/27/51, JC14/39; twelve months' imprisonment.

Verdict – all rapes

Analysis of rape trials at England's Old Bailey between 1921 and 1926 revealed that only 56 per cent of juries included one female (on average 1.6 women per twelve-person jury), which dropped to 27 per cent when broadened to include all sexual offence indictments.[37] For the same period in Scotland and where records of jury divisions are available, except one case in 1922 with three women jurors, in all other cases no fewer than four women served on rape juries, which is significantly different from the English experience. As the decade progressed, the minimum number of women per jury increased, regularly exceeding six individuals. However, the impact of significant numbers of women serving appears not to be reflected in a greater number of guilty verdicts. Of all rape charges for all victim age groups, after guilty pleas are removed, 63 per cent of the remaining jury-heard cases resulted in a conviction (49 per cent if guilty pleas are included), and there is no evidence in the early years of the decade when all-male juries sat that these years returned fewer guilty verdicts suggesting some male sympathy for the panel.[38] However, in jury-heard cases involving minors, the percentage of convictions increased significantly and may reveal jury sympathies towards this age group.

Verdict – rape of minors

Research conducted on the late Victorian Middlesex Assizes reveals that the younger the victim, the greater the likelihood of a conviction, particularly when the child was aged under nine years, whereas unlawful sexual violence against girls in the contentious age group of thirteen to fifteen years was the least likely to win a conviction (Figure 7.2).[39]

In Scotland, in all-age minor jury-heard rape cases, 77 per cent resulted in some level of conviction, either as indicted or on a lesser sexual violence charge. For children under nine years, 78 per cent of cases resulted in a conviction, with cases involving girls aged nine to sixteen years having a 75 per cent conviction

---

37 Anwar, Bayer and Hjalmarsson, 'Jury of Her Peers', 16.
38 Conley calculated that the conviction rate for rape in Victorian England was 40 per cent. However, it is unclear whether this figure included guilty pleas or was based solely on jury-heard rape cases; Conley, 'Rape and Justice', 521.
39 L. A. Jackson, *Child Sexual Abuse in Victorian England* (London, 2000), 91; L. Jackson, 'Child Sexual Abuse in England and Wales: Prosecution and Prevalence 1918-1970', *Policy Papers*, 7, http://www.historyandpolicy.org/policy-papers/rss_2.0, accessed October 2022.

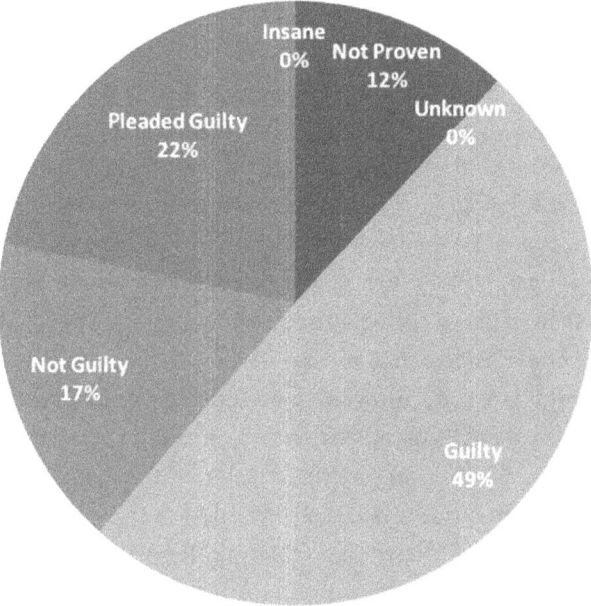

Figure 7.2 Rape verdicts: All age groups including adult females.

rate.[40] This marginal difference between the two age groups differs from the English records. However, the evidence reveals that sexual crimes perpetrated against children were much likelier to result in a conviction than for all-age (including adult female) rapes: 77 per cent compared with 63 per cent. Despite difficulties experienced in collecting corroborated evidence from the youngest girls, and the inconsistency and unreliability of medical and forensic reports, prosecuting a sexual violence charge involving a minor in 1920s Scotland appears to have had a high probability of success.

In Scots Law, because a conviction could not be secured on the evidence of a child accuser alone, consequently Scottish juries hearing child sexual violence cases understood that the evidence presented was corroborated, even if it were deficient in adult eyewitness statements, and that in testing the child's testimony in court, any sexual precocity on her part was evaluated.[41] Thus, in rape cases, the probability of conviction was in excess of the chances of success in incest cases (63 per cent of all-age rapes compared with 36 per cent of all incest cases).

Frustratingly, the HCJ records do not contain the definitive explanation for this difference in success rates for two sexual violence crimes committed

---

40 These figures do not include cases where the panel pleaded guilty.
41 L. A. Jackson, 'The Child's Word in Court: Cases of Sexual Abuse in London 1870-1914', in *Gender and Crime in Modern Europe*, eds C. Usborne and M. Arnot (London, 2001), 224 and 226.

against girls under the age of consent. However, the evidence suggests several possibilities. Potentially, jurors were more reticent to convict in incest cases unless the evidence was watertight because they were reluctant to break up a family and add shame to an already difficult predicament. However, this would suppose jurors did not believe the girls' complaints or, if they did to some extent, that they were prepared to allow an abusive male relation to return to the home in the hope he would not re-offend – the impact of arrest and a prosecution being hopefully sufficient warning to him. Or were jurors disbelieving of the idea that incest was occurring in their midst? If the welfare officers investigating the living conditions of Scotland's poor failed to detect and report incest as evidenced by their absence from the HCJ records, could jurors be expected to understand the intra-familial abuse these girls suffered? Jurors' potential distrust of the evidence, their lack of sympathy with the girl physically presented to them, their possible empathy with the panel before them needs to be balanced against the possibility that jurors had no personal experience of incest; it was beyond their comprehension. Whereas non-familial sexual abuse of minors was more believable because it fitted societal 'rape myths' more readily: young girls were vulnerable to predatory males whether they were neighbours, local shopkeepers or complete strangers. Without other sources to explain jurors' decisions, the statistics alone suggest that non-familial rape of young girls was a more plausible crime on which to convict.

Verdict – rape of adult women

If it was difficult for Victorian men who populated the justice system to understand the enormity of rape as a crime, by the 1920s in Scotland, this difficulty had been partly resolved with women serving on juries, although not yet acting as counsel.[42] Female jurors relied on male defence and prosecution lawyers to construct the evidence, the participants' 'characters' and their conclusions. However, the verdicts returned for rape of adult women do not suggest significant male influence once the jury retired. Research on Victorian rape prosecutions concluded that 81 per cent of rape cases involving men with a higher status than labourer or soldier were indicted as attempt to rape or indecent assault and not rape.[43] By comparison, the Scottish HCJ rape records reveal that the majority of panels fulfilled an occupational status above labourer and a concomitant number

---

42 Conley, 'Rape and Justice', 532.
43 Conley, 'Rape and Justice', 523.

of lesser indictments was not used to indict panels with better occupational and social status. In fact, such lower indictments were rarely singly cited; if assault of an adult female had a sexual component it was usually indicted in combination with rape while the majority of cases charged as simple 'assault' were seemingly exactly that. Therefore, the HCJ records suggest that Scottish prosecutors did not allow a panel's status to influence their indictment decisions.

However, the received opinion was, and remains, that the bar was set much higher for women complaining of sexual violence, with rape of adult females the least likely sexual crime not only to secure a conviction but also to be prosecuted in the first place.[44] Then, and now, rape cases relied on establishing consent: had the victim consented? Had her assailant acknowledged her lack of consent or was he oblivious to her non-participation?[45] The legal concept of *mens rea* (Latin: guilty mind) was crucial to understanding whether the assailant had believed he was committing rape at the time of the assault. In a murder case, *mens rea* requires the prosecution to establish that there was intent to kill or at least a reckless indifference to the outcome of interpersonal violence. In rape terms, this translates as intent to have sex without regard for the woman's consent or consequences. Thus, defence counsel endeavoured to prove that 'a man who acts on an unreasonable belief in consent will not believe that he has committed rape, [while] a woman who is subjected to the act of sexual intercourse without her consent will believe that she has been raped'.[46] The obverse is *actus reus*: the prosecution must establish that consent was, and is, absent.[47] Essentially, if the panel was confused about his 'partner's' consent and this could be proved in court, he could be acquitted.[48]

From the HCJ jury returns of guilty – either unanimously, by majority or on a lesser charge – the panel's 'guilty mind' at the time of the crime had been established in court because 50 per cent of adult female rape cases secured a conviction. However, this percentage reveals that adult females were less successful in obtaining guilty verdicts than minor victims of rape. As adult women, they were less likely to be virginal; as working-class women their testimony did

---

44 Jackson, 'Child Sexual Abuse', 7; L. Olsson, '"Violence that's wicked for a man to use": Sex, Gender and Violence in the Eighteenth Century', in *Interpreting Sexual Violence, 1660-1800*, ed A. Greenfield (Abingdon, 2016), 141.
45 Jackson, 'Child Sexual Abuse', 7.
46 G. H. Gordon, 'Criminal Responsibility in Scots Law', unpublished PhD thesis (University of Glasgow, 1959), 270; D. F. Alexander, 'Twenty Years of *Morgan*: Criticism of the Subjectivist View of *Mens Rea* and Rape in Great Britain', *Pace International Law Review*, 7 (1995): 233.
47 H. Bows and J. Herring, 'Getting Away with Murder? A Review of the "Rough Sex Defence"', *Journal of Criminal Law*, 84, no. 6 (2020): 528.
48 A. McColgan, 'Common Law and the Relevance of Sexual History Evidence', *Oxford Journal of Legal Studies*, 16, no. 2 (1996): 292.

not have the same credibility and any previous sexual history, especially if it had resulted in illegitimate pregnancy, detracted from their case.[49] Without court transcripts or juries' notes, it is impossible to understand jury discourse concerning an adult woman's previous sexual experience or whether courting activities or marital status actively influenced the juries' verdicts. However, in the sole case of a prostitute bringing a rape charge against two panels, the jury of four women and eleven men returned a unanimously guilty verdict. The victim had sustained 'bruises to her face and thighs', although there was no evidence 'of ill-usage to her genitals', but she had convinced the jury of her two assailants' guilt and her non-consent when confronted with overwhelming evidence of her 'immoral' occupation; she had, however, had a civilian witness.[50] Research on rape in nineteenth-century England suggests that the conviction rate was reduced to 10 per cent if a complainer was a prostitute or drunkard, and more recent research reveals that unless a prostitute sustained terrible injuries during her ordeal, the immorality of her profession was likely to outweigh evidence of rape.[51] This Scottish woman may be an anomaly in the records, but her case suggests that in 1920s Scotland it was possible for a prostitute to appeal to a jury who employed the same set of values used for more socially acceptable females.

Verdict – social rapes

The same nineteenth-century research discovered that consent was assumed by judges and juries if the panel and complainer were acquainted.[52] The general absence of acquaintance rape cases prosecuted in Scotland between 1885 and 1910 suggests that Procurators Fiscal (PFs) may have decided consent was established before a case could proceed, if any cases were presented. However, a few decades later, the number of social rape cases that reached court suggests the situation had improved. In the ten HCJ cases where the perpetrator and victim had socialized, the juries' returns were: six acquitted, one found guilty of a lesser charge and three found guilty: a 40 per cent conviction rate. Of the three guilty-as-indicted verdicts, two have a listed jury. The first was a minority female jury with a division of five to ten; the second was a majority female jury divided

49 J. Bourke, *Rape: A History from 1860 to the Present* (London, 2010), 80 and 9; McColgan, 'Sexual History Evidence', 277–81.
50 AD15/22/73, JC14/36; seven years' penal servitude.
51 Conley, 'Rape and Justice', 531; Stanko, *Intimate Intrusions*, 93.
52 Conley, 'Rape and Justice', 524.

eight to seven. Both cases returned a unanimously guilty verdict suggesting that jury composition did not necessarily have an impact on outcome.[53] Similarly, in the acquitted cases, the verdict was unanimous irrespective of jury composition. Thus, anticipated feminine sympathies and male prejudices are not evident in the prosecuted social rape cases; and establishment of consent and non-consent appears to have been evaluated on the evidence rather than the degree of relationship between panel and complainer.

Verdict – rape of older women

There are only three rape cases involving victims over sixty years. In one, the panel pleaded guilty and in the other two, juries of six women to nine men both returned unanimously not proven verdicts. These verdicts implied not only that the evidence was insufficiently compelling to convict but also a margin of doubt may have remained over the actual occurrence of the crimes.[54] These verdicts may also suggest the juries' possible lack of empathy with an elderly woman; she was beyond emotional harm and reputational damage.

Verdict – group rapes

In group rape cases, it was the complainer's word from first reporting to the police office to an appearance in court against the evidence of two or more panels, often with no eyewitnesses. The fact that of sixteen cases of group rape, none pleaded guilty indicates that the panels anticipated corroboration of one another's evidence would be a sufficient defence. Four cases were acquitted including two not proven verdicts.[55] Twelve cases were found guilty including three returns on a lesser charge: two of indecent assault when the charge had been the single indictment of rape and one convicting the lead panel as charged and his accomplice with intent to ravish (not on the original charge sheet).[56] Thus 75 per cent of group rape trials returned guilty verdicts, all of which were unanimous decisions. There is no correlation between the age of the victim

---

53 AD15/21/192, JC12/55; AD15/23/79, JC11/119.
54 AD15/21/175A, JC11/119; AD15/27/92, JC11/120.
55 AD15/19/85, JC13/132 and AD15/21/183, JC11/119; unanimous verdicts. AD15/20/34, JC5/14 and AD15/21/75, JC13/133 majority verdicts.
56 AD15/23/76, JC11/119; AD15/24/42, JC15/35; and JC26/1929/34, JC15/40, respectively.

and verdict which might suggest greater sympathy for younger group rape victims. Clearly, in the majority of group rape cases, the complainer's evidence was sufficiently well-corroborated and the girls' stories satisfactorily credible irrespective of the panels' version of events. As the PF wrote in a 1922 group rape by two men against an underweight sixteen-year-old girl: 'she is little more than a child, to behave as the defence suggests, she must either have been a depraved woman or a mental defective'.[57]

Verdict – forensic influence

In the late Victorian period when forensic medicine was a nascent discipline, legal counsel and medical experts often engaged in professional conflict in court.[58] By the 1920s, despite forensic physicians' evidence remaining inconclusive due to the limitations of the scientific methods available, the opinions of expert witnesses such as Professor Glaister could be accepted as definitive, and yet even he acknowledged the inconsistent relationship between rape and injury:

> It is easy to conceive the possibility of the legal commission of the crime [rape] without any physical evidence whatever being found on the body of the female to justify a medical examiner in doing more than reporting the negative facts.[59]

Thus, not everyone was convinced of the validity of the new forensics, including sitting jurors, and conversely, forensic physicians could be frustrated by the legal process's lack of understanding and reticence towards their scientific 'evidence'. In 41 out of 101 rape cases 'definitive' forensic and medical opinions of partial or complete penetration were given, but in only 50 per cent of these cases was a guilty verdict returned, with a further 22 per cent of cases resulting in a lesser charge. Thus, medical expert witness opinion was not necessarily the defining detail on which juries relied to convict.

Insanity defences further illustrate the competition for authority between legal and medical experts and the jury. The HCJ records offer ten cases where the panel entered, or attempted to enter, an insanity plea, which was accepted by the PF and proceeded to the HCJ. These include one rape-homicide case, three incest cases, two cases of ravishment and four trials for LLPB. All cases were tried after 1925, except one of ravishment in which the panel was a repeat offender

---

57 AD15/22/91, JC122/55.
58 R. Smith, *Trial by Medicine: Insanity and Responsibility in Victorian Trials* (Edinburgh, 1981), 90.
59 J. Glaister, *A Text-Book of Medical Jurisprudence and Toxicology* (Edinburgh, 1915), 482.

having indecently assaulted a nine-year-old in 1916. His trial in 1919 was for a similar offence.⁶⁰ If tendered prior to 1925, it appears that PFs were not inclined to accept insanity pleas which may illustrate a delay in the acceptance of forensic and psychological medical opinions. However, after 1925, the panel's insanity was only disallowed in one case: a rape homicide involving a male attendant at a Greenock mental hospital in 1926 accused of raping and murdering a nurse. In this case, possibly the jury had not believed defence counsel's argument that the panel had not been responsible for his actions at the time of the crime or their verdict of guilty on the lesser charge of rape with culpable homicide indicated their reluctance to convict on a murder charge for which they knew the sentence would be capital punishment.⁶¹

Of the incest cases, the medical reports include such details as 'he is simple, childish and [has] a peculiar look in his eyes typical for a state of dementia' as well as 'emotionally unstable' and 'pleads ignorance of his behaviour'.⁶² These diagnoses conform with contemporary ideas of congenital mental illness and inability to function normally in society.⁶³ However, one 1927 case mentioned: 'since he came back from the Army, we have had a very unhappy time in the house. He has been very quarrelsome and even violent'. A work colleague remarked that the panel had been making mistakes at work for nearly seven years. What no one connected was this now 51-year-old's war service and possible untreated war neurosis.⁶⁴ Except the rape-homicide case, all panels after 1925 who entered an insanity plea were accepted and detained at 'His Majesty's Pleasure'.

Interestingly, in the sampled years from 1885 to 1905, no panels indicted for rape or incest were incarcerated at 'Her/His Majesty's Pleasure', and in 1910 there were no insanity pleas entered in bar of trial, which suggests a potential medical and legal indifference towards mental illness as mitigation for sexual violence in the lead-up to the war or that the genuinely seriously mentally disturbed were already incarcerated and not at liberty to commit crime.⁶⁵ The absence of insanity pleas in the immediate post-war years may be a continuation of this pre-war trend with shell-shock and other war injuries either disregarded by PFs and Advocates Depute (AD) or already receiving treatment in an asylum. This may also explain the equal absence of attempts by defence counsel to tender insanity pleas in the first half of the 1920s. However, by the latter half of the

60   JC26/1919/7; at HM Pleasure.
61   AD15/26/81, JC15/37; fifteen years' penal servitude.
62   AD15/30/52, JC13/138 and AD15/29/39, JC13/138; both at HM Pleasure.
63   Smith, *Trial by Medicine*, 116.
64   AD15/27/47, JC26/1927/88; at HM Pleasure.
65   Smith, *Trial by Medicine*, 90.

decade, it might have been considered that anyone committing crimes provoked by war neurosis would have perpetrated them earlier and thus the small number of insanity pleas after 1925 suggests a reluctance to accept mental aberration as mitigation.

Verdict – ethnicity

The English judge McCardie declared that 'it matters not in what realm a man has been born. . . . The moment he sets foot on British soil, he falls within the King's peace . . . and shall be protected by the ordinary rules of British justice'.[66] Despite the law's declared blindness to ethnicity, it did not prevent societal prejudice in all social classes from which the elites operating the legal system were unlikely to be immune.[67] There are very few clearly identifiable Irish families in any of the sexual violence indictments surveyed, although Italian, French and German cases are recognizable.

It has been estimated that 10 per cent of the Scottish population was Irish-born, with 70 per cent concentrated in the west's industrial and urban centres.[68] On her journalistic tour of Scotland in 1936, Cicely Hamilton stated: 'Clydeside has an Irish population of something like six hundred thousand . . . considerably more than a tenth of the total population of Scotland' and that 'the Irish population of Glasgow and its neighbourhood' accounted for 'more than its due proportion of crime'.[69] Her correlation between Irish ethnicity and crime was supported by her contemporary George Pryde, whose research revealed that 'slightly more than one-quarter of the prisoners and inmates in Borstal institutions were Roman Catholics' and since they only accounted for 'one-eighth of the population, the inference that their criminality is twice the normal rate is unavoidable'.[70] However, Pryde conflated Roman Catholics, Irish immigrants and Scots-Irish as a single body whom he viewed as non-Scots and ethnically criminal. Thus, his statistics do not correlate with modern surveys of 1920s criminality. A survey of nineteenth-century Scottish newspaper trial reports reveals that reports might only give the accused's nationality but no name, not out of regard for

---

66 Lentin, *McCardie*, 42.
67 Bourke, *Rape*, 294.
68 J. Darragh, 'The Catholic population of Scotland, 1878-1977', in *Modern Scottish Catholicism*, ed. D. McRoberts (Glasgow, 1979), 232, quoted in I. Maver, 'The Catholic Community', in *Scotland in the Twentieth Century*, eds T. M. Devine and R. J. Finlay (Edinburgh, 1996), 271.
69 C. Hamilton, *Modern Scotland* (London, 1937), 50–1.
70 G. S. Pryde, *Social Life in Scotland since 1707* (London, 1934), 29.

the man's reputation but to reinforce perceptions of criminal 'types'.[71] Despite the prevailing and pervasive prejudice against the ethnic Irish, the absence of pejorative comment on them in the HCJ case papers suggests ambivalence on the part of PFs and their colleagues or again a clear indication of the fairness of the Scottish legal system. A 1924 case illustrates the diversity of nationalities in Glasgow all of whom were considered reliable witnesses irrespective of ethnicity. A seventeen-year-old domestic servant accused two perpetrators with distinctively Irish surnames of rape. Non-eyewitness corroboration was provided by the girl's Polish landlady and a Russian émigré fish-shop owner, who saw the girl leave his shop with the two men.[72] This case illustrates that not only was corroboration sometimes tenuous, which may have affected the jury's verdict of indecent assault only, but that testimony from non-natives was sought despite prejudices towards their communities.

Glasgow was also home to the third largest community of Italians in Britain with approximately 3,000 living in the city.[73] The HCJ records include a single case of rape by an Italian, in which racial prejudice may be evident from the long list of previous convictions for everything from contravention of shop-closing hours to indictments under the Children's Act from 1911. This may have been harassment by Glasgow police, although the final indictment for LLPB, rape and CLAA sections 4 and 5 (1) against four girls under thirteen years, who he assaulted in his ice cream parlour, suggests real criminality rather than racism. The jury returned a unanimously guilty verdict on the non-penetrative charges, with the indictments for rape and unlawful carnal knowledge not proven.[74] A French national accused of the rape of a nine-year-old girl in Dumfries in 1923 pleaded guilty 'to dispose of the case quickly' and was recommended to deportation.[75] The AD's request to deport criminal foreign nationals may demonstrate *post judice* racism – a disinclination to incarcerate aliens at tax payers' expense and a desire to prevent repeat offences from an ethnic group perceived not to uphold 'Scottish values'. However, sentencing for ethnic groups did not exceed sentences imposed on Scottish nationals, implying that the law was not discriminatorily employed. However, two decades earlier in 1905, it would be too easy to suggest that a travelling-show horse groom, originally from Mafeking in South Africa,

---

71 D. Barrie, 'Naming and Shaming: Trial by Media in Nineteenth Century Scotland', *Journal of British Studies*, 54 (April 2015): 363.
72 AD15/24/46, JC15/35; three and six months' imprisonment.
73 T. Colpi, 'The Scottish Italian Community: senza un campanile?', *Innes Review*, 44, no. 2 (1993): 161.
74 AD15/21/163, JC11/118; two years' imprisonment, recommendation for deportation.
75 AD15/23/10, JC5/16; four years' penal servitude.

was the victim of an unduly severe capital sentence because of jury bias only five years after the famous Boer War siege.[76]

Jury responses and deliberation

Analysis of jury responses for rape shows that most verdicts were unanimously decided. It is impossible to ascertain if majority male juries persuaded female jurors to follow their decision or vice versa, because the juries' deliberations and gender divisions on verdicts were not recorded. Additionally, the duration of their deliberations was rarely noted except in a 1928 incest case where a unanimously guilty verdict was returned after twenty-three minutes, which is only known because the trial transcript has survived, and a group rape case with only twenty-five minutes' deliberation, which is known because the case went to appeal.[77] However, this degree of unanimity after jury deliberation suggests the lack of ambiguity in and the persuasiveness of the evidence presented. Unanimity might also suggest elite bias against working-class perpetrators and complainers, but the inclusion of males on the jury socially close in status to the accused would refute this. Admittedly, the unskilled were unrepresented, but skilled workers such as plumbers, warehousemen and joiners were present. Thus, the efficacy of the Scottish judicial system would appear robust: neither social background nor gender, with its perceived inherent sympathies, appears to have influenced a trial's outcome, except possibly in rape cases involving minors.

Jury returns appear to have relied on the facts of the case rather than the more pejorative details such as a complainer's previous sexual history or other 'character' traits deleterious to her case. Sometimes that factual evidence was considered so repulsive and disturbing that the judge excused the jury from further service for a period of time. This occurred in the case of the hospital attendant convicted of raping and killing a nurse and in a group rape by four men against an adult woman. In the latter case, Professor Glaister's report stated clearly the severity of the woman's injuries, the state of her clothing and that she 'broke down during the interview and wept bitterly'. All jury members were excused further service for four years.[78] This demonstrates again the equal treatment of both juror sexes, which differs from the English experience

---

76 AD15/05/112, JC26/1905/6; executed November 1905.
77 JC36/58; JC34/1/81 and JC34/1/82, respectively.
78 JC26/1928/103, JC15/39; seven years' penal servitude each.

in the 1920s when numbers of women jurors were declining because they had demurred to serve and court clerks were second-guessing judges' preferences for all-male juries.[79]

Judges' directions and opinions

Of the limited number of court transcripts to have survived, a few offer judges' directions to the jury and summings-up, revealing legal and social attitudes of members of the bench prosecuting sexual crimes. Three cases provide useful comment from the bench. In 1921, Lord Sands sitting in Glasgow on an incest trial involving two girls aged nine and five, assaulted by their father, summed up the case in damning terms of abhorrence with a historical punishment of burning alive. Having thus impressed the jury and panel, he continued to describe the panel's previous clean record, 'successful business' as a house painter, war service and wounds and the wife's 'very great matrimonial wrong'. Lord Sands explained that men of virtue also committed crime, and equally a wife could falsely or mistakenly accuse a husband, and lastly, that even partial or attempted penetration of a female family member would suffice for a conviction. He concluded that the evidence of little girls, possibly influenced by a disaffected mother, might not be as credible as hoped.[80] This summing-up demonstrates the careful direction given: firstly, to frame the crime in its historical context; secondly, to draw unbiased attention to the virtue of the accused and the complainer's possible causal influences; and lastly, the integrity of the evidence. Irrespective of the despicable nature of the alleged crime, the jury was directed to give a fair hearing regardless of any personal prejudices.

In a 1928 Glasgow group rape of an adult woman heard by Lord Moncrieff, his summing-up reflected the repercussions of the crime on the victim: 'the effect of it will tell upon the memory of outrage and shame which will accompany that young woman through life'. These comments and the sentence handed down conveyed his personal compassion; all four panels received seven-year penal servitude sentences.[81] In another group rape case in 1930 involving three men and a 23-year-old woman, Lord Hunter explained the concept of collective culpability ensuring that none of the panels escaped justice:

---

79   Crosby, 'Keeping Women Off', 17.
80   AD15/21/132, JC14/36; majority guilty of attempted incest; five years' penal servitude.
81   JC26/1928/103.

If one man did the ravish but the other two were in concert, then these two are equally guilty with the one, and it is unnecessary for the Crown to establish that each of the other two committed the act himself. If he is art and part with the man who committed the crime, he is actually guilty of the crime.

The jury was out for twenty-five minutes before returning a unanimously guilty verdict.[82]

In the two group rape cases, the HCJ papers contain no comment on the woman's social standing, any previous sexual experience or observations concerning her physical resistance. It was the judge's responsibility to ensure the jury discarded character assessment and personal background in favour of evidenced facts. Further, in the last case the jury's speed of return suggests their credibility in the strength of the evidence supporting Lord Hunter's direction.

Sentencing

In 1920s Scotland, the welfare system's focus on prevention of sexual violence, particularly against the youngest females in society, was not effective in detecting and reporting crime; they were not involved in these nearly 700 cases prosecuted at the HCJ during the decade. Thus, sentencing was the last instrument available to punish criminals and was the ultimate reflection of the bench's opinion on sexual violence and its perpetrators. Lengthy sentences might also deter potential miscreants. However, contemporary investigators of sexual offences commented that 'many instances were given of sentences of widely different severity imposed for offences of apparently the same character'. They attributed this perception to 'slip-shod newspaper reports', which aggregated all sexual crimes under the single title 'indecent assault'. Popular indignation against 'inadequate sentences for child assault' was attributed to 'ignorance of the true nature of the offences'.[83] Their report surveyed opinions on sheriff courts, where indecent assaults and cases attracting shorter sentences were heard, and public and journalist attendance allowed, which promoted public perceptions of the court system and the amount of sexual violence perpetrated.

The public was largely ignorant of the difference between statute and common law, as the report's investigators explained, and the implications the difference

---

82 JC34/1/81 and JC34/1/82; one panel appealed.
83 *Departmental Committee on Sexual Offences against Children and Young Persons in Scotland*, Report of the Committee appointed by the Secretary for Scotland (Edinburgh, 1926), 17.

had for sentences. Sentencing for the former was restricted by the statute, thus an *attempt* at carnal knowledge of a girl under thirteen indicted under the 1885 CLAA carried a maximum of two years' hard labour and was heard at the sheriff court, whereas carnal knowledge of a girl under thirteen carried a lengthier sentence and, if pleaded guilty at sheriff court, would proceed to the HCJ for sentencing or otherwise jury trial.[84] A conviction of rape, prosecuted under common law attracted 'penal servitude for life, or for a long term of years' and was heard at the HCJ.[85] Not understanding the legal minutiae could promote disgruntlement with the judicial system.

Analysing the HCJ records for convicted rape trials, there are no obvious trends correlating sentencing to age of victim, number of victims, medical confirmation of penetration or whether the panel pleaded guilty. In a 1919 Glasgow rape case involving a victim aged 7 attacked by a 37-year-old male, the panel received ten years' penal servitude for partial penetration; whereas three years later in another case involving another 7-year-old victim, the adult rapist also received ten years' penal servitude but Professor Glaister had confirmed a ruptured hymen and sperm present in the child's vagina.[86] Similarly in 1921, an adult rapist assaulted a six-year-old and was given seven years despite pleading guilty (forensic details not available).[87] In these examples, the victims were of similar age as were the perpetrators, but medical evidence or a voluntary guilty plea appear to have made little impact on their sentences. In cases involving adult women and single rapists, similar erratic sentencing occurred, which did not correlate with the case details. Equally, in group rape cases, although sentencing was always suitably harsh ranging from three to ten years, it does not appear to have taken into account the number of perpetrators. In the few cases where the jury returned only a majority guilty verdict, no pattern emerges which might correlate a judge's leniency towards a non-unanimous conviction.

Despite contemporary attitudes arguing that 'penal servitude [is] incompetent where he is under 16 years of age', judges appear to have imposed penal servitude on boys as young as fifteen years.[88] For example, there were two cases in 1922, one involving a fifteen-year-old who pleaded guilty to rape of a girl aged six and another involving a sixteen-year-old and his victim aged five. The former boy's guilty plea may have influenced a shorter sentence of three years, while

---

84 *Departmental Committee*, 21–2.
85 R. Macgregor Mitchell, *A Practical Treatise on the Criminal Law of Scotland by the late Right Honourable Sir J H A MacDonald*, fourth edition (Edinburgh, 1929), 177.
86 AD15/19/49, JC14/34 and AD15/22/49, JC14/36.
87 AD15/20/19, JC9/16.
88 *Departmental Committee*, 22.

the latter boy received seven years – both penal servitude.[89] In 1920s Scotland, these were harsh sentences for teenage perpetrators and do not follow trends discovered for Victorian Kent where sentences were reduced if the boy was young, irrespective of being above or below sixteen years.[90] If delinquency rates were rising throughout the 1920s, as has been suggested by the enactment of the 1933 Children and Young Persons Act, these severe sentences may signal the beginning of a judicial response to a rise in youth crime.[91]

In incest cases involving fathers and step/daughters, sentencing appears to have complied largely with the guidelines of the 1908 Children Act, with nearly all sentences falling inside three to ten years, most at the lower end of the tariff.[92] However, like rape cases, irrespective of a step/daughter's age, a guilty plea did not necessarily attract a shorter sentence. For example, in two 1924 cases, one father pleaded guilty to incest with his fourteen-year-old stepdaughter and received 12 months' imprisonment, while another father found guilty by a majority jury of assaulting his twelve-year-old stepdaughter received the same sentence.[93] Equally, the number of victims per case appears not to have had an impact on sentences. In two 1919 cases both found unanimously guilty, one panel had committed incest against two teenage daughters making one pregnant and was sentenced to four years, while another father who assaulted a single teenage daughter without pregnancy received five years.[94]

In incest cases committed by brothers, sentences were generally relatively light, in terms of only months' imprisonment. Consanguineous uncle/niece incest cases also received lighter sentences, and when these relationships appeared to be causing no harm, there was increasing leniency. In a 1927 case of consensual consanguineous incest between a 66-year-old uncle and his 37-year-old niece, the AD reflected that 'it is unfortunate that proceedings for incest should have to be taken now after the parties have been living as married people for so long'.

---

89   AD15/22/92, JC12/55 and AD15/22/50, JC14/36.
90   Conley, 'Rape and Justice', 533.
91   B. Weinberger, *The Best Police in the World* (Cambridge, 1995), 148.
92   The 1908 Incest Act stipulated sentences 'up to seven years and not less than three'; A. Wohl, 'Sex and the Single Room: Incest among the Victorian Working-Classes', in *The Victorian Family: Structure and Stresses*, ed A. Wohl (New York, 1978), 210. Discussing incest several decades later, Lord Justice Ackner reflected that 'no cases are more difficult to deal with from the penological aspect' and described English judges' sentencing approach between 1910 and 1919 spreading 'very evenly over 6 months to five years with a slight preponderance of sentences of the 1 to 3 year bracket' and non-custodial sentences increasing between 1920 and 1929; Lord Justice Ackner, 'The Crime of Incest', *Medico-Legal Journal*, 48 (1980): 79 and 87. His observation of non-compliance with the minimum three-year sentence may be attributed to convictions on lesser indictments, for example, attempted incest or indecent assault.
93   AD15/24/12, JC5/19; and AD15/24/24, JC5/16.
94   AD15/19/45, JC15/30; and AD15/19/52, JC15/30.

Their incest had been discovered when a neighbour accused the male panel of lewd practices with her daughter. That charge was found not proven at sheriff court, but their other 'crime' had been disclosed. The HCJ jury found the couple unanimously guilty and recommended them to leniency; the AD did not move for sentence, and Lord Ormidale dismissed them from the bar.[95] His compassion was echoed in a 1928 incest-by-affinity case heard by Lord Fleming, who having explained the accuracy of a charge of incest even between consensual non-blood adults, proceeded also to dismiss them despite a unanimously guilty verdict from a jury of six women and ten men.[96]

Thus, analysis of the HCJ records suggests that sentencing strategies were inconsistent depending on an individual judge's reaction to the facts before him. Punishment was erratic and trends by circuit court and judge are not apparent. However, the deterrent message inherent in longer sentencing seems to have been effective because during the 1920s contemporary investigators remarked that recidivism affected 'only 10 per cent of convicted sexual offenders against children and young persons' and appeared least in more serious sexual crimes. Few HCJ indictment sheets recorded previous sexual crimes including those heard at a lower court and the investigators concluded that 'present methods of dealing with offenders are sufficiently deterrent'.[97]

* * *

Conclusion

When judging sexual crimes, prisons commissioner Norwood East explained that 'the subject impinges upon social morality and religious doctrine, and the ordinary citizen is tempted to appraise sexual misconduct in accordance with the manner in which it personally affronts him'.[98] However, when case details are compared with verdicts, the responses of 1920s Scottish juries for the most serious indictments of incest and rape suggest that, in the majority of cases, any prejudices a jury might have held beforehand disappeared once they were

---

95 AD15/27/78, JC13/137.
96 JC26/1928/91, JC14/40.
97 *Departmental Committee*, 18. One incest case tried in 1929 included details of two previous charges heard at sheriff court, one for lewd practices in 1923 incurring sixty days' imprisonment and another in 1924 charged under the CLAA 1922 receiving 18 months; these were non-familial crimes, AD15/29/68, JC15/40; three years' penal servitude.
98 Norwood East, 'Sexual Offenders', 527.

presented with a case. However, in rapes against minors, the records suggest that juries' sympathies may have influenced their verdicts.

Recent research has argued that male behaviour was increasingly criminalized during the Victorian period which meant that explanations for male violence which had previously been acceptable no longer were and so harsher punishment was meted out.[99] In the 1920s Scottish sexual crime context this meant that once found guilty, men could expect considerable sentences that followed earlier Victorian attitudes. The Great War appears not to have created a watershed between the Victorian and post-war eras in this respect; a sexual violence case perpetrated against a girl under ten in 1885 could receive a five-year sentence as much as a similar one in 1929.[100] Early twentieth-century Scottish juries appear not to have been moving towards alignment with the argument that if penalties are too severe juries are more reluctant to convict sex offenders; they do not wish to be responsible for imposing lengthy sentences.[101] This is the 'hanging argument' also used to support acquittals in murder cases where the only sentence available to the judge was death.

Instead, the HCJ records suggest that 1920s Scottish juries evaluated each case at face value whether they were called to an assize in Inverness or Glasgow and their verdicts do not demonstrate reluctance to convict because of the possibility of lengthy incarcerations. Whether they all realized the judge's sentencing powers cannot be completely ascertained, but if they read the *Glasgow Herald* or *The Scotsman*, or any number of local newspapers, they cannot have failed to understand the severity of penalties handed down from the brief court reports printed. To be eligible for jury service in the 1920s, jurors would have been born before the war and their understanding of the bench's reaction, if found guilty, suggests continuing Victorian attitudes towards convicted sexual violence criminals: they needed to be incarcerated.

---

[99] J. Carter-Wood, 'Criminal Violence in Britain', *History Compass*, 4, no. 1 (2006): 84.
[100] AD14/85/299, JC12/54; and AD15/29/65, JC14/40.
[101] Bourke, *Rape*, 402.

8

Sexual entitlement and arrogance
Conclusion

In the aftermath of the Great War, writers and journalists such as Cicely Hamilton and Philip Gibbs anticipated that the brutalizing impact of war would make it difficult for society to adjust. Fears were expressed among elite groups that women would be targets for the frustrations and stresses accompanying the process of adjustment. Yet, these fears proved unfounded. Prosecuted cases in the High Court of Justiciary (HCJ) suggest that combatants were no more likely to perpetrate sexual violence than non-combatants. Thus, sexual violence in Scottish society in the 1920s was a more complex phenomenon than elite groups imagined.

The HCJ case papers describe sexual violence as a set of crimes committed by working-class men of different occupations and social backgrounds. In prosecuted cases of incest, the perpetrators' actions relied on their victims' silence and weak maternal authority, and victims of incest who managed to prosecute a case were predominantly pubertal females. While incest occurred indoors, rape could be perpetrated either privately or in unobserved external loci. Further, rape mainly occurred between an assailant and victim who were to some degree acquainted. Rape could be premeditated, particularly when committed against minor females, or an opportunistic crime. However, once detected, families' recourse to the law was immediate, which may have aided their success in proceeding to a prosecution.

The HCJ cases conform with a combination of social mythology and legal requirements: women required protection from depraved men; sexual violence was perceived by the elites as endemic in working-class communities, and corroboration was required in order to prosecute. However, panels' motives for committing sexual violence have not survived within the case papers, if indeed they were ever voluntarily explained. Thus, potential judicial bias against certain 'types' of working-class male is invisible in the HCJ records.[1] So, there remains an unanswered question: what caused sexual violence in 1920s Scotland?

Firstly, factors connected with lifestyle and location were important. The urban working classes largely lived their lives on the streets, and rural working classes lived and played outside. As individual cases have revealed, young women returned from work or entertainment without chaperones and young girls played in scraps of vacant land as well as running late-night errands. If females were forced onto the streets, then so too were males. Young men sought similar entertainments to their female peers, while older men associated in pubs to escape overcrowded homes. These separate spheres of leisure re-intensified in the interwar years.[2] The streets and closes of cities and towns were transformed into male-dominated locations in which females could be vulnerable to predation. When the need to court in private is considered, then walking home through dark alleys might provide 'somewhere to cuddle' but could also become spaces where courtship activities could escalate beyond the female's wishes, without chaperoning or other witnesses to intervene.[3]

However, while urban geography and lifestyle might provide clues for cases of rape, they cannot explain the number of incest cases. Many precognosced females described complicated sleeping arrangements. Unable to remain indoors for leisure yet closely packed together to sleep, was the housing of the working classes a catalyst for incest? By the 1931 census, 80 per cent of Scotland's population lived in towns and cities, with Glasgow and Dundee experiencing the worst densities, with over 60 per cent of their inhabitants in single-end and two-roomed homes.[4] However, the majority of urban residents lived in Glasgow and its satellite towns.[5] Contemporary social investigators believed that overcrowded apartments, where families grew up without privacy, resulted in depraved behaviour, a theory emphasized nine years later when a further Royal Commission commented that 'few people realize the closeness of the connection

---

1   M. N. Christoffersen, K. Soothill and B. Francis, 'Who Is Most a Risk of Becoming a Convicted Rapist? The Likelihood of a Rape Conviction among the 1966 Birth Cohort in Denmark', *Journal of Scandinavian Studies in Criminology and Crime Prevention*, 6 (2005): 41.
2   L. A. Jackson, 'Women Professionals and the Regulation of Violence', in *Everyday Violence in Britain 1850-1950*, ed. S. D'Cruze (Harlow, 2000), 121.
3   Carnegie United Kingdom Trust, *Disinherited Youth* (Edinburgh, 1943), 109, quoted in T. C. Smout, *A Century of the Scottish People 1830-1950* (London, 1986), 175.
4   G. S. Pryde, *Social Life in Scotland since 1707* (London, 1934), 26; W. W. Knox, *Industrial Nation: Work, Culture and Society in Scotland, 1800-Present* (Edinburgh, 2009), 192.
5   W. W. Knox, 'The Political and Workplace Culture of the Scottish Working-Class 1832-1914', in *People and Society in Scotland Volume II 1830-1914*, eds W. Hamish Fraser and R. J. Morris (Edinburgh, 1990), 41.

between bad housing and the offences with which we are dealing'.[6] However, not all men who lived in cramped conditions committed incest.

Details of sleeping arrangements were only asked in precognitions for incest and rapes perpetrated by lodgers, which emphasizes contemporaries' correlation of overcrowding with sexual violence. However, in their precognitions victims and their supporters failed to evince accommodation-related reasons for sexual violence. None of the girls or their female guardians blamed bed or room sharing; no male sibling witnesses mentioned sexual interest or knowledge gained in the home and female siblings did not describe being observed or touched until incest commenced. Therefore, contemporary elite anxieties regarding incest may have stemmed from social segregation and fear of the unseen 'other'. Greater separation of housing types had occurred in the late nineteenth century, with previously mixed-class districts becoming lower status.[7] By the 1920s, the greater number of sexual crimes in Glaswegian families living in the socially isolated, densely packed slums contrasted with fewer complaints brought by families inhabiting the new housing estates such as Mosspark.

Although more spacious homes removed much of the need for bed sharing, the new low-density estates disrupted working-class social patterns, forcing families to live as single units rather than as part of a close-knit community.[8] This new arrangement may have interrupted traditional patterns of neighbourly detection and reporting and might account for the lower number of prosecutions emanating from addresses in the new housing estates. However, prosecutions remained concentrated in Glasgow. Sexual violence was not prosecuted to anywhere near the same extent in Scotland's other urban centres, namely Edinburgh, Dundee or Aberdeen. Neither was it prosecuted to any great degree in rural regions, such as the Highlands.

The demographic composition of the population should also be considered: did the ratio of women to men have an impact on the incidence of sexual violence? The only other Scottish city with comparable housing conditions to Glasgow was Dundee. Here the industrial employment base and gender balance were different. Dundee's predominant industry was jute manufacture, which relied on a female workforce, many of whom were married women.[9] Many

---

6   *Report of the Departmental Committee on Sexual Offences against Children and Young Persons in Scotland* (Edinburgh, 1926), 40–2.
7   J. Carter-Wood, 'Self-Policing and Policing the Self: Violence, Protection and the Civilizing Bargain in Britain', *Crime, Histoire and Societies*, 7, no. 1 (2003): 113.
8   R. Rodger, 'Urbanisation in Twentieth-Century Scotland', in *Scotland in the Twentieth Century*, eds T. M. Devine and R. J. Finlay (Edinburgh, 1996), 124.
9   http://www.visionofbritain.org.uk/unit/10150553/cube/AGESEX_85UP, accessed October 2022.

men worked away from the city because employment opportunities in jute fell to women in their twenties and thirties, financially empowering working wives in their domestic sphere.[10] Historians have recognized the agency possessed by Dundee's women which was not apparent among Glasgow's women.[11] This empowerment combined with fewer men physically living in the city may have provided a safer environment for young women seeking after-work leisure and female children on night errands. Also, with mothers alive and present in their families' lives, and respect between spouses predicated on a more equitable marital balance, this may have provided respite for teenage daughters potentially at risk of incest.[12]

Edinburgh also contained pockets of working-class, overcrowded single-end homes. Yet, while the capital's women were predominantly economically inactive without independent financial resources to enjoy leisure time or contribute to the household income, their lack of 'domestic voice' does not appear to have resulted in a greater number of sexual violence prosecutions. Their husbands lived and worked at home, unlike in Dundee, but Edinburgh's men worked in different sectors from Glasgow's male-dominated heavy industries. Edinburgh's main employment base in 1911 was manufacturing, transport and storage (warehousing). By 1931, there had been a considerable increase in men employed in public administration, wholesale and retail.[13] On the whole, Edinburgh's men did not work in physically arduous occupations and they were engaged in a wider range of activities. Thus, working men did not exist in the same concentrations in either Dundee or Edinburgh as they did in Glasgow, where the shipyards and associated industries employed the majority of men in trades associated with dirt and danger.

Furthermore, in the Highlands and rural north-east, decades of migration had altered the demographic composition so that there were fewer young families, and women outnumbered men to a greater extent than elsewhere in Scotland, although women did not necessarily enjoy greater empowerment in these traditional communities. Different social behaviours slowed the process of

---

10 *Census of Population: Occupations of the People of Scotland*, 3 (1901): 680–1, quoted in S. Browne and J. Tomlinson, 'A Women's Town', in *Jute No More: Transforming Dundee*, eds J. Tomlinson and C. A. Whatley (Edinburgh, 2015), 1, chapter 5.
11 Research on abortion rates in Scotland shows that unwanted sex and subsequent pregnancies were lowest in Dundee; R. Davidson, *Illicit and Unnatural Practices: The Law, Sex and Society in Scotland since 1900* (Edinburgh, 2019), 76.
12 E. Gordon, 'The Family', in *Gender in Scottish History since 1700*, eds L. Abrams, E. Gordon, D. Simonton and E. Janes Yeo (Edinburgh, 2006), 252.
13 GB Historical GIS, University of Portsmouth, Edinburgh City through time, Work and Poverty Statistics Economically Active by Sex, A Vision of Britain through Time, http://www.visionofbritain.org.uk/unit/10211104/cube/CENSUS_ACTIVE_GEN, accessed October 2022.

change and practices in the Highlands were no longer evident in the Lowlands.[14] In the Highlands and north-east, rural women fulfilled traditional roles as mothers and wives; their financial contribution to the household was based on their limited earnings from fishing and agriculture. Also, although rural communities did not live in the same densities as the cities, they often inhabited homes just as small and mean as those in Glasgow. Yet sexual violence was not as visible as it was in the densely populated urban south-west. Its absence may have been due to several factors.

Firstly, rural communities may have employed 'rough justice', with local men taking matters into their own hands. Such summary justice would be invisible to the historical record. Secondly, different societal attitudes to illegitimate pregnancies may have affected the number of rape prosecutions. Christopher Smout argues that illegitimacy was on average higher in Scotland than in England, and higher still in rural areas.[15] In the rural north-east, a bothy or chaumer system operated with young farm workers occupying segregated communal living spaces where they lived beyond parental control, potentially with easy access to the opposite sex. If sexually indulgent courtship produced pregnancy, then illegitimate births may not have attracted the same degree of disapprobation. In the north-east, accusations of rape to cover an illegitimate pregnancy were less likely because young women possessed acceptable alternative options for child-rearing with grandparents raising babies, allowing young single mothers to return to work.[16] In the more socially conservative Highlands and Islands, young people lived at home, employed in the fishing industry and on family crofts, where parental surveillance of courtship may have reduced opportunities for intercourse, consenting or otherwise. Also, problems of land inheritance in a struggling rural economy may have disinclined young people to have sex before a home was available to them. Thus, premarital attitudes to sex may have had a significant impact on the statistics of prosecuted sexual violence in rural areas.

Overcrowding and poor living conditions affected so many working-class families that alone they were not catalysts for familial and non-familial sexual violence despite assumptions made by contemporary welfare officers. Female

---

14 R. H. Campbell and T. M. Devine, 'The Rural Experience', in *People and Society in Scotland, volume II 1830-1914*, eds W. H. Fraser and R. J. Morris (Edinburgh, 1990), 50.
15 Smout, *Century*, 166.
16 L. Jamieson, 'Changing Intimacy: Seeking and Forming Couple Relationships', in *A History of Everyday Life in Twentieth Century Scotland*, eds L. Abrams and C. G. Brown (Edinburgh, 2010), 78; A. Blaikie, 'Scottish Illegitimacy: Social Adjustment or Moral Economy?', *Journal of Interdisciplinary History*, 20, no. 2 (Autumn 1998): 230.

agency may have had some impact in Dundee where women enjoyed independent means or contributed significantly to the household, and it is possible that less arduous male trades in Edinburgh resulted in a more harmonious family life. Regional attitudes in the rural north-east also may have reduced the number of prosecutions, although not necessarily the actual amount of sexual violence. This leaves the industrial south-west where men engaged in heavy industry had a reputation for hard drinking, fighting and violence in general.[17] Such aggressive masculine behaviour could be generationally learned so that fathers' attitudes towards women and children were passed on to their sons, potentially resulting in an ultra-masculine dominance of society.[18] Did an exaggerated sense of 'male rights' exist in the industrial south-west? Rachel Jewkes explains that male violence towards women originates from male vulnerability in societies that place too many expectations on men. She argues that 'societies with stronger ideologies of male dominance have more intimate partner violence' – and by extension, more familial and non-familial sexual violence.[19] In Scotland's industrialized south-west, where post-war economic hardship hit the shipyards particularly badly, unemployment might have affected some men differently.[20] With elements of their outward masculinity constrained by unemployment and inability to provide for their families, it is possible that male frustrations resulted in spousal, familial and extra-familial sexual violence. Thus, did cultural configurations in Glasgow shape 'hard men', who, intent on risk-taking – a further manifestation of masculinity – indulged in incest, rape, ravish and lewd practices to enforce their assumed and inherent hegemonic masculinity?[21] Possibly, but they have left no written record of their sexual motivations, just the legend of their tough masculinity.

That aside, the concentration of sexual violence prosecutions in Glasgow may have been the result of better community relations with the police facilitating an easier conduit for reporting crime. Although very few cases were detected by the police on the beat, the greater density of policing in Glasgow may have assisted

---

17 R. Johnston and A. McIvor, 'Dangerous Work, Hard Men and Broken Bodies: Masculinity in the Clydeside Heavy Industries', *Labour History Review*, 69, no. 2 (August 2004): 138.
18 L. Abrams and E. Ewan, 'Interrogating Men and Masculinities in Scottish History', in *Nine Centuries of Man: Manhood and Masculinities in Scottish History*, eds L. Abrams and E. Ewan (Edinburgh, 2017), 2.
19 R. Jewkes, 'Intimate Partner Violence: Causes and Prevention', *The Lancet*, 359 (2002): 1424–5.
20 N. Penlington, 'Masculinity and Domesticity in 1930s South Wales: Did Unemployment Change the Domestic Division of Labour?', *Twentieth Century British History*, 21, no. 3 (2010): 281–99.
21 A. Bartie and A. Fraser, 'Speaking to the "Hard Men": Masculinities, Violence and Youth Gangs in Glasgow, c.1965-75', in *Nine Centuries of Man: Manhood and Masculinities in Scottish History*, eds L. Abrams and E. Ewan (Edinburgh, 2017), 266.

reporting thus leading to a greater number of prosecutions.[22] Contemporary criminologist Hermann Mannheim understood that a localized increase in a certain crime type in a certain place would stimulate watchfulness within the community and the police enabling the arrest of a higher number of miscreants. This may also explain the predominance of Glasgow in the prosecution records.[23] Or possibly that Glasgow's Procurator Fiscal (PF) exerted a personal campaign against sexually violent men, resulting in more prosecutions. Frustratingly, Glasgow's PF appears to have left no personal commentary on his decisions other than those contained within the HCJ papers.

However, despite the investigations of contemporary welfare officers and changes to the law protecting females since the mid-nineteenth century, the judicial authorities were unable to deter serious sexual violence. When it occurred, families and victims inclined to do so reported it; the authorities very rarely detected it. If the 'dark number' of unreported sexual crimes and the unquantifiable number that failed to progress to a prosecution are as numerous as historians and criminologists fear, then sexual violence was probably endemic in society. However, only certain men were prepared to commit it. Jane Caputi contends that 'the violent male is actually society's ultimate man'.[24] He may have been among certain peer groups in Glasgow and its environs, but society's efforts to detect, report, indict and convict violent men suggests that, universally, the sexually violent male was, and is, reviled.

Lindsay Farmer concludes in his study of Scots criminal law that there has been 'a gradual convergence between the underlying wrong (the infringement of sexual autonomy) and the content of the law', a development that is a form of 'civilizing process', in which legal reforms reflect society's anxieties surrounding sexual crime.[25] Thus, if the law has responded to societal anxieties by creating more criminal offences to remove sexually violent individuals from the community while also sending a message of deterrence, has the strategy worked? As a result of legal developments, are more sexual assaults being prosecuted and more criminals convicted?

In her study of mid-nineteenth century crime, Carolyn Conley calculated that the conviction rate for rape in Victorian England was 40 per cent. It is unclear whether this figure includes guilty pleas or was based solely on jury-heard rape

22 L. A. Jackson, with N. Davidson, L. Fleming, D. M. Smale and R. Sparks, *Police and Community in Twentieth-Century Scotland* (Edinburgh, 2020), 54–5.
23 H. Mannheim, *Social Aspects of Crime in England between the Wars* (London, 1940), 79.
24 J. Caputi, *The Age of Sex Crime* (London, 1988), 62.
25 L. Farmer, *Making the Modern Criminal Law: Criminalization and Civil Order* (Oxford, 2016), 293.

trials.[26] However, comparing this with Scottish rape prosecutions for 1885, of twenty-five prosecutions at the HCJ a guilty verdict was returned in twenty-one cases; the prosecution to conviction conversion rate was 84 per cent. In 1890, 1895, 1900 and 1905, the conversion rates were 69, 71, 78 and 50 per cent, respectively.[27] By the 1920s, as discussed in the last chapter, once guilty pleas are removed, in 63 per cent of prosecutions for rape for all age groups the panel was found guilty.[28] A hundred years later in a survey conducted for the mayor's office for policing and crime in London in 2016, of rape cases that proceeded to trial, 61 per cent resulted in a conviction.[29] In Scotland in 2017, in a survey of all sexual crime indictments heard at the HCJ, in 65 per cent of prosecutions either the panel pleaded guilty or the jury returned a guilty verdict.[30] While the figures are not precisely comparable, they reveal that if a rape victim reaches court, there is a high probability of a jury listening to the case, scrutinizing her appearance and performance as well as the accused's in the court room and, after debating the evidence and the 'characters' of the key protagonists, concluding that the accused is guilty. The prosecution to conviction conversion figures over 150 years have not varied significantly. However, the scientific methods supporting forensic medicine have developed considerably. Rather than simply identifying mammalian sperm, forensic science can now pinpoint its rightful owner. Given these advances, why are conviction rates not higher? Why do so many reported assaults in the two modern surveys not reach the prosecution stage? These unprosecuted cases are not part of the 'dark number'; they have been reported but for some reason failed to secure a prosecution. The causes of this attrition may help us to understand the nature of cases which remain completely unreported to the police.

Perhaps an answer to the first question lies in answering the second. There are many reasons why cases fail to proceed to court, but the key factors affecting the attrition of rape reports in modern surveys are that the victim withdrew their complaint at some point before prosecution and/or there was insufficient evidence with which to proceed. The *London Rape Review* found that generally victims withdrew their complaint early in the investigative stage, which concurs

[26] C. Conley, 'Rape and Justice in Victorian England', *Victorian Studies*, 29, no.4 (Summer 1986), 521.
[27] 1890: nine out of thirteen cases returned guilty; 1895: five out of seven cases; 1900: seven out of nine cases; 1905: three out of six prosecuted cases.
[28] 49 per cent if guilty pleas are included.
[29] *The London Rape Review: A Review of Cases from 2016*, Mayor's Office for Policing and Crime (July 2019), 13.
[30] Chart 2 'Cases Proceeding to Trial', *Investigation and Prosecution of Sexual Crimes Review*, Justice Directorate, Scottish Government, 16 November 2017.

with research conducted in 2005 commissioned by the UK's Home Office.[31] Research revealed that early withdrawal occurred because the investigative process was too traumatic to continue; women feared for their own safety if the sexual assault was domestic abuse and some simply wished to get the matter off their chest – reporting alone had assuaged that need.[32]

The trauma experienced during a rape investigation through recalling events in minute detail and undergoing intimate medical examinations is understandable. However, insufficient evidence to proceed is perplexing unless the type of rape is considered. While the medical evidence required from the victim remains the same for all types of rape whether stranger, group or acquaintance assault, the number and quality of witnesses does not. In the London review, 35 per cent of rapes were committed by an intimate partner and a further 34 per cent were committed by an acquaintance or friend. In both situations, an independent witness to all aspects of the assault is rare and therefore the case becomes the perpetrator's word against the victim's: did she consent or not?

Until 2009 when the Sexual Offences Act (Scotland) updated, among other clauses, those concerning consent, the situation had continued that the victim had to prove she had not consented, whereas after the 2009 Act, the onus was on the defendant to prove she had consented. The temporality of consent allows it to be withdrawn at any time during a sexual act and although the situation regarding consent is in a healthier position for victims, it relies as it always has on the legal definition of consent which is often different from its societal interpretation.[33] The jury as representatives of society operating under judicial guidance must act on the legal definition but cannot necessarily set aside their personal understanding of consent. A similar paradox exists, or is perceived to exist, among the police when a complainer first reports an assault. Thus, it appears that a victim's 'performance' throughout the judicial process remains pivotal because prejudicial attitudes towards rape victims – the 'dominant rape mythology' – persist. A victim presenting at a police office who does not correspond with the 'ideal victim' characterization and the circumstances of whose rape are also not 'ideal' may struggle to be convincing: presenting as angry or quietly vacant are not 'typical' rape responses, whereas a broken and sobbing victim fits the 'typical' profile.

---

31   L. Kelly, J. Lovett and L. Regan, *A Gap or a Chasm? Attrition in Reported Rape Cases*, Home Office Research Study 293 (London Metropolitan University, 2005), x.
32   *London Rape Review*, 14.
33   Age of Consent podcast, episode 1, https://www.narrativematters.scot/the-age-of-consent-podcast.

Fiona Leverick identifies four commonly held beliefs concerning the victim and her evidence. Firstly, there is an element of blame attached to the victim if she was intoxicated at the time of the assault, if she did not or could not scream or defend herself and if she failed to 'sufficiently communicate her lack of consent to the accused'. Secondly, false allegations are made to revenge a broken relationship. Thirdly, women send mixed signals on which men, who are constructed as unable to control their sexual desires unlike women, act believing in the woman's consent. And lastly, ideas of 'real rape', that is, the cases reported by the media which correspond with society's expectations of rape: a violent crime committed by a complete stranger in a public space which may end in murder.[34]

In the 1920s as the HCJ precognitions show, judicial officers were keen to understand how much resistance an adult victim had offered to her assailant, how long she had screamed, whether she had been drinking before the attack. Among the cases that reached the HCJ, many did not fit a perfect model. Juries did not always require their victims to have put up the greatest amount of resistance to return a guilty verdict. However, what will never be known is the number of cases in which the victim herself decided not to report, because her own understanding of the assault and what her part in it might look like complied with society's dominant rape mythology. Leverick's second belief concerning false accusations is confirmed by Joanna Bourke who states that women do not lie about rape, yet the idea that they might persists.[35] This is rooted in a long history of women characterized as unreliable witnesses, as emotional and hysterical, and therefore potentially vindictive. Wrongful accusations of rape from revengeful 'little minxes' were debated in Parliament before the Criminal Law Amendment Act was passed in 1885; it was contended that women's behaviour and their motives for reporting rape included revenge for being jilted or a refusal of marriage once pregnancy was confirmed. The third belief that men's libido is uncontrollable once roused and that women send confusing signals leading to a complicated *mens rea* situation in which the man thought the woman had said yes, but she had only been flirting with no intention of participating in sex, has enduring tenacity: this inequitable notion of gendered libidos is founded in outdated ideas of masculinity in which men need sex and respectable women

---

34 F. Leverick, 'What Do We know about Rape Myths and Juror Decision Making?', *International Journal of Evidence & Proof*, 24, no. 3 (2020): 256–7.
35 J. Bourke, *Disgrace: Global Reflections on Sexual Violence* (London, 2022), 177; J. Bourke, *Rape: A History from 1860 to the Present* (London, 2010), 322, discussing marital rape.

do not. And lastly, 'real rapes' are not perpetrated after dark in public parks and back alleys by unknown assailants.

The statistics for Scotland in the 1920s reveal that 35 per cent of prosecuted adult rapes were committed by a stranger; if rapes of all age groups are included, that figure decreases to 19 per cent. In London in 2016, stranger rapes accounted for 7 per cent of all reported rapes.[36] A Scottish survey conducted in 2005 found that 22 per cent of rapes were perpetrated by someone the victim had become acquainted with within the previous twenty-four hours of which 7 per cent were committed by a total stranger.[37] The widely reported Sarah Everard case, a rape-homicide perpetrated by a police officer in London in early March 2021, fits the 'real rape' scenario. A teacher and respectable young woman Sarah was walking home alone late at night when her assailant Wayne Couzens kidnapped her, raped her and then murdered her before dumping her burned body. Rightly, the case was met with outrage in the newspapers and around the country, but the amount of reporting was not equal to the exceptionality of this form of rape. The same can be said of the quantity of reporting surrounding the 1926 Greenock rape-homicide which involved a nurse and a hospital attendant. In 2021, Sarah's rape and murder fitted a persistent societal belief in what real rape looks like. Whereas the reality is 'everyday rape', which occurs indoors perpetrated by an intimate partner or friend or neighbour and rarely makes the press.

Everyday rapes are described in the 1920s precognition statements and in both the recent London and Scottish surveys. This continuity extends to the age groups most frequently assaulted. In Scotland in the 1920s, 53 per cent of rapes were perpetrated against young women aged between sixteen and twenty-four years. In the London review, 66 per cent of victims were aged under thirty years; in the 2005 Scottish report, 53 per cent of victims were also under thirty years.[38] Other continuities exist in the evidential challenges facing victims. Until recently, sexual history evidence was admissible in court. Thus, a complainer's previous relationships, their frequency and longevity – one-night stands in particular – could be employed by defence counsel to discredit her. Research conducted in the 1990s found that juries responded less favourably the further a complainer's report of rape wandered from the 'ideal' of an innocent woman raped without any hint of provocation, by a stranger in an isolated place. Further,

---

36　*London Rape Review*, 4.
37　M. Burman, L. Lovett and L. Kelly, 'Country Briefing: Scotland', in *Different Systems, Similar Outcomes? Tracking Attrition in Reported Rape Cases in Eleven Countries*, European Commission Daphne II Programme (May, 2009), 6.
38　*London Rape Review*, 16; Burman, Lovett and Kelly, 'Country Briefing', 5.

possessing a sexual history diminished a complainer's 'probative credibility' in the jury's eyes. Societal attitudes concerning 'loose' women who lie about rape prejudicially affected jury decision-making because they perceived women with a sexual history as less 'rapeable' than those with 'unblemished' characters. The admissibility of the complainer's sexual history in court precluded juries from 'considering the possibility of the defendant's guilt'.[39] Adducing a complainer's sexual history evidence in court is now restricted under section 274 of the Criminal Procedure (Scotland) Act 1995, and it is hoped that public awareness of this change will encourage more victims to report assaults now that the fear of their entire social media and mobile phone history being revealed – a 'digital strip search' – is largely removed.[40] It is a step towards dislodging societal preconceptions and constructions of victims and rapists.

Other continuities exist among the individual sexual violence indictments. A Scottish Law report revealed that in 1951 there were twenty reports for incest made known to the police which peaked at forty-four reports in 1968 and again in 1971 before declining to twenty-three reports in 1978. In the year 2020 to 2021, that figure has fallen further to seven complaints recorded by the police.[41] These peaks and troughs follow a similar trend for the 1920s, with largely inexplicable differences year on year. However, the most recent single-figure statistics may be attributable to incest being indicted under a different charge, as in the 1920s, to avoid reputational damage to the family and the individual child.

Studies examining group rape, more usually known as multiple perpetrator rape in the twenty-first century, suggest that 'rape culture' and 'rape myths' continue to influence men's sexual behaviour in groups. These social groups, such as a sports team or drinking partners, comprise men who have sought out the company of other men with similar beliefs about and attitudes towards women. Explanatory theories attribute multiple perpetrator rape to sociocultural factors concerning belonging, leading and dominating within the group and beliefs which the group projects externally: women's lack of value in society and patriarchy.[42] These characteristics of multiple perpetrator rape readily map onto

---

39 A. McColgan, 'Common Law and the Relevance of Sexual History Evidence', *Oxford Journal of Legal Studies*, 16, no. 2 (1996): 281, 286 and 297.
40 Scottish Government Consultation Paper, 'Improving Victims' Experiences of the Justice System: Consultation', May, 2022, chapter 6; 'Rape: Where Are We Going Wrong?', *The Times*, 1 June 2022.
41 *The Law of Incest in Scotland*, Memorandum no.44, *Scottish Law Commission* (April 1980), 79 appendix II; 'Recorded Crime in Scotland 2020-21', Scottish Government (2022), 93 Table A1 'Sexual Crimes Recorded by the Police, Scotland 2011-12 to 2020-21'.
42 T. da Silva, J. Woodhams and L. Harkins, 'Multiple Perpetrator Rape: A Critical Review of Existing Explanatory Theories', *Aggression and Behavior*, 25 (2015): 151–3.

group rapes in Scotland in the 1920s where heavy industry working cultures emphasized group identity through idealized masculinity.

However, throughout the twentieth century and into the twenty-first, notable changes in approaches to sexual violence prosecutions have evolved. Possibly the most publicly debated development is the naming of alleged perpetrators in the press and the right to anonymity of victims. Naming a victim publicly may deter reporting of sexual violence because individuals fear public discussion and potential shaming which press attention could bring. Although, publishing victims' names may encourage other victims to come forward. Victims voluntarily recounting their experience of sexual assault has been effective in the ongoing #metoo campaign. However, it continues to be the victim's personal decision whether to remain anonymous during the prosecution process because society's prejudicial construction of sexual assault victims, irrespective of having secured a conviction for their assailant, is tenacious. Even the use of the term 'accuser' in the press insinuates lack of credibility in the complainer's account of the assault. A further development has been the pre-prosecution naming of alleged perpetrators of sexual violence. This practice is often accompanied by detailed and nuanced news reporting of the alleged perpetrator's actions. It does not necessarily allow him a fair trial because it cannot be assumed that jurors have not been influenced by the press. Also, if acquitted, a named individual may suffer reputational damage.[43]

The continuities apparent across a century of sexual violence in Scotland outweigh the changes. The majority of 'everyday rapes' are now perpetrated in one of the parties' homes with a number also committed in semi-public locations such as a club or social gathering.[44] These assaults may still be spontaneous and/or opportunistic, but their locus of perpetration has changed. Where once the behaviour of courting couples might descend into sexual assault on the walk home from the cinema, nowadays such incidents occur at parties and in student bedrooms. Yet, one factor in these prosecutions continues to dominate. Wherever a rape or other sexual assault occurs and whoever perpetrates it and how, one element connects cases from the late nineteenth century, the 1920s and the present day in Scotland and in England: speed of reporting.

Of over 700 HCJ prosecutions for sexual assault examined for Scotland in the 1920s, only one complainer delayed reporting her assault to the police because

---

43 D. Denno, 'The Privacy Rights of Rape Victims in the Media and the Law: Perspectives on Disclosing Rape Victims' Names', *Fordham Law Review*, 61 (1993): 1129–30; M. Sharpe, 'Who's a Victim? Who's an Accuser?', *Washington Post*, 27 September 2018.
44 Burman, Lovett and Kelly, 'Country Briefing', 6.

she was a domestic servant whose employer did not allow her to return home until her scheduled weekend off when she told her mother who then supported her in reporting to the police. The delay was one week and the jury returned a not proven verdict.[45] All other assaults were reported immediately after their commission or as soon as a mother discovered the evidence on her child. This does not mean that speed of reporting proved the truth of the accusation, but there appears to have been a correlation between speed of reporting and reaching the prosecution stage. Writing in 1957, criminologist Leon Radzinowicz confirmed that 'a complaint is admissible only when it is made at the first opportunity after the offence' and that the definition of a reasonable 'first opportunity' was a matter for the court to decide.[46] There was an underlying interpretation that a delay in reporting implied indecision about the true nature of the incident or, worse, a false accusation. In Scotland in the 1920s, it is possible that reports made late to the police and passed to the PF which did not reach prosecution exist among the 'dark number'. The PF would have been unable to precognosce the victim and witnesses within the guidance of the *Book of Regulations* and any attempt to gain forensic medical corroborating evidence would have been too late. Thus, speed of reporting enabled swift precognoscing before any insinuation could enter a victim's testimony and medical evidence gathering, however inconclusive it might be.

More recently, the London and Scottish surveys report an increasing number of historical reports. In London, there has been an increase from 18 per cent of reports in 2012 being made over a year after the assault to 27 per cent in 2016. Same-day reporting decreased from 40 per cent of rapes in 2012 to only 29 per cent in 2016. This has been attributed to the influence of celebrity cases in the media which not only encourage young women to come forward but also suggest that justice will be automatic. Despite enormous advances in forensic science, a delay in reporting an assault effectively wipes away any physical evidence; in London there was a noted correlation between the presence of evidence and the length of time elapsed between offence and first report.[47] Likewise in Scotland, there is now 'a significant increase in historical crimes' being reported combined with more cases providing insufficient evidence to proceed.[48] Therefore, the picture is distorted as the increase in historical reports and recorded sexual

---

45 AD15/21/183, JC11/119.
46 L. Radzinowicz, *Sexual Offences: A Report of the Cambridge Department of Criminal Science* (London, 1957), 379–80.
47 *London Rape Review*, 22 and 6.
48 *Investigation and Prosecution of Sexual Crimes Review*, chapter 1.

crime in general coincides with decreasing numbers of prosecutions and successful convictions. The London report suggests that the general increase in sexual assault reports is due to 'improved crime data integrity', but it may also be the result of media campaigns promoting awareness of the possibility of success even months and years after an assault.

However, media reporting on sexual crime statistics often fails to explore the expectation of a prosecution and the disappointment when insufficient evidence forces the judicial system to discontinue investigations and proceedings. The possibility of success in a rape prosecution appears much worse if an increasing number of reports to the police is compared to the low number of convictions, rather than explaining the more hopeful outcomes if the conversion rate of prosecutions to convictions is used. In 2017, Rape Crisis Scotland reported that 43.3 per cent of rape cases *prosecuted* secured a conviction, whereas only 11 per cent of *reported* cases resulted in a conviction; in England and Wales the conversion of reports to convictions was 3.8 per cent in 2019.[49] These sets of figures rely on reports to crisis centres, not reports collected by the police, therefore many of these cases continue to reside within the 'dark number'.

Thus, the positive continuity across the previous century and a half appears to be that speed of reporting to the police may facilitate reaching the prosecution stage and possibly securing a conviction. The petrifying trauma of rape is deeply acknowledged, but if a sexual assault victim can reach a police office or hospital where testimony and physical evidence can be taken immediately, then the insinuation of uncertainty, embellishment or inaccurate or imperfect recall of the event and even a false claim may be erased or at least diminished. Closing the gap between the crime and reporting prevents 'rape myths' from filling it. Speed of reporting may be part of the solution to better outcomes for rape complainers. Going home to shower and call a friend or parent instead of an immediate report allows space for persistent 'rape myths' to be insinuated into the socio-judicial process.

Clearly, not all men rape or indulge in other acts of violent misogyny. Transgressions such as 'up-skirting' and 'down-blousing' have been enshrined in recent UK legislation, although it is unlikely that wolf-whistling will become an indictable crime, yet these non-violent assaults all upset or infuriate some women and girls.[50] They are small acts of sexual antagonism and aggression on a sliding scale the other end of which is rape homicide. In early February 2019, Libby Squire,

---

49   www.rapecrisisscotland.org/help-facts/, accessed July 2022; 'Give us your iPhone or We'll Drop the Case', *The Times*, 29 April 2019.
50   Up-skirting is the practice of taking a photograph beneath someone's skirt; down-blousing similarly involves taking a photograph; both are perpetrated without consent.

a student at Hull University in the UK, was raped and murdered after a night out. Her mother argues that the perpetrator's history of deviant sexual behaviours were gateway crimes which escalated to rape homicide. Mrs Lisa Squire acknowledges that 'flashing' and other micro-sexual aggressions do not always proceed to rape, but that all rapists started somewhere on the sexual crime spectrum. She argues that each and every transgression should be reported to the police, and if at first not believed, continue until you find a police officer who will listen.[51]

Across time the indecent assault and rape landscape is unlikely to have been any different. Women suffer, or at best put up with, sexual assaults of varying severity. Some men have always, and continue, to behave with impunity towards women's sexual and bodily autonomy. When Cicely Hamilton described the post-Great War decade as an 'ugly epoch' in respect of sexual violence, the HCJ records bear out her accusation, but it was perhaps no uglier than any preceding or subsequent decade. Annual crime statistics may fluctuate, more legislation is introduced, but a century later, sexual violence has not disappeared: young men continue to be charged with 'social rape'; group rape has become gang rape. Incest remains an unspoken crime. However, middle-class crimes now reach the newspapers and courts.

The HCJ records of prosecuted crime surveyed here can only divulge so much historical information; they do not constitute the entire picture. Narrowly, the records suggest that sexual violence was committed by working-class men, particularly working-class men in the overcrowded slums of Glasgow. Yet common-sense and modern experience strongly suggest that prosecuted crime can only be assumed to be the visible surface of the sexual violence iceberg. The current debate on the low report-to-conviction conversion rate responds to public outcry and explores ways in which the judicial system may improve its approach to victims of sexual crime, supporting victims through the judicial process to reduce the attrition rate thus enabling more reports to become prosecutions. The public's and victims' confidence in the judicial process is critical to improving the sexual violence landscape, because the evidence from history suggests that victims and their supporters who had confidence in the judicial system, who discarded any personal interpretation of 'dominant rape mythology' and reported a crime as speedily as possible on the understanding their complaint would be believed, were the victims who reached court and of whom more than half secured the conviction and incarceration of their assailant.

51 'Flashing Isn't a Minor Crime. It Can End in a Nightmare', *The Times*, 23 October 2022. Also J. Grant, BBC Radio 4, *Today* programme, 6 March 2023 for further discussion on pre-cursor and red flag sexual crime.

Bibliography

Manuscript and archive sources

Court Papers of the High Court of Justiciary (ref. series numbers), held at the National Records of Scotland:
JC26 Records of Criminal Trials case papers
AD15 Crown Office Precognitions (including other case correspondence)
JC5 Edinburgh Court Books of Adjournal
JC9 Edinburgh Court Minute Books
JC10, JC11, JC12, JC13, JC14 Circuit Courts Minute Books
JC15, JC16 Circuit Courts Books of Adjournal
JC34 Records of Criminal Appeals
JC36 Trial transcripts (on appeal only)

Acts of Parliament

Age of Marriage Act (Scotland) 1929, 19 Geo 5. London, 1929.
Children Act 1908, 8 Edw 7, c67. London, 1908.
Criminal Law Amendment Act 1885, 48 & 49 Vict. C.69. London, 1885.
Sex Disqualification (Removal) Act 1919.

Government reports and papers

Criminal Statistics: Statistics Relating to Police Apprehensions, Criminal Proceedings, and Reformatory and Industrial Schools, for the year 1925. Edinburgh, 1928.
Fifty-Fifth Annual Report of His Majesty's Inspectorate of Constabulary for Scotland, for the year Ended 31st December 1912. London, 1913., Parliamentary Papers, Cmd.6712.
First And *Second Reports of her Majesty's Commissioners for Inquiring into the Housing of the Working Classes, Scotland*. London, 1885.
'The Law of Incest in Scotland', *Scottish Law Commission*, Memorandum no.44. Edinburgh, April 1980.

'The Law of Incest in Scotland: Report on a Reference under 3(1)(e) of the Law Commissions Act 1965', *Scottish Law Commission*, No.69. Edinburgh, December 1981.
'Minutes of Evidence of the Committee on the Employment of Women on Police Duties', Parliamentary Papers, 1921, Cmd.1133.
Police Manual, McCorquodale & Co. Ltd, prepared by a Committee of Chief Constables of Scotland, fifth edn. Glasgow, 1910.
Registrar General's Annual Review for Scotland 1921: Marriage Statistics and Regular and Irregular Marriages in Scotland, tables 10 and 11.
Report of the Departmental Committee on Reformatory and Industrial Schools in Scotland, Minutes of Evidence taken before the Young Offenders Committee, 1925, Cmd. E878/73.
Report of the Departmental Committee on Sexual Offences against Children and Young Persons in Scotland. Edinburgh, 1926, Cmd. E878/79.
Report of the Departmental Committee on Sexual Offences against Young Persons, 1925, Hansard, Cmd. 2561.
Report of the Royal Commission on the Housing of the Industrial Population of Scotland, Rural and Urban. Edinburgh, 1917.
Scottish Law Review and Sheriff Court Reports (1921–30), vols XXXVII–XLVI. London: William Hodge & Co., 1921–1930.

Contemporary newspapers

Glasgow Herald
Manchester Guardian
Pall Mall Gazette
The Scotsman
The Times

Contemporary sources: Books and articles

Anderson, A. M. *The Criminal Law of Scotland*. Edinburgh, 1892.
Anon. 'Sexual Offences against Young Persons', *The Howard Journal of Criminal Justice* 2, no. 1 (1926): 48–51.
Bloch, I. *The Sexual Life of Our Time*. New York, 1908.
Booth, W. *In Darkest England and the Way Out*. London, 1890.
Cassity, J. H. 'Psychological Considerations of Pedophilia', *The Psycholanalytic Review* 14 (1927): 189–99.
Cox, E. W. *Principles of Punishment*. London, 1877.

Ellis, H. 'The Play Function of Sex', *British Society for the Study of Sex Psychology*, Pamphlet no. 9. London, 1921.
Gibb, A. D. *A Preface to Scots Law*. Edinburgh, 1944.
Gibb, A. D. *Scotland in Eclipse*. London, 1930.
Gibbs, P. *Now It Can Be Told*. London, 1920, facsimile edn. South Carolina, 2015.
Gibbs, P. *Since Then*. London, 1930.
Glaister, J. *Medical Jurisprudence and Toxicology*. 3rd edn. Edinburgh, 1915.
Goodwin, J. C. *Insanity and the Criminal*. London, 1923.
Grant, I. F. 'The Law of Incest in Scotland', *Juridical Review* 26, no. 4 (1914): 437–47.
Hamilton, C. *Life Errant*. London, 1935.
Hamilton, C. *Modern Scotland*. London, 1937.
Hollander, B. *The Psychology of Misconduct, Vice and Crime*. London, 1922.
Hume, D. *Commentaries on the Law of Scotland, Respecting Trial for Crimes*. 4th edn. Edinburgh, 1844.
Juridical Review. 1910–30.
Justiciary Cases. Glasgow University Law Library, 1917–26 and 1926–30.
Keedy, E. R. 'Criminal Procedure in Scotland', *Journal of the American Institute of Criminal Law and Criminology* 3 (1912): 728–53.
Keedy, E. R. 'Criminal Procedure in Scotland II', *Journal of the American Institute of Criminal Law and Criminology* 3, issue 6 (1913): 834–54.
MacGregor Mitchell, R. *A Practical Treatise on the Criminal Law of Scotland, by the Late Right Honourable Sir J. H. A. Macdonald*. Edinburgh, 1929.
Mannheim, H. *Social Aspects of Crime in England between the Wars*. London, 1940.
Norwood East, W. 'Sexual Offenders – A British View', *The Yale Law Journal* 55, no. 3 (April 1946): 527–57.
Pryde, G. S. *Social Life in Scotland since 1707*. London, 1934.
Scots Law Times. Edinburgh, 1908–30.
Sherwell, A. *The Drink Peril in Scotland*. Edinburgh, 1903.
Smith, S. *Forensic Medicine: A Text-Book for Students and Practitioners*. London, 1925.
Stead, W. T. 'Close Time for Girls', *Pall Mall Gazette*, 8 July 1885.
Tod, M. C. 'Gonorrhoeal Vulvo-Vaginitis in Children', *British Journal of Venereal Diseases* 3, no. 2 (April 1927): 113–21.
Webb, B. *My Apprenticeship*. London, 1926.
Woolf, V. *Moments of Being*. London, 2002.

Secondary sources: Books and chapters

Abrams, L. 'From Demon to Victim: The Infanticidal Mother in Shetland 1699–1899', in *Twisted Sisters: Women, Crime and Deviance in Scotland since 1400*, edited by Y. Galloway Brown and R. Ferguson, 180–99. East Linton, 2002.

Abrams, L. and C. G. Brown. 'Introduction: Conceiving the Everyday in the Twentieth Century', in *A History of Everyday Life in Twentieth Century Scotland*, edited by L. Abrams and C. G. Brown, 1–18. Edinburgh, 2010.

Abrams, L. and E. Ewan. *Nine Centuries of Man: Manhood and Masculinities in Scottish History*. Edinburgh, 2017.

Anderson, M. *Scotland's Populations from the 1850s to Today*. Oxford, 2018.

Archer, J. E. 'Men Behaving Badly?: Masculinity and the Uses of Violence 1850–1900', in *Everyday Violence in Britain 1850-1950*, edited by S. D'Cruze, 41–54. Harlow, 2000.

Arnold, J. H. and S. Brady. *What Is Masculinity? Historical Dynamics from Antiquity to the Contemporary World*. Basingstoke, 2013.

Barclay, K. 'From Rape to Marriage: Questions of Consent in Eighteenth-Century Britain', in *Interpreting Sexual Violence, 1660–1800*, edited by A. Greenfield, 35–44. Abingdon, 2016.

Bartie, A. and A. Fraser. 'Speaking to the Hard Men: Masculinities, Violence and Youth Gangs in Glasgow, c. 1965-1975', in *Nine Centuries of Man: Manhood and Masculinities in Scottish History*, edited by L. Abrams and E. Ewan, 258–77. Edinburgh, 2017.

Bland, L. 'Marriage Laid Bare: Middle-Class Women and Marital Sex 1880s-1914', in *Labour and Love: Women's Experience of Home and Family 1850–1940*, edited by J. Lewis, 123–46. Oxford, 1986.

Bland, L., *Modern Women on Trial: Sexual Transgression in the Age of the Flapper*. Manchester, 2013.

Bourke, J. *Disgrace: Global Reflections on Sexual Violence*. London, 2022.

Bourke, J. *Dismembering the Male: Men's Bodies, Britain and the Great War*. London, 2009.

Bourke, J. *Rape: A History from 1860 to the Present*. London, 2010.

Bourke, J. *Working-Class Cultures in Britain 1890-1950*. London, 1994.

Boyd, K. 'Knowing Your Place: The Tensions of Manliness in Boys' Story Papers, 1918-1939', in *Manful Assertions: Masculinities in Britain since 1800*, edited by M. Roper and J. Tosh, 145–67. London, 1991.

Brookman, F. 'Homicide', in *Handbook on Crime*, edited by F. Brookman, M. Maguire, H. Pierpoint and T. Bennett, 217–44. Cullompton, 2010.

Browne, S. and J. Tomlinson. 'A Women's Town', in *Jute No More*, edited by J. Tomlinson and C. A. Whatley, chapter 5. Dundee, 2015.

Cameron, E. A. 'The Scottish Highlands: From Congested District to Objective One', in *Scotland in the Twentieth Century*, edited by T. M. Devine and R. J. Finlay, 153–69. Edinburgh, 1996.

Campbell, R. H. and T. M. Devine. 'The Rural Experience', in *People and Society in Scotland vol. II 1830–1914*, edited by W. H. Fraser and R. J. Morris, 46–72. Edinburgh, 1990.

Caputi, J. *The Age of Sex Crime*. London, 1988.

Carson, K. and H. Idzikowska. 'The Social Production of Scottish Policing 1795–1900', in *Policing and Prosecution in Britain 1750-1850*, edited by D. Days and F. Snyder, 267–97. Oxford, 1989.

Chalmers, J., F. Leverick and V. E. Munro. 'Beyond Doubt: The Case against "Not Proven"', *Modern Law Review* 0 (2021): 1–32.

Cheadle, T. 'Music Hall, "Mashers" and the "Unco Guid": Competing Masculinities in Victorian Glasgow', in *Nine Centuries of Man: Manhood and Masculinities in Scottish History*, edited by L. Abrams and E. Ewan, 223–41. Edinburgh, 2017.

Checkland, S. and O. Checkland. *Industry and Ethos: Scotland 1832–1914*. London, 1984.

Clark, A., 'Domesticity and the Problem of Wife Beating in Nineteenth Century Britain: Working Class Culture, Law and Politics', in *Everyday Violence in Britain 1850-1950, Gender and Class*, edited by S. D'Cruze, chapter 1, 27–40. Harlow, 2000.

Clarke, P. *Hope and Glory: Britain in 1900–1990*. London, 1996.

Conley, C. *Certain Other Countries: Homicide, Gender and National Identity in Late Nineteenth Century England, Ireland, Scotland and Wales*. Ohio, 2007.

Conley, C. 'Sexual Violence in Historical Perspective', in *The Oxford Handbook of Gender, Sex and Crime*, edited by R. Gartner and B. McCarthy, 191–205. Oxford, 2014.

Conley, C. *The Unwritten Law: Criminal Justice in Victorian Kent*. Oxford, 1991.

Connell, R. W. *Masculinities*. London, 2018.

Crowther, M. A. and B. White. *On Soul and Conscience: The Medical Expert and Crime, 150 years of Forensic Medicine in Glasgow*. Aberdeen, 1988.

Daly, M. and M. Wilson. *Homicide*. New Brunswick, 1988.

Davidson, R. *Dangerous Liaisons: A Social History of Venereal Disease in Twentieth-Century Scotland*. Amsterdam, 2000.

Davidson, R. *Illicit and Unnatural Practices: The Law, Sex and Society in Scotland since 1900*. Edinburgh, 2019.

Davies, A. *City of Gangs: Glasgow and the Rise of the British Gangster*. London, 2014.

Davis, J. 'The London Garrotting Panic of 1862: A Moral Panic and the Creation of a Criminal Class in Mid-Victorian England', in *Crime and the Law: The Social History of Crime in Western Europe since 1500*, edited by V. A. C. Gatrell, B. Lenman and G. Parker, general editor N. McKendrick, 190–213. London, 1980.

D'Cruze, S., ed. *Everyday Violence in Britain 1850-1950*. Harlow, 2000.

D'Cruze, S. and L. A. Jackson, eds. *Women, Crime and Justice in England since 1660*. London, 2009.

de Courcy, A. *The Viceroy's Daughters: The lives of the Curzon Sisters*. London, 2000.

Denys, C. 'Geography of Crime: Urban and Rural Environments', in *The Oxford Handbook of the History of Crime and Criminal Justice*, edited by P. Knepper and A. Johansen, 1–25. Oxford, 2016.

Devlin, P. *Trial by Jury*. London, 1956.

Donnelly, D. *The Scottish Police Officer*. Abingdon, 2014.

Edwards, S. S. M. '"Provoking Her Own Demise": From Common Assault to Homicide', in *Women, Violence and Social Control*, edited by J. Hanmer and M. Maynard, 152–68. London, 1990.

Evans, S. *Queen Bees: Six Brilliant and Extraordinary Society Hostesses between the Wars*. London, 2016.

Farmer, L. 'Criminal Law', in *A Compendium of Scottish Ethnology, Series: Scottish Life and Society*, edited by M. Mulhern, 177–90. Edinburgh, 2012.

Farmer, L. *Criminal Law, Tradition and Legal Order: Crime and the Genius of Scots Law 1747 to the Present*. Cambridge, 2005.

Farmer, L. *Making the Modern Criminal Law: Criminalization and Civil Order*. Oxford, 2016.

Fiske, A. P. and T. S. Rai. *Virtuous Violence*. Cambridge, 2015.

Fletcher, J. *Violence and Civilization: An Introduction to the Work of Norbert Elias*. Cambridge, 1997.

Flinn, M., ed. *Scottish Population History from the 17th Century to the 1930s*. Cambridge, 1977.

Fraser, D. *The Christian Watt Papers*. Ellon, 1988.

French, H. and M. Rothery. 'Hegemonic Masculinities? Assessing Change and Processes of Change in Elite Masculinity, 1700–1900', in *What Is Masculinity? Historical Dynamics from Antiquity to the Contemporary World*, edited by J. H. Arnold and S. Brady, 139–66. Basingstoke, 2013.

Fussell, P. *The Great War and Modern Memory*. Oxford, 2013.

Gaskill, M. *Crime and Mentalities in Early Modern England*. Cambridge, 2000.

Gatrell, V. A. C. 'The Decline of Theft and Violence in Victorian and Edwardian England', in *Crime and the Law: The Social History of Crime in Western Europe since 1500*, edited by V. A. C. Gatrell, B. Lenman and G. Parker, general editor N. McKendrick, 238–337. London, 1980.

Gatrell, V. A. C. and T. B. Hadden. 'Criminal Statistics and their Interpretation', in *Nineteenth Century Society: Essays in the Use of Quantitative Methods for the Study of Social Data*, edited by E. A. Wrigley, 336–96. Cambridge, 1972.

Gibbon, L. G. *A Scots Quair*. Edinburgh, 2006.

Gilbert, S. M. 'Soldier's Heart: Literary Men, Literary Women, and the Great War', in *Behind the Lines: Gender and the Two World Wars*, edited by M. R. Higonnet, J. Jenson, S. Michel and M. C. Weitz, 197–226. Yale, 1987.

Gittins, D. 'Marital Status, Work and Kinship, 1850–1930', in *Labour and Love: Women's Experience of Home and Family 1850–1940*, edited by J. Lewis, 249–67. Oxford, 1986.

Glasser, R. *Growing up in the Gorbals*. London, 1986.

Godfrey, B., C. Emsley and G. Dunstall, eds. *Comparative Histories of Crime*. Cullompton, 2003.

Gordon, E. 'The Family', in *Gender in Scottish History since 1700*, edited by L. Abrams, E. Gordon, D. Simonton and E. Janes Yeo. Edinburgh, 2006.

Gordon, E. 'Women's Spheres', in *People and Society in Scotland vol. II 1830–1914*, edited by W. H. Fraser and R. J. Morris, 206–35, Edinburgh, 1990.

Gordon, P. *Policing Scotland*. Glasgow, 1980.

Grant, D. *The Thin Blue Line: The Story of the City of Glasgow Police*. London, 1973.

Graves, R. and A. Hodge. *The Long Weekend: A Social History of Great Britain 1918–1939*. London, 1995.

Gray Kyd, J. *Scottish Population Statistics Including Webster's Analysis of Population 1755*, vol. 44, series 3. Edinburgh, 1952.

Greenfield, A. *Interpreting Sexual Violence, 1660–1800*. Abingdon, 2016.

Greer, G. *Germaine Greer on Rape*. London, 2018.

Hay, D. 'Property, Authority and the Criminal Law', in *Albion's Fatal Tree: Crime and Society in Eighteenth-Century England*, edited by D. Hay, P. Linebaugh, J. G. Rule, E. P. Thompson and C. Winslow, 17–63. London, 2011.

Herman, J. L. *Father-Daughter Incest*. Harvard, 1981.

Hobsbawm, E. J. *Industry and Empire: The Birth of the Industrial Revolution*. London, 1999.

Holy Bible, authorized King James version. Edinburgh, 1952.

Jackson, L. A. *Child Sexual Abuse in Victorian England*. London, 2000.

Jackson, L. A. 'The Child's Word in Court: Cases of Sexual Abuse in London 1870–1914', in *Gender and Crime in Modern Europe*, edited by C. Usborne and M. Arnot, 222–37. London, 2001.

Jackson, L. A. 'Family, Community and the Regulation of Child Sexual Abuse, London 1870–1914', in *Childhood in Question: Children, Parents and the State*, edited by A. Fletcher and S. Hussey, 133–51. Manchester, 1999.

Jackson, L. A. 'Girls and Delinquency', in *Women, Crime and Justice in England since 1660*, edited by S. D'Cruze and L. A. Jackson, 143–60. Basingstoke, 2009.

Jackson, L. A. 'Women Professionals and the Regulation of Violence in Interwar Britain', in *Everyday Violence in Britain 1850-1950*, edited by S. D'Cruze, 119–35. Harlow, 2000.

Jackson, L. A., with N. Davidson, L. Fleming, D. M. Smale and R. Sparks. *Police and Community in Twentieth-Century Scotland*. Edinburgh, 2020.

Jamieson, L. 'Changing Intimacy: Seeking and Forming Couple Relationships', in *A History of Everyday Life in Twentieth Century Scotland*, edited by L. Abrams and C. G. Brown, 76–102. Edinburgh, 2010.

Jamieson, L. 'Limited Resources and Limiting Conventions: Working-Class Mothers and Daughters in Urban Scotland c.1890-1925', in *Labour and Love: Women's Experience of Home and Family 1850–1940*, edited by J. Lewis, 49–69. Oxford, 1986.

Johnson, E. A. and E. H. Monkkonen. *The Civilization of Crime: Violence in Town and Country since the Middle Ages*. Chicago, 1996.

Kellas, J. G. *Modern Scotland*. London, 1980.

Kilday, A. M. *Crime in Scotland 1660–1960: The Violent North?*. Abingdon, 2019.

Kilday, A. M. and D. Nash, eds. *Histories of Crime: Britain 1600-2000*. Basingstoke, 2010.
King, P. *Crime, Justice and Discretion in England, 1740–1820*. Basingstoke, 2000.
King, P. 'Moral Panics and Violent Street Crime 1750-2000', in *Comparative Histories of Crime*, edited by B. Godfrey, C. Emsley and G. Dunstall, 53–71. Cullompton, 2003.
Kingsley-Kent, S. *Making Peace: The Reconstruction of Gender in Interwar Britain*, 74–143. Chichester, 1993.
Knafla, L. A. 'Structure, Conjuncture and Event in the Historiography of Modern Criminal Justice History', in *Crime History and Histories of Crime: Studies in Historiography of Crime and Criminal Justice in Modern History*, edited by C. Emsley and L. A. Knafla, 33–46. Westport, 1996.
Knepper, P. *Writing the History of Crime*. London, 2017.
Knox, W. W. *Industrial Nation: Work, Culture and Society in Scotland, 1800-Present*. Edinburgh, 1999.
Knox, W. W. 'The Political and Workplace Culture of the Scottish Working Class, 1832–1914', in *People and Society in Scotland vol. II 1830–1914*, edited by W. H. Fraser and R. J. Morris, 138–66. Edinburgh, 1990.
Knox, W. W. J. and A. McKinlay. 'Crime, Protest and Policing in Nineteenth Century Scotland', in *A History of Everyday life in Scotland 1800–1900*, edited by T. Griffiths and G. Morton, 196–224. Edinburgh, 2010.
Kuper, A. *Incest and Influence: The Private Life of Bourgeois England*. Harvard, 2009.
Lentin, A. *Mr. Justice McCardie 1869-1933*. Newcastle upon Tyne, 2016.
Mahood, L. 'Family Ties: Lady Child-Savers and Girls of the Street, 1850–1925', in *Out of Bounds: Women in Scottish Society 1800–1945*, edited by E. Breitenbach and E. Gordon, 42–64. Edinburgh, 1992.
Mayer, I. 'The Catholic Community', in *Scotland in the Twentieth Century*, edited by T. M. Devine and R. J. Finlay, 269–84. Edinburgh, 1996.
McArthur, A. and H. Kingsley Long. *No Mean City*. London, 1989.
McGarry, R. and S. Walklate, eds. *The Palgrave Handbook of Criminology and War*. London, 2016.
McIvor, A. 'Gender Apartheid? Women in Scottish Society', in *Scotland in the Twentieth Century*, edited by T. M. Devine and R. J. Finlay, 188–209. Edinburgh, 1996.
Meek, J. *Queer Voices in Post-War Scotland*. Basingstoke, 2015.
Meek, J. '"That Class of Men": Effeminacy, Sodomy and Failed Masculinities in Inter- and Post-War Scotland', in *Nine Centuries of Man: Manhood and Masculinities in Scottish History*, edited by L. Abrams and E. Ewan, 242–57. Edinburgh, 2017.
Moody, S. R. and J. Tombs. *Prosecution in the Public Interest*. Edinburgh, 1982.
Murdoch, A. and R. B. Sher. 'Literary and Learned Culture', in *People and Society in Scotland, volume 1 1760-1830*, edited by T. M. Devine and R. Mitchison, 127–42. Edinburgh, 1988.
Newburn, T. and E. A. Stanko, eds. *Just Boys doing Business: Men, Masculinities and Crime*. London, 1994.

Olsson, L. '"Violence that's wicked for a man to use": Sex, Gender and Violence in the Eighteenth Century', in *Interpreting Sexual Violence, 1660-1800*, edited by A. Greenfield, 141-8. Abingdon, 2016.

Overy, R. *The Morbid Age*. London, 2010.

Radzinowicz, L. *Sexual Offences: A Report of the Cambridge Department of Criminal Science*. London, 1957.

Rodger, R. 'Urbanisation in Twentieth Century Scotland', in *Scotland in the Twentieth Century*, edited by T. M. Devine and R. J. Finlay, 122-52. Edinburgh, 1996.

Rogers, H. 'Making their Mark: Young Offenders' Life Histories and Social Networks', in *Law, Crime & Deviance since 1700 - Micro-Studies in the History of Crime*, edited by A. M. Kilday and D. Nash, 227-49. London, 2017.

Rolph, C. H. *Common Sense about Crime and Punishment*. London, 1961.

Roper, M. and J. Tosh. *Manful Assertions: Masculinities in Britain since 1800*. London, 1991.

Roth, R. 'Gender, Sex and Intimate Partner Violence in Historical Perspective', in *The Oxford Handbook of Gender, Sex and Crime*, edited by R. Gartner and B. McCarthy, 163-76. Oxford, 2014.

Sharpe, J. 'History from Below', in *New Perspectives on Historical Writing*, edited by P. Burke, 25-42. Cambridge, 2001.

Smith, R. *Trial by Medicine: Insanity and Responsibility in Victorian Trials*. Edinburgh, 1981.

Smout, T. C. *A Century of the Scottish People 1850-1930*. London, 1986.

Spierenburg, P. *A History of Murder: Personal Violence in Europe from the Middle Ages to the Present*. Cambridge, 2008.

Spierenburg, P. *Men and Violence: Gender, Honor, and Rituals in Modern Europe and America*, edited by P. Spierenburg. Ohio, 1998.

Stanko, E. A. *Intimate Intrusions: Women's Experience of Male Violence*. London, 1985.

Stanko, E. A. 'Typical Violence, Normal Precaution: Men, Women and Interpersonal Violence in England, Wales, Scotland and the USA', in *Women, Violence and Social Control*, edited by J. Hanmer and M. Maynard, 122-34. London, 1990.

Stevenson, K. 'Ingenuities of the Female Mind: Legal and Public Perceptions of Sexual Violence in Victorian England, 1850-1890', in *Everyday Violence in Britain 1850-1950*, edited by S. D'Cruze, 89-103. Harlow, 2000.

Strachan, H. 'The Scottish Soldier and Scotland, 1914-1918', in *A Global Force: War, Identities and Scotland's Diaspora*, edited by D. Forsyth and W. Ugolini, chapter 3. Edinburgh, 2018.

Thom, D. 'Wishes, Anxieties, Play and Gestures: Child Guidance in Inter-war England', in *In the Name of the Child: Health and Welfare 1880-1940*, edited by R. Cooter, 200-19. London, 1992.

Tosh, J. 'Domesticity and Manliness in the Victorian Middle Class: The Family of Edward White Benson', in *Manful Assertions: Masculinities in Britain since 1800*, edited by M. Roper and J. Tosh, 44-73. London, 1991.

Tosh, J. 'The History of Masculinity: An Outdated Concept', in *What Is Masculinity? Historical Dynamics from Antiquity to the Contemporary World*, edited by J. H. Arnold and S. Brady, 17–34. Basingstoke, 2013.

Ward, E. *Father-Daughter Rape*. London, 1988.

Weinberger, B. *The Best Police in the World*. Cambridge, 1995.

Weinberger, B. 'Urban and Rural Crime Rates and their Genesis in Late Nineteenth- and Early Twentieth-Century Britain', in *The Civilization of Crime: Violence in Town and Country since the Middle Ages*, edited by E. A. Johnson and E. H. Monkkonen, 198–216. Chicago, 1996.

Weston, J. *Medicine, the Penal System and Sexual Crimes in England, 1919-1960s: Diagnosing Deviance*. London, 2018.

Wiener, M. *Men of Blood: Violence, Manliness and Criminal Justice in Victorian England*. Cambridge, 2006.

Wiener, M. *Reconstructing the Criminal – Culture, Law and Policy in England 1830- 1914*. Cambridge, 1990.

Wiener, M. 'The Victorian Criminalization of Men', in *Men and Violence: Gender, Honor, and Rituals in Modern Europe and America*, edited by P. Spierenburg, 197–212. USA, 1998.

Wohl, A. 'Sex and the Single Room: Incest among the Victorian Working-Classes', in *The Victorian Family, Structure and Stresses*, edited by A. Wohl, 197–216. New York, 1978.

Yarrow, S. 'Masculinity as a World Historical Category of Analysis', in *What Is Masculinity? Historical Dynamics from Antiquity to the Contemporary World*, edited by J. H. Arnold and S. Brady, 114–38. Basingstoke, 2013.

Young, H. 'Being a Man: Everyday Masculinities', in *A History of Everyday Life in Twentieth Century Scotland*, edited by L. Abrams and C. G. Brown, 131–52. Edinburgh, 2010.

Secondary sources: Journal articles

Abrams, L. 'The Taming of Highland Masculinity: Interpersonal Violence and Shifting Codes of Manhood, c.1760-1840', *The Scottish Historical Review* 92, no. 233 (April 2013): 100–22.

Ackner, Lord Justice. 'The Crime of Incest', *Medico-Legal Journal* 48 (1980): 79–91.

Alexander, D. F. 'Twenty Years of Morgan: A Criticism of the Subjectivist View of Mens Rea and Rape in Great Britain', *Pace International Law Review* 7, no. 1 (1995): 207–46.

Anwar, S., P. Bayer and R. Hjalmarsson. *A Jury of Her Peers: The Impact of the First Female Jurors on Criminal Convictions*. Working Paper No.21960, 1–47. Cambridge: National Bureau of Economic Research, 2016.

Barrie, D. G. 'The Media as a Judicial and Police Resource: Police Courts and the Printed Word in Scotland, c.1800 to 1850', *Cultural and Social History* 12, no. 3 (2015): 385–410.

Barrie, D. G. 'Naming and Shaming: Trial by Media in Nineteenth Century Scotland', *Journal of British Studies*, no. 54 (April 2015): 349–76.

Begiato, J. 'Between Poise and Power: Embodied Manliness in Eighteenth- and Nineteenth-Century British Culture', *Transactions of the Royal Historical Society* 26 (2016): 125–47.

Bingham, A. '"It would be Better for the Newspapers to Call a Spade a Spade": The British Press and Child Sexual Abuse, c.1918-90', *History Workshop Journal*, issue 88 (2019): 89–110.

Bingham, A., L. Delap, L. Jackson and L. Settle. 'Historical Child Sexual Abuse in England and Wales: The Role of Historians', *History of Education* 45, no. 4 (2016): 411–29.

Blaikie, A. 'Scottish Illegitimacy: Social Adjustment or Moral Economy?', *Journal of Interdisciplinary History* 20, no. 2 (Autumn 1998): 221–41.

Bourke, J. 'Police Surgeons and Victims of Rape: Cultures of Harm and Care', *Social History of Medicine* 31, no. 4 (2019): 711–31.

Bows, H. and J. Herring. 'Getting away with Murder? A Review of the "Rough Sex Defence"', *Journal of Criminal Law* 84, no. 6 (2020): 525–38.

Burman, M., L. Lovett and L. Kelly. 'Country Briefing: Scotland', in *Different Systems, Similar Outcomes? Tracking Attrition in Reported Rape Cases in Eleven Countries*, 1–10. European Commission Daphne II Programme, May 2009. www.cwasu.org.

Carter Wood, J. 'Self-Policing and Policing the Self: Violence, Protection and the Civilizing Bargain in Britain', *Crime, History & Societies* 7, no. 1 (2003): 109–28.

Christie, D. J. and S. R. Moody. *The Work of Precognition Agents in Criminal Cases*, 1–30, Scottish Executive Central Research Unit. Scottish Government, 1999.

Christoffersen, M. N., K. Soothill and B. Francis. 'Who Is Most a Risk of becoming a Convicted Rapist? The Likelihood of a Rape Conviction among the 1966 Cohort in Denmark', *Journal of Scandinavian Studies in Criminology and Crime Prevention* 6 (2005): 39–56.

Coldrey, B. 'The Sexual Abuse of Children: The Historical Perspective', *Studies: An Irish Quarterly Review* 85, no. 340 (Winter 1996): 370–80.

Colpi, T. 'The Scottish Italian Community: Senza un campanile?', *Innes Review* 44, no. 2 (1993): 153–67.

Conley, C. 'Rape and Justice in Victorian England', *Victorian Studies* 29, no. 4 (Summer 1986): 519–36.

Conley, C. 'War among Savages: Homicide and Ethnicity in the Victorian United Kingdom', *Journal of British Studies* 44 (October 2005): 775–95.

Crosby, K. 'Keeping Women off the Jury in 1920s England and Wales', *Legal Studies* 37, issue 4 (2017): 1–23.

Damaska, M., 'Criminal Procedure in Scotland and France', *Yale Law School Faculty Scholarship Series 1588* (1976): 779–84.

da Silva, T., J. Woodhams and L. Harkins. 'Multiple Perpetrator Rape: A Critical Review of Existing Explanatory Theories', *Aggression and Behavior* 25 (2015): 150–8.

Davidson, N., L. Fleming, L. A. Jackson, D. Smale and R. Sparks. 'Police and Community in Twentieth-Century Scotland: The Uses of Social History', *British Journal of Criminology* 57 (2017): 18–39.

D'Cruze, S. 'Sex, Violence and Local Courts – Working-Class Respectability in a Mid-nineteenth Century Lancashire Town', *British Journal of Criminology* 39, no. 1 (1990): 39–55.

Denno, D. W. 'The Privacy Rights of Rape Victims in the Media and the Law: Perspectives on Disclosing Rape Victims' Names', *Fordham Law Review* 61 (1993): 1113–31.

Dobash, R. E. and R. P. Dobash. 'The Nature and Antecedents of Violent Events', *British Journal of Criminology* 24, no. 3 (July 1984): 269–88.

Eisner, M. 'Long term Historical Trends in Violent Crime', *Crime and Justice, a Review of Research* 30 (2003): 83–142.

Ferreira, L. T. H. and M. Grasten. 'Law's Lolita Paradox: Translating "childhood" in Statutory Rape Jurisprudence', *Australian Feminist Law Review* 47, no. 2 (2022): 229–49.

Gane, C., 'The Scottish Jury', *Revue international de droit penal* 72, no. 1 (2001): 259–72.

Giles, J. 'Playing Hard to Get: Working-Class Women, Sexuality and Respectability in Britain, 1918–40', *Women's History Review* 1, no. 2 (1992): 239–55.

Goodwin, J., L. Cormier and J. Owen. 'Grandfather-Granddaughter Incest: A Trigenerational View', *Child Abuse and Neglect* 7 (1983): 163–70.

Gordon, G. and J. Robb. 'Small-Scale Residential Differentiation in Nineteenth Century Scottish Cities', *Scottish Geographical Magazine* 97, no. 2 (1981): 77–84.

Gorham, D., '"The Maiden Tribute of Modern Babylon" Re-examined: Child Prostitution and the Idea of Childhood in Late-Victorian England', *Victorian Studies* 21, no. 3 (Spring 1978): 353–79.

Hall, L. A. 'Impotent Ghosts from No Man's Land, Flappers' Boyfriends, or Crypto-Patriarchs? Men, Sex and Social Change in 1920s Britain', *Social History* 21, no. 1 (January 1996): 54–70.

Holligan, C. and R. Deuchar. 'What does It Mean to be a Man? Psychosocial Undercurrents in the Voices of Incarcerated (violent) Scottish Teenage Offenders', *Criminology & Criminal Justice* 15, no. 3 (2015): 361–77.

Jackson, S. 'The Social Context of Rape: Sexual Scripts and Motivation', *Women's Studies International Quarterly* 1 (1978): 27–38.

Jewkes, R. 'Intimate Partner Violence: Causes and Prevention', *The Lancet* 359 (2002): 1423–9.

Johnston, R. and A. McIvor. 'Dangerous Work, Hard Men and Broken Bodies: Masculinity in the Clydeside Heavy Industries', *Labour History Review* 69, no. 2 (August 2004): 135–51.

Jones, J. G. 'Sexual Abuse of Children: Current Concepts', *American Journal of Diseases of Children* 136, no. 2 (1982): 142–6.

Kelly, C. 'Continuity and Change in the History of Scottish Juvenile Justice', *Law Crime and History* 1 (2016): 59–62.

Kelly, L., J. Lovett and L. Regan. *A Gap or a Chasm? Attrition in Reported Rape Cases*, Home Office Research Study 293, 1–136. London Metropolitan University, 2005.

King, P. 'Female Offenders, Work and Life-Cycle Change in Late Eighteenth-Century London', *Continuity and Change* 11, issue 1 (May 1996): 61–90.

Kingsley Kent, S. 'The Politics of Sexual Difference: World War One and the Demise of British Feminism', *Journal of British Studies* 27, no. 3 (July 1988): 232–53.

Lawrence, J. 'Forging a Peaceable Kingdom: War, Violence and Fear of Brutalization in Post-First World War Britain', *The Journal of Modern History* 75, no. 3 (September 2003): 557–89.

Leeming, W. 'New Taboo? Some Observations on the Late Arrival of Changes to the Law of Incest in Scotland', *International Journal of the Sociology of Law* 24 (1996): 313–36.

Levack, B. 'The Prosecution of Sexual Crimes in Early Eighteenth-Century Scotland', *The Scottish Historical Review* LXXXIX, 2, no. 228 (October 2010): 172–93.

Leverick, F. 'What do we know about Rape Myths and Juror Decision Making?', *International Journal of Evidence & Proof* 24, no. 3 (2020): 255–79.

Litin, E. M., M. E. Griffin and A. M. Johnson. 'Parental Influence in Unusual Sexual Behaviour in Children', *The Psychoanalytic Quarterly* 25 (1956): 37–55.

Loughran, T. 'A Crisis of Masculinity? Re-writing the History of Shell-shock and Gender in First World War Britain', *History Compass* 11, no. 9 (2013): 727–38.

Mahood, L. 'Give Him a Doing: The Birching of Young Offenders in Scotland', *Canadian Journal of History* 37 (December 2002): 439–57.

Mahood, L. and B. Littlewood. 'The "Vicious" Girl and the "Street-corner" Boy: Sexuality and the Gendered Delinquent in the Scottish Child-Saving Movement, 1850–1940', *Journal of the History of Sexuality* 4, no. 4 (April 1994): 549–78.

McColgan, A. 'Common Law and the Relevance of Sexual History Evidence', *Oxford Journal of Legal Studies* 16, no. 2 (1996): 275–307.

Meek, J. 'Boarding and Lodging Practices in Early Twentieth Century Scotland', *Continuity and Change* 31, no. 1 (2016): 79–100.

Monkkonen, E. 'Estimating the Accuracy of Historic Homicide Rates', *Social Science History* 25, no. 1 (Spring 2001): 53–66.

Monkkonen, E. 'New Standards for Historical Homicide Research', *Crime History and Societies* 5, no. 2 (2001): 5–26.

Morris, R. M. 'Lies, Damned Lies and Criminal Statistics', *Crime, History and Societies* 5, no. 1 (2001): 111–27.

Munday, R. J. C. 'Reflections on the Criminal Evidence Act 1898', *The Cambridge Law Journal* 44, no. 1 (March 1985): 62–86.

Penlington, N. 'Masculinity and Domesticity in 1930s South Wales: Did Unemployment Change the Domestic Division of Labour?', *Twentieth Century British History* 21, no. 3 (2010): 281–99.

Randolph, J., 'Rape and Resistance: Women and Consent in Seventeenth-Century English Legal and Political Thought', *Journal of British Studies* 39, no. 2 (April 2000): 157–84.

Robertson, S. 'Signs, Marks and Private Parts: Doctors, Legal Discourses and Evidence of Rape in the United States, 1823–1930', *Journal of the History of Sexuality* 8, no. 3 (January 1998): 345–88.

Robertson, S. 'What's Law got to do with it? Legal Records and Sexual Histories', *Journal of the History of Sexuality* 14, no. 1/2 (2005): 161–85.

Ross, E. '"Not the Sort that Would Sit on the Doorstep": Respectability in Pre-World War I London Neighborhoods', *International Labour and Working Class History* 27 (Spring 1985): 39–59.

Shiels, R. S. 'The Crown Practice of Precognition in Mid-Victorian Scotland', *Law, Crime and History* 2 (2015): 29–43.

Shiels, R. S. 'The Mid-Victorian Codification of the Practice of Public Prosecution', *The Scottish Historical Review* 98, supplement no. 248 (October 2019): 410–38.

Smart, C. 'A History of Ambivalence and Conflict in the Discursive Construction of the "Child Victim" of Sexual Abuse', *Social and Legal Studies* 8, no. 3 (1999): 391–409.

Smart, C. 'Reconsidering the Recent History of Child Sexual Abuse, 1910–1960', *Journal of Social Policy* 29, no. 1 (2000): 55–71.

Smith, T. B. 'Bail before Trial: Reflections of a Scottish Lawyer', *University of Pennsylvania Law Review* 108, no. 3 (January 1960): 305–22.

Smythe, W. E. and M. J. Murray. 'Owning the Story: Ethical Considerations in Narrative Research', *Ethics and Behavior* 10, no. 4 (2000): 311–36.

Stevenson, K. '"Not just the Ideas of a Few Enthusiasts": Early Twentieth Century Legal Activism and the Reformation of the Age of Sexual Consent', *Cultural and Social History* 14, no. 2 (2017): 219–36.

Stevenson, K. '"These are cases which it is inadvisable to drag into the light of day": Disinterring the Crime of Incest in Early Twentieth-Century England', *Crime, History & Societies* 20, no. 2 (2016): 1–25.

Stevenson, K. 'Unearthing the Realities of Rape: Utilising Victorian Newspaper Reportage to Fill in the Contextual Gaps', *Liverpool Law Review* 38 (2007): 405–24.

Storch, R. 'The Plague of Blue Locusts: Police Reform and Popular Resistance in Northern England, 1840–1857', *International Review of Social History* 20, issue 1 (April 1975): 61–90.

Storch, R. 'The Policeman as Domestic Missionary: Urban Discipline and Popular Culture in Northern England, 1850–1880', *The Journal of Social History* 9, issue 4 (1976): 481–509.

Strachan, H. 'The First World War as a Global War', *First World War Studies* 1, issue 1 (2010): 3–14.

Takayanagi, M. 'Women and the Vote: The Parliamentary Path to Equal Franchise 1918-28', *Parliamentary History* 37, no. 1 (2018): 173-7.

Taylor, K. J. 'Venereal Disease in Nineteenth-Century Children', *Journal of Psychohistory* 12, no. 4 (1985): 431-64.

Tidefors, I., H. Arvisson, S. Ingevaldson and M. Larsson. 'Sibling Incest: A Literature Review and a Clinical Study', *Journal of Sexual Aggression* 16, no. 3 (November 2010): 347-60.

Tylee, C. M. 'Maleness Run Riot: The Great War and Women's Resistance to Militarism', *Women's Studies International Forum* 11, no. 3 (1988): 199-210.

Willock, I. D. 'The Jury in Scotland', *Stair Society* 23 (1966): 1-290.

Wood, J. C. 'Criminal Violence in Modern Britain', *History Compass* 4, no. 1 (2006): 77-90.

Woollacott, A. 'Khaki Fever and Its Control: Gender, Class, Age and Sexual Morality on the British Homefront in the First World War', *Journal of Contemporary History* 29, no. 2 (April 1994): 325-47.

Theses & unpublished papers

Bates, V. '"Not an Exact Science": Medical Approaches to Age and Sexual Offences in England, 1850-1914'. PhD thesis, University of Exeter, 2012.

Brown, A. 'Social History of Scottish Homicide, 1836–1869'. Unpublished thesis, University of Leicester, 2015.

Duvall, N. E. 'Forensic Medicine in Scotland, 1914–39'. Unpublished PhD thesis, University of Manchester, 2013.

Goldsmith, A. L. 'The Development of the City of Glasgow Police c. 1800-1939'. Unpublished PhD thesis, University of Strathclyde, 2002.

Gordon, G. H. 'Criminal Responsibility in Scots Law'. Unpublished PhD thesis, University of Glasgow, 1959.

Willock, I. D. 'The Origins and Development of the Jury System in Scotland'. PhD thesis, Aberdeen, 1963.

Online sources

Age of Consent Podcast. https://www.narrativematters.scot/the-age-of-consent-podcast

England and Wales Crime Statistics. www.gov.uk/government/statistics/historical-crime-data

Godfrey, B., T. Hitchcock and R. Shoemaker. 'The Ethics of Digital Data on Convict Lives'. www.digitalpanopticon.org/The_Ethics_of_Digital_Data

Greer, G. 'BBC Radio 4', *Today*, 20 March 2018.
Investigation and Prosecution of Sexual Crimes Review, Justice Directorate, Scottish Government, 16 November 2017.
Jackson, L. A. 'Child Sexual Abuse in England and Wales: Prosecution and Prevalence 1918–1970'. http://www.historyandpolicy.org/policy-papers/rss_2.0
Jackson, L. A. 'Sexual Assault, Criminal Justice and Policing since the 1880s'. www.historyandpolicy.org
The London Rape Review: A Review of Cases from 2016, Mayor's Office for Policing and Crime, July 2019.
Rape Crisis Scotland. www.rapecrisisscotland.org/help-facts/
Scots Law definitions. https://www.copfs.gov.uk/involved-in-a-case/glossary-of-legal-terms#N -
UK 1921 Census Data. http://www.visionofbritain.org.uk/census/table/EW1921GEN_M1 -

Modern newspapers

'Flashing Isn't a Minor Crime. It can End in a Nightmare', *The Times*, 23 October 2022.
'Give us your iPhone or We'll Drop the Case', *The Times*, 29 April 2019.
'The Problem with Calling Someone an "accuser" when they Allege Sexual Assault', *Washington Post*, 27 September 2018.
'Who's a Victim? Who's an Accuser?', *Washington Post*, 27 September 2018.

Index

Aberdeen   2, 5, 48, 83, 164, 199, 219
   Aberdeenshire   158, 169
Acts of Parliament, *see under* individual entries
actus reus   203
Advocate Depute   35, 39, 84, 106, 140, 166, 167, 182, 185–7, 207, 209, 214, 215
alcohol   16, 57, 65, 75, 78, 110, 118, 135, 137, 147
   addicted to drink   61
   alcoholic confusion   66
   drink   66, 69, 81, 101, 130
   drunken activities   62
   influence of   65, 67
   liquor   132
   mitigation of   85, 110, 118
   payday drinking   66
   stupor   198
   'unbuttoning effects of'   147
   uninhibiting effects of   67, 76
Aliens Order Act, (1920)   84
American Institute of Criminal Law and Criminology   39
Arbroath   63
Armistice   58
Arnold, John H.   22
Astor, Viscountess   13
Austria   14
   Austria clinic patients   64
Ayr   116, 131, 158, 169

Bail (Scotland) Act, (1888)   44
Ballantyne, Henry, Sir   12
Belgium   42
Bingham, A.   13
'black locusts'   162
Bland, Lucy   18
Blantyre   69
Bloch, Iwan   54
'blue bottles'   162
Boer War   210

Book of Adjournal   21, 111, 193
Book of Regulations (1868)   36, 141, 167, 168, 230
Booth, General   84
Borstal   92, 184, 185, 208
Bourke, Joanna   20
Brady, Sean   22
Britain   2, 3, 6, 14, 54, 156
   UK   2, 5–7, 18, 84, 139, 232
      Home Office   225
Buchan   29

Canada   57, 69
Caputi, Jane   223
Cassity, John Holland   97
Children Act, (1908)   97, 102, 192, 209, 214
Children and Young Persons Act, (1933)   214
civilizing process   9, 223
Clapham Set   16
Conley, Carolyn   18, 223
contraception
   contraceptive precautions   74
   prophylactic precautions   66
   quinine   66, 67
   'salts'   57
Court of Summary Jurisdiction   188
Couzens, Wayne   227
Cox, Edward   175
   Law Times   175
Crimean War   125
criminal appellate court   38, 47
   appellate judge   136
Criminal Evidence Act, (1898)   38, 46
Criminal Law Amendment Act, (1885)   21, 42, 48, 54, 60, 78, 87, 88, 97, 104, 105, 115, 118, 121, 124, 183, 213, 226
   1922 revision   21, 42, 43, 60, 88, 97, 115, 124, 187, 189, 190, 193

'young man's defence'   43, 187, 189, 190
  1928 revision   43, 60
  Section 4   42, 209
  Section 5   107, 189, 209
Criminal Procedure (Scotland) Act, (1995)   228
Criminal Statistics for Scotland, (1925)   84, 88
Crown Agent   39, 40, 68, 106
Crown Counsel   21, 25, 35, 36, 39, 56, 91, 94, 102, 103, 115, 122, 130, 136, 138, 159, 162, 166, 168, 176, 181, 183, 189–91
Culross   148

'dark number'   19, 23, 25, 27, 65, 82, 84, 95, 150, 151, 159, 161, 164, 223, 231
Davidson, Roger   17
D'Cruze, Shani   19, 20
Departmental Committee on Sexual Offences against Children and Young Persons in Scotland, (1926)   13, 164
Devlin, Lord   45
'digital strip search'   228
'dominant rape mythology'   19, 28, 132, 150, 166, 167, 225, 226
'down-blousing'   231
Down's syndrome   106
Dumfries   107, 209
Dundee   2, 5, 71, 122, 129, 218–20, 222
Dunoon   106

East Wemyss   131
economic depression   60, 86, 222
  global recession   60
  Great Crash   2
Edinburgh   2, 5, 13, 39, 61, 71, 74, 76, 95, 122, 128, 133, 148, 171, 178, 179, 219, 220, 222
  High Court   116
  Sheriff Court   116
Eisner, Manuel   7
Elgin   44, 142, 143
Elias, Norbert   9
  Uber den Prozess der Zivilisation   9
England   6, 10, 16, 17, 20, 40–2, 45, 53, 102, 136, 155, 193, 195, 196, 204, 221, 223, 229

'English Law'   17, 33, 35, 36, 44, 46, 135
England and Wales   6, 17, 20, 40, 41, 56, 73, 115, 194, 231
  Old Bailey   200
epilepsy   13, 70
  epileptic fits   80
Essex   167
ethnicity   83–4, 208–10
  French   208, 209
  German   83, 208
  Irish   24, 83, 208–9
  Italian   83, 84, 194, 208, 209
  Polish   209
  Russian   209
  South African   209
Europe   5, 111
  homicide   7
  violence   9
Everard, Sarah   227
'everyday rape'   227, 229

Fairfield, Letitia, Dr.   53
Farmer, Lindsay   20, 223
Fife   94, 122, 144, 179, 182
First Report of Her Majesty's Commissioners for Inquiring into the Housing of the Working Classes, (1885)   12
Fleming, Lord   78, 215
forensic medicine   176–81, 224
Fort William   114
France   10
  French   208, 209
Freud, Sigmund   14, 64
Fry, Margery   13
Fussell, Paul   3

Gaelic   49
gang rape   134, 232
Gatrell, V. A. C.   7
Germany   10, 54, 75
  anti-German   84
  German   83, 208
Gibb, Andrew Dewar   27, 53, 83, 88
Gibbs, Philip   2, 3, 95, 151, 217
Gilbert, Sandra   3
Giles, Judy   18
Glaister, John, Professor   67, 98, 104, 110, 132, 139, 147, 171, 174, 178–80, 186, 189, 190, 206, 210, 213

Index

Glasgow   1, 5, 10–14, 24, 26, 55, 58, 63, 66, 69, 71, 72, 75, 88, 93, 95, 98, 99, 101, 102, 108, 111, 113, 114, 118, 122, 123, 130, 131, 133, 137, 145, 148, 149, 151, 156–8, 160–3, 166, 173, 174, 177, 179, 180, 182, 184, 185, 192, 208, 209, 211, 213, 216, 218–23
   Assizes   190
   Barlinnie (prison)   138
   Barrhead   93, 160
   Bloody Friday   1
   Broomielaw   1
   Central Police Office   137
   Clyde Corridor   5
   Clydeside   2, 11, 208
   County Buildings   63
   Glasgow Herald   139, 149, 216
   Glaswegian men   10
   Govan   93
   Jail Square   139
   Maryhill   158
   Mossend   92
   Mosspark   219
   park   92, 114, 171
   Partick   92
   police   163, 209, 222
   Rutherglen   136
   Sauchiehall Street   30
   second court   50
   Shettleston   95
   slums   4, 232
   University of   88, 98
Glasser, Ralph   10, 14, 72–3
Goodwin, Jean   15
Grassic Gibbon, Lewis   14
   A Scots Quair   14
   Sunset Song   14
Graves, Robert   2, 3, 141, 194
Great Crash   2
Great War   1, 3–5, 33, 39, 55, 63, 64, 75, 95, 111, 123, 132, 159, 216, 217, 232
   Armistice   58
   demobilization   60
      demobilizing troops   3
   Menin Gate   33
   military service   148
   post-traumatic stress   75
   post-war   86, 118, 119, 151, 159, 207, 216, 232
   economic hardship   222
   marriages   63, 64, 130
   trenches   2
   war neurosis   207, 208
   war service   71, 89, 106, 109, 111
   war trauma   111
Greenock   109, 138, 192, 207, 227

Hadden, T. B.   7
Hamilton, Cicely   1–5, 95, 151, 208, 217, 232
Heritable Jurisdictions Act, (1747)   35
Herman, Judith   15
High Court of Justiciary   7, 8, 15–23, 25–32, 35–7, 39, 40, 43–5, 47–50, 56, 61, 63, 72, 73, 76, 78, 82, 84–7, 89, 95, 99, 101, 102, 104–11, 113, 114, 116, 118, 121–4, 127, 128, 130, 134, 135, 139, 140, 142, 145, 147–51, 155, 157–61, 163–8, 170, 172, 173, 177, 181, 182, 184, 189–91, 193–6, 201–4, 206, 209, 212, 213, 215–17, 223, 224, 226, 229, 232
Highlands   4, 24, 34, 106, 122, 126, 163, 184, 219–22
   Culross   148
   dancing   170
   Highlanders   5, 24
   & Islands   5, 221
Hobsbawm, Eric   6
Hollander, Bernard   9, 13, 31, 109, 113, 137, 147, 150
homicide   79, 207
   rape-homicide   227, 231
homosexuality   18, 186
   homosexual prosecutions   195
   sodomy   195
Howard League for Penal Reform   13
   Howard Journal   25
Hull University   232
Hunter, Lord   211–12

illegitimacy   67–8
   pregnancies   141, 142, 204, 221
Incest Act, (1567)   40
India   70
infantile paralysis   106
insanity   70, 139
   plea of   43, 70, 108, 207

sadism   139
special defence   70
Inverness   5, 216
    Assize   106, 194
Irish   24, 83, 208–9
    anti-Irish   83
    Irish-born   208
    Irishman   83
    Scots-Irish   208
    surnames   209
Italian (national)   83, 84, 194, 208, 209

Jackson, Louise A.   16, 17
Jackson, Stevi   19
Jewkes, Rachel   222
Johnson, Eric   7, 22
judges
    Fleming, Lord   78, 215
    Hunter, Lord   211–12
    MacKenzie, Lord   194–5
    McLaren, Lord   189
    Moncrieff, Lord   211
    Ormidale, Lord   139, 215
    Salvesen, Lord   78
    Sands, Lord   53, 211

Keedy, Edwin   39, 45, 47
Kent   18, 134, 214
King, Peter   22
Kingsley-Kent, Susan   3
Kuper, Adam   16

Law and Customs in Scotland in Matters Criminal   20
Law Times   175
Legitimation of Children Act, (1926)   68
Leverick, Fiona   225
Leviticus   40, 68, 78
Littlejohn, Henry   171, 178
Littlewood, Barbara   18
London   16, 30, 64, 102, 112, 113, 224, 227, 230, 231
    Chief Medical Officer   53
    School of Economics   111
London Rape Review, (2016)   224–5, 227, 230
Lord Advocate   35, 166, 189
Loughran, Tracey   3

McArthur, Alexander   10, 11
    & Kingsley Long   10
    No Mean City   10
McCardie, Justice, Mr   193, 208
McColgan, Aileen   19
Macdonald, J. H. A., Sir   183
MacKenzie   20
MacKenzie, Lord   194–5
McLaren, Lord   189
Macready, Nevil, Sir   125
Mafeking   209
Mahood, Linda   18
Maitland, Dorothea   53, 61
Mannheim, Hermann   111, 117–18, 188, 223
Marriage Act, (1929)   110, 190
Married Love   121
masculinity   9, 10, 12, 19, 76, 118, 222, 226
    hegemonic masculinity   9, 11, 222
    hyper-masculine   11, 136
    idealized   229
    masculine behaviour   93, 222
    masculinized society   86
    pay-packet masculinity   11
    rampant   149
    ultra-masculine   222
Meek, Jeffrey   18
mens rea   203, 226
mental condition   98, 106–8
mental illness   70, 207
    'mental defectives'   105–7, 206
    mental incapacity   105
    'weak intellect'   78
    'weak minded'   71, 78, 105
methylated spirits   57
#metoo   229
Middlesex Assize   16, 102, 200
Minute Book   21, 71, 111, 118, 193, 194
Moncrieff, Lord   211
Monkkonen Eric   7, 22
Moray   160
multiple perpetrator rape   134, 135, 148, 228
    gang rape   134, 232
murder   8, 14
    homicide   79
    rape-homicide   138–40, 227, 231

National Society for the Prevention of Cruelty to Children   84
    General Booth   84

Nesbit, Edith   28
'New Portias', the   193–5
New York   107
Norwood East, William   13, 80, 100, 105, 109, 110, 215

Offences against the Person Act, (1828)   21
Orange Lodge   173
Ormidale, Lord   139, 215

paedophilia   97
  'pedophilia'   97
  'sexual psychopath'   97
Paisley   168
Pall Mall Gazette   42, 118
Parliament   3, 13, 188, 226
  Members of   195
patriarchy   9, 228
  patriarchal assumption   20, 161
  patriarchal attitudes   176
  patriarchal hurdles   161
  patriarchal prejudices   161
payday drinking   66
pay packet   11
  pay packet rape   148
Perth   47, 106, 133, 166
  Perthshire   97
police   24, 25, 27, 38, 72, 75, 80–4, 93, 99, 100, 113–15, 117, 131, 134, 156, 160, 164, 229, 231, 232
  'black locusts'   162
  'blue bottles'   162
  constable   24, 37, 69, 133, 137, 146, 149, 155, 166, 184
  court   25, 115, 162, 188
  dual role   26, 99, 118, 156, 162
  employment   24
  female police   160
  Metropolitan   125
  office   15, 36, 59, 67, 70, 74, 85, 114, 156, 157, 159, 160, 225, 231
  Police Manual, (1910)   40
  station   72
  superintendent   162
polio   106
pregnancy   16, 54, 55, 57, 58, 66, 67, 69, 70, 74, 76, 78, 80, 99, 107, 190, 199
  conception   67
  siblings   74–6

Procurator Fiscal   17, 19–25, 27, 28, 33, 35–40, 44, 45, 49, 56, 58, 60, 62, 68, 71, 73, 76, 79, 83, 84, 89, 91–4, 97, 99, 102, 103, 106, 114–16, 124, 130, 133, 134, 136–8, 141–4, 158, 159, 162, 165–70, 172, 174–6, 178–84, 189–91, 204, 206, 207, 209, 222, 230
  fiscal depute   162
  fiscal service   35, 168
  Glasgow's   37, 103, 140, 168, 170, 177, 223
  Inverness's   168
prophylactic precautions   66
prostitute   137–8, 158, 174, 204
Pryde, George   208
Punishment of Incest Act, (1908)   40

Radzinowicz, Leon   230
Rape Crisis Scotland   231
'rape culture'   228
'rape myths'   32, 134, 192, 228, 231
  'dominant rape mythology'   19, 28, 132, 150, 166, 167, 225, 226
  'everyday rape'   227, 229
  'ideal victim'   225, 227
  'real rape'   226, 227
'rape script'   49, 121, 133, 172, 174
  'sexual script'   129
recidivism   116–17, 149–50, 215
Registrar General's Annual Review for Scotland, (1921)   130
Report of the Royal Commission on the Housing of the Industrial Population of Scotland, Rural and Urban, (1917)   12
Representation of the People Act 1918   3
'Roaring Twenties'   141
Roman Catholic   81, 83, 208
Roper, Michael   16
Rothesay   132
rough justice   162–5, 221
Royal Commission on the Housing of the Working Classes, (1884)   54, 56
Royal Scottish Society for the Prevention of Cruelty to Children   71
R v Sweenie (1858)   175

Salvation Army   55
Salvesen, Lord   78

Sands, Lord   53, 211
Scotland   2, 4–6, 10, 11, 16–18, 20, 26, 29, 33–5, 45, 53, 55, 56, 71, 73, 82, 83, 85, 86, 89, 97, 102, 117, 122, 125, 126, 134, 138–40, 146, 150, 155–7, 162, 167, 170, 178, 181, 182, 189, 192, 194, 195, 200, 202, 204, 208, 212, 214, 218, 220, 221, 224, 227, 229, 230
  north-east   29, 34, 220–2
  south-west   151, 221, 222
Scots Law   16, 35, 37, 44, 46, 62, 68, 102, 142, 143, 183, 196, 201
  criminal law   223
  Lord Advocate   35, 166, 189
  Lord President   32, 175
  Macdonald   183
  MacKenzie   20
Scotsman, the   216
Scottish Law Commission   56
Second Report of Her Majesty's Commissioners for Inquiring into the Housing of the Working Classes, (1885)   12
Secretary of State for Scotland   36
Sex Disqualification (Removal) Act, (1919)   3, 45, 193–5
Sexual Offences (Scotland) Act, 2009   225
'sexual script'   129
Sheriff   44, 145
  court   25, 35, 43, 72, 76, 99, 115, 116, 145, 184, 190, 212, 213
sibling incest   16, 72–6, 199
Smart, Carol   15, 17
Smout, T Christopher   221
Solicitor General   35, 138, 166, 167
South Africa   140, 209
  Boer War   210
  Mafeking   209
Squire, Libby   231
  Mrs   232
Stanko, Elizabeth   15, 19

Stead, W. T.   42, 118
  'Maiden Tribute of Modern Babylon'   30, 42
Stevenson, Kim   19
Stirling   91
Stopes, Marie   121
  Married Love   121
Strathaven   135
Strathern, John Drummond   37

Tancred, Edith   157
Thurso   105, 160
Tidefors, Inga   16
Tosh, John   16
tri-generational incest   15, 77
Tweed, the   5

Union 1707   21
  Act of   35
United States   7, 20, 81–2, 84, 97
  America   44
  American women   84
  New York   107
'up-skirting'   231

venereal disease   17, 111, 121, 186
  gonorrhoea   177, 180
'vicious girls'   87, 104

Wales   6, 17, 20
  South Wales   60
Watt, Christian   29
Webb, Beatrice   54
welfare authorities/investigators/officers   28, 54, 71–3, 79, 102, 111, 115, 185, 186, 212, 215, 221
Wells, H. G.   28
Wiener, Martin   7, 20
Wishaw   95
Wohl, Anthony   14
Woolf, Virginia   14, 28

'young man's defence'   43, 187, 189, 190

www.ingramcontent.com/pod-product-compliance
Lightning Source LLC
Chambersburg PA
CBHW071816300426
44116CB00009B/1340